Teaming Up

Teaming Up

THE SMALL-BUSINESS GUIDE TO

COLLABORATING WITH OTHERS

TO BOOST YOUR EARNINGS

AND EXPAND YOUR HORIZONS

PAUL AND SARAH EDWARDS
AND RICK BENZEL

A JEREMY P. TARCHER/PUTNAM BOOK
published by G. P. Putnam's Sons
New York

Most Tarcher/Putnam books are available at special quantity discounts for bulk purchases for sales promotions, premiums, fund-raising, and educational needs. Special books or book excerpts also can be created to fit specific needs. For details, write or telephone Special Markets, The Putnam Publishing Group, 200 Madison Ave., New York, NY 10016; (212) 951-8891.

———————

A Jeremy P. Tarcher/Putnam Book
Published by G. P. Putnam's Sons
Publishers Since 1838
200 Madison Avenue
New York, NY 10016
http://www.putnam.com/putnam

Library of Congress Cataloging-in-Publication Data

Edwards, Paul, date.
    Teaming up : the small-business guide to collaborating with others to boost your earnings and expand your horizons / Paul and Sarah Edwards, and Rick Benzel.
        p.   cm.
    Includes index.
    ISBN 0-87477-842-5
    1. Small business—Management.   2. Partnership.   3. Strategic alliances (Business)
I. Edwards, Sarah (Sarah A.)   II. Benzel, Rick.   III. Title.
    HD62.7.E346   1997   96-33515 CIP
    658.02'2—dc20

Book and cover design by Susan Shankin

Printed in the United States of America
10   9   8   7   6   5   4   3   2   1

This book is printed on acid-free paper. ∞

Contents

Acknowledgments

FROM: PAUL AND SARAH

This book marks a transition for our publisher of fourteen years. Jeremy Tarcher retired just prior to publication of this book. So we want to express for the last time in a new book our appreciation to Jeremy for supporting our vision of the need for information tailored to home and small-business people. We also want to thank the people who have worked with Jeremy, such as Robert Welsch, whose guidance and help shaped this series of books, and Jeremy's able assistant, Lisa Chadwick.

We now have the opportunity to also thank for the first time a new Tarcher/Putnam team, including our supportive and wise editor, Irene Prokop; her able assistant, Jennifer Greene; David Groff, associate editor; Joel Fotinos, publisher; Maria Liu, marketing coordinator; and the folks in publicity who enable you and others to know about this book, Joanna Pinsker and Ken Siman.

Others to whom we express special appreciation include Barbara Grenquist, the copyeditor; and Coral Tysliava and the people she works with, who facilitate the production of our books. Deserving of special note, too, is our assistant, Joyce Acosta, who enables us to complete the manuscripts that come from our home office. We also thank Les Klinger of Kopple & Klinger of Los Angeles for reviewing chapter 4, and for his sharing sage advice for us to pass along to you the reader. And, of course, special thanks to our co-writer and long-time valued collaborator, Rick Benzel.

FROM: RICK

I want to first thank Paul and Sarah Edwards for inviting me to coauthor this book with them. It seemed quite fitting that we all recognized the value of working closely together to fashion this book about the collaborative experience. I thank Paul and Sarah for their encouragement, support, and trust in this endeavor.

I also thank lawyer Clifford Ennico of the firm Pepe and Hazard in Southport, Connecticut. Cliff graciously reviewed various sections of this book containing legal information and advice, especially in chapter 4, to be sure it was accurate and sound. His suggestions on wording to help keep the information understandable and approachable by the average nonlawyer reader were enormously useful.

Similarly, I would like to thank Lita Schloss for her review of various portions of the book relating to the financial and tax issues of partnerships and corporations. Her assistance was very helpful.

Finally, I want to thank my wife, Terry, and my two daughters, Rebecca and Sarah, for being there for me during the months I had to research and write. They made my life complete.

FROM ALL OF US:

Most of all, we acknowledge the hundreds of people we interviewed, many of whose stories provide examples in this book. Without their openness and honesty in sharing their experiences, both the war stories and the victories, we could not have made this book as practical as we hope you will find it.

Preface

For the raindrop, joy is entering the river. —GHALIB

TEAMING UP IS ABOUT a new way of working. It's about the variety of innovative and collaborative ways self-employed individuals and small and home businesses are going about doing business these days. Whereas the traditional entrepreneur has long been viewed as a "lone eagle," going solo in the competitive, cutthroat, dog-eat-dog world of commerce, *Teaming Up* presents an entirely new scenario for what it means to become your own boss.

In this book, you'll discover that contrary to the idea that being on your own is a lonely, each person-for-him- or -herself experience, today's self-employed individuals are linking up in a broad spectrum of mutually beneficial relationships that could enable them to not only become more successful, but to do so with less effort and better results. In fact, often those who are linking up with others by mutual agreement are greatly enhancing each other's capabilities, clientele, and income.

The growing tendency toward teaming up is not something that's being done out of despair and desperation. It's not about some grasping last-ditch effort to stay afloat. Quite the contrary. The phenomenon we're observing is taking place both instinctively and purposefully, sometimes even strategically, from a position of strength and confidence. It's arising from a desire to grow and expand, to achieve and accomplish. Sometimes it's about growing larger and sometimes it's about growing financially without having to get any larger. Sometimes it's even about being able to grow a smaller and more enjoyable enterprise.

Teaming Up is based on the recognition that individuals on their own have substantially more to gain by working together than by working solo, or worse, by competing against each other. In fact, we believe a significant shift is taking place in how people are doing business. It seems that we're moving from a time of *competition* and *self-reliance* to an era of *cooperation* and *interdependence*. Actually, the trend toward teaming up reflects a "paradigm" shift in the way growing numbers of small and home-based businesses will be working in the future.

In the traditional paradigm, or "world view," entrepreneurs, small-business owners, and people leaving the corporate environment to go out on their own were taught to view their success as the result of singular dedication, brute force, and persistence. The business world has been, and often still is, thought of as a battlefield that demands a "military" mentality to survive and thrive. Everyone has been viewed as a competitor and competitors are adversaries, enemies, fighting over "market share," each trying to capture as big a piece as possible of some fixed or dwindling pie. This traditional view of doing business is reflected in such commonly heard metaphors as:

- It's a dog-eat-dog world out there in the trenches.
- You've got to stay ahead of the pack.
- You've got to swim with the sharks.
- Prepare for a shark attack.
- Use guerrilla warfare tactics.
- If you want to survive, never say die.
- You've got to beat your competitors to the punch.
- You've got to be number one.
- Never mind the other guy; just CYA (Cover Your Ass).

But people going out on their own today are finding that this paradigm is no longer useful, efficient, productive, or appropriate. As we move into the twenty-first century, we're witnessing the emergence of a radically changing economic environment. We live in a larger, more competitive global market, subject to complex financial and social forces. Corporations everywhere are "restructuring" and "downsizing" to cut costs while somehow increasing efficiency. At the same time, tremendous advances in high technology are completely altering the methods and operations of work, as computers, cellular phones, CD-ROMs, and multimedia infiltrate the office and the consumer market, putting the power and capabilities of the many into the hands of the individual.

The marketplace itself is also shifting, as consumers have new demands for quality, service, lower cost, and speed. In short, the business world is much more *dynamic* and *complex* than ever before, and it will only become increasingly so. This new reality calls for a new way of doing business, one better suited to independent individuals working cooperatively to create new expanding possibilities than to large organizations with legions of workers doing battle with one another over the same pie.

Ironically, as the economy is getting more complex and competitive, it's requiring that businesses of all sizes become more collaborative and cooperative. We're all being compelled to create and share a multiplicity of new pies instead of fighting over a limited number of existing ones. As a result, we see large corporations teaming up, not only with each other, but also with the growing numbers of small businesses and one-person and home-based businesses. With new opportunities abounding and ever tighter competition, even old-style entrepreneurs are wanting to team up. As our title suggests, today you may be on your own, but you no longer need to work alone! It's a time to team up so everyone can win.

HOW TO USE THIS BOOK

As you will see from reading the many examples and stories on the following pages, *Teaming Up* is written for self-employed professionals and small- and home-based business owners who are already in business or are in the process of deciding to go out on their own. It addresses the needs of and opportunities for self-employed individuals with as few as no employees up to as many as ten employees, whether you're located in a small office, a home office, a garage, or a retail storefront. Whether you're a programmer, designer, writer, publisher, artist, craftsperson, legal and accounting professional, independent sales rep, retail store owner, or any one of the growing number of small-office, home-office businesses forming today, this book outlines many ways you can team up with others to better achieve the success you're seeking.

We designed *Teaming Up* to be the most comprehensive source available for information about how self-employed individuals and small or home-based businesses can collaborate with one another and with larger businesses, as well. While other books may focus on one particular way to team up such as networking or partnering, this book describes the pros and cons of a wide range of collaborative strategies and techniques, so you can identify which ones will work most effectively for you. It's divided into eight chapters. Here's an overview of what you can expect:

Chapter 1: Teaming Up: A New and Better Way of Doing Business

This chapter describes in greater detail the paradigm shift that's occurring in the way we need to work if we are to succeed on our own in today's economy. You'll discover why now is actually a golden age for independent workers. You'll see why so many people are deciding to team up and the specific benefits teaming up provides for overcoming the challenges self-employed individuals and small and home businesses face. If you're still skeptical about the idea of joining efforts with others, you're not alone. Not everyone has had a good experience with teaming up. Like others, you may fear that you'll get left with the short end of the stick, or maybe you already have been. But in this chapter, we'll discusses why operating from the traditional competitive frame of reference was better suited to the Industrial Age and how it can actually be counterproductive to your success in today's burgeoning information and service economy.

You'll see why working cooperatively seems to be ideally suited to the new economy and may well enable you to achieve your goals more quickly, easily, and inexpensively. Teaming up does call for a new set of skills and competencies, but they are ones that can be learned on the job, so to speak, and this book is designed to familiarize you with what's required to successfully navigate the new economic terrain.

Chapter 2: Ten Win-Win Ways of Teaming Up

In this chapter, you'll learn about the ten ways we've seen people team up for greater success. You're undoubtedly already familiar with some of these methods, but you may or may not have discovered how to make them work for you. Other methods you'll read about will probably be new to you. They were to us. So, we outline what we've found to be the pros and cons of these various arrangements and provide basic guidelines as to how to best make each of these arrangements work. They include:

- Networking
- Making mutual referrals
- Doing cross-promotions
- Forming interdependent alliances
- Joint venturing
- Satellite subcontracting
- Creating consortiums
- Forming family/spouse collaborations
- Partnering
- Joining virtual organizations

Chapter 3: Finding the Right People and Making the Right Choices

Teaming up to do business in any form has often been compared to meeting a mate and is subject to the same perils and pitfalls. As with finding a mate, picking a person or persons to team up with is critical to the success of any shared effort. But finding the right match in business is often no easier than finding the right match in a mate, so this chapter presents a six-step process to help you understand your own personality, work habits, and business needs, so you can identify which ways of teaming up are best suited to you and your business and better select the right associates to team up with. This chapter also includes a list of warning signs you can watch out for to avoid teaming up with the wrong people, companies, and organizations.

Chapter 4: Taking Care of Business: Legal and Financial Issues

In this chapter, we discuss the legal and financial aspects of teaming up and how such arrangements can not only protect you but also serve as a foundation for making sure your collaborations or alliances proceed as you intend. You'll learn how and when to create formal agreements or contracts with those you team up with and how to clarify your relationships to keep problems from developing in the future. You'll find sample agreements that walk you through specific wording and various clauses typically used when formalizing today's new working relationships. And most important, you'll learn how to establish equitable ways to share your profits, expenses, and workload so that regardless of what each party brings to the table, everyone will feel that your collaboration is a win-win deal.

Chapter 5: The Psychology of Making Your Relationships Work

Since a mutually beneficial business relationship can be invaluable, doing everything you can to make it succeed is critical. This chapter identifies several important issues you'll want to address to help make your teaming-up activities successful. First, we discuss the four-stage process you can expect any teaming-up relationship to go through regardless of how many people are involved. You'll see that some of the bumpiest times are a natural, normal, and important part of developing a strong working relationship. We describe three different styles people slip into when teaming with one another. Each of these styles can be useful, but by understanding all three you'll be able to select the style that best suits you, your business, and those you're working with in various circumstances.

We also identify the key habits we've found people use to build good working relationships, including what we call the "VELCRO" approach to good communication. VELCRO is an acronym for six things that we've found to compose the glue that holds good working relationships together. This chapter also includes advice for special needs involved in collaborating with family members in such situations as husband/wife or parent/child teams.

Chapter 6: A Teaming-Up Troubleshooting Guide

It's only natural that in working closely with another person, there will be some disagreements over business strategy or implementation. But when conflicts arise, each party must be sensitive to the expectations and needs of the others involved. In this chapter, we review the most common conflicts that occur when independent business people decide to team up. And we present a number of strategies that can be employed to reduce or overcome the problems involved in each. The goal of the chapter is to show you how to prevent conflicts from ruining a potentially valuable relationship.

Chapter 7: When Breaking Up Is Best

Teaming up relationships won't always be forever. Times change and needs change, so business relationships must often change too. But as you'll see, these changes can be done amicably. Also because some conflicts cannot be resolved, this chapter provides specific advice on terminating a relationship when there's no longer any chance of resolving the problems involved. The chapter also covers what to do when one partner or associate wants to end a business relationship and the other doesn't, and how to handle one partner's wanting to buy out the other.

Chapter 8: Creating Magic Together

Teaming up can launch your business in new directions you never imagined. As a result, you need to be prepared to respond when your business evolves to a new level. In some cases, an informal arrangement will need to be formalized. In other cases, if your business has grown substantially and you see an even brighter future ahead for you and those you've teamed with, you may want to expand your venture by seeking outside capitalization such as obtaining loans or bringing in investment money from a limited partner, an angel, or even a venture capitalist. This chapter explores these options and helps you to analyze the advantages and disadvantages of each.

A Note on the Case Histories and Personal Stories

Throughout the chapters, you'll find many case histories and stories from the thousands of people we've interviewed over the years in researching this and our other books. Most of these cases include specific names of the people and companies involved. However, because we want to provide illustrations of why teaming-up relationships fail and what happens between people when a joint effort doesn't work out, we also discuss many highly sensitive issues. Therefore, in presenting information of this nature, we've refrained from mentioning names and have sometimes disguised the identity of the individuals and companies involved, and even the businesses they're in. This was done to protect the parties and provide them with the security of knowing that their personal stories won't lead to any repercussions from former partners or future clients and customers.

A LOGICAL PROGRESSION

In many ways, *Teaming Up* is a natural progression from the other books the three of us have written on self-employment. A decade and a half ago, we, Paul and Sarah, first noticed a significant trend toward home-based business and wrote our first book, *Working from Home*. It was one of the seminal books published to teach people how to initiate and run a professional home-based business and continues to be updated regularly. It's now in its fourth edition.

Clearly *Working from Home* hit a nerve in the American psyche, as tens of thousands of people began considering the home-based option we were outlining. So following the success of that book, we realized that people heading out on their own wanted other specific information on how to make self-employment more successful. At that point, we teamed up with Rick Benzel as our trusted editor and wrote four other books: *Getting Business to Come to You,* which is about how to market and promote yourself effectively as a self-employed individual; *Secrets of Self-Employment,* which focuses on the skills and attitudes necessary to survive and thrive as your own boss; and *Best Home Businesses for the 90s* and *Making Money with Your Computer at Home,* which were written in response to a demand from people wanting to know what kinds of businesses they could run on their own from home. Our most recent book, *Finding Your Perfect Work,* is for the millions of people who would like to become their own boss but they're not sure how to decide what kind of work to do.

We've also teamed up to create books on other specific businesses, but to do that we reversed roles with several writers. For two of these books, Paul and Sarah served as editors while Rick Benzel did the writing for his books *Health Service Businesses on Your Home-Based PC* and *Legal and Paralegal Services on Your Home-Based PC* (the latter with coauthor Kathryn Sheehy Hussey).

So, as you can see, this book has itself grown from our experience of the needs for and benefits of teaming up. Over the years, we've learned how important it is to understand and recognize the trends that affect all of us who are self-employed so that we can approach what we do from a forward-thinking, visionary perspective. We hope you'll agree that *Teaming Up* is indeed the logical next step in your future success.

PAUL & SARAH EDWARDS AND RICK BENZEL

Teaming Up

1

Teaming Up:
A New and Better Way of Doing Business

One finger can't lift a pebble. —HOPI INDIAN SAYING

YOU PROBABLY LIKE the idea of being your own boss. Most people do. But whether you're already on your own or just thinking about it, if you're like most of us, you've already realized that as wonderful as being on your own can be, doing it all alone can be tough at times. So, in all likelihood you've probably already considered the possibility of teaming up in some way with other people. Maybe you're already working with others on a formal or informal basis. Or maybe you'd like to be but haven't made the right connections yet.

Nonetheless, you may also have some mixed feelings about getting involved financially and professionally with someone else. You may be wondering if it will be more hassle than it's worth. You may fear you could end up holding the short end of the stick. You may be concerned about whether you could count on someone else to follow through. These are just a few of the reservations most self-employed people have when it comes right down to deciding to work with someone else. And like most of us, you've undoubtedly heard partnership horror stories. Maybe you've even lived through one.

After all, as an entrepreneur or someone who's working on your own or wants to be, you're probably somewhat independent minded and self-directed by nature. You probably enjoy calling the shots and being in charge of your own fate. Or, while you might wish to be more independent, you may feel that your best chance for success on your own will be to team up with someone who has certain skills and aptitudes you don't feel confident of. Or you may simply enjoy being part of a team and working together with others while maintaining your independence.

Either way, paradoxical as it may be, if you're self-employed, the best way to compete right now and in the upcoming twenty-first century is to start making what's often referred to as "strategic alliances." Of course, teaming up will never be a cure-all or panacea and should never be thought of as a guaranteed route to personal and economic survival. Still, in our view, teaming up with other independent individuals as well as companies and organizations of various sizes will soon become the modus operandi for all business—a new paradigm for success in an evolving global marketplace. After all, our nature is to affiliate with others. Social inventions for associating with others predate history, including such entities as family, tribe, clan, gang, club, and group, to name just a few. As millions leave behind the social organizations we call corporations and agencies, it's only natural that we turn to new ways of joining with others.

But this doesn't mean you have to become entangled in unpleasant or unwanted interpersonal complexities. In fact, avoiding such complications may have a lot to do with why you want to be your own boss in the first place. Clearly there's no sense in teaming up unless doing so enhances your work and your life. So, while your urge to "merge" is right on target for meeting the challenges of today's economy, so is any hesitancy you may be feeling about involving others in your business. Teaming up productively requires a new set of skills, different from the ones involved in working for someone else and different from those called for in working independently. But that's exactly what we've observed literally tens of thousands of people doing so effectively these days.

When teaming up works, no one gets taken advantage of. No one gets the short end of the stick. Quite the contrary. When teaming up works, each party brings something valuable to the table. Everyone involved seeks to win through their joint efforts, *while preventing the others from losing. Conflict* and *competition* are not part of the dynamic new teaming-up relationships we've been observing. *Cooperation* and *mutual benefit* reign supreme.

In fact, we're using the term *teaming up* to refer to a broad spectrum of positive, proactive alliances self-employed people are entering into intentionally and strategically not just to survive, but to thrive, on their own. To fully understand the new role these alliances play these days, it's useful to step back and examine the reasons they've become so appealing. From this broader perspective, you'll see that today as an independent worker or small-business owner you can enjoy unparalleled opportunities, despite new pressures and limitations, when you can find colleagues and allies with whom you can affiliate to maximize your time, energy, and resources.

WHY ALL THIS TEAMING UP?

Today's economy has changed radically from the corporate America of the past, and the way we do business is changing along with it. Teaming up is one result. It's happening at all levels of the business world, among both large and small businesses. The past five years have seen large companies begin making alliances of all kinds: airline companies are doing cross-promotions with car-rental companies, soft drink companies are teaming up with food outlets, footwear and clothing companies are aligning with sporting-goods firms, competing auto dealers form alliances for collective advertising. Everywhere you turn today, you'll find major businesses exploring new ways of collaborating.

For the self-employed and small business, the shift toward teaming up is perhaps even more vital. Small and home-based businesses are discovering they can be more successful, prosper, and survive more easily by teaming up in new and creative ways. In fact, some of the most innovative teaming-up activity is taking place among the growing numbers of people who are working on their own. In 1970 fewer than seven million Americans were self-employed. Almost everyone was working for someone else. Even as late as 1986, it was estimated that only eight million people worked in small or home-based businesses. But by 1993, Americans were filing over twenty-one million business tax returns, reflecting the mushrooming growth of small businesses. Literally millions of people are turning away, or being turned away, from traditional corporate jobs to discover the joys and challenges of being their own boss.

But while they're on their own, they're discovering they need not be alone. Growing numbers of individuals and small businesses are rejecting the long-standing belief that doing business is a competitive dog-eat-dog proposition. They are replacing this outdated competitive model with a new model of cooperation and collaboration. Here's why.

A Wealth of New Opportunities

According to the Commerce Department, small businesses with fewer than four employees are providing the vast majority of new jobs. This new economic reality, coupled with new personal goals and new technology, is transforming not only the work we do but also how and when we can do it. In other words, three forces are creating new opportunities to go out on your own and succeed at levels never before possible by making various strategic alliances with other independent individuals, small businesses, and companies of all sizes.

1. A New World of Work. Perhaps the single most critical factor spurring so many people to go out on their own and link up with others in new ways is the relentless shrinking of the corporate workforce that's occurred over the past decade. As tens of thousands of corporations have been forced to cut costs and "reengineer themselves" for a new global information and service economy, they've laid off millions of workers and reduced future hiring in proportions never seen before. The new American corporation has shed its hierarchical layers of management to emerge lean and trim, as what Charles Handy, author of *The Age of Reason,* calls a *cloverleaf organization* composed of three types of personnel: (1) a small core staff of employees, (2) out-sourced contract services which are called upon when needed, and (3) strategic alliances with partner organizations.

TODAY'S CLOVERLEAF ORGANIZATION

As a result of this fundamental restructuring of the workplace, millions of displaced workers are starting their own businesses and millions of others, feeling overworked and undervalued, are voluntarily forsaking their corporate jobs for the freedom and flexibility of self-employment. And at the same time, corporations are turning to these very same people to help them carry out the work that still must be done on an outsourced basis. Large companies are teaming up with independent contractors, consultants, freelancers, and small businesses of all kinds who are in turn are doing business with one another to provide a vast array of products and services more effectively and productively. In fact, construction contractors, event planners, cleaning and maintenance personnel, public-relations and advertising agencies, production and design firms, and even lawyers and health practitioners routinely work as part of project teams that assemble and disband as needed.

Increasingly today's workforce operates more like a Hollywood studio making a movie than a factory assembling automobiles or executives climbing a corporate ladder. Just as movie producers assemble a team of professionals to work on their movie projects, today's organization pulls together teams of corporate employees, small businesses, and self-employed individuals to work on a project-by-project basis. When a project is completed, the team disbands and the individuals involved go on to work on other projects, often as part of entirely new teams. This process has been called "flocking," because a company deploys and redeploys its resources, flocking them around the demands of the hour. Teams of employees and outsourced personnel are combined and recombined as the situation demands.

These *"recombinant work teams,"* as we call them, provide the flexibility, creativity, and freedom to make working in the new economy profitable for everyone. Large organizations, small businesses, and independent work-

RECOMBINANT WORK TEAMS

This diagram shows three work teams, composed of seven different people, each with their own specialized role. Each team has been pulled together for a particular project. Team members may be employees of various allied companies, small businesses, or self-employed individuals. Note that Person #2 is part of all three teams and was instrumental in recommending persons #1, #4, and #6 who are each part of two of the teams. At a future date, any one of these individuals may recommend any other to work on other projects in which they're involved.

ers all benefit from working together in this way; and increasingly these fluid, time-limited interdependent projects offer the best-paying, most promising work. Flocking into recombinant work teams is generating a new work culture that's centered on maintaining personal relationships forged through networking, mutual referrals, and other forms of strategic alliances. Here are just a few examples of how recombinant work teams are providing new opportunities for more flexible, and profitable, work.

Deb Watering is a marketing consultant who works with telecommunications companies. To meet the needs of her clients, she draws from a wide circle of other independent professionals whom she brings in to work with her on particular projects. Sometimes she works as a member of an in-house team; at other times she serves as a project leader of a team composed of her client's employees, other consultants the client has engaged, and personnel from allied companies. Sometimes consultants she meets on such projects bring her in to work with them on other projects, and with each project she adds to the base of professionals she can call on in working with her clients.

We (Paul and Sarah) met Watering on a project team pulled together for Northern Telecom. She was serving as the project leader. We were among a number of consultants brought in to work with the Northern Telecom staff and staff from their PR and advertising agencies. We often work as part of such recombinant teams. In the past, the teams have usually been composed of people we'd never met before and never expected to work with again, but as the years go by, we increasingly find ourselves working with consultants and other personnel we've worked with on previous projects for various other clients. Sometimes they've recommended that we be part of the team; other times we've been asked to suggest people we know to work on a project.

Dena Levy used the "Hollywood" flocking model to expand Two-D Productions, her television commercial and infomercial production company. To compete with larger production companies and provide a high degree of personalized service for her clients, Dena realized that she had to find the best talent for each project while keeping her expenses low. So, rather than hire permanent employees, she chooses from a pool of freelance talent she has cultivated over the years, bringing in writers, editors, camerapeople, production managers, caterers, and others who best meet her needs for a particular production. On working with freelancers, she says,

> Choosing from a pool of people gives me the freedom to say this person is right for this job and that person is right for that job. When I get a new job, I put together a schedule, and somebody in my office calls the people I want and puts them on hold for the dates I want them. It takes only half a day. [Working this way] gives me the opportunity to have the small company I want and still do the kind of projects I want.

Sometimes, small businesses and self-employed individuals feel that in order to bid on and win outsourced contracts they must go beyond simply networking, making mutual referrals, and being part of loose-knit affiliations with colleagues. So they're forming formal partnerships, consortiums, and even "*virtual organizations*" of their own. For example, Mary Vandergrift of Columbia, Maryland, had eighteen years of experience working with computers for IBM, but when she started her medical billing company she realized she didn't have the sales and marketing skills she needed to land outsourced contracts from medical offices. So she took on a partner, a woman she knew who had twenty years of sales experience. Working together, within a few months, they had a flourishing business with a half dozen doctors' offices as clients. They each attribute their success to their partnership, and both readily acknowledge that they couldn't have done it alone.

Bill Vick has operated a successful executive recruiting business from his home since 1988. Two years ago he obtained a large search assignment he couldn't do alone. He turned to people he knew on the Internet as candidates for the positions he was filling. From this experience, he realized there was potential for developing a Century 21–like organization for recruiters on the Internet. In two years, he has attracted 1,800 members who pay $395 to participate in his virtual organization which he calls Recruiters Online Network. Vick says, "The Internet has changed the recruiting business. As video and web chat come on, the whole model of recruiting is changing. It is becoming more distributed, collaborative, and partnering oriented."

2. New Priorities for How to Live and Work. An equally important factor that's causing people to team up in new and different ways is the dramatic shift that's taking place in our personal and social values. Men and women of all ages are giving up the traditional trappings of financial "success" in order to find a more satisfying and personally rewarding way of life. Growing numbers of people are trading in office politics, the daily commute, and the stress of a high-speed lifestyle for the freedom of working reduced or more flexible hours on their own. For many people this means moving away from large metropolitan areas to smaller cities or rural locations in search of a higher quality of life with more affordable housing, reduced crime, and a slower, more family-friendly pace. But finding a balance between making a good living and enjoying a good life often means teaming up with colleagues and others who might once have been considered competitors.

Rolf Rudestam, for example, was a public-relations agent who had a long and rewarding career working in the fast-paced corporate world of advertising. But one day, he realized that his work no longer involved doing the things he most enjoyed. Instead of working directly with clients, he was spending most of his time supervising and communicating through a staff of junior agents. He knew it was time for a change, so he left the firm and moved to Big Bear, California, a small mountain community miles away from the hectic world of traditional public relations. There, in this land of crisp, clean air and crystal blue skies, he set up his own PR company working from his home. And to make sure he can continue working on challenging and lucrative projects, he has linked up with a legion of other PR agents from around the world whom he's met throughout his career. By funneling work to these colleagues, he can take on jobs of any size and have a presence in virtually any region of the country.

Often the desire to create a better way of life means teaming up with the one person closest to you: your spouse or significant other. In fact, many of today's independent workers are husband-and-wife teams looking for ways to better balance their family lives and their careers. The Small Business Administration reports that husband-and-wife businesses were the fastest-growing segment of new business start-ups between 1980 and 1989. Couples are teaming up in record numbers for a number of reasons.

For Anita and Al Robertson, the reason was purely economic. They started their business together after Al lost his job. For some time Anita had been earning extra income doing calligraphy, an interest that began as a hobby. She reasoned that, working with Al, she could earn more than she could at her job. So she quit and they joined forces to turn her part-time business into a full-time endeavor. Long believers in home schooling, they traveled for fifteen years with their children from city to city to sell their work at craft shows.

For Donald and Paige Marrs, it was the desire to spend more time together and share a lifelong relationship of meaningful work. Theirs was a second marriage for both of them and they didn't want to spend the majority of their waking hours apart in separate careers, so after they got married, Paige joined Donald in Marketing Partners which they run from their home. She already knew quite a bit about the business, however, because she'd been one of Donald's clients. That's how they met. Having worked together, they were impressed with each other's skills and believed they could complement each other in business as well as in their personal relationship. So Paige sold her import business and the two have been working together ever since.

For Susan Pinsky and David Starkman, working together in their own business means having the flexibility to do what they love most: travel. They operate Reel 3-D, a home-based mail-order-catalogue company that sells equipment to 3-D photographers. What they like best about their lifestyle is the flexibility it provides to close the doors on their business and take to the road, or air, as the case may be, whenever they want.

When Wendy Gladney's event-planning business grew to being more than she could handle, she much preferred to bring her husband, Fred, into the business than to try to find a stranger with whom to share her business. They find working together makes it easier to share caring for their young daughter as well. Tom Koehler also joined his wife's business. He had thought about starting his own business, but his wife's company was booming and he realized he could use his skills to help her business grow. They have been a two-career couple throughout their marriage; now, working together allows them to spend more time together than ever before.

3. New Technologies That Break the Barrier. A last and pivotal factor spurring people to head out on their own and then join together in innovative ways is the availability of powerful, inexpensive technology that enables us to work independently yet stay connected to the world from our home office, small office, kiosk, or virtually anywhere. Technology has, for all intents and purposes, leveled the playing field for *big* and *small* enterprise. With everything from desktop computers and fax machines to laser printers, scanners, and cellular phones, individuals can easily obtain the technological power and sophistication that formerly was affordable only in the corporate world. In a sense, advances in technology have removed both the practical and the psychological barriers that prevented people from becoming their own boss in the past. Few companies these days are concerned if those they do business with are located in a plush high-rise or in a pink garage so long as the work is done well at a good price.

In fact, technology is making the size and location of one's operation essentially invisible. It's also enabling those of us who want to work independently to link up with others almost seamlessly whenever we want and need to. With today's technology, you can team up with others whose expertise or resources you need irrespective of your geographical location. And using these tools to work together, you can better serve the growing number of clients and customers who need your products or services. You can respond more easily to new consumer needs and keep up with today's massive information overload. And by teaming up, you also can more easily tap into a growing global marketplace it would otherwise be difficult to reach.

In fact, today's home business is twice as likely to be engaged in business travel as the average American worker. Thirty-eight percent of home businesses do business nationally and 14 percent do business internationally. By teaming up with a software manufacturer, for example, Gordon Driver has been able to establish an international computer consulting company that he runs from the den of his suburban home. When a company located outside the United States needs help installing networking software, the manufacturer refers the company to Driver, who, using his computer, a modem, and the telephone lines, can tap into the client's computer system and get their system operating smoothly without setting foot outside his office.

New Challenges

Despite this rosy perspective, the changes we've described, coupled with the increasingly global marketplace, are drawing so many new people into business for themselves each year that everyone's facing more competition than ever before. At the same time, consumers are demanding higher quality products and they want them faster, cheaper, and delivered with a smile. An excellent job done with speed at a reasonable price is becoming a requirement for success; and those who can't meet a promised delivery date will not be around for long.

Such demands are making it all the more important for us as individuals and small and home-based businesses to join efforts both among ourselves and with larger organizations. Even with the advances in technology like computers and fax machines to simplify our work, the level of complexity we must manage and master can become greater than imagined, especially as we become more successful. Often, all alone, we simply don't have the time, money, or expertise to make the most of all the opportunities that await us.

Also too often we're operating without the institutional support systems that have been developed to spur the growth of larger businesses. Few public policies or institutions are in place to address the needs of today's rapidly growing independent workforce. Existing health and disability insurance policies, credit lines, tax laws, and the like often don't meet our needs. In fact, too often they place limitations on us and saddle us with burdens that make achieving our goals all the harder. Of course, as our numbers grow, such barriers are falling, but change is slow. So in the meantime, we need to find creative solutions to make the most of our opportunities within the options open to us. Usually, this boils down to generating more business or increasing our fees to compensate for the higher costs and higher taxes we must pay for our independence.

Some independent individuals and small businesses are unable to overcome these challenges alone, and others overcome only a few. The former decide to return to the world of salaried employment if they can find a position; the latter struggle by, merely *surviving,* but not really *thriving.* And while surviving is enough for some, living in a survival mode is a risky proposition and it's becoming even more so. As the economic environment gets more complex and sophisticated, and as competition continues to heat up, those who settle for mere subsistence risk going under. The truth is, in order to survive and thrive, today's new economic realities are requiring us as self-employed and small business owners, to join efforts and team up to use smarter, more creative strategies to rise above the limitations of being a small, home-based, or geographically remote operation.

THE BENEFITS OF TEAMING UP

Teaming up enables many people to both seize the opportunities and overcome the challenges of being their own boss. The following box summarizes the benefits people most frequently mention when telling us about why and how they're teaming up. As you read through the list, consider how any of the reasons might help you better overcome any of the challenges you're facing and make the most of being on your own.

Fifteen Reasons to Team Up

1. Get more business and increase your income.
2. Serve more clients in the same period of time and become successful faster.
3. Avoid downtime between jobs.
4. Bid on larger contracts and take on bigger, more interesting projects.
5. Make sure people take you seriously.
6. Add on or expand into additional sources of income.
7. Test out new business ideas with less risk.
8. Respond more quickly and easily to the demands of change.
9. Reach clients and make contacts in other geographic locations.
10. Enhance your credibility or reputation.
11. Boost your effectiveness, creativity, and energy.
12. Do a better job more quickly.
13. Share expenses to stretch a tight budget.
14. Avoid professional isolation and get inside information.
15. Get needed support without hiring employees.

Benefit 1: Get More Business and Increase Your Income

By teaming up, you can gain access to new clients, new markets, and new distributors. Having a steady stream of clients is crucial to any one-person or very small business. Yet the amount of time and energy you can spend marketing and getting business is limited, because you need to spend as much time as possible actually doing paying work. But teaming up can help you keep an ample supply of new clients and customers coming to you without having to expend inordinate amounts of time and energy.

Working strictly on your own, you may be limited, for example, to doing business within your local community. Like many of us, you may get all or most of your business primarily from people you already know or even from a single company such as your former employer. Or, as is often the case, you may be focusing your efforts on developing a highly specialized niche. At times, and especially while you're building your reputation, any of these situations can lead to dry spells that wreak havoc on your cash flow. In the worst case, such situations make you vulnerable to the whims of market downturns that could stall or even wipe out your industry.

But by teaming up, you can gain access to OPC—Other People's Contacts. Through networking, collaborations, partnerships, or alliances of various kinds, you can develop new avenues for reaching more clients, discovering opportunities, and expanding your client and customer base. By teaming up you can vastly expand your sphere of contacts, meet new people and gain access to contacts you wouldn't otherwise have.

That's what Chris Beal did. Beal is the founder of ReComp, a company that rehabilitates computers and sells them in secondary markets. Although he was already growing at the rate of 500 percent a year on the West Coast, Beal knew that if he had the manpower, he could cover the entire nation and do even better. Fortunately, a Seattle-based company also recognized the possibilities for ReComp and contacted Beal to sound out the idea of forming a partnership. He didn't want to enter into a formal partnership, but he did begin collaborating with the firm, granting them an exclusive territory in certain college markets that he couldn't reach himself. The firm lines up orders in their region and Beal drop-ships the computers. Their collaboration has proved profitable for both parties, enough so that Beal has started to set up similar collaborative arrangements overseas.

When you run out of names of people or companies you know of who need what you offer, you can purchase mailing lists or make cold calls from directories, but that's the hard way to get business. It's time-consuming and can be discouraging. But by teaming up, you can gain access to the eyes and ears of others who will provide you with fresh sources of names and contacts with companies who have needs for your products and services. Chellie Campbell, until she recently sold it, operated Cameron Diversified, a bookkeeping service in Pacific Palisades, California. Over only two years' time, Campbell doubled her client base by networking extensively and consistently. Her networking contacts led to dozens of referrals from people in her networking groups whom she would never have met otherwise.

Usually establishing yourself as an expert in a specialized niche is important in becoming truly successful, but developing your own niche can take time. In the meantime, by teaming up you can do work outside your specialty for associates and keep your cash flowing without having to dilute either your image as a specialist or your marketing efforts in your niche. For example, if you're a makeup artist and you're working to build a reputation for doing weddings, while you're getting established in this niche, you can provide backup for busy colleagues who have other specialties. That's what Stephanie Miller does. She's marketing herself successfully as a wedding makeup artist, but since she's just getting established, she doesn't always have enough wedding business. So to fill in, she works as a subcontractor for other makeup artists she's affiliated with. Sometimes she works on video shoots, sometimes for photographers.

These kinds of affiliations also work well when the niche you prefer to work in isn't large enough or lucrative enough to provide you with a full-time income. If you're an information researcher, for example, who prefers to do on-line medical searches for people with life-threatening illnesses, you may not always have enough clients with the financial wherewithal to provide you with a full-time income. But by arranging to team up with other information brokers, you can supplement your income by doing other types of searches for them while continuing to devote your marketing efforts to developing your medical specialty.

In addition, while you may not want to become a large organization, you can expand your business without expanding your costs and overhead by adding a variety of other people's products and services to your own. For example, Mary Cordoro is a certified bau-biologist and environmental consultant. She works closely with many architects and real estate agents who refer clients to her who are concerned about the environmental health of a building or home they are about to buy. In turn, Mary's company, A Room of One's Own, teams up with another firm, The Art of Placement, operated by Kathyrn Metz who is a feng-shui consultant. Mary's clients are often interested not only in her environmental consulting services but also in designing their homes and furnishing them for maximum health and pleasure, which is what Kathyrn offers through her knowledge of the ancient Chinese art of feng-shui. So Mary can bring Kathyrn in on such projects, and vice versa.

In Oregon, teaming up in ways like these has been recognized as so vital to the state's economic development that the government has established a grant program called Flexible Networks. The program helps small businesses form alliances to find new markets or identify new niches that aren't being filled. One such alliance brought together a video production company, a graphic design firm, a software company, and a marketing and sales specialist who joined together to develop a new video project that will become a CD-ROM as well.

Also, consortiums and arrangements of various kinds are facilitated by county extension agents such as Ann Lastovica of Virginia, who brought together a millinery maker with a home-based subcontractor to provide buttons, benefiting both businesses.

Benefit 2: Serve More Clients in the Same Period of Time and Become Successful Faster

There are only twenty-four hours in a day, and most of us want to work only eight or ten of them. To make matters worse, usually not all the hours you work can be billable ones. You have to devote a certain amount of time to carrying out the tasks involved in the administrative aspects of your work and preparing for work that you cannot justify billing to a client. So, there's a finite limit on the amount of paying work you can personally take on. At times, you may find yourself faced with having to turn down new business because you don't have time to do it, or you may have to postpone taking on new work until you've finished the projects you're working on. To do otherwise is a Catch-22 because if you take on more work than you can do well, you risk disappointing the client and jeopardizing your reputation.

But if you'd like to take on more business and grow faster than your personal time allows, teaming up can solve this problem. Here's an example of how teaming up can help. Let's say you accept a three-month contract for $12,000. Two months into that contract, you get a call from a major company in your area with whom you've been wanting to do business for over a year. They're offering you an assignment for one month at $5,000 but they need the work done immediately. You try to postpone their rush, but in the end, you're forced to turn down their business, while earnestly appealing to them to call you again for a future assignment. On the one hand, you have lost $1,000 in business because the remaining month on your existing contract is worth only $4,000. But on the other hand, the lost opportunity may be worth more than $5,000 in new business because if the company finds a satisfactory way of meeting their need without you, you may also lose out on the opportunity to work on even more profitable contracts with the new company in the future.

Although you may never know what might come from a situation like this, why risk losing such opportunities? By calling in the resources of others, you can avoid the dilemma of either overcommitting and not meeting your promised delivery dates, or undercommitting and cheating yourself out of potential income and new clients. Vicki Fite, who operates a medical transcription service in San Diego, confronts such dilemmas all the time. Because her profit depends entirely on how many words she can keyboard in each day, Vicki realized that working alone would severely limit her income. Rather than turning down clients, she set up a network of other home-based transcriptionists to whom she sends work. This allows her to accept and even bid on more contracts than she could ever handle alone. And by teaming up, instead of taking on the overhead of full-time staff, she can keep her overhead down and doesn't need to worry about always having enough business to keep full-time employees busy.

Benefit 3: Avoid Downtime Between Jobs

Downtime is the enemy of a healthy cash flow. Large companies have staff to market what they do while other personnel are busy doing paying work. But as a one-person or small business, you may hit periodic downtimes because you don't have time to market while you are busy working on existing projects. Once your busy period is over, a week, a month or even more can pass before you're able to do enough marketing to generate new work. We hear this complaint all too frequently from people doing everything from desktop publishing to programming, technical writing to editorial services, consulting, and many other professions.

But by teaming up, you can quickly fill in downtimes by drawing upon other people's marketing efforts, and you can do the same for them in return. For example, computer trainer Jan Bernstein maintains a consistent mutual-referral agreement with several other trainers. When she's not available for an assignment, she passes it on to a colleague. In turn when she has downtime, Jan often gets clients right away from those same colleagues who are too busy to take work that's coming their way.

One of the best ways to avoid downtime is to make sure you don't shy away from bidding on new business because you're too busy. Unfortunately, many people worry about bidding on new jobs because if they get the work, they fear they'll get overcommitted. Again this is where teaming up can help. When you know you can easily get a helping hand from a collaborator, you are more apt to bid on several projects at a time even if they overlap.

Benefit 4: Bid on Larger Contracts and Take on Bigger, More Interesting Projects

Since you have only so many hours in the day to work and only know how to do certain things well enough to feel confident about charging for them, there may be times when you feel restricted in the size, scope, and nature of projects you can take on by yourself. While this limitation doesn't necessarily prevent you from becoming successful, it may affect what you can accomplish and even the type of business you can obtain. This can be particularly problematic when you're just starting out or when you'd like to grow faster than you can by taking on one small project at a time.

By teaming up, however, you may be able to bid on and/or accept larger, better-paying projects than you could handle alone. In fact, when several individuals or small businesses team up as associates or a consortium, they can often charge more because of their combined expertise and energy. Jordan Ayan, a management consultant in Chicago, teams up frequently with Deanna Berg, a consultant from Atlanta, to win larger, better-paying contracts for his seminars and workshops. As Jordan points out, "We try to do as much work as we can together, because our collaboration adds value to what we each can offer individually. By working together, we can give longer and more in-depth workshops that reflect both of our backgrounds. Deanna has more academic expertise in organizational behavior and I have many years of successful management experience. We each have our own clients, but working together translates into larger fees for both of us." Together, Jordan and Deanna have worked on contracts with AT&T, NASA, Kimberly Clark, and Freddie Mac.

Joint projects of this nature can bring in tens of thousands of dollars instead of just several thousand. For example, a husband-and-wife team we know who began a home-based marketing and communications business from their living room teamed up with other freelancers to win increasingly larger and larger contracts. They produce marketing and customer-support materials for some of the best-known high-tech companies in the country. They network and subcontract with more than thirty freelancers and produce total revenues approaching $3 million. Teaming up catapulted them into an entirely new level of success, far beyond anything they imagined when they originally decided to become a home-based business.

Carolyn Colby had a similar experience. She had been running a home-health agency in her community for eight years when she began losing business to larger companies. Her problem was that HMOs and other managed-care companies were giving their business to large agencies that had offices throughout the state. So Colby joined forces with other small agencies located in other parts of the state to found the National Independent Nursing Network, which consists of thirty-four independent home-health agencies. They're all independent businesswomen who have joined together, incorporated, set up a joint fee structure, developed contracts and joint marketing materials, and hired an executive director. By being part of this network, Colby is now competing head-to-head with larger statewide agencies. She's been able to retain her independence and continue to grow her local business.

Benefit 5: Make Sure People Take You Seriously

Sometimes as a one-person or very small business, potential clients, customers, suppliers, and referral sources don't take you seriously, especially when you're just starting out. They lump you in with the growing numbers of "consultants" and "temps" who are in between jobs. You have to convince them that you're serious about who you are and what you do. Of course, there are many ways to do this, but if clients, suppliers, or distributors are perceiving you as too small to handle their needs but you know you can do a good job for them, teaming up can help you correct this misconception.

That's what Peter Lloyd did. Lloyd, a business creativity consultant in Ohio, was presenting solo workshops to small companies for several years with moderate success. Then one day when he was bidding on a presentation to a major *Fortune* 500 client he decided to ask them if they'd be interested in an innovative "live theater" workshop that would combine his skills in teaching creativity with those of a colleague who could beam the program to each of their branch offices via video and satellite transmissions. The company jumped at the idea and signed a contract that netted each of the two consultants more than double their individual rates. In other words, by teaming up Lloyd could offer something of more perceived value to the client than either he or his colleague could have offered alone. Since then, the two men have been successful at attracting much larger projects because they are no longer viewed as simply "small-time" consultants.

Wendy Gladney, owner of Personal Services Plus, a special-events planning company, also recognized the value of teaming up for making sure people take her business seriously. Although Wendy and her husband, Fred, are basically a two-person business, she regularly collaborates with other self-employed individuals so they can bid on larger contracts. In one instance, Wendy teamed up with a local graphic artist who specializes in "corporate image enhancement," and together they won a contract from Nestlé to handle all the planning for a charity event that included a dinner, an auction, and a celebrity basketball game. Of course, adding Nestlé to the client list on her marketing materials has done wonders for getting other large companies to take her business seriously.

Benefit 6: Add On or Expand Into Additional Sources of Income

Generally we don't advocate trying to start multiple businesses at the same time, because trying to build more than one business diffuses your efforts, dilutes your credibility, and confuses your potential clients as to what business you're in. But once you've sufficiently established yourself in one business activity, there are a variety of circumstances when it makes good sense to team up so you can add on or expand into other complementary sources of income. These include:

- When the potential customer base for your business is not sufficient to support you full-time
- When your primary business in a broad field enables you to provide several related services to your existing or new clients, as in the case of a writer who could also offer editing or publishing services
- When the income potential from your business is substantially less than your income goals
- When you can turn a long-standing hobby or interest into additional income
- When you want to make the transition from one business to another more desirable one

Unfortunately even when it would be advantageous to add additional businesses, most people simply don't have the time, money, or energy to launch more than one business at a time. That's where teaming up can make the difference. By working with a collaborator or partner, you can tap into other people's time, expertise, and resources without taking away unduly from your primary work.

For example, by teaming up, Wally Bock, a small-business consultant in Oakland, California, was able to simultaneously expand his consulting practice into four additional areas: marketing consulting, employee training, publishing, and on-line technology consulting. By teaming up formally or informally at different stages of expansion into each of these activities, Bock was able to juggle several different businesses at once by drawing on the skills, time, and energy of others. Here's how he did it: he entered into a formal partnership with another consultant who could provide marketing consulting; he teamed up with a writer so he could publish his first book; and he collaborated with a computer expert to develop interactive employee training materials and do on-line consulting—all this while he was still running his primary consulting business!

Jan Caldwell is a home-based lawyer in Maryland who specializes in working with small businesses. By working with partners, however, she has been able to expand into two other income-producing activities while continuing to run her full-time law practice. One venture, The Front Desk, is an editorial services company that helps authors get their books published and does legal desktop publishing. The other venture, Pantera Enterprises, specializes in exporting autos and auto supplies to South America and Europe. These two ventures are part-time businesses for Jan, but each supplements her income significantly. Her interest is not just in the additional money, however. These part-time activities add spice to Caldwell's life and enable her to look forward to a future even more to her liking. She intends to build the export company into a full-time occupation that will allow her to move to rural Wyoming where she'll live and run her business from a ranch.

Benefit 7: Test Out New Business Ideas with Less Risk

If there's one fortunate truth about today's new economy, it's that people are constantly seeking new products and services to improve their lives and to entertain or please themselves. So when you're in business or looking for a business, it's easy to identify a variety of trends or client needs that could turn into a good source of income. But the problem is, how do you as a one-person or small business find the time, expertise, and resources to test out these opportunities. Large companies have resources for research and development and product testing—even if they have to absorb a loss when an idea fails—but we often don't have the time, capital, or expertise to research, develop, and bring such new ideas for products or services onto the market by ourselves. And we usually can't afford to fail at such explorations.

In many cases, teaming up can be the obvious solution. Some business ventures require a tremendous leap of faith and some cold cash to get off the ground. But that's where teaming up can be especially helpful. By teaming up you can share the investment of time, money, and risk to test the viability of good ideas. And you can make use of each other's expertise and double check each others' thinking so your new venture will be more likely to succeed. An engineer, for example, with a passion for gemstones and stonecutting teamed up with an investor to open a gem shop in St. Croix. While leaving the country to start a business as speculative and untested as a gem shop might seem like a pretty risky proposition, by pooling their resources, their shop has been successful. It's led to a new life and a dream come true that neither of them would have been able to risk alone.

By teaming up, Mara Seibert and Leonore Rice were also able to undertake a venture that would otherwise have been too risky. They were both Wall Street professionals—the former a mergers-and-acquisitions specialist, the latter, a lawyer—when, while traveling together on vacation with their families, they visited Imprunetta, Italy. There they happened upon what they considered to be some of the world's most beautiful pottery. As they admired its beauty, an idea came to them: they could import this pottery to the United States! There was no pottery in the United States with such unique coloring and Italian design, so although importing can be expensive and risky, they agreed to work together and test out the idea. They split an initial investment of $4,000 to import a container load of spectacular pottery and, just as they expected, it was an immediate hit. They sold much of the first shipment to landscape designers in their home state of New Jersey. Then they split the cost of having a booth at a trade fair, where they won best-of-show for their booth presentation. Within two years, their company, Seibert & Rice, has gone from sales of $20,000 year to over $100,000, thanks to their hard work and collaborative efforts.

Chelsi Sholty and Melanie Johnson also teamed up to develop an inspired business idea. The two women met when they were working in the human resources (HR) department of a large Boise, Idaho, corporation, but they shared a dream of running their own business someday. Quite by chance, Chelsi began noticing how many small companies in the Boise area could not afford to maintain an in-house HR department. So, inspired by her insight, the two women quit their jobs and established an independent HR consulting firm. By sharing the work and the challenge, they each had less at risk and both felt more confident to go out on their own. As Chelsi told us, "Working with Melanie not only helped me develop the idea for our business, it also gave me the impetus to quit my job and begin thinking about having my own business. I don't think I would have done this if I weren't working with Melanie. We both have different skills, and that allowed us to set larger goals for our business than we could have done alone."

Benefit 8: Respond More Quickly and Easily to the Demands of Changes in the Economy, Your Field, and the Marketplace

Products or services come and go more rapidly today than ever before, sometimes in a period of only a few months or a few years. Not long ago, for instance, Total Quality (TQ) management consulting was popular, whereas today diversity training and expertise in the field of reengineering are in demand. In the 1980s, travel writers could hardly find a publisher for their articles, but today, dozens of newsletters, magazines, and book publishers are seeking out good travel writers.

Such rapid changes require us to shift quickly in response to the quixotic needs of our clients and customers. Teaming up can enable you to shift what you offer more easily so you can stay current with the popular trends of the moment. By forming an alliance with others who already have a foot in the door, you can move quickly into a new milieu, or you can team up with others to introduce a new product or service more readily.

Consider the experience of Mike Hakimi and Joshua Schneider who founded American Information Systems, an Internet service provider and consulting company in Chicago. Mike and Joshua became fascinated with electronic bulletin boards while studying at the University of Illinois and saw a business opportunity they could pursue in this emerging field. Best friends since childhood, they teamed up in 1992 to start a consulting firm helping companies understand and use electronic bulletin board services. By 1994, though, they foresaw that the Internet was becoming the center of on-line activity and people would need services to establish their own on-line presence. So they joined with two other partners who helped them acquire the capital to expand. With hard work and savvy, their business has become one of Chicago's premier private Internet service providers. From their small bootstrap start-up, Mike and Joshua's teaming-up venture now employs twenty-five people and projects 1996 revenues of over $3 million—and they're not even thirty years old!

Similarly, Sharon Crawford and Charlie Russel are a husband-and-wife writing team, specializing in computer books. Although they work on most of their books together, Sharon was approached by a publisher who wanted her to write a book on the Internet, but of course he needed it *immediately.* Rather than pass up the opportunity, Sharon teamed up with another writer who already had experience with the ins and outs of the information highway. Coincidentally, her husband was soon after approached by a different publisher who wanted a book on computer operating systems, also with a deadline of just a few months. He, too, took on that project by teaming up with other writers. In this way, both Sharon and Charlie were able to take on two new cutting-edge writing projects even while they continued working together on the book they'd been under contract to write for over a year. Not only did the two writers create three books within a short period of time, but they were also able to tackle two hot trends before the trends became old hat.

Benefit 9: Reach Clients and Make Contacts in Other Geographic Locations

Despite wondrous advances in communications like teleconferencing, cellular phones, E-mail, and fax, there are times in every business when meeting face-to-face with a client is critical to winning a contract or getting a job done right. In some situations, you still can't beat personal contact. But how can a solo business owner be in more than one place at a time? By teaming up with people in other locations, of course.

For example, Patricia McGinnis and Dottie Hall are partners in a marketing communications company. Specializing in the computer industry, they took advantage of the fact that Patricia lives in Seattle, while Dottie lives in San Francisco. By having an office in each of these locations, they can both cultivate clients in the two leading hotbeds of computer activity in the nation: Silicon Valley and Seattle, home to Microsoft and many other computer companies. If needed, they fly to each other's location when an important meeting comes up, but for the most part, their partnership allows each woman to remain home based while serving a multistate clientele.

Teaming up has enabled business consultant Jordan Ayan and his partner to attract international business. A Brazilian organizer who puts together business workshops was impressed with their joint expertise and invited them to participate in his seminar series in Brazil, all expenses paid. Such opportunities are not unusual; teaming up can be an excellent way to expand into today's international marketplace.

Chiropractor Stuart Garber had always wanted to go to Italy, and thanks to a variety of teaming up activities he now lectures there regularly. It all began when Garber teamed up with several holistic practitioners to open an alternative health center. Through one of his associates at the center, he met a doctor from Curaçao and arranged for the doctor to see clients at the center whenever he was visiting the United States. During one of his visits, the doctor mentioned that he was lecturing in Italy, to which Garber responded, "I'd like to do that!" Not long thereafter he got a fax from Curaçao; the doctor had lined up a lecture series for him in Italy! While lecturing in Italy, Garber teamed up with an alternative medical society there and arranged for them to sponsor future seminars. Through contacts he's made from lecturing internationally, he has been able to team up with practitioners in other countries as well and has lectured in Holland, Curaçao, and Japan.

Benefit 10: Enhance Your Credibility and Reputation

There are many times when a small and home-based business can use added credibility to obtain a particular type of client. So tying in with someone who's already well known or has a reputation in a particular field, industry, or area of expertise can open doors to bigger and better opportunities. This can be especially true when you're just starting to build your reputation, but it can be to your advantage at any time.

Robert Tucker, for example, was an award-winning writer and leading chronicler of social change. His trend-setting articles had appeared in *Esquire*, *Omni*, *Inc*, and *Success!* as well as been syndicated via the *Los Angeles Times* in more than fifty other major newspapers. But to boost his reputation as a professional speaker on social change and innovation, he teamed up with Dennis Waitley to write his first book, *Winning the Innovation Game*. Waitley, an internationally recognized authority on high performance who addresses thousands each year through his speaking engagements for *Fortune* 500 companies, already had several best-selling books on the market including *Seeds of Greatness*. With the added boost of Dennis's reputation, Tucker was soon booked on radio and television shows across the country to talk about innovation. His speaking career has flourished, and he has since written another book of his own, *The Win Value Revolution*.

Often teaming up to boost one's reputation can be a two-way street. If you already have a reputation in your field, it's likely there are other people whose stature can be enhanced by affiliating with you, as yours can by affiliating with them. Here's an example. A professional trainer who specializes in creativity training developed an intriguing idea for a business book. While he had a publisher that was interested in his idea, they weren't willing to publish the book because the trainer wasn't known as a business writer. In other words, the publisher didn't think the trainer had the "credibility" the book needed to be competitive among other business books. Fortunately, a friend introduced the trainer to the vice president of a *Fortune* 500 company who, as it turned out, desperately wanted to have her name on a book to enhance her stature within the company. They agreed to write a book together, making use of each other's credibility, talents, and connections. The writer was able to bring in an agent and a potential publisher, while the VP had the credentials the book needed to be marketed to business audiences. It was a perfect match.

Benefit 11: Boost Your Effectiveness, Creativity, and Energy

To keep the ball rolling in a highly competitive, fast-changing economy, you must remain creative, productive, and energized. Midsize and large companies have access to staff who can pool their various talents to keep pace, but as a small or home-based business, your success depends entirely on your own intelligence, personality, and energy.

By teaming up, however, you too can tap into the creative ideas and energy of others. Carolyn Colby, for example, found that not only was she able to get more business through the home nursing network she founded, but she also enjoyed not having to rely solely on her own brain power all the time. She appreciates having others around to help her problem solve and share ideas and suggestions. Mike Hakimi, who runs the Internet service American Information Systems discussed earlier, told us he values the input of his three partners highly and attributes the success of his company to their ability to work together creatively.

Teaming up also enables you to gain access to skills that don't come naturally to you. For example, some self-employed individuals and small-business owners have a wealth of "right-brain" creativity to come up with new services or products, but they lack the logical "left-brain" organizational ability to follow through on the details and practicalities of implementing their ideas. Others are excellent at providing their particular product or service but detest having to market, promote, and sell what they do. By teaming up with the right person, such individuals can build a business that neither one could launch successfully working alone. Indeed, many of the best-known partnerships, such as Jobs and Wozniak (Apple Computer), Hewlett and Packard (HP), and Ben and Jerry (Ben and Jerry's Ice Cream) are said to be collaborations that grew out of complementing each other's creative skills and abilities.

When twenty-five-year-old Daryn Ross of Orrich, Missouri, started a business imprinting T-shirts and other novelty items for college fraternities and sororities, his father was about to retire from his job teaching industrial arts. Due to Daryn's sales skills and campus contacts, his business doubled every year right from the start, but he needed someone to handle the actual imprinting side of the business. So it seemed like a natural to ask his dad to help out. By teaming up with his parents, Don and Teresa, who run the entire printing operation of his company, Daryn's company, Innovative Concepts, has become a million-dollar business.

Teaming up can help you tap into "personality traits" that round out your strengths and compensate for your weaknesses. Some people, for example, lean toward being introverted, while others are extroverted. Some people are better at problem solving, while others are more creative by nature. Some people are a whiz with numbers, while others shine at marketing. Examine the list below, for instance, and determine which side of the spectrum you tend to be on.

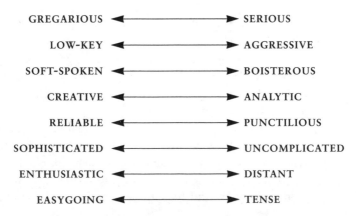

GREGARIOUS	SERIOUS
LOW-KEY	AGGRESSIVE
SOFT-SPOKEN	BOISTEROUS
CREATIVE	ANALYTIC
RELIABLE	PUNCTILIOUS
SOPHISTICATED	UNCOMPLICATED
ENTHUSIASTIC	DISTANT
EASYGOING	TENSE

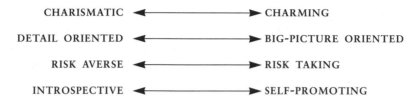

CHARISMATIC ←——————→ CHARMING

DETAIL ORIENTED ←——————→ BIG-PICTURE ORIENTED

RISK AVERSE ←——————→ RISK TAKING

INTROSPECTIVE ←——————→ SELF-PROMOTING

Whatever your personality, can you imagine how useful it might be to work with someone with a complementary set of traits? Dave Lakhani and Liane Lemon have found such a match as business partners in a Boise, Idaho, consulting firm. Dave is a marketing consultant and Liane is a CPA. Dave acknowledges that Liane is more detail oriented, better with numbers, and tends to be more cautious in her outlook. Liane acknowledges that Dave is more energetic, perceptive, and tends to be more of a risk taker than she is. They both attest that, together, they complement each other in ways that make them better able to analyze their clients' businesses and give more balanced business advice. By combining their knowledge and complementary skills, they're able to specialize in helping small businesses develop practical business strategies.

Complementary personalities can be particularly useful in negotiations. We're all familiar with the "good cop, bad cop" routine in which two people take opposite roles in a tough negotiating situation: one person takes the easygoing, affable, and cooperative approach, while the other assumes an aggressive, no-nonsense demeanor. Actually such a team effort can be quite effective in moving negotiations along to a win-win conclusion if it becomes clear that you're no pushover, but you're also willing to cooperate and be reasonable. We've found that partners or associates often tend to fall naturally into these complementary roles and can assist one another to reach agreements either one would have difficulty reaching on his or her own.

Teaming up can increase your effectiveness in other more subtle ways as well. Sometimes a particular client is more responsive to working with a man or a woman, for example, or with someone of a particular ethnic background. Despite laws against such bias, many businesspeople swear they've gotten business because the client was more receptive to a partner of a particular sex or ethnic background. Of course, larger companies with many employees can gain such advantages easily by assigning particular projects to the most advantageous staff person. But by working with others, you can gain this decided advantage too.

For example, special-event planner Wendy Gladney, whom we mentioned earlier, is of mixed African-American and Caucasian ancestry. Wendy is certain she has experienced prejudice in her business dealings on some occasions, and so in some situations she collaborates with other independent contractors as a way to avoid such problems. On one occasion, a client was balking at using her services to run a particular event, so she turned to an older Caucasian woman she subcontracts work to. The woman accompanied Wendy to the next client meeting and, just as she suspected, her colleague was able to close the deal because the client assumed Wendy was the employee rather than the owner of the company. Now, whenever Wendy feels there may be a problem with a client who seems uncomfortable working with a young African-American woman, she knows to team up with others to "get around" this barrier.

Ultimately, teaming up can create unparalleled synergy for your business. Chellie Campbell, whom we mentioned earlier as operating a professional bookkeeping and financial consulting firm, quotes her father who offered her this advice.

> Collaborations lead to the highest achievements of mankind because they combine the special resources and skills of many people. Like the space shuttle, which was built using the intellect of over four thousand people, most of us can achieve astonishing feats by learning to focus on what we do best and leaving other tasks to those who have the right talent to get them done.

Benefit 12: Do a Better Job More Quickly

As we mentioned before, providing high quality on a fast timetable is increasingly important these days. Just as corporations are under the gun to deliver more in less time and still get it right, most small and home-based businesses are equally pressured to handle whatever deadlines are demanded and deliver exactly as promised.

And once again, teaming up with others can be one answer to meeting such pressures. In fact, if your business involves providing outsourced work like desktop publishing, copywriting, marketing, or public relations for larger companies, teaming up to share your workload and make sure it all gets done on time can be particularly advantageous. Mary Beth Mason, for example, is a desktop publisher and owner of Word Mason, in Silver Springs, Maryland. Her clients are large companies that always seem to be a in a big hurry for their jobs, so Mary Beth has created an extensive network of other desktop publishers to whom she can send work when a critical deadline looms. In exchange, she provides backup for her colleagues as well, thus filling in the occasional downtime she experiences.

Benefit 13: Share Expenses to Stretch a Tight Budget

As the saying goes, you need to spend money to make money. While large companies have hefty financial resources at their disposal, most one-person or small businesses have much tighter budgets to work within. We may not be able to afford to buy a new piece of office equipment every year, or advertise as much as we might like in the most desirable media, or exhibit at all the trade shows we could benefit from, or invest in attending all the seminars and training programs we hear about that could help us run our businesses better. But by teaming up with others, we may be able to do these very things despite budget limitations.

Several businesses can share advertising costs, for example, split the costs of booth space at a trade show, chip in to purchase new equipment, or the rental of an office. Sharing marketing expenses, in particular, can be a welcome relief to small and home-based businesses who may need to spend thousands of dollars each year to make sure people know about their products and services. A magician, a musician, and a poet, for example, joined together to have a booth at a Seattle Chamber of Commerce small-business expo. Each of these creative people is selling his or her services to corporate trainers and event planners. By pooling their resources, they were able to have an attractive booth where they could demonstrate firsthand their effectiveness by attracting prospective clients and other spectators to their booth.

Through a professional networking group, the Secretarial Association Services, Barbara Taylor participated in an innovative co-op ad campaign. She joined with nine other secretarial services to take out a large space ad in the Yellow Pages. If she had taken an ad of this size herself, it would have cost her $900; by joining with other services she split up the price and was able to get the benefit of a large ad for only $90. Each service got much more than this cost savings, however. By listing individually under the Secretarial Association Services ad, they were able to present themselves as part of a larger organization that could handle whatever work a client needed. If one person was too busy to take on work, others could; and since they were located throughout San Diego County, a caller could always find someone nearby. Because the ad included the association logo, they also could benefit from the prestige of a professional affiliation.

As a rule of thumb, the higher your cost of doing business, the more worthwhile it is for you to team up and split expenses. In particular, if you're undertaking any kind of new product research and development, you'll almost certainly benefit from sharing such costs with a partner or collaborator of some kind. For instance, Ray DiMarini recognized the value of teaming up when he came up with a concept for designing more powerful softball bats. Given that the softball bat industry was completely dominated by large companies, Ray knew he would need to join up with someone else to pursue his vision. He found engineer Mike Eggiman, and together they formed Dimarini Sports, Inc., in Hillsboro, Oregon. The two began working out of a barn, where they built their own manufacturing equipment to produce Ray's specially designed bats that pack more punch than older bat designs. When their first-year sales hit $65,000, they knew they had a potential business, so they obtained a loan from the Small Business Administration to increase their distribution. Between 1991 and 1995, their sales skyrocketed to $2.5 million, and they now have distribution to over 27,000 sporting goods stores.

Benefit 14: Avoid Professional Isolation and Get Inside Information

Personal contacts and up-to-date information are key to anyone's success when you're on your own. You have to keep up with the trends and issues in your field, and better yet, keep an eye on the future as well as ever-changing government regulations, new technologies, and the latest industry gossip. But working alone in a small or home office, it's easy to feel cut off from what's going on unless you stay connected with others.

Teaming up can be a great antidote for such isolation. By networking, collaborating, partnering, or otherwise teaming up, small and home-based businesses can get tuned in to the "grapevine" through which the latest word on industry developments is so often conveyed. In some cases, partners, formal or informal, can agree to carry out specific aspects of keeping up-to-date with the latest information as part of their responsibilities. Wendy Gladney relies on her collaboration with a graphic arts company for much of the inside information in her industry. As Wendy told us,

> The biggest thing about teaming up for me is that it helps me get and understand a lot of new information. There are certain proposals I get that I don't know quite what to do with it, so I always team up with Brian on these. He not only has the time to help me, but he used to be an executive with IBM and so he understands corporate America, and what buzzwords they might be looking for. He also has a lot of contacts I can make use of.

For professional organizer Priscilla Young of Providence, Rhode Island, the statewide Home Business Association sponsored by the state Chamber of Commerce has kept her from feeling isolated. She says, "I don't know how I would have survived without it. The moral support I get from the group has been important to me. Working for yourself you may not even see the same clients every day so it can get very, very lonely. But through the association, I have a chance to connect with others on a regular basis like you do on a job. I've made some wonderful friends and I no longer have any fear of walking up to someone, putting out my hand, and saying hello. The key is we're a real down-home, down-to-earth group, very warm. We know we're all in this together and we really care about each other. I know I speak for the whole group when I say this."

In some cases, teaming up may be a way to share the responsibility of keeping up-to-date with the latest information. Liane Lemon and Dave Lakhani, mentioned above, have decided for example that because of Dave's voracious reading habits, he'll take charge of reading the variety of journals in their field and pass on the pertinent information to Liane. She handles other matters for them, thereby allowing Dave the time to keep up on his reading. Through this arrangement, both Dave and Liane can keep current.

Benefit 15: Get Needed Support Without Hiring Employees

While adding staff can be costly and at odds with the lifestyle many self-employed individuals are seeking, through collaborations or partnerships, it's often possible to harness the manpower you need to get more work, take on larger projects, and carry out administrative tasks without the hassle of hiring employees.

Many husband-and-wife ventures originate for this very reason. One spouse may start as a solo enterprise, but when the business grows to a certain level, the other spouse decides to join in the business rather than hiring an outside individual. Debra Goldentyre, for example, was a health-care lawyer for several years when her husband, Mark, a videographer who specialized in producing corporate and educational training videos, won a large contract and needed to bring in someone else to help out. Partly because Debra didn't like her job, and partly because Mark needed legal research for his project, Debra agreed to come on board and assist her husband. That was more than six years ago, and today the couple runs a successful videography business, Schaeffer & Goldentyre, from their home in Oakland, California. For each of their projects, Debra does most of the research and script writing, while Mark directs and handles postproduction editing.

Similarly, Lu Howell and her husband work together in their company, Computer Dust Busters in Salt Lake City, Utah. In this case, Lu began the business on her own but soon found that the market was so vast and customers so eager for her computer maintenance and repair services that she decided to hire her husband, an alternative they both preferred to her bringing in an outside employee.

Photographer Helen Garber has developed a variety of innovative ways of teaming up to get help with her business. Photographing publicity events is one of Garber's specialties, and so she joined the L.A. Publicity Club as a way to market her business. Attendance at the meetings was light, however, so she asked for information about how she could advertise in the organization's newsletter. Much to her surprise, she received a call the next morning asking if she would be interested in taking photographs for the club's upcoming awards banquet in exchange for advertising space in their newsletter. She was delighted! Not only did she get several ads featuring her work in the newsletters, but three of her photographs and her client list were also featured in the program guide for the banquet. So by the time she met publicists at the banquet, they'd already seen her name and her photographs twice.

To demonstrate that she had the capability of handling large-scale publicity events, Helen teamed up with another photographer, Joseph McDougall II, who accompanied her to the awards banquet. They formed PRP, Public Relations Photography, and had special cards made in time for the event. The contacts they've made have been fruitful and they plan to team up in this way with other organizations and galleries. And, of course, she's added the L.A. Publicity Club to her client list. Interestingly, Garber had initially approached

The Mental and Physical Health Benefits of Teaming Up

In addition to the financial benefits teaming up provides, research shows that collaborating offers many psychological, physical, and spiritual benefits as well. In fact, according to noted cardiologist and author Dr. Dean Ornish, recent studies reveal that people who are lonely or feel isolated have a greater risk of dying prematurely. Furthermore, research shows that middle-aged men who live relatively isolated from others have a higher risk of developing heart disease.

As Americans have become more and more mobile moving from job to job and city to city, we have become a more disconnected society in which many of us no longer have family or friends nearby. With our high-pressured, fast-paced lives, many high achievers develop unhealthy lifestyle habits such as hypercompetitiveness, overeating, drinking, or workaholism to compensate for their loneliness and lack of social ties.

Teaming up with others, however, can help solo business owners who find themselves working harder and enjoying it less to put the joy back into their work and their lives. Even when they are making more money than they ever did before, solo entrepreneurs who are driven relentlessly to compete can burn out quickly, suffer high levels of stress, and experience psychological problems such as depression and anxiety. So as a self-employed or small-business person, don't just think about what teaming up can do for your business and financial success, also consider what it can do for your physical and psychological well-being.

another photographer about teaming up in this way, but the woman couldn't see the benefit of sharing future fees coming from such events. Now, while Helen and Joseph are working on other client projects together, this photographer is having to fill in part-time with secretarial work.

MAKING THE SHIFT FROM COMPETITION TO COOPERATION

As you can see, the benefits of teaming up are considerable and go a long way toward neutralizing many of the challenges self-employed individuals and small businesses face as they pursue today's many opportunities. But most of us have been trained to believe that we have to compete to win. We've been taught that competition spurs us on to victory, to constantly produce superior performance, and ultimately to defeat our opponents. In fact, we live in a competition-driven world. Just glance at any newspaper or tune in to any newscast and you'll hear not only the sports statistics but also the ratings for virtually every industry from what TV shows win their time slots each week to what songs top the chart, from what software packages sell the most to what movies have the highest box office, and from what network wins the sweeps to what airline has the best on-time record.

College applicants compete based on SAT scores and class standing; graduates compete based on GRE scores and grade point averages. Corporate success of one company is measured against another in terms of their percentage share of the market, stock prices, and annual revenues. Cars are rated against one another for frequency of repair records and average resale value. And so on and so on.

Our drive to compete is so ingrained that sometimes we're propelled as much by the fear of losing as by the desire to win. In fact, competition is so ingrained in our thinking and behavior that trainers who have developed exercises to teach team-building skills find that many people will not forsake the idea of beating their teammates in training exercises, even if their competitive approach means their team will score poorly again and again. Even after participants are shown mathematically that the only way to amass a winning score in an exercise is to cooperate, many people still continue to compete instead. As one participant said in such an exercise, "In the end, I was afraid my teammates would try to get all the points for themselves instead of cooperating, and I didn't want to be the one with the lowest score, so I didn't cooperate either."

While for the self-employed, the tide is turning dramatically toward cooperation, we still live in a competitive society. So it's natural to feel somewhat wary or apprehensive about teaming up. In many ways, it goes against some of our most basic cultural programming, particularly when it comes to working with colleagues who could just as easily become competitors. Quite naturally, in the back of your mind, you may wonder, "Why should I team up? Someone might end up stealing my clients. They might gain an advantage and take away my share of the market. They might undercut me. I might lose what I've worked so hard to gain." And, if any of those things has ever happened to you, even once, it will be even harder to consider cooperating the next time around.

Common Concerns About Teaming Up

The following is a list of the top reservations men and women have about teaming up. Check off any that concern you.

    ___ **1.** I'll get the short end of the stick, doing most of the work and putting in most of the costs but splitting the money.

    ___ **2.** Teaming up will take more time and slow down my ability to respond.

    ___ **3.** There won't be enough money coming in to make it worth everyone's while.

    ___ **4.** I'll experience a loss of control.

    ___ **5.** People will perceive me as less than capable since I have to bring in others.

___ 6. Ego issues and conflicts will be time-consuming and unpleasant.

___ 7. Not everyone will have the same level of commitment.

___ 8. Handling interpersonal issues will be uncomfortable.

___ 9. Of necessity, everyone will put their own needs first, so they may pull out and leave me in the lurch.

___ 10. The reward won't be equal to the amount of time, energy and effort I'll have to put in.

Our intention in the chapters that follow is to outline practical ways to avoid these concerns so you can limit your involvement to mutually rewarding, conflict-free relationships with other individuals and organizations. But even under the best of circumstances, we've found, everyone has her or his own comfort zone when it comes to working with others. At one end of the continuum are people who are highly cooperative by nature. Working with others comes naturally to them. They prefer working in teams and do their best work as part of a joint effort. In fact, they have a hard time working alone. At the other end of the continuum are the true "lone eagles." They prefer to work by themselves and find working with others interferes with their progress and slows them down. Most people, of course, fall somewhere in between these two extremes. Most people are comfortable with varying degrees of cooperative interaction under various circumstances, sometimes preferring to work solo and other times liking some degree of involvement with others. How would you describe yourself?

YOUR TEAMING COMFORT ZONE

|__|__|__|__|__|__|__|__|__|__|__|__|__|__|

STRICTLY   TEAM

A LONE EAGLE   PLAYER

Fortunately, today there's a wide spectrum of opportunities for working with others. Some involve virtually no commitment or risk; others require a level of commitment that does leave you vulnerable, exposing you not only to loss, but to liability as well. As we outline the various ways people are teaming up, we invite you to identify what level of involvement you feel comfortable with at this time and to begin building relationships that match your comfort level. You can use the skills and guidelines outlined in the chapters that follow to build a track record of successful alliances, and as you do, you may become comfortable with making more such affiliations and even want to get more involved with others than you do at this time.

Overcoming Skepticism

If you're still skeptical about the idea of teaming up, rest assured you're not alone. As we said, it's difficult for many people to imagine a world that's not based on "healthy competition." But if you'd like to enjoy the benefits teaming up affords, consider the downside of operating from the traditional competitive model we've grown so familiar with. As noted teacher and consultant Alfie Kohn points out, in his book *No Contest: The Cases Against Competition,* many of our assumptions about competition are actually incorrect and no longer practical at this point in history. Kohn believes that these days competition can cause more harm than good. He believes it can lead to a "win at all costs" philosophy that leads us to lie, cheat, steal, and even harm ourselves or others physically or psychologically in an effort to get ahead. A *USA Today* survey supports this contention. It found that 55 percent of workers say their co-workers lie to supervisors, 41 percent falsify records, and 35 percent steal from their employers. Similar studies show that college students are equally willing to cheat or falsify information in order to get in, stay in, and graduate.

In the end, says Kohn, we can benefit greatly by reframing our view of the world and shifting our perspective from competition to cooperation. Kohn's research makes the following convincing arguments that contradict the popular notions about competition.

1. Competition is not inevitable. Many people think that competitiveness is an instinct, an inveterate aspect of human nature. There is actually little evidence, however, to demonstrate a biological component to competition. Instead competition seems to be a learned trait that we must be carefully taught from the earliest years of our socialization process. In fact, the degree of competitiveness varies greatly from society to society and culture to culture. In Japan, for example, the level of competitiveness among children is far less than in the United States. Unfortunately, however, as the training exercises described above demonstrate, competition reinforces itself as those who are competitive tend to think others are competing against them. Ultimately, as you will see from the many success stories throughout this book, staying in such a competitive rat race is by no means inevitable.

2. Competition is not necessarily productive. Perhaps the most detrimental assumption about competition is that it makes us perform better and achieve more. But this, too, says Kohn, is a fallacy, as many self-employed individuals are discovering. There's nothing inherent in human nature that prevents us from achieving our best and producing superior performances without having to compete against others. In fact, much research shows that competing against yourself and working toward your own goals is a more important indicator of success than focusing your efforts on beating out the competition. As Kohn writes, "Superior performance not only does not *require* competition; it usually seems to require its absence."

Furthermore, a great deal of research shows that, depending on the task, people can actually be more productive by working cooperatively in groups. It has been shown in over 120 studies that students learn better when cooperating; people are better at problem solving when cooperating; and even artistic creativity blossoms more readily with cooperation. As Kohn concludes, "Trying to do well and trying to beat others are two different things," and competition actually detracts from one's ability to do well. In addition, whereas competition often squanders resources, cooperation maximizes them.

3. Competition is not necessarily enjoyable. Many people believe that competition adds spice to life, particularly in the context of sports, games, and recreation. However, once again, Kohn shows that play is more enjoyable when it doesn't have a competitive focus or a "goal to win orientation." Adults in particular are happier when play and sports have a "process focus," meaning when your motivation isn't focused on whether you win or lose, but on how well you play the game. Perhaps this is why cooperation is flourishing among the self-employed, because most people going out on their own today want their work to be as fun and stress free as it is profitable.

4. Competition doesn't necessarily build character. In Kohn's view, instead of building character, all too often, competition is a means of compensating for low self-esteem, and as a result, competing becomes like a vicious cycle that leads, not to greater self-confidence, but to greater insecurities. The more you compete, the more you want to win and the more you want to win the more you want to compete until it becomes an addiction. Kohn goes so far as to contend that there is no such thing as "healthy" competition. He finds the two terms are actually antithetical to each other.

5. Competition doesn't necessarily forge strong relationships. Kohn suggests in no uncertain terms that instead of strengthening relationships, competition poisons them. Living in a society that trains us to regard others as our adversaries strains our ability to form high-quality relationships. Kohn writes, "Camaraderie and companionship—to say nothing of genuine friendship and love—scarcely have a chance to take root when we are defined as competitors." When "I can succeed only if you fail," we become rivals, not colleagues. In contrast, when we think well of ourselves while being empathic to others, we're more likely to develop a better and deeper understanding of one another.

Think for example of the way we used to view the Olympic Games when the Soviet Union was considered to be our national adversary. And think about how differently we can view the games now that we no longer fear the

Eastern bloc countries. Today, we can more easily enjoy an outstanding gold-medal performance whether it's that of a U.S. athlete or one from Russia, Ukraine, or Romania.

Kohn concludes that by replacing our competitive view of life with a more cooperative one, we can both accomplish more and get enjoyment from our work and our personal lives. As he concludes, we don't need to "act as if cooperation is something for which we must passively sit and wait, like a beautiful sunset." Instead, we can change our personal attitudes and habits and free ourselves from the limitations of viewing everything we do in terms of how we stack up against others. We can proactively replace our societal competitive psyche with a larger cooperative framework in which everyone can win through his or her own honest efforts.

So, if you're still wary about teaming up, if you still harbor doubts that collaborating with others can make sense for your business, we invite you to set aside your doubts and bad memories of past teaming-up experiences. Open your mind to the new thinking and creative ideas you'll find in this book. You'll find that we're entering a new era, a time in which collaboration and building alliances can produce an exciting array of new possibilities for you. You'll discover a growing number of forward-looking approaches for teaming up that can foster healthier, more positive ways of working with others so that each person's success contributes to the other's. Today, winning is more often than not a shared game, not a zero-sum proposition in which only the lucky few can win. We believe that economic survival today no longer needs to be a dog-eat-dog world, but rather a matter of running with the right pack. As poet Rudyard Kipling wrote many years ago,

> Now this is the Law of the Jungle—
>   as old and as true as the sky;
> And the Wolf that shall keep it may prosper,
>   but the Wolf that shall break it must die.
> As the creeper that girdles the tree trunk,
>   the Law runneth forward and back—
> For the strength of the Pack is the Wolf
>   and the strength of the Wolf is the Pack.

The goal of teaming up today is to allow everyone to gain whatever it is she or he is most hoping for, be it greater financial rewards, less stress, a higher level of creativity, answers to technical problems, networking contacts, or just plain friendship with a close business partner. Obviously since each person's situation is different, you'll want to customize the recommendations in this book to your needs. However, as you read through the chapters that follow, you'll find the basic structure and fundamental procedures for prospering from teaming-up efforts and you may become an enthusiastic convert to a new and more cooperative way of working.

Confessions from a Convert

Not everyone we talked with in writing this book started out feeling enthusiastic about teaming up, but most of them feel differently today. Sometimes they've been quite startled by the profound impact working with others can have on their lives. That was certainly true for the following person whose confession provides a touching glimpse of what teaming up can be like at its best.

> When I decided to go out on my own, I relished the freedom of not having to confer with anyone about anything I wanted to do. I'd had it with meetings and office politics and interoffice memos. I could do anything I wanted whenever I wanted and that gave me the ultimate in flexibility and responsibility. I could act quickly and with abandon, or hold back and put off what didn't feel right. I could watch my ideas take root, see what became of them, learn from my mistakes, redirect my efforts, use my ingenuity, and let intuition be my guide. I felt my confidence soar as, for better or worse, I experienced controlling my own destiny for the first time in my life.
>
> When things weren't going well, there were lonely, sleepless nights. Even nights of desperation. But I survived these crises and each one I overcame made me stronger. The more successful I became, the more I realized I didn't *need* other people to survive, yet the more I felt *drawn* to share and communicate and interact with others. I had come to genuinely enjoy other people's success. And I genuinely enjoyed contributing to it. And as if by magic, more and more people were offering to help me in ways I would never have imagined.
>
> One day, for example, quite by accident I ran into someone at a bookstore who I'd known years before. After learning about my work, he became excited and offered to promote my work on his Web page. Soon someone he knew called me with suggestions for how I could create my own Web page for very little cost. Not long after that I had another serendipitous experience that changed the way I wanted to work from that point forward.
>
> A business trip took me to a small college community in upstate New York that happened to be the home of a colleague I knew from our national trade association. On a whim, I decided that since I was going to be in town I'd call to see if she'd like to get together for dinner while I was there. She was delighted and began telling me about a team of colleagues she'd been collaborating with who she thought I might enjoy meeting. Although they lived in various parts of the state, she offered to pull the team together for what she referred to as a brainstorming dinner.
>
> As we all gathered around the dining table in a quiet corner of a comfy health-food restaurant, the group began telling me about how

they'd met, the projects they were undertaking both individually and together, and the various ways they were involved with one another, some working together on one project, others on another, and so on. What became clear was that these individuals shared a common vision for advancing and contributing to our field and to one another's success. As one person would speak, the rest would listen with rapt attention, not interrupting, not elaborating or correcting, or upstaging, but seemingly hanging on the speaker's every word. Each speaker became increasingly articulate in the glow of the group's attention. And after a time, whoever was speaking would pause and after a moment, someone else would begin talking, at which point everyone's rapt attention would shift to that person, almost as if we were watching a championship tennis match.

Within no time, we were all bouncing ideas off one another and growing increasingly excited about ourselves and one another's work. The room became electric. I can't remember a time I felt more alive, more attuned to life's rich possibilities. I can't remember a time in my professional career that I'd felt so supported or so able to be supportive. As we left the restaurant to each go our separate ways, our eyes were aglow. We looked like children on Christmas Eve waiting for Santa to arrive. Or perhaps like a group of carolers setting out to spread holiday cheer to all we met.

Since that time, we've collaborated in a variety of ways in various combinations, communicating via phone, fax, or E-mail and occasionally in person. I feel sure we'll continue to do so in the future in ways I can't even begin to imagine at this moment. But the most significant impact from the evening was how it changed forever my view of what it meant to work with other people. For the first time in my life, I'd had a firsthand experience with what noncompetitive, win-win collaboration within a group of like-minded people could be. And I was hooked.

Since that time I've participated in innumerable joint ventures, both formal and informal, with many other people, from sharing booth space to writing a book with a colleague, from doing a joint research project to cosponsoring a series of workshops. I work only with people who share my goals and values and who have as little time or desire for hassle and discord in their lives as I do. And it seems there's no end to the success we can lavish upon one another.

IMAGINE THE FUTURE

All in all, we believe that the impact of this shift toward teaming up will have enormous implications for the way we live and work. We foresee an emerging new economic environment that's gradually reshaping our society, causing people to lessen their conditioned competitive instincts so they can learn to work together for the good of all. As we approach the millennium, we will likely all be living more in what Marshall McLuhan called the global village, a world in which one's work and personal life commingle in one peaceful worldwide market that freely shares information, ideas, and lifestyles. Although there will still be competition among businesses, it will occur in a friendlier, lighter fashion that demonstrates respect and support for one another. As each person wins one by one, we all win!

Consider this visual image of the future: Imagine a large map board, similar to the classic world map that hangs on the wall at the NASA space control center. The board is covered with millions of interconnected, flashing points of light. At any instant, one light signals another nearby, then a third one way across the board. The third then links up with a fourth and a fifth at the opposite end of the board, and the fifth eventually sends back a signal to light up the first. As the signals spread, this type of linking happens all across the board, as groups of lights intermittently flash on and off, signaling within their own clusters as well as to and from other clusters from one end of the map to another.

This is the image we see for our future: vast networks of homes and small offices all interconnecting in crisscrossing patterns, buzzing and blinking as they link with one another. Indeed, this will be the global commerce of the future, one in which people working from their separate homes and offices interact freely, passing information and work back and forth from one to another, communicating and collaborating as needed, building upon one another's expertise, and earning a living in the process.

We wrote *Teaming Up* to help you join in creating this future.

RESOURCES

The Age of Unreason. Charles Handy. Boston: Harvard Business, 1990.

Managing in a Time of Great Change. Peter F. Drucker. New York: NAL/ Dutton, 1995.

No Contest: The Case Against Competition. Alfie Kohn. Boston: Houghton Mifflin, 1992.

The Virtual Corporation. William H. Davidow and Michael S. Malone. New York: Harper Business, 1993.

2

Ten Win-Win Ways
of Teaming Up

The power of We is stronger than the power of Me.
—Red Holzman, basketball coach
New York Knicks

Some of the ways small and home-based businesses are teaming up to enhance their mutual success are already familiar to most of us and seem to have been used throughout time. Other ways people are teaming, however, are quite innovative and represent new ways for people to work together.

In this chapter, we've organized the various ways people are teaming up into ten win-win options, any one or a combination of which you may find to be beneficial for your business. Each of these options has its own pros and cons. Some methods are more structured; others, more informal. Some are more complex and involve considerable time, energy, money, and legal implications. Others are quite simple and involve little commitment. So to help you decide which options will be most appealing to you we've included examples of how people are benefiting from each of these options, and we list the general circumstances and situations in which each option may work best for self-employed individuals and small businesses.

As we mentioned in the previous chapter, everyone has his or her own comfort level for working with others, so we've sequenced the ten teaming-up options along a continuum from the least involving, most simple of relationships to the more complex and formal ones. We'll begin by describing ways to team up that allow you to continue operating with as much independence as you desire, without any legal or financial formalities. As we proceed along the continuum, we'll discuss increasingly involved arrangements that require greater levels of commitment over longer periods of time and require more legal and financial negotiations.

Our goal is to help you identify where along this continuum your teaming up comfort level lies at this time. As you read through the ten ways people are teaming up, you might want to make notes on the options that seem most appealing to you—and those that don't—as well as the ones you've already used or are using and your overall satisfaction or dissatisfaction with them.

We recommend that you begin by experimenting with simpler relationships before committing to more complex and formal ones. In this way, you can test the waters, so to speak, see how well teaming up works for you, and develop your skills at identifying the right associates or partners. You can also use this "gradual" approach when getting involved with a particular individual or group, working with them more informally at first. In other words, you can think of teaming up as a process that's somewhat like dating and mating. You can begin "dating" a variety of individuals until you find someone you'd like to date on a more or less exclusive basis. Figuratively speaking, you may ultimately want to get engaged, live together, or even get married to one person or business you find the most mutually rewarding and compatible.

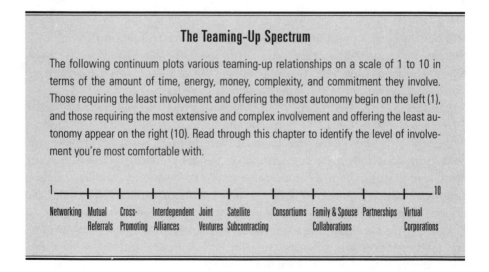

The Teaming-Up Spectrum

The following continuum plots various teaming-up relationships on a scale of 1 to 10 in terms of the amount of time, energy, money, complexity, and commitment they involve. Those requiring the least involvement and offering the most autonomy begin on the left (1), and those requiring the most extensive and complex involvement and offering the least autonomy appear on the right (10). Read through this chapter to identify the level of involvement you're most comfortable with.

1 —————————————————————————— 10

Networking | Mutual Referrals | Cross-Promoting | Interdependent Alliances | Joint Ventures | Satellite Subcontracting | Consortiums | Family & Spouse Collaborations | Partnerships | Virtual Corporations

OPTION 1: NETWORKING

Networking is by far the most popular, and one of the most effective, marketing methods for small and home-based businesses, so you're undoubtedly already quite familiar with it. You may already be a proficient networker and find it to be an effective way to get business. But networking can be far more than a business-generating tool. It can also be a nonthreatening, low-risk, infinitely flexible and rewarding way to team up with others.

That certainly was what Beverley Williams made of networking. Beverley helped start the Women's Business Owners of Montgomery County, Maryland, primarily to help promote her desktop publishing business. Through the organization's Desktop Publishing Special Interest Group (SIG), she discovered just how much more than a lead-generator networking could be. The twelve to fifteen women in the Desktop Publishing SIG developed into a true team, assisting each other when needed on one another's projects, doing joint ventures together, and actively promoting one another's businesses. Williams has gone on to create the American Association of Home-Based Businesses (AAHBB), a national organization with eighty-some chapters in development through which others can enjoy the values of teaming up through networking.

Experiences like Beverly's have convinced us that when viewed from a broader perspective, networking can be an entrée to a rich array of teaming-up experiences and one of the easiest ways to begin working with others.

Networking Defined

Perhaps networking can best be summed up with the expression "You help me, and I'll help you." As you can see from the box on page 44, a wealth of networking organizations exists in virtually every community across the country. As a teaming-up activity, however, networking goes beyond being a convenient way to make contacts and get business leads. A network can become a team of individuals who actively work together for one another's success in any combination of the following three ways.

1. Networking As a Marketing Team. Many networks are, in fact, or could be, highly effective marketing teams in which each person takes on the responsibility of learning as much as she or he can about the businesses of other members and each actively works to promote and sell the others' services. In some networking groups, for example, like LeTip International, members are required to bring referrals to each meeting and actually carry a business card case containing one another's cards. Such groups are essentially mutual-referral networks, and they consider one another to be extensions of their own businesses.

One well-known network that views their activities as a team marketing effort is Business Network, International (BNI), a networking association founded by Dr. Ivan Misner in 1985. BNI now has more than five hundred chapters across the U.S. and in several other nations as well. According to Misner, in 1995, the collective efforts of all BNI chapters accounted for almost 400,000 referrals, which generated over $130 million in business for BNI's 10,000-plus members. Virginia Devine is a good example of how networking as a team within BNI can pay off for a small business. As a home-based accountant, Virginia joined one of the first BNI chapters in the mid-1980s and by attending the weekly meetings and working with those in her group, within one year she had doubled her gross income through referrals from the other group members. Virginia stayed in her BNI chapter for six years, by the end of which she had quadrupled her business!

Even more informal networking arrangements can become effective "marketing teams." Barry Allen, for example, had been a member of a formal networking group, but he didn't enjoy the pressure of having to attend every meeting and having to be constantly referring clients to other members. So he formed the Consumer Business Network (CBN), a more informal type of group that nevertheless allowed people to help one another exchange leads and referrals. CBN groups meet for breakfast once a week, and there is no annual fee or requirement to attend meetings. People can come as often as they wish at any time. This approach to team marketing worked for interior designer Victoria Alberty. Thanks to the referrals from members of three CBN groups she's active in, Alberty was able to build her business from scratch.

The key to making networking a marketing team effort lies in joining networks or linking up with others in a network who are willing to view networking activities as more than a quick chance to meet new business prospects. When a group takes a longer-term perspective of working to build one another's businesses, there are multiple mutually beneficial marketing activities they can explore. The Seattle Chamber of Commerce, for example, offers an annual business expo as part of its member services. These annual business expos provide a way for members to jointly market their businesses. And as we mentioned before, several members of the San Diego–based Secretarial Association Services have taken the initiative to link their marketing efforts by taking out a collective Yellow Pages ad under the name of the association.

2. Networking As a Support Team. Networks can also become highly effective support teams in which members view one another almost as "family," helping one another in whatever ways are needed. Networking associations can become a source of encouragement and feedback on new ideas, a problem-solving arena for finding answers to sticky business questions, a source of advice from experienced individuals, and a chance to belong to a community where you can get the support you need as well as contribute to the success of others.

When Peggy Glenn started her own secretarial service, she felt isolated and cut off from colleagues and associates, so she decided to create a network for herself. As she told us, "I called a few other people who ran secretarial businesses and invited them to lunch, Dutch treat. Six or seven of them came, and right then and there was the birth of what has become a great network. We support one another. We help with overload. And best of all, there is somebody to call on a bad day (or on a good day), somebody you can learn from if you've just received a job that is something you've never done before, somebody to refer others to if you don't want to take the job."

When an Oakland wildfire destroyed Sue Rugee's home and her home-based information research company along with it, colleagues from the professional association she'd been active in sent her gifts and pitched in to help her get started again. When a major account pulled their business back in-house, Chellie Campbell's bookkeeping service almost went under. But by joining a mentor program sponsored jointly by the National Association of Women Business Owners (NAWBO) and the Small Business Administration, Campbell was assigned to a successful woman-business owner who provided specific direction and emotional support to help Campbell rebuild her business.

Networking as a support team is a two-way street. Not only do you benefit, but you also are able to provide advice, encouragement, referrals, leads, and introductions to everyone else within your network.

3. Networking As a Springboard to Other Generative Relationships. Networking is probably the most effective way to create, discover, or stumble upon a wealth of other serendipitous opportunities. Networking provides a doorway to meet interesting people to team up with, a low-risk platform for exploring and testing the potential of new relationships, and a way to hear about projects and activities you can engage in. In other words, networking is a way to find relationships that will lead to other relationships and to become involved in activities that evolve into still other activities you would never otherwise have known about or been included in.

For instance, Chicago business consultant Jordan Ayan who was mentioned in chapter 1 met his teaming-up collaborator, Deanna Berg, when he was attending a conference for professional consultants in the Boston area. Their meeting was actually a fortuitous occurrence, because Jordan had just lost a very important bid on a major contract. While networking that evening with people at the conference, Jordan met Deanna and began telling her about his plight. Much to his surprise, it turned out that Deanna was the person who'd won that very same contract. Since winning the bid, Deanna had decided that she needed help on the contract, so she invited Jordan to join her in doing the project, while splitting the fees. After that project, Jordan and Deanna have continued to do workshops and consulting jobs together, pooling their complementary strengths and expertise. While they are not formal business partners, they work together as frequently as they can.

Through her participation in CBN, Sharon Merino, a business consultant who specializes in helping small minority- and women-owned businesses get certified with state and local governments to get business from those governments, met Jack Friery, a lawyer from Manhattan Beach. They began doing seminars and training sessions together, and this association has led to unexpected new business for both of them.

Professional organizer Julie Morgenstern is a member of the National Association of Professional Organizers (NAPO) which has its online head-quarters on the Working from Home Forum on CompuServe. Through online connections Julie and other NAPO members are generating a wealth of ways to support one another's businesses. Their goal is to develop a list of 101 ways to promote one another's work. Here are six relationships that are already under way from which many more can be expected.

1. Morgenstern sells colleague Stephanie Schur's videotape, *How to Organize Your Home,* at her own workshops on getting organized.
2. Various members are selling one another's time-planning systems to their clients.
3. Members are subcontracting work to other organizers.
4. Two NAPO members are collaborating on writing a book; others are collaborating on developing new organizing products.
5. Members are helping to get one another's books and products into retail outlets in their area. For example, when Morgenstern noticed that organizer Barbara Hemphill's book, *Taming the Office Tiger,* was not in her local Office Depot store, she wrote a note to the manager suggesting they carry the book and asking him to direct the request to the national buyer.
6. Members are including information about one another's products in their mailings or catalogs. For example, Morgenstern was thrilled when fellow organizer Sandra Felton included her *How to Be the Organized Women of Proverbs 31* in her *Messies Anonymous* catalog.

"We each move in different circles," Morgenstern points out, "and by promoting each other's products and or businesses, we can expand our collective effectiveness and reach more people. And isn't that why we do what we do—help others in organizing?"

Of course, not all networks think of or conduct themselves as a team. And not everyone wants to network as a team. As you can see in reviewing the following box, some groups are strictly civic, social, or educational in nature. Networking is purely an ancillary activity or side benefit so to speak. Others are strictly grab-what-you-can-and-run propositions with large numbers of people flowing in and out of meetings madly promoting themselves before moving on to more fertile fields. Still other networks are simply casual professional arenas where people can create whatever opportunities arise. You may have participated in all such types of networking events. But the true beauty of networking is that you can pick and choose and mold your networking experiences into whatever type of interaction you wish, even to the point of creating your own network that's custom designed to your particular needs.

Five Types of Networking Groups

There are basically five different types of networking groups you might want to consider participating in. Any one of them can become a doorway to a rich array of teaming-up activities. For names and addresses of such organizations see the Resources list at the end of this chapter.

1. Business Organizations. The local Chambers of Commerce found in virtually every city around the country are one of the most popular examples of this type of network. Other examples include women's referral networks, singles or women's business organizations like the National Association of Women Business Owners (NAWBO), home-business associations, and other small-business organizations. Any number of people from all kinds of professions can network through such organizations. Their goals are to share information among members, listen to business presentations of general interest to the entire group, lobby for local legislation that might be useful to the business community, and mingle informally with one another to develop friendships and business leads. They usually meet monthly for lunch or dinner, although they may also sponsor seminars, expos, or conferences throughout the year. Members are free to come to as many or as few meetings as they wish.

2. Leads Clubs. These networks exist for the expressed purpose of generating business leads and referrals for the members. Each group or chapter usually restricts membership to one person from any given profession or specialty. In other words, each leads club opens its doors to just one accountant, one lawyer, one management consultant, one dentist, one chiropractor, etc. Meetings are usually held weekly over breakfast, lunch, or dinner. Members are expected to attend all meetings, which often follow a formal procedure that begins with a member giving a presentation about his or her business so other members can make more effective referrals. Members then exchange leads or referrals, and of course there is usually time for informal networking. Some leads groups require members to bring at least one referral to each meeting or pay a fine. Some groups also require chapter members to carry the business cards of other members with them to further facilitate making referrals. National leads clubs with local chapters throughout the country include such organizations as Business Network International, LEADS Clubs, and Le Tip International.

3. Community-Service Clubs. Community-service clubs are dedicated to performing public service for various causes through fund-raisers and volunteer activities. These include groups like Rotary International, Lions, and Kiwanis as well as religious-affiliated associations. In general, overt networking for business purposes is discouraged; however, informal networking can still be quite effective. In the process of "giving something back" to your community, you can meet movers and shakers in your area and often, as a by-product of volunteering time or cash contributions, you can make valuable contacts that lead to future business relationships.

4. Professional Associations. Professional associations are a valuable way to establish relationships with colleagues in your field. Such contacts can often be sources of valuable leads, referrals, cutting-edge information, support, and overload exchanges. But contacts can also grow into long-term teaming-up arrangements of a more committed nature. Participation at national, regional, and local levels can each provide many teaming-up opportunities.

5. On-Line Networking Groups. A growing wealth of on-line computer networks provide rich opportunities to link up with potential partners and associates across the nation and around the world. Networking through services such as CompuServe, America Online, and the Internet magnifies your ability to make contact a hundredfold. You can join interest groups, chat with people over bulletin boards, access E-mail, and attend live conferences at any time, twenty-four hours a day. The Court Reporter's Forum or the PR and Marketing Forum on CompuServe, or the Medical Transcriptionist bulletin board on America Online are examples of the type of formal on-line network organizations available to businesspeople in almost every profession.

If you can't find a networking group that meets your needs, you can do what so many others have done and form your own. Many of the organizations we've mentioned provide assistance in establishing new chapters, or you can simply create your own group. That's what we (Paul and Sarah) did when we moved from our hometown of Kansas City to Los Angeles. We began what we called the Community Network, and each month we hosted a potluck dinner for about twenty of our neighbors and suppliers. During the evening each person would introduce himself or herself to the group, explain what they did, and what kind of contacts they were hoping to make. Through this informal social network, we ended up meeting contacts, some of whom we continue to do business with today. We also made many friendships that have lasted for years.

When fiber artist Cameron Taylor-Brown moved to Los Angeles, she too found no ready-made networking group to affiliate with. However, when one of her works was published in *Fiber Arts* magazine, she had an idea. Cameron contacted all the other artists whose work had been displayed in that issue of the magazine and invited them to join with her in putting together a portfolio and presentation binder. She then began showing the joint portfolio to galleries around in the area. The portfolio attracted the attention of the cultural affairs department of Los Angeles, and they agreed to do a show in a Woodland Hills gallery featuring her and her newly created "network" of artists.

Forming Your Own Networking Group

If you don't find a networking group that provides the type of relationships you're looking for, you can form your own. While your group can be formal or informal in nature, we recommend starting small and informally until you find a cohesive group of like-minded individuals who want to establish a more formal identity. The group you start can remain an informal support group for a long time, or it can evolve into any one or more of the other teaming-up options you'll read about throughout this chapter.

Here are a few tips on starting a group of your own.

1. Identify what you want from creating such a group and what you're willing to contribute. Do you want to share leads and referrals, or are you more interested in providing problem-solving and personal support? What type of individuals do you want to have in your group? Do you want to join with people in the same field, for instance, or interact with people from a variety of compatible fields? Do you have a preference for meeting weekly, every two weeks, or monthly? Do you want to meet over breakfast, lunch, dinner, or some other time?

2. Begin by finding two to four like-minded individuals who share your desire for a networking group. Once you've identified your needs and preferences, look for a few other people you'd enjoy and benefit from meeting with regularly. If necessary, build your group one person at a time. Try to find successful, win/win people with a proven attitude of success. Select individuals who believe there's plenty of opportunity in the world for everyone to profit and who enjoy sharing their success with others. Get to know these individuals as well as possible.

3. Hold a few initial meetings. Early meetings can focus on getting to know one another personally and professionally. These meetings can also address the logistics and procedures you wish to establish. Be flexible at this stage, however, because you are forming a group of colleagues and peers, the group will probably want to evolve its own format over time.

4. Ask each person to think ahead of time what they'd like to accomplish in each meeting. Do they need ideas and options for their businesses? Do they want feedback on their ideas? Is there a problem that the entire group could brainstorm and help solve? Are there resources each of you can recommend to the others? Is there a particular frustration you can sympathize with and help resolve?

5. Agree upon a structure for your meetings. Decide when, where, and how often you'd like to meet and agree upon what you'll do at your meetings. A sample structure for your meeting might be as follows:

- We'll meet once a month for dinner at a centrally located restaurant.
- We'll begin each meeting with fifteen to twenty minutes of casual conversation during which we all can talk informally about whatever is on our minds.
- Then each person will have a chance to identify what he or she would like to get from the meeting.
- We'll divide the remaining time into quadrants focused either on each person's need or on any shared topics that have been raised.

With a simple structure like this, each meeting can be valuable to everyone involved in a variety of ways. You might help one another find new ways of doing business, getting new clients, coping with problems, developing new goals, expanding business, developing a five-year strategy, and whatever other issues fit your group.

6. Be prepared for your group to go through a "forming" process as you get to know one another and learn to work together. At first, your group will go through an "orientation period" as people get acquainted. Then most new groups experience "second thoughts" or a "resistance" phase as people begin "feeling each other out" to discover how much they can safely share about their business and personal lives with other members. Once people find their comfort level with one another, the "commitment" stage begins and members agree on goals, structure, and so forth. This period is often quite exciting and creative, as members come up with many ideas for what they can do together. Finally, the group begins "performing," working together as members begin trusting one another and working together.

7. Don't let meetings get bogged down in negativity. A networking group should be willing to help its members through thick and thin, yet each meeting also needs to be a positive experience or people will begin losing interest. So it's important that your meetings don't turn into extended gripe sessions focused only on complaining about problems and lamenting miseries. You can avoid this by setting aside a specific time in each meeting for what we call "Ain't-It-Awfuls." During this time those who need to can complain and air their feelings about difficult situations, disappointments, troublesome clients, and so forth. When someone needs time for Ain't-It-Awfuls, everyone else can provide appropriate sympathy and support. Then after five minutes or so, the group can get on to other business, including, if desired, problem solving and positive-action steps for addressing difficulties.

With Whom and How to Network

If networking is to be a rewarding experience, it's vital to connect with the right people. Every networking group has its own "personality," and you'll want to find one that suits you. It's also vital that you network with people who can actually be of service to you and you to them. The most common problem people have with networking is investing a lot of time and energy in a group without getting a commensurate return. As one woman told us, "I've been attending meetings now for almost a year. I reach out to people. I've donated my services. I've volunteered to help out on many activities, but nothing's happened. I like the people and they seem to like me. I just haven't gotten any new business or developed any relationships that have led anywhere for my business."

Clearly this woman is networking in, what for her, is barren ground. She needs to find a group that will be fertile soil where her contributions can grow. The right group will be "generative" in nature. In other words, as you participate and contribute actively, your contributions should begin bearing fruit. One contact should be leading to another, and another to another. The right group will become like a beehive of activity for you and those you meet, abuzz with energy and ripe with possibilities. One way to make sure this happens is to determine if you share similar interests, goals, challenges, and clientele. So gravitate toward groups that you know have a need for and interest in your work and you in theirs.

As photographer Helen Garber told us,

> I'd been to a lot of networking groups, and although the people were always nice and very professional, I still felt somewhat like a stranger until I went to the Advertising Photographers Association of America (APA). The minute I walked into their meeting, I knew I was in the right place. These people were like me. They were my compatriots. We were dressed alike, we were talking about the same things. We had the same needs and concerns. I felt right at home.

As with Helen, finding the right group for you may take some time and exploration. You may need to attend many different group meetings before you find the right one or two. But when you do, it will have been worth the effort and you may have met other interesting people along the way.

Tips for Effective Networking

Of course, each group will have its own expectations of members and variations in how it operates, but here are six basic tips you can use in developing or improving your networking skills.

1. Sample a variety of networking groups with different styles. Attend several networking meetings before making a commitment to join. Find a group where you feel comfortable that offers what you're looking for and where you can make a contribution that will be appreciated. Most groups are happy to have people come one or more times as a visitor.

2. Attend the meetings of the group(s) you join regularly and become an active participant. Don't waste your own time or that of others with a half-

hearted effort. You won't reap the rewards of networking unless you participate fully and actually get to know the other members over time. Be friendly.
Talk to people and let them know what you do. Aim to spend at least ten minutes talking with new people you meet to establish an initial rapport. Don't
try to "sell" or close deals at your networking meetings. Focus on getting to
know people. Save selling and deal making for follow-up contact.

3. Go to meetings with your eyes and ears open to new possibilities. Regardless of what kind of group you join, be aware that you can benefit in
many ways, sometimes unexpectedly, from the relationships you're developing. View your networking as a long-term strategy. Even if an individual or
group activity doesn't seem to hold the promise of immediate business referrals or leads, be open to meeting people with whom you get along well and
could work with in other ways in the future. For example, while networking,
you might get computer training, learn general marketing skills from others,
find a way to expand to another geographic area, or augment your financial
resources from someone seeking to invest. Opportunities like these could far
outweigh a one-time lead or referral for possible business.

4. Follow the credo "Givers gain." According to Ivan Misner, the first
law of professional networking is to have a positive and supportive attitude.
This law is predicated on the age-old notion that "What goes around comes
around." In other words, the more you give, the more you get. We agree
wholeheartedly with this principle. If you view networking first as an effort to
help others rather than as a way to quickly get something for yourself, you
could be surprised at the opportunities that develop.

*5. Spend time developing a catchy description of your business along
with a lighthearted short "hook"* to pique interest. Use the short hook whenever you meet people who ask what you do. Don't bore them with all the details unless they're interested and ask you to explain more. For example, to
introduce being in the bookkeeping business, Chellie Campbell told people
she did "financial stress reduction." That was her short hook. Use your
longer description whenever you're invited to tell others more about your
business capabilities.

6. Don't expect yourself to be a master "networker" immediately. Give
yourself time to develop your skills at meeting people, giving presentations
about your business, generating leads, offering assistance, and establishing relationships. Networking is an acquired skill. And in the process of acquiring
it, you'll be honing your skills for teaming up in other ways.

When you think about networking as a springboard to teaming up, it can
be an excellent way to explore, test, and enjoy rewarding business relationships.

Summary—Pros and Cons of Networking

Pros

- You can draw upon other people's time, information, and advice when needed.
- You can avoid isolation, keep abreast of new developments, and contribute to your field.
- More people learn about your business, and you get the chance to make new business-generating contacts.
- You have flexibility as to if, how, and when to relate to a wide variety of people.
- You can explore and test out other possible teaming-up relationships with low risk.
- The cost is low. Most networking groups have low membership fees. Often your greatest cost is the price of the meal that is part of most meetings.
- There is high potential for making new business relationships in groups that are fertile ground for your business.

Cons

- Successful networking is time-consuming. You must take time out to attend meetings regularly, and you must get involved. Just showing up usually isn't enough. You must follow up on the contacts you make and work at being sure you also reciprocate by helping those you meet.
- Not everyone is comfortable promoting themselves directly. Some people don't like mixing business and personal activities. Others feel that networking for leads and referrals is somewhat crass.
- There's no guarantee of results from informal networking. Success depends on the quality of contacts you make and your own efforts. You may or may not get worthwhile referrals, and you may not meet people you want to team up with.

OPTION 2: MUTUAL REFERRALS

Like networking, giving and getting referrals is a common marketing practice among small businesses. In fact, most successfully established self-employed individuals tell us they get the majority of their business through "word-of-mouth" referrals. But making referrals among colleagues and peers is fast becoming more than a marketing strategy. Developing mutual referral agreements is blossoming into a popular way to run your business more effectively by teaming up.

Dan Silverman, for example, is a financial planner specializing in insurance and estate planning. In order to provide creative solutions to clients with particularly challenging insurance issues, Silverman has a mutual referral agreement with insurance agent Julian Movsesian, who specializes in underwriting. Their relationship began with casually referring business to each other on occasion, but over the years as their relationship developed, mutual referring has become a standard aspect of both of their businesses. Movsesian refers smaller clients to Silverman; Silverman refers large, complex cases to Movsesian. They split commissions on the work they refer to each other fifty-fifty. Their arrangement enables them both to focus on their own specialty without having to limit their business.

Mutual Referrals Defined

A mutual-referral agreement involves a conscious decision between two or more people to refer business to one another on a regular basis. While most businesspeople make occasional referrals to a variety of colleagues and professionals, developing a mutual-referral relationship involves a higher degree of commitment and trust. For example, when I, Sarah, began my private psychotherapy practice, I had an unspoken agreement that I would send clients who needed to work with a male therapist to my colleague Richard Nadeau, and he in turn sent clients who needed to work with a female therapist to me. This arrangement worked quite well for both of us and kept our clients happy. Over the years, our mutual-referral agreement became explicit and we expended our referral network to include a variety of other types of therapists who could handle special cases neither of us was prepared to take on. Ultimately we had weekly meetings with key network participants.

To Whom and When to Make Mutual Referrals

You can make mutual-referral agreements on a one-to-one basis with various individuals you select or, like Sarah, you can join with others to create a mutual-referral network. In either case, you can make such agreements either among colleagues in your own field or among people in other fields who in the course of doing what they do come into regular contact with people who need what you offer.

REFERRALS AMONG COLLEAGUES

At first blush it might not seem as though people in the same business or field would be a very promising source of referrals. After all, aren't they supposed to be your competitors? And wouldn't it be detrimental to your interest to give business to a competitor? But referrals among colleagues work very well in two situations.

1. When you have a lot of business coming in. When you have more business than you can handle, instead of turning down work or disappointing your clients or customers by getting behind in your work, it could make sense for you to call upon a colleague to handle your overflow. And in return, you can work out an agreement that when they've got more work than they can do, they'll refer their overflow to you. Everyone wins in such an ad hoc arrangement. You each can rest assured that you'll have backup when you've got more work than you can do or when an emergency occurs. And when times are slow, you've got a ready-made prospect for getting new business. In some fields where fee splitting or commissions are appropriate, you can also share in the revenue generated from the business you referred.

2. When your business is highly specialized. Often the more specialized your business, the more successful you'll be, but by specializing you may want to decline business that doesn't fit with your specialty. By setting up mutual-referral agreements, however, you won't need to lose out when business comes along that doesn't fall within your specialty. You can refer that business to a colleague whose specialty is more in line with the client's needs and expect to get referrals in return when his or her clients need what you have to offer. Mutual referrals among highly specialized businesses are a win/win situation for everyone, including the clients who get reliable referrals without having to spend time locating sources who can offer what they need.

REFERRALS AMONG PEOPLE IN DIFFERENT PROFESSIONS

Setting up mutual-referral arrangements with people in other professions is an especially valuable way to team up. These people become, in effect, gatekeepers for you, leading you to new clients. Virtually every day, your gatekeepers may come in contact with people who need what you offer; and since they already have a relationship with these clients, what better recommendation can you get? Of course, in return, those you serve may need your gatekeeper's services, so you can make referrals to them as well. Such arrangements can be a perfect fit! The more you refer to your gatekeepers, the more likely they will be to refer to you in return.

Here are four situations when having a mutual-referral agreement with people in other fields can work especially well.

1. When customers have many choices. Mutual referrals work especially well in an urban or suburban area where there are many competing businesses. In fact, whenever there's a wealth of choices available, customers and clients usually prefer getting a referral. Referrals help them find what they need more quickly and with less risk of being disappointed. The CPA who can refer clients to a lawyer, financial planner, or real estate agent is not only appreciated by his or her clients but can also realize a wealth of referral business in return.

2. Whenever those who need what you offer also need help from a variety of other related businesses. Often if customers need one type of service, it's likely they'll need help in other, related areas as well. For example, someone planning a wedding or buying a home usually needs a host of services all at once. If you're a wedding makeup artist, for example, it makes sense to set up a mutual-referral arrangement with a wedding planner, a caterer, a florist, a wedding-dress and tuxedo shop, a bakery, a musician, a travel agent, and so forth, because anyone planning a wedding also needs all these services. By cross-referring to one another, you can help each prosper. Similarly, a real estate appraiser would benefit from setting up mutual-referral arrangements with real estate agents, contractors, home inspectors, and others who regularly work with people who might need to have their homes appraised.

3. When your business is highly specialized. If you've specialized in related fields, getting referrals from others is a low-cost way to get a steady flow of business. For example, if you're an artist who does unique paintings, you might do well to have a mutual-referral arrangement with an interior designer who comes into regular contact with people wanting to redecorate their homes. Naturally you can refer your own clients to the decorator too. Similarly, if you are a corporate trainer, you could have a mutual referral agreement with a management consultant. Such relationships can help build your reputation as an influential person and become a reliable source of business.

Vivian Shimoyama, a jewelry designer, is also a member of the Los Angeles chapter of the National Association of Women Business Owners. At one NAWBO meeting, Vivian met another member whose business, Pieces of Art, Inc., is selling items like gold-plated pens to corporations which use them as premium giveaways. The two women hit it off because their highly specialized businesses were perfect matches for each other. Since their meeting, the two women have collaborated together on several deals using Vivian's jewelry designs as part of the premium the other woman sells. Although they decided not to become formal business partners, they work with each other on a regular basis either by mutual referrals or by combining forces for a special promotion one of them sells to a large corporation.

4. When you can draw on a marketable group identity. People often prefer to do business with other people who belong to their same professional association, religious group, or civic organization. For example, people often prefer to do business with owners and entrepreneurs who belong to their church or synagogue. Hence, the popularity of various ethnic interest group "yellow pages." If you belong to an affinity group, it can be useful to create specific mutual-referral agreements with other members of organizations you're active in.

Basic Tips for Effective Referrals

Making mutual-referral arrangements or joining a mutual-referral network involves a closer, more personal level of commitment than networking. As a result, your relationship becomes somewhat more complex as well. Referral arrangements tend to increase the expectations people have of one another. Those to whom you're referring business are no longer casual acquaintances or ancillary to your business. Indeed, you now have higher hopes that they will come through for you just as they have high hopes that you will be helpful to them. If the level of referrals doesn't live up to your expectations, you'll be disappointed. Likewise, if referrals aren't roughly equal in number or quality between you, disappointment may also be the result. The one holding the short end of the stick may become angry, bitter, or suspicious, and your future relationship may be jeopardized.

Also, sometimes a mutual-referral arrangement can invite associates to become more critical of one another. When you make referrals, you expect them to serve the customers or clients well, just as they expect you to do a good job for their customers. Both your reputations are on the line. While there are no cut-and-dried formulas for how to manage these issues, here are a few tips that can help.

1. Start small and take it slow. Begin with a more casual referral agreement until you get to know the individuals involved and feel confident you have shared goals and expectations, can rely on them to provide high-quality products and services, and can expect reciprocity. Then you can consider making a more formalized agreement and perhaps creating a referral network among those with whom you work well.

2. Spell out the details of how you'll refer to each other and write them down in a letter. Discuss how you want each other to make contact with those you refer. Do you want to give your clients the phone number of your associate and let her or him initiate the client contact, or do you feel comfortable getting permission to give the clients' phone numbers to your associate directly? It's important to clarify such issues to define what you each consider a "referral" to be. Sometimes, people can have very different ideas of what constitutes a referral. For instance, consider these situations.

- Jane is a desktop publisher and, one day, her client happens to mention that he is about to buy new office furniture. Jane has an informal agreement with an interior designer, so she calls him to let him know the potential customer's name. The problem is, Jane has never mentioned to her client that she's making this referral, so when the designer calls, the client is confused and indicates that he's already shopping elsewhere. This isn't a useful referral. It's not even a very good lead.
- Robert is a career counselor. He has made a mutual-referral arrangement with a psychotherapist. In thinking about people he could refer to get the relationship off the ground, he concludes that since his sister has been having lots of problems with her teenage son, he'll give her the psychotherapist's name and phone number. This, too, isn't a true referral. The sister has yet to express interest in or a need for a psychotherapist.

- Marjory is a bookkeeper. In the process of serving one of her clients, she discovers that he has yet to computerize the accounting system for his dry cleaning business, so she gives the dry cleaner's name to a computer consultant in her referral group network. But again, this isn't a true "referral." This will be little more than a cold call for the computer consultant because the dry cleaner has yet to decide that he wants to computerize and Marjory hasn't talked with her client to find out if he wants a referral.

As you can see, there is plenty of room for misunderstandings in making referrals, so always be sure to clarify the referral process you and your associates will be using. Similarly, be sure your customers are aware that you're making a referral—and that they want one—so they won't be surprised when they get a call from your colleague seeking their business. A good-quality referral is one in which the person not only needs the product or service, but also realizes the need for it and is actively seeking it. A good-quality referral also involves asking if the person would like a referral and, if so, telling him or her something about who you'll be referring them to, along with why you believe this referral is the right one for the situation.

3. Clarify your expectations. Make sure you each understand when and to whom you'll be referring. Don't just assume that you will get the number and type of referrals you want to serve. And check to be sure you each can expect to make such referrals.

Being precise will avoid misunderstandings. Connie, for example, is a massage therapist. She met a facialist at a networking meeting and they talked about making mutual referrals. Soon Connie had sent her colleague several new clients but had gotten no referrals yet in return. So finally she raised the issue and discovered the facialist felt she could only refer people when the massage therapist at the salon where she rented space was too busy to take on additional clients.

4. Always make a referral immediately when an opportunity arises. Don't let a hot lead turn cold with time, or worse, don't think you have helped your colleague by referring someone to him or her who never calls. From the colleague's point of view, if there's been no contact, there's been no referral. So when you give an associate's phone number to someone, call and give the referral's name to your associates and say he or she can be expecting to get a call.

5. Don't give the same referral to more than one business, unless the person asks for several names. When you have a mutual-referral agreement, it's your job to make sure you perceive a good fit for the person you're referring to. If you can't wholeheartedly recommend your colleague's products or services, don't team up with him or her. And if you can endorse someone wholeheartedly, don't put them in competition with others, thinking they're getting a referral.

6. When you get a referral from a colleague, follow up right away. No matter how busy you are, always call the person who's been referred to you immediately to discuss his or her needs. Never give the impression you're too busy to respond to your colleague's referrals.

7. Express appreciation for each referral you get. Always thank your colleagues for each referral you get. In fact, thank them frequently. A thank-you note or phone call will usually suffice, but if a colleague has sent you a lot of business or a very substantial piece of business, you may want to send an appropriate gift or express your appreciation by inviting her or him to be your guest for dinner.

8. Adjust your referral arrangements as needed. When problems develop, approach them openly from a problem-solving perspective (see chapter 5). But if a referral relationship doesn't appear to be working out, ending it can create an uncomfortable situation that should be handled with care. If the arrangement has been a casual one, chances are you can let it die a natural death while keeping your relationship cordial. If the person continues referring to you, however, or if you have an explicit agreement to refer to each other exclusively, you'll need to diplomatically let the person know you need to change your plans. Otherwise, you'll risk her or his becoming bitter, disgruntled, or even vindictive.

In ending your relationship, unless the person has behaved unethically or improperly, there is nothing to be gained from itemizing all the "reasons" you don't want to work together anymore. Of course, if you're really unhappy, it may be tempting to complain. You'll be best served, however, by simply letting them know that your situation has changed and that while you can no longer be counted on to make regular referrals, you do continue to wish them the best.

Should You Give and Get a Referral Fee or Commission?

One question that always comes up when making referrals is whether or not to offer a commission on them. Many people feel that if a referral results in a sale, the referring party should share in the profit by receiving a referral fee of either some set dollar amount or some percentage of the business ranging from 5 to 50 percent. Those who advocate referral fees believe that they increase the motivation to refer. But others are adamantly opposed to the idea of a referral fee, believing it diminishes the value of a referral by giving the impression that it's made from the standpoint of vested self-interest instead of a belief in the quality of the product or service.

Clearly, you need to discuss with those you're mutually referring whether or not to give referral fees. If you don't know where you stand on this issue, here are several questions you can ask to reach a mutually agreeable decision.

1. *Will you be making referrals to each other on an ongoing basis?* If so, it probably makes more sense to avoid giving referral fees. What you're offering each other for referrals is to make referrals in return. So unless otherwise stated, the expectation is that no referral fee is needed. However, when referrals are made to someone with whom you have no particular ongoing referral agreement, paying a commission could be appropriate, especially when the dollar amount of the business is sizable.

2. *Will the pattern of referrals actually be mutual?* When someone will be consistently making referrals without getting any referrals in return, then a commission or referral fee might be appropriate. So, if you're getting referrals regularly from someone but are unable to provide any in return, you may want to offer a referral fee as a way to keep those referrals coming to you.

On occasion, Mary Vandergrift and her partner, who run a medical billing company in Columbia, Maryland, have paid a commission for referrals. For example, the owner of another medical billing company referred a doctor to them who needed a complete computer system installed in his office. The owner made this referral because, unlike Mary, he didn't have a background in working with hardware. In return for the business, which was considerable, Mary paid a 15 percent commission on the fee.

To build BaLooney Balloons, Ray Bichenest gives commissions to party planners, caterers, and equipment rental companies who send him new business. These referrals helped him build business up quickly, so after a year he could quit his job and concentrate full-time on his business. "It's like having a part-time sales force out there," he says. In business now for four years, Bichenest has three employees and has served 550 clients.

3. *Would you prefer some other form of exchange?* If you don't feel comfortable taking a commission—or someone you're getting referrals from is uncomfortable with your paying one—you might consider exchanging services or helping out each other's business in some other way. This accomplishes two things: first, it diplomatically acknowledges the value of the referral and assures that everyone gets some benefit from making it; second, it puts you on a "business-to-business" footing in the event you want or need to collaborate further in the future.

For example when Carla Young opened her private practice as a marriage counselor, her mentor, whose practice was full, referred clients to her regularly. She appreciated the referrals but felt uncomfortable with the one-sided nature of their relationship, so she volunteered to assist at seminars the mentor held each month. He appreciated the help, and after working together in this way they eventually began offering other seminars together as business partners.

4. Are commissions or fee splitting ethical in your business field? In some professions fee splitting is considered unethical, and even suggesting it will cause your colleague to question your credibility. So be sure to find out how referral fees and commissions are regarded in your field before raising this issue.

Summary—Pros and Cons of Mutual Referrals

Pros
- Mutual referrals are by far the least time-consuming, most cost-effective way to get steady business.
- The majority of successfully self-employed individuals and small businesses get most of their business from word of mouth.
- Mutual referrals work so well because they enable you to get business coming to you without your having to spend inordinate amounts of time marketing yourself.
- Mutual-referral arrangements are flexible, easy to set up, and can be as formal or informal as you feel comfortable negotiating.

Cons
- Referrals may or may not be of the nature or quality you are seeking.
- You have to make sure the people you refer to will, in fact, provide high-quality services to those you send them. Your reputation is going to be affected when you make a referral. If clients or customers are disappointed with a referral, they'll be disappointed and perhaps angry with you too.
- The number and frequency of referrals between you and an associate may turn out to be lopsided, in which case one of you may start to feel resentful.
- By aligning yourself with a particular person, you could cut yourself off from other possible referral sources.

OPTION 3: CROSS-PROMOTING

Graphic designer Elyse Chapman set up a successful cross-promotion with five other small businesses. She wanted to produce a high-quality, information-intensive promotional newsletter that featured her business, but she didn't want to shoulder the financial burden of the thousands of dollars required to do a top-notch job of producing and disseminating it. So she conceived a plan for joining with other professionals who would donate their time and expertise to produce a newsletter that would be called *Ad News, Tips & Tricks,* which would include ads and feature articles about each of their businesses and expertise.

With this in mind, she approached photographer David Gautreau. He liked the idea and contributed the photography for the entire six-page piece in exchange for an ad and an article by him entitled "Take Your Best Shot." The article is accompanied by a head shot of him, photos of his studio equipment, and a biographical line describing his expertise. Elyse then presented her joint promotion idea to illustrator Dave Arkle. Dave also liked the idea and contributed illustrations for the newsletter along with an ad. Copywriter Ron Cogan edited the newsletter in exchange for an ad and article entitled "The Successful Press Release," which included a picture and bio material about him.

In order to show off Elyse's graphic designs, the newsletter needed to be printed using a sophisticated two-color process, so she approached S. G. Advanced Color Graphics, and sure enough they liked the idea of joining her cross-promotion, so they printed the newsletter in exchange for an ad.

The only remaining cost was for mailing out the newsletters, which could be considerable, so Elyse contacted Nancy DeDiemar, owner of Quality Mailing, about participating in the joint effort. Nancy, too, liked the idea and contributed an article showcasing her expertise entitled "Shrink Direct Mail Costs & Improve Your Return." Quality Mailing also had a display ad in the newsletter.

In the end, all five participants benefited from this joint promotional effort. Some, including Elyse, got business immediately from the actual mailing. And everyone involved now has an excellent high-quality promotional piece to use as a brochure or handout and, in doing so, each is cross-promoting the other. Anytime one of them distributes the newsletter, they will all get the added exposure at virtually no cost. Elyse's total out-of-pocket investment was only $150!

Cross-promotions like this can take your teaming-up results one step further than trading referrals. Cross-promoting enables you to actively join forces with others to promote each other's products and services. In some cases, cross-promotion also means spending *your* money to help others' business because they are spending *their* money to help yours. In addition, sometimes including a well-known business as part of one of your promotions can improve the perception of what you offer.

Cross-Promoting Defined

In the book *Walk Your Talk,* business consultant Kare Anderson defines the concept of cross-promotion in the following way.

> Cross-promoting means pooling your promotional resources (time, money, ideas, contacts, etc.) with others who share the same market, so that everyone gets more visibility and positive impact for a fraction of the effort and expense . . . cross-promotion might involve a joint advertising campaign, media event, or mailing; offering discounts on one another's products or services; promoting one another with signs and flyers in your places of business; or having the Blue Angels write

your names across the sky. It can be anything that you and your partner think will capture the attention of the customers you share.

With Whom to Cross-Promote

Essentially you want to cross-promote with others who are trying to reach the same clients and customers you're wanting to reach. So, the first step is to identify precisely whom you want to reach, and then figure out who else wants to reach these same individuals or companies. To develop an in-depth profile of your potential clients or customers, begin by asking yourself these questions.

- Who are my customers?
- Where do they live or work?
- How much money do they make?
- How frequently do they buy my product or service?
- What motivates them to buy from me?
- What characteristics are they looking for in a product? Are they more interested in quality, quantity, or a mix of the two?
- What are their interests?
- How quickly do they need my product or service after they contact me?
- If they don't buy from me, who would they buy from?

If you still don't feel you have a handle on who your customers are, create a questionnaire and ask your existing customers to fill it out in exchange for a gift certificate or a small gift of some kind. Once you have answers to these questions, write up as explicitly as you can a customer profile to describe the people or businesses you're seeking. Try to describe them in detail so another person reading your profile can actually visualize precisely whom you're wanting to reach.

The next step is to ask yourself who else wants to serve these same customers. Your potential allies in cross-marketing needn't be limited to profit-making businesses. In some cases you can also team up with nonprofit associations or community organizations. For example, you may identify a potential partner in a nonprofit health association such as the Cancer Society, or in a volunteer group that helps teenagers or unwed mothers.

Armed with your list of other businesses or groups who want to reach your customers, you can then begin approaching them and brainstorming about how you might combine your efforts to help promote one another. For instance, you could:

- Combine resources to pay for display advertising that features you both.
- Give out coupons offering discounts on one another's businesses to your clients.

- Put business cards, brochures, even signs or posters in one another's workplaces or print promotional messages for one another's businesses on your receipts or enclose them in your mailings.
- Hand out promotional items like pens, calendars, etc., with one another's businesses' names imprinted on them.
- Provide testimonials for one another's products or services.
- Give free speeches for one another's clientele.
- Offer discounts on any business you refer to one another.
- Provide your service as a gift or reward to one another's special customers.
- Agree to work together on a community project so you can all get free publicity from the event.
- Jointly sponsor a contest, street fair, trade show booth, or special event.

And so on and so on. The point is, there are many, many options for cross-promoting. You can even team up with one business for one kind of campaign and another business for another type of campaign.

Here's an example of how hair stylist Edward Salazar made cross-promotion work for him. Salazar specializes in doing hair for media personalities, all of whom need to have their hair styled for publicity photos and media appearances. So he teamed up with a photographer whose clients need to have their hair styled before having their head shots taken. Salazar gave gift certificates for a free photo session with the photographer to his "preferred" client list at the holiday season, and in turn the photographer gave gift certificates for a free hairstyling with Salazar to his "preferred" clients.

Ultimately, your choice of a cross-promoting partner depends on many factors, such as:

- The nature of your business. Do you serve other businesses or do you serve consumers?
- The size of your business. Are you home based versus a larger small business?
- The amount you're willing to spend. Do you have only a few hundred dollars to spend or can you invest big bucks?
- The time you have. Are you working overtime to serve your clients and customers or do you have more time than money?
- The life cycle of your sales. Is your work year-round or is it seasonal?

In evaluating the potential of cross-promoting with someone, take into account how reliable and trustworthy the person or company is or has the reputation for being. Aim to team up with people who share similar goals, ethics, and values with you. After all, if you are devoting this level of energy to helping someone else's business and perhaps even splitting expenses for certain promotional items, you want to be sure that the other party will treat you fairly and squarely and that your association will enhance, not detract from, your reputation and image.

In thinking about potential partners, however, don't limit your options unnecessarily. If you're a small business, don't assume that you can only cross-promote with other small companies. Even if you're just starting out on your own with little capital on hand, you can find ways to cross-promote with much larger businesses in a community. For instance, a home-based graphic designer or writer might cross-promote with a large print shop; a home-based clothing designer/seamstress might cross-promote with a trendy dress store or dry cleaning chain; and so on. We even get brochures in the mail from a local Chinese restaurant that appears to be cross-promoting with an auto body shop on the same block. Their brochure not only includes the dinner menu for the restaurant but also a personal endorsement from the chef about the quality of the auto body work done by his neighbor. So let your imagination and creativity take you where ever it leads; there is no limit to the kind of cross-promoting you can to do.

Tips for Effective Cross-Promoting

Here are a few tips for successful cross-promotions.

1. Write down your goals for promoting your business. By having your goals in mind, when you talk with people you could potentially cross-promote with, you'll be better prepared to share your ideas and present what you could offer them.

2. Approach your strongest possible promotional partners first. If you are going to cross-promote, try to do it with the best possible "partners," whose contacts and reputation will do each of you the most good. You will become identified with the people you do cross-promoting with, so choose the most advantageous and desirable relationships right from the start.

3. Focus on what the other person has to gain. Don't focus your discussions with a potential cross-promotional partner on the litany of things this campaign will do to help you and your business. Use your early discussions to show how the cross-promoting with you will help them, then you can talk about a cross-promotion that will produce win-win results. This will be a more convincing and realistic approach. You don't want those you talk with to think that you're planning to use them strictly for your gain. You want to build a mutually advantageous relationship for all involved.

4. Be flexible in planning a cross-promotional strategy. Brainstorm together about your many opportunities for cross-promotion and figure out which options would be the most helpful to each of you. Be open to potential ideas you might never have considered. That's one of the advantages of cross-promoting.

5. Value time, money, and reputation. Don't think you each have to contribute equal amounts of cash to your promotion.

When magician Kelly Muldrow took a booth space at the annual Seattle Chamber of Commerce Expo with musician Corina Lapid and corporate poet Doug Nathan, he paid all the fees but got the help he needed to cover the booth twelve to fourteen hours per day with knowledgeable professionals.

When one person contributes the money, give credit if the other contributes the time doing such things as going to the printer and doing other nitty-gritty footwork. It's a good idea to calculate a reasonable "in-kind" hourly fee that can be used to match the dollar amount the other is contributing. Such calculations will help make sure no one feels taken advantage of.

6. Don't rush into an agreement. Allow ample time for both you and those you're considering working with to get to know one another. Explore and give thought to what will actually work for each of you. You may want to brainstorm about new promotional ideas. If appropriate, try out, sample, or otherwise experience one another's work so you can be genuinely enthusiastic.

7. Start small and go slowly. As with all teaming-up ventures, we recommend that you experiment with a small initial promotion to learn more about what will and won't work for each of you. Test the waters first before risking your time, money, or reputation. Neither of you wants to get involved in a promotion that ties up your time and money without producing results.

8. If you are successful with one promotion, establish longer-term goals and strategies. If your initial activities work splendidly, plan a larger, longer-term campaign for the upcoming year so you can take advantage of the momentum and track record you've established.

9. If you are working with several parties in a cross-promotion, be aware of the group dynamics. As Kare Anderson points out in her book, *Walk Your Talk,* "Groups take on a life of their own, and working as a group can be more challenging than working alone." Even in performing as focused an activity as a promotion together will require what Harvard Business School professor Rosabeth Moss Kanter calls relationship management. So it's important to take the group's "pulse" regularly to make sure everyone is satisfied and, if there is a problem, address it together.

Summary—Pros and Cons of Cross-Promoting

Pros

- Cross-promotions can be done at whatever scale or level of involvement you feel comfortable with.
- Participants can continue or easily back out after an initial effort if the relationship doesn't work out.
- Because those involved are actively putting in time and/or money to help each other get results, you have a better chance of producing a return from your efforts than from more informal relationships that require less investment.
- Often, you can get better results for the same amount of time and money you would put into your marketing or advertising independently.

Cons

- Cross-promoting requires investing a higher level of time and energy for planning and coordinating your efforts than other more informal teaming-up relationships.
- A financial contribution is often necessary to implement a meaningful cross-promotion, and trusting others when money is involved not only increases the risk but also puts added pressures on your relationship.
- While the increased investment increases expectations among participants, there is no guarantee of results. Customers still make the decisions about whether or not to use your services. Also, one of you may draw a better response from the promotion than the others, thereby creating bitter rivalry.
- The higher investment and visibility of a cross-promotion increase potential conflicts.

OPTION 4: INTERDEPENDENT ALLIANCES

Like many people, you may want to work more closely, regularly, and interdependently with others but still not want to enter into a full-blown formal partnership. If so, establishing one or more interdependent alliances may be a workable solution.

That's what PR consultants Risa Hoag and Mindy Hermann decided to do. When they first met at a local National Association of Women Business Owners meeting, both Hoag and Hermann were running independent home-based public-relations businesses in Westchester County outside of New York City. After several discussions, they realized they had many shared interests and values and that working together might prove fruitful. However, they also wanted to maintain their separate business identities.

So, to make use of their complementary professional skills, they began by including each other in their proposals when bidding on projects. Every time one of them would bid on a new contract, she'd list the other's name as an associate, impressing upon potential clients the range of expertise and work experience her company could provide. Then, when one of them won a contract, she would hire the other to do a portion of the work, paying an agreed-upon discounted hourly rate. The amount of work the other did varied. Sometimes, they simply reviewed or edited each other's writing. At other times, they jointly worked on the entire contract, even meeting with the clients together. Today, the extent of their mutual support depends on the needs of each client, the nature of the project, the deadline required, and how much help each woman feels she needs. Whatever the arrangement, however, they always pay each other for whatever work is done.

Risa and Mindy believe they have benefited from their interdependent alliance in many ways. First, their arrangement has helped them each to get more business. As Risa explained, they each have been able to tout the expertise of the other in order to get new accounts they would probably not have gotten without their alliance. Furthermore, they each have been able to garner larger, more profitable accounts than they could have gotten on their own because some clients are more comfortable knowing there are two qualified people available to do the work. This gives clients the feeling they're dealing with a PR "agency." The two women also report that working together has helped improve the quality of their work, which also makes their clients happier. Their interdependent collaboration has blossomed over time to the point that Risa and Mindy now work together on nearly every project—regardless of who generates the original contract.

Interdependent Alliances Defined

As this example shows, an interdependent alliance enables two businesses to work *regularly* and *consistently* with each other on actual projects originated by either party. Each business remains independent yet depends on the other for added capabilities, expertise, and competence. This form of teaming up is similar to forming a partnership or a joint venture (both of which are discussed below), except that in an interdependent alliance the parties involved continue to operate as separate and distinct legal and financial entities, working alone at times on some projects while teaming up on others.

When to Form an Alliance

Interdependent alliances are a beneficial choice in several types of situations.

1. *When the parties involved are in the same business and have workloads that can fluctuate greatly.* Some companies seem to experience feast-or-famine conditions. One week or month, they have lots of business—even more than they can handle—and the next week or month, they have practically none. When this occurs, it can be very useful to have one or more inter-

dependent alliances with other companies with whom to share projects on a regular and consistent basis.

Chris White, a freelance technical writer in Sacramento, has an interdependent alliance with two other writers in the area. Their alliance enables both of them to better handle their fluctuating workloads, and also to present themselves as a more substantial company to bid on larger contracts. They pay each other by dividing whatever fees are received according to how many chapters each person writes. As Chris told us, "The advantage of this arrangement is that we've become known as writers who work fast and can turn out a good book. In addition, we can do projects for a client who is looking to hire a firm instead of an individual freelance writer."

2. When the parties involved can provide complementary products or services to the same client. Many types of businesses provide a service that by its nature requires other businesses. A company hiring a computer consultant, for example, will often need to locate an equipment vendor. A new dog owner who's selecting a vet may also need a dog groomer, a pet-sitter, an obedience trainer, and so forth. Someone who's hiring a copywriter may also need to work with a graphic designer or desktop publisher. An organization using the services of a management consultant may also need help from a corporate trainer. In such situations, linking up with others who provide related services can give everyone involved an edge on getting business because they can bring in an entire team and save time, aggravation, and money for the client.

By establishing an interdependent alliance, a business related to yours, when approaching a prospective client, can automatically include you as part of what they can offer, either as a supplier or as a coworker. And, in return, you can include those you're allied with as part of what you have to offer.

Beverley Williams owned a desktop publishing service in suburban Maryland, outside of Washington, D.C. She had an interdependent alliance with several other desktop publishers to handle one another's overload work, and this arrangement worked well over the years. Of more interest, though, is the fact that Beverley also teamed up with a photographer and a reporter who work with her to develop newsletters for clients. Whenever any one of them had a client who would benefit from having a newsletter published about their company or organization, he or she offered to provide the entire team to supply all the services needed to put together a first-class newsletter, from providing the articles to taking the photographs, which Beverley then typeset and published.

Management consultant Peter Lloyd, mentioned in chapter 1, and his associate Dave Dufour, also have an interdependent alliance that serves several purposes. While each has his own independent consulting company, the number of clients they can attract varies greatly in any given month. As a result, they often pass on tips and leads to each about business they couldn't handle on their own. They also frequently include each other in proposals they make for new contracts. This makes their proposals stronger and more appealing to clients since each offers special skills the other alone can't provide. Dave specializes in live theater presentations making use of his background in drama and acting, while Peter specializes in more straightforward motivational speaking. By combining their work, they have been able to come up with more clever and unique presentations than any others a client may have been considering.

On the other hand, being part of an interdependent alliance is more involved and requires a greater degree of relationship than simply referring business or doing a cross-promotion. All parties are making the decision to include one another as part of their work rather than having the customer make the decision to buy each one's products or services. In addition, in an interdependent alliance, money actually changes hands among the parties involved because they're essentially subcontractors with one another. Whoever initiates getting the work usually deals directly with the client, oversees the project, collects the fee, and then pays the others for whatever work they've done once it's completed.

Tips for Effective Interdependent Alliances

Since interdependent alliances require a higher level of commitment and closer involvement, the possibilities for complications and problems are greater as well. Here are several issues you'll need to deal with to create successful alliances.

1. Take a long-term view of each alliance. Interdependent alliances have an inherent chicken-before-the-egg problem. One of you has to be the first to hire—and *pay*—the other to get the alliance going. In some cases, you may end up feeling that you could have done the work yourself without having hired your colleague, or that you're taking money out of your own pocket when it comes time to write your colleague a check. While such feelings are common at first, they reflect a shortsighted view. The value of an interdependent relationship is that in the long run, you'll benefit by being able to take on more business and larger projects knowing you have someone other than yourself to do the work—or to get the work when you need it!

2. Make sure you respect each other's work or product. Because you'll be working together with clients, you'll need to depend on each other to come through as promised. You'll need to be familiar with how each of you works and be satisfied with each other's capabilities, quality of work, and ability to adhere to and deliver on deadlines. An interdependent alliance will not last if you must resort to criticizing, correcting, or chastising each other in order to get the work done. For this reason you may want to do a few one-time short-term joint projects before committing to an ongoing interdependent alliance.

3. Subcontract with or involve each other in enough projects to justify your relationship. Without a relatively high degree of reciprocity, an alliance will become nothing more than a typical subcontracting arrangement in which Business A occasionally hires Business B. The purpose of an interdependent alliance is to enhance *each other's* income, business opportunities, and reputation. In essence, you're aiming to create a synergy between your businesses so that the sum of the parts will be greater than the whole. As you pass business back and forth, your capabilities should grow so you can do a better job on more work, more quickly. Eventually, by working together you should be able to move your businesses to a new plateau where you can handle larger, more profitable projects and get work with more substantial clients, just as Risa and Mindy were able to do with their PR businesses over several years of working together.

4. Agree that whoever originates and brings in the business will be the project leader. Usually the person who obtains the contract knows more about that client and has already developed a relationship. So unless circumstances call for doing otherwise, don't confuse the client by introducing some other person or company as their primary contact. Unless for some reason the client prefers to subcontract separately, all legal and financial agreements should be with whoever originates the business. This should make things simpler for your clients and reduce potential conflicts and disagreements.

Also, to avoid delays and confusion, someone needs to have the final say and the final responsibility for a given project. That should be the person who established the relationship and it should be clear to all involved that everyone else will adhere to the decisions of the project leader. Of course, to work effectively, the project leader will need to solicit and consider everyone else's input.

5. All parties should agree in advance in writing on what fees will be paid. Because interdependent alliances are essentially subcontracts in which one party pays the other for work completed, you need to know up front how much each of you will charge for any given project. Whatever rates you decide upon, it's critical that all involved be scrupulously honest and frank about the billing and payment process. If, for example, either of you intends to mark up your associate's fees to the client, you should both know this before work begins to avoid jealousy and any embarrassing confusion for your clients. Always make clear when and how everyone will be paid. Usually in interdependent alliances, no one is paid until the client pays the bill, after which subcontractors are paid immediately. But such arrangements need to be spelled out clearly in writing.

Also, be sure each of you knows what can be counted as billable time, what expenses are considered reimbursable, and what rate is being charged. For example, will you bill each other for travel time? Will you bill each other for paper and supplies? Will you bill each other per hour rounded to the nearest fifteen or thirty minutes? All these details need to be worked out in a written agreement beforehand.

It's also useful to charge each other a discounted rate below what your other customers pay, so both parties feel there is a special incentive for working together. This practice also allows each business to submit proposals and bid on contracts with the best possible price, thereby increasing your chances of getting the business.

6. If a project incurs cost overruns, negotiate in good faith about how to absorb added expenses. This issue is perhaps one of the stickiest for an interdependent alliance. For example, if you finish a project that required one of you to invest ten more hours than the contract called for and spend $250 more on supplies and expenses than was projected, you'll need to determine from whose pocket the lost profit will come. If one of you is clearly responsible for a cost overrun, perhaps that person should voluntarily take the loss and then learn to make better cost estimates in the future. But if the profit margin was high enough, perhaps those involved can split the loss in the spirit of building your long-term relationship.

Whichever solution you come to, do not hold such overruns over each other's head at a later date. If many errors are made in estimating costs and you believe your associate needs help to do a better job of projecting time and expenses, work together the next time around to better calculate what your costs will be so you can avoid problems after a project is completed.

Beware: Special Consideration for Working with Independent Contractors. Whatever you do, avoid giving the impression that one of you is an "employee" of the other as defined by IRS standards.

If you are working regularly and consistently with another individual, the IRS may consider that one of you is actually the employer while the other is an employee instead of an independent contractor. If the IRS makes this determination, it can have undesirable consequences for both of you, but especially for the person who is viewed as the employer. If the IRS considers an independent contractor to be an employee, you may be subject to severe tax penalties at both the federal and the state levels for not withholding appropriate taxes and social security benefits.

Avoiding this perception is easy if both of you make efforts to demonstrate your independent contractor status through the following actions or steps.

- Perform the work at your own locations.
- Perform the work on your own schedule so that you clearly set your own hours.
- Arrange to be paid in a lump sum for the entire job rather than by the hour.

- Furnish your own tools, equipment, and supplies.
- Make sure you're each bringing in new clients so that your alliance is reciprocal.
- Most important, be sure you each do work for more than one client at a time.

See the box on page 79 for more information on this topic.

Since an interdependent alliance is the closest business relationship you can have without becoming an actual partnership, many of the skills that are required in having a successful partnership apply to building a successful alliance as well. So be sure to review the tips in the section on partnerships below.

Summary—Pros and Cons of Interdependent Alliances

Pros

- You can accept whatever projects come your way at any time, knowing you have backup available to help you. This allows you to expand your business faster and take it to a new level where you can work on more complex projects.
- You can take on larger, more demanding projects that have fast turnaround time knowing that you have additional resources available to help you meet deadlines or fulfill projects with more work than you could handle on your own, thus not having to decline work you might otherwise have to.
- You have the possibility of getting work from other projects when you don't have business at hand, thereby increasing your chances of having a steady income. Having an interdependent alliance is like an insurance policy against downtimes and a feast-or-famine lifestyle.
- You can enhance your reputation for being able to handle significant projects.
- Alliances provide an opportunity to build rewarding interpersonal relationships.

Cons

- Alliances require a high level of mutual trust, cooperation, and planning. Therefore there's a higher risk of conflicts, disappointments, complications, and even problems affecting your reputation if an associate doesn't deliver top-quality work in a timely fashion.
- There are tax and legal implications relative to maintaining independent contractor status that must be taken care of, including filing a 1099 Form for each associate whose services you use.
- There is always a risk that, in the future, a client or customer will have only enough work for one of you and will prefer working with your associate even if their initial contact was with you. That could mean losing a valued customer or client.
- An interdependent alliance requires keeping additional records and doing increased administrative work to track time and expenses, process invoices, and meet tax obligations.

OPTION 5: JOINT VENTURES

If you're ready to truly share and share alike with someone else, but you're not sure you want to enter into a full-scale partnership that absorbs your entire business, a joint venture could be an ideal way for you to team up. Entering into a joint venture worked well for newsletter publisher Steve Dworman in Los Angeles. A few years ago, Dworman began a newsletter to cover the infomercial business. Recognizing that there would be tremendous growth in this field, Dworman also realized it could be very profitable to publish a "sourcebook" listing all the companies involved in this industry, from producers and directors to graphic artists and cameramen. However, Dworman knew that it can cost a lot of money to assemble, print, and market a book, so he decided that a joint venture would be the best way to get his project off the ground. He contacted one of the largest business magazine publishers and convinced them to give his idea a try. Dworman put up the money to print the book and the magazine handled the distribution, taking a cut from the price of each copy. Just as Dworman expected, the sourcebook, *The Infomercial and Direct Response Television Sourcebook,* has gone on to be a best-seller in his industry and has become an annual publication that everyone in the entire industry feels compelled to buy.

As you can see, a joint venture can allow you to test new opportunities while not losing your primary business focus.

Joint Ventures Defined

A joint venture is essentially a one-time or limited-purpose partnership. It can even be thought of as a trial partnership, because sometimes successful joint ventures lead to full-scale partnerships. Whereas in an interdependent alliance each party brings in the other only on specific projects, and each is still legally and financially responsible for the projects he or she brings in, in a joint venture, you literally link up to act as one entity on a given project. In other words, in an interdependent alliance, you take turns going for a ride on each other's coattails; in a joint venture, you head out together arm in arm, sharing full responsibility from start to finish for whatever happens.

Unlike a full-blown partnership, joint ventures are usually limited to a single event or activity. Two writers, for example, who write a book together or two videographers who agree to produce a video on a particular topic together have teamed up for a single-event joint venture. Similarly, two business consultants who join efforts to give a certain type of workshop together or two programmers who come together to develop a software game are also examples of joint ventures for a limited activity.

When and with Whom to Enter into a Joint Venture

Although not as complex as a full-scale partnership, from a legal point of view joint ventures technically are partnerships, and when you enter into a joint venture, you and your partner(s) are in business together. Such short-term or one-time partnerships, however, can be a wise choice in several types of situations.

1. When you are presented with a unique opportunity you can pursue only by teaming up in a particular way. As they say, opportunity only knocks once, so when self-employed, the savvy person realizes that he or she must move quickly to seize an opportunity when it becomes available. Money—or lack of it—can often be the driving force that brings people together to capitalize on an opportunity. We know of two women in Texas who were interested in going into the medical billing business. When they found out that the Texas Medical Association meeting was going on in their city the next month, they quickly teamed up to purchase booth space that would have been too expensive for either to manage on her own and arranged to conduct a workshop on medical billing. At the conference, their efforts paid off; they were able to sign up five doctors as clients for their medical billing practices. This was a very short-term joint venture but one that served the two parties well.

But money isn't the only driving force behind joint ventures. Sometimes, capturing an opportunity requires joining forces with someone else who can contribute expertise or manpower you don't have. For example, you may hear about a particular contract you'd love to work on, but you may not have the experience required to meet all the specifications. Rather than give up on the opportunity, however, it might make sense for you to team up with another company or individual who has the needed expertise and make a proposal as a joint venture between your two companies.

Joint ventures can be for as long or as short a time as you want and need them to be. Rob Mermin, founder and artistic director of Circus Smirkus, a children's theater company based in Vermont, uses short-term joint ventures to help his troupe take an annual summer tour through New England. To fund a performance in each city or town along the tour, Mermin teams up with a local museum, association, or children's charity to bring his troupe to the town in exchange for splitting the profits and getting some free promotion. Technically speaking, Mermin's joint ventures last for only one performance. Steve Dworman's venture, on the other hand, to publish the infomercial sourcebook in collaboration with the magazine publisher, has lasted five years as of this writing, and Steve expects it to continue indefinitely. His venture is limited in focus to producing the sourcebook, but it's not limited in terms of time.

2. When you can create a new opportunity outside the normal sphere of your operations. In some situations, a joint venture can be the way to carve out an entirely new enterprise that extends, supplements, or even replaces your existing business. In other words, by combining talents, expertise, and brain power, a joint venture can provide an opportunity to create an entirely new business beyond what either of the parties was doing before or could have done on their own.

Dave Lakhani and Liane Lemon of Boise, Idaho, are an example of how to use a joint venture to create new opportunities. Their affiliation began when Dave, a marketing consultant and owner of a computer store met Liane, a CPA, whose office was in the same complex as his store. Over neighborly chats, they soon realized that they could pool their expertise and offer a one-stop consulting service for small businesses that want to grow. Dave and Liane then formed a separate joint venture, called the Small Business Network, in which each is a 50 percent partner.

Their enterprise combines Dave's knowledge of marketing with Liane's financial and tax expertise. Together they're able to provide small companies with sophisticated feedback on how to expand and grow. Within a few years, their joint venture has grown to produce more income than each of their individual businesses. And surprisingly, Dave and Liane point out, their joint venture has enabled them to charge more per hour when they work together than their individual rates multiplied by two!

3. When you want to explore an opportunity without risking all your resources. In many instances, a joint venture is the only chance you may have to explore an idea or a market when you're not in a position to devote 100 percent of your time or money to test out the possibilities. A joint venture can allow you to share with someone else the time and money involved in doing the research, undertaking the financial risk, and handling the start-up work involved in pursuing a new idea.

For example, I, Rick, used a joint venture once to explore a potential opportunity in another field vastly different from writing. Working with a husband/wife team whom I had met while editing their book, I did a joint venture with "play experts" Mark and Denise Weston. Together we developed several new ideas for children's games. Merging our collective creativity and finances, we produced several models of games and presented them to a half dozen companies, one of whom expressed interest and paid us to take an idea one step further to a real working prototype. Although our joint venture ultimately did not pan out because the toy company decided not to pursue our concept, it proved worthwhile for the three of us to explore a potential business venture without risking all our resources. By working together and equally contributing cash and time to the enterprise, we were able to learn about the toy business and meet executives in a number of major companies as we attempted to sell a new concept.

4. When you have an idea or invention that could be developed or applied to another field but you don't have the contacts or resources needed. Sometimes we're lucky enough to have a great idea, but we're not so lucky as to have the resources to maximize the potential of that idea. In such cases, a joint venture may the only way you can grow beyond your limited resources.

Deborah Camp, for example, is a successful businesswoman in Tennessee who founded a new business-to-business directory called *Doing Business in Memphis*. Deborah's directory collects over two hundred pieces of detailed data on nearly every business in the Memphis area, including such information as their address, zip code, number of employees, percentage of minorities, type of computer systems used, square footage, year established, and names of officers. Needless to say, this information is highly valuable, so Deborah sells her directory to thousands of companies that want up-to-date financial and marketing information for doing business in Memphis. The guide has been so successful that Deborah realized she could expand her business into other cities—if only she had the resources. But she didn't.

Deborah lacked both the time and the financial resources to expand until she was approached by two successful businessmen who believed her concept could be franchised and proposed entering into a joint venture to take her business nationwide. Now the new partners are busily developing business directory franchises in other cities across the country while Deborah continues to maintain her Memphis-based business.

Basic Tips for Effective Joint Ventures

As with a full-blown partnership, a joint venture requires attention to many details concerning your working relationship. Here are a few basic tips for creating a successful joint venture.

1. Keep your joint venture in perspective. In the beginning, a joint venture is often an opportunity to experiment with an exciting new idea or possibility. So, it's easy to get caught up in the excitement and let your primary business suffer. Don't let this happen. Make sure the time and money you and your partner(s) commit to your joint venture doesn't detract from the success of your regular businesses. Otherwise, should your primary business begin to suffer, you could find yourself having to suddenly drop the venture just to keep afloat, leaving your venture partner on the line. So in undertaking a joint venture, don't "rob from Peter to pay Paul."

2. Clearly define and focus on the goals for your joint venture. Make sure everyone involved shares the same goals for your joint venture. In general, a joint venture is a partnership that's limited to accomplishing one or two goals, but it's easy to let the scope of a joint venture get out of hand. Be careful to prevent the joint venture from encroaching on your normal business by allowing it take off in many different directions at once. In the beginning, it's best to draw up a mission statement; that is, write down what you want to accomplish with your joint venture so you and your partners clearly identify your goals and objectives.

3. Be sure you trust and respect your joint venture partner. Just because a joint venture is more limited in scope than a full partnership, don't assume that you'll be able to tolerate a colleague's quirks or serious differences in ethics, values, or work style. You'll still be working together as partners, and underlying distrust, conflict, and irritation will jeopardize your ability to work together effectively. Technically speaking, you're also legally liable for any actions of your joint venture partner. If your partner pulls out, you'll still be liable to deliver on any contracts you've undertaken. If your partner is sued for misconduct, you most likely will be sued too. And what your partner does in this venture or any other could affect your reputation as well.

4. Put all your agreements in writing. A joint venture is as close to a partnership as you can get without making a total commitment. Therefore, it is vital to make sure you have written down all your agreements as to what and how each person will contribute in terms of time and/or cash, how you'll be dividing your responsibilities, and how you'll split any profits or losses. You should also make sure your written agreement indicates the time span for your joint venture, and what will happen if the enterprise becomes successful. One woman we interviewed began a joint venture with a friend to explore selling a new product, and as their enterprise gained momentum, her friend resigned from the joint venture to sell the very same product herself, much to the first woman's dismay. This unfortunate situation might have been avoided if the two had created a written agreement between them. We'll be describing how you can protect yourself with written agreements in chapter 4.

Summary—Pros and Cons of Joint Ventures

Pros
- A joint venture provides the opportunity to explore a new idea or market you don't have the time or money to pursue on your own.
- You can garner the energy and creativity of others.
- You can boost your reputation by associating with your joint venture partner(s).
- A joint venture can open doors previously shut to you alone.
- You can have most of the benefits of a partnership without as many risks.
- A joint venture can be a productive way to test the waters before entering into full-scale partnership.

Cons

- Usually you are truly interdependent in a joint venture. You must depend on someone else to accomplish the joint goals. This added vulnerability creates greater potential for conflicts, disappointments, and disagreements.
- You're legally liable for the actions of your joint venture partner.
- To protect your legal and financial interests, you need to get all joint venture agreements in writing. This can take time and energy and add complications to your life.
- The joint venture can drain time, energy, and money from your primary business.
- It's harder to back out if things don't work out because others are dependent on you and you're legally liable for whatever you've jointly contracted to do.

OPTION 6: SATELLITE SUBCONTRACTING

Ron Wohl of Gaithersburg, Maryland, started In Plain English, a company that specializes in designing business forms and writing training manuals. Ron is a premiere marketer with artful selling skills and widespread contacts in many corporations. As a result he's able to obtain plenty of business, including some projects that are quite large in scope requiring many months and/or several people to complete. Since Ron can't possibly do all the work he generates by himself, he teams up as needed with up to a dozen independent subcontractors he has established long-term relationships with. Combining talents in this way allows him to bid on a wide variety of projects of all sizes and scopes. In bidding on any given project, Ron consults his subcontractors to obtain estimates of their time and fees. He then puts together a proposal, adding a percentage of profit for himself for finding and supervising the work.

This successful approach to teaming up is an example of what we call *satellite subcontracting*. It could be an excellent way for you to team up with others if, as a matter of course, you have more business than you can handle alone or if you're good at what you do and want a steady stream of work coming in without having to spend your time marketing.

Satellite Subcontracting Defined

Whereas an interdependent alliance involves two or more companies subcontracting reciprocally with each other, *satellite subcontracting* occurs when one person's company becomes the "marketing hub" or business generator and subcontracts the business out to other self-employed individuals or small companies. Someone who's operating as the hub of a satellite subcontracts out work either horizontally or vertically. In a horizontal satellite arrangement, you subcontract out to people who do the same type of work you do; in a vertical satellite arrangement, you subcontract out to people who do work that either precedes or follows what you do. For example, a word processor who subcontracts out to many other word processors has created a horizontal satellite; a general contractor who subcontracts out to architects, carpenters, electricians, and so on is involved in a vertical subcontracting arrangement.

When to Do Satellite Subcontracting

There are a variety of situations when satellite subcontracting can work well.

1. When you have excellent marketing skills and can generate more business than you can do yourself. Some people are simply rainmakers; they're better than others at drumming up lots of business. If you fit this description, satellite subcontracting will allow you to take on as much work as you can bring in without the added cost, time, and energy required to hire full-time employees. As the rainmaker, you can farm the work out to others who don't have the interest or skill to market themselves as well as you do.

Desktop publisher Mary Lou Remy is an example of a rainmaker. Having been in her business, 9 to 5 Etc., for seven years, she has a large and steady clientele of repeat customers. Mary Lou also spends about $5,000 a year advertising in local phone directories. Overall, she has been able to build her business to the point that she now has more business than she can handle herself, and frequently she also takes on very large and complex publishing projects. In order to handle all this work, Mary Lou has become a rainmaker for several other home-based word-processing services whose owners are not as aggressive in their marketing and who do not have the reputation she has.

At any given time, Mary Lou assigns work to any one of three people who handle many of the typing jobs she gets while she carries out the more complex desktop publishing assignments. In some cases, she makes a good profit on the subcontracted work, but in other cases, she does it just to keep her clients happy knowing that they can always rely on her for getting a job done. In a typical year, Mary Lou farms out between $5,000 and $10,000 in business to others. As she points out, "This allows me to keep my customers happy, because I never have to refuse a job, and I know that if they're satisfied, my clients will keep coming back. It also lets me spend some of my time exploring other interesting work for my clients, like computer training and Web page design. Overall, it has helped me increase my income by at least 10 percent per year."

2. When work you can generate involves providing products or services in addition to those you can provide yourself. If you're good at marketing, you may be able to serve as rainmaker for other people who do different aspects of the projects you're already lining up for yourself. For instance, Derry

Prosser runs a cleaning service. Often his clients have specialized cleaning needs, so Derry subcontracts with companies that specialize in floors, carpets, windows, venetian blinds, power washing, and awning cleaning.

3. When you don't have clients yet and you want to get started—or when you're not very good at or interested in marketing yourself. Teaming up with a rainmaker can be an excellent way to build or sustain your business when marketing is not your forte. It can be particularly useful if you want to become self-employed but you're not ready to quit your full-time job yet. By connecting with someone who can get business, you can test the waters and see if you enjoy being in business.

For example, Joan DeLoise is a wardrobe artist and the sole support of two small children. She has little spare time to market, but almost everyone in her field is an independent contractor. So Joan stays busy by working through two or three television producers who regularly need to pull together a team of professionals on the spur of the moment. Of working in satellite arrangements, she says "It was very hard breaking into this field, but by volunteering for producers I proved my abilities and now there's always some producer who needs me."

Tips for Effective Satellite Subcontracting

Several issues need to be addressed in order for satellite subcontracting to work well.

1. If you are the rainmaker, let your clients know that you will be subcontracting work to others and have all the work flow through you. In most cases, clients prefer knowing there will be other people working on their project, who they are, and what they will be doing. But usually they also prefer dealing with only one person. So letting everyone know up front that you will always be the primary client contact reduces misunderstandings and avoids possible problems later on.

2. If you are the rainmaker, recognize that you are responsible to the client for the quality of the work. In subcontracting out work, be sure to allocate time to supervise the subcontractors to make sure their work is done to your client's specifications. If a subcontractor produces less than satisfactory work, you'll be the one who suffers most because you could lose a client and damage your reputation. In short, be aware that the responsibility for the quality of all the work will generally fall on you.

Such responsibility does put added pressure on a rainmaker. Other people will be counting on you to provide them with work. Graphic designer Susan Shankin knows this type of pressure firsthand. Because of the high quality of her work and her long-standing reputation in both the publishing and entertainment industries, Susan was in demand as a designer and thought she would enjoy subcontracting out work to other good designers she knows have a hard time getting assignments themselves. However, supervising the work of others and making sure she always had enough work for them became more of a burden for Susan than she wanted to carry. After five years of operating a fast-paced and very lucrative satellite subcontracting business, Susan decided to cut back and take only those jobs that she could handle herself. Although her decision has reduced her income, she learned over time that being responsible for the income and performance of others was not a role she wanted to play.

Similarly, in another case, a marketing communications firm we spoke to had grown to the point of using thirty-two subcontractors who were generating $1.2 million in business. Ultimately, the wife, who was a partner in this enterprise, told her husband she felt their business had gotten too large to manage and she wanted to return to running a simpler and calmer two-person, home-based operation. The husband finally agreed, and they scaled back their business and their lifestyle to be more in keeping with their original goals.

3. Get a clear agreement for each assignment on all financial details. To avoid potential miscommunication and other problems, whether you're the subcontractor or the rainmaker, discuss each assignment fully beforehand. Define clearly the estimated amount of time the subcontractor will need to complete the work, the level of effort involved, the equipment and supplies to be used, what expenses are involved, and how and when fees will be paid. If there is any doubt about the difficulty or amount of time required on a project, agree to negotiate in good faith as the project progresses. Do not wait until the project is completed to have these discussions. Discuss such matters as they develop so there will be no surprises when invoices are submitted. If there are cost overruns, or extra time is required, or unreasonable expectations emerge on the part of the client that cause a subcontractor to spend more time than planned for on a project, all parties need to find a mutually acceptable solution before conflicts develop. When negotiating compensation for difficult jobs, it's best that rainmaker and subcontractors alike take a long-term view of their relationship.

Ron Wohl, for example, makes every effort to help his subcontractors with their time and cost estimates for each project. On occasion, he even warns subcontractors that they have estimated too low, and he will double their time estimate in making his bid. Then, if a project takes more time because of client demands, if possible, he splits some of his fee with the subcontractor. This philosophy has allowed Ron to continue to work with some of the same subcontractors for fifteen years.

4. Agree up front on who "owns" the clients. This issue is the most common source of dissension between rainmakers and subcontractors. In general,

Beware: Special Considerations in Satellite Subcontracting

Avoid unfair competition and unfair rewards. In our view, one of the prime rules for successfully teaming up is that whoever gets the business owns the client. Violating this principle usually results in bad feelings and too often leads to lawsuits, bad-mouthing, and other retaliatory behavior you'll be better off avoiding. Honoring this principle builds trust and increases respect that will enhance your reputation and boost your chances of working successfully with others in the future. So, if a rainmaker has cultivated a client list that has allowed a satellite arrangement to flourish, it behooves all the subcontractors to either wait for an agreed-upon period of time before directly soliciting business from any of those clients or to arrange to share any profits earned from work done independently for those clients for a specified time.

Either solution can work: a time-limited noncompete agreement acknowledges the principle of fair competition; the sharing of profits acknowledges the principle of fair rewards.

Note: combining both ideas, however, is unfair; the hub firm should not ask a subcontractor to hold off competing with it for some specified amount of time *plus* ask it to share profits on any contracts won from that point on.

Watch out for employee versus independent contractor status issues. As mentioned in the section on interdependent alliances, when one independent worker works frequently and consistently with another, the IRS may determine that one of them is actually an employer and the other, an employee. To avoid this, make sure that all involved take steps to maintain their independent contractor status (see p. 68). You don't want to end up like one couple who regularly hired several "freelancers" in satellite subcontracting arrangements. Then a whole year later, after one of their freelancers hadn't gotten work from them for several months, she filed a claim for unemployment insurance, stating that she had been their employee. Because the couple was away from the city, they missed seeing a notice of the claim in time to reply to it. The resulting problem cost the couple thousands of dollars in attorney's fees, tied up their time in untangling this unpleasant hassle, and caused them a lot of mental pain and suffering. Had they consulted a lawyer when developing their subcontracting agreement, they might have avoided this problem.

If you are concerned about your status as an independent contractor, or to get more information about the IRS regulations, read the IRS list of twenty questions that serve as guidelines for determining the status of employees versus independent contractors. It's available in IRS Publication 937. We provide specific steps you can take to meet these twenty guidelines in our book *Working from Home*.

rainmakers believe if they find and develop a client, all future business with that client should flow through them to the subcontractors, thereby precluding the subcontractors from competing with the rainmaker for future contracts with that client. Frequently, however, subcontractors wanting to expand and move in their own direction will decide at some point to directly approach the clients they've been working with through the rain-maker about doing business with them directly. To avoid this competitive situation, many rainmakers establish a ground rule embodied in a written agreement that subcontractors cannot directly solicit business from their clients until six months to one year after the time of their last subcontracting assignment.

Summary—Pros and Cons of Satellite Subcontracting

Pros

- Rainmakers can take on more business than they can handle on their own.
- Rainmakers can increase their profits by keeping a percentage of the fees they pay to sub-contractors.
- Rainmakers can grow their business without the costs, risks, and administrative hassles of taking on permanent employees.
- Subcontractors can maintain their independence without the time, expense, and frustra-tion of having to market themselves.
- Subcontractors can concentrate their time and energy on providing their services or carrying out other responsibilities in their lives instead of having to devote time to marketing.
- Subcontractors can bring in an initial income and build experience during what would otherwise be a lean start-up period.

Cons

- Subcontracting can be time-consuming for rainmakers who must invest time in arranging for, administering, and overseeing subcontractors' work. In fact, your business could grow larger and more complex than you intend or want it to.
- Rainmakers must simultaneously look for good subcontractors as well as for new clients.
- Rainmakers are essentially agents for other businesses, which can lead to a double bind. On one hand, you must make sure that your subcontractors do a good job for your clients or your business and reputation will suffer. On the other hand, you must find as much work for your subcontractors as possible to keep them happily working with you. These two is-sues may lead to conflicts, because you may push your subcontractors to work quickly while at the same time expecting high-quality output.
- Subcontractors may eventually step around you and take your clients as their own.
- As a subcontractor, your success is dependent on someone else's ability to get business for you. There's no guarantee you will always have projects to work on, and yet your time may be totally tied up working on the projects you do get, leaving you little time to market.
- As a subcontractor your fee will probably be less than if you had gotten the business your-self.

OPTION 7: CONSORTIUMS

When bookkeeper and financial consultant Phillip Greenberg went into business for himself several years ago, he realized from his own experience that many small businesses could use a wide range of professional help to get through the difficulties of entrepreneuring. He therefore set out to put together a team of people who could advise small businesses on just about any problem they might encounter. Through his own contacts and referrals from others, Greenberg spent a few months organizing a group of people who would agree to work with him. His team, which he calls the Greenberg Group, includes a CPA, a professional writer of business plans and advertising copy, a financial management consultant, a human resources consultant to create benefit programs and employee manuals, an Internet consultant and Web master, a strategic planning consultant, a secretarial service, a graphic artist, a public relations firm, and himself.

Greenberg developed a unique procedure for enabling the group to function as a team. Any time one member of the group gets a new client, he or she is supposed to offer the services of the entire group to that business. If the business is interested, the team will go in and do an initial survey for $500, which is split among any participating team members. Through the survey, the team does an analysis of what areas the business needs to improve and how they can help. If the business decides to pursue the help, it can sign a contract for one year which entitles it to a certain number of consulting hours per month from any of the Greenberg Group members, as needed. The consulting hours can be split in whatever way the business owner deems best. One month, the business owner may opt to use five hours of PR consulting and five hours of accounting, but another month, it may take ten hours of the writer's time.

In exchange for the opportunity to get this new business, each member of the Greenberg Group discounts his or her usual rate. They also keep track of their time by billing in "units" rather than dollars, and each member of the Greenberg Group has agreed to bill a certain amount of units per hour. For example, the CPA bills at four units per hour; whereas the secretary bills at one unit per hour. Meanwhile, the clients pay Phillip Greenberg who keeps track of the units each member bills, and he pays each person according to his or her units of work at the end of each month.

The Greenberg Group is an example of another way people are teaming up for success: a consortium, in which a group of independent individuals or small companies agree to work together *collectively,* pooling their knowledge and marketing their skills for the good of all.

Consortium Defined

In a consortium, different types of businesspeople work together as a group to attract or obtain business for one another. They may also actually do some of the work together. In this sense, a consortium is actually an expanded form of an interdependent alliance in that it includes many self-employed individuals or small businesses. The word *consortium* originates from *consort* which means keeping company with and, sharing or working in harmony with a companion, associate, or partner.

Consortiums aim to make use of each member's contacts, abilities, and reputation to get work for the group they could not get alone. As in the Greenberg Group, each business goes out into the world seeking contracts or projects the entire group can work on. If necessary, they all work together to write proposals or bids. This collective effort enhances the capability of all the members. This has been Sue Feldman's experience as well. Sue, whose company is Datasearch, of Ithaca, New York, is an information consultant specializing in digital library studies. She participates in a loose consortium with three other information consultants so that they can all provide a complete range of digital library search services. She says, "Being part of a consortium is so much easier than trying to be an expert on everything."

When and with Whom to Form a Consortium

Basically, a consortium can work well when many similar or even dissimilar businesses can work together on large projects or assignments they could not undertake as successfully on their own. A jeweler, for example, working on his own couldn't supply a catalog with an order for ten thousand handcrafted pieces, but as part of a consortium of jewelers, he could.

As the Greenberg Group demonstrates, a consortium can work well for a group of diversified consulting and service businesses who all complement one another through their common focus on a specific niche such as small businesses. In fact, if you are interested in forming your own consortium, Greenberg sells his business concept and plans for implementation (see the Resources list at the end of this chapter).

But there are other types of possible consortiums, too. Consider the following examples.

- A group of writers, editors, graphic designers, desktop publishers, multimedia specialists, and videographers might form a consortium to obtain large corporate or government training contracts.
- A group of programmers, multimedia specialists, writers, graphic artists, and marketing consultants could form a consortium to develop software and CD-ROM materials for high-technology companies.
- A group of educational specialists, graphic designers, marketing consultants, and writers might form a consortium to develop children's games and books for publishers or toy companies.

Consortiums are also a popular avenue for craftspeople and artisans to sell their work. Potters, stained-glass artists, woodworkers, jewelers, and other artisans are joining together all across the country to share expenses for setting up and staffing a booth at fairs or trade shows or to jointly operate a retail storefront. In fact, many parts of the country have intentionally refurbished old factories or mills and converted the space to studios and retail space for lease to consortiums of artists.

Gallery 510, in Decatur, Illinois, for example, came about when twenty-four independent visual artists shared the concern that being in a small town without a single gallery, they were not selling as much of their work as they could. To deal with this problem, they formed a "guild," a sort of cooperative in which they pooled both money and ideas. They applied for a bank loan to buy an old Victorian house, which they restored and transformed into a gallery. The gallery provides each artist permanent exhibit space, plus each member also gets a special month-long exhibit every twenty-four months. The gallery keeps 20 percent of sales revenue for administrative expenses. The artists find they get more press coverage operating as a gallery than they did from their individual efforts. Working together has paid off in another way: the gallery has applied for and received several arts grants and has been listed by the Bureau of Illinois Tourism as a worthy tourist stop.

Another unique artists' consortium is called the Collections of the Country Market in Durham, North Carolina. Actually, this group operates both as a consortium and a satellite subcontractor. The Collections was started by four women artists with exceptional marketing skills. According to cofounder Joanne Hodgson, the Collections began in the early 1980s when the four women teamed up to market their own crafts by convincing a real estate agent to lend them for one weekend the use of a house that was for sale. The women set up their crafts in the house and soon had a slew of visitors and craft buyers. (What a great joint promotion!) Within a few years, though, the weekend crowds they attracted were too large for a loaner house, so the women convinced a local shopping center to lend them an entire vacant store for a weekend, and they took on the job of "repping" (representing) other artists. Today, Joanne and her partners Alana Parrish, Eleanor Batchelor, and Susie Smith run a two-to-three-week-long show twice a year that includes arts and crafts produced by over one hundred craftspeople from North Carolina and a few other Atlantic states. The four women set up the show, help the artists determine their pricing, and take complete charge of advertising and promotion. Each artist must work a few hours at the show and learn enough about the work of the other artists to sell it.

This operation is not strictly a consortium, since the four women owners keep a portion of the cash intake from the shows to compensate themselves for their time. It borders on being a satellite subcontractor arrangement because the organizational and marketing efforts of the four women are essentially what provides the work for so many other artists. Whatever title you give it, though, this collaborative effort makes money for everyone involved and, like the Greenberg Group, is a good model other businesses might emulate.

Tips for Participating in a Successful Consortium

Unfortunately, forming a successful consortium can be quite a challenge, given the number of people involved and the varying financial and psychological needs of the members. Alma Lopez, a desktop publisher in Silver Spring, Maryland, knows this challenge well. She has tried twice to put together a consortium of publishing-related people to bid on large government contracts. In her first try, she was encouraged by the attendance at a preliminary meeting she hosted for prospective members. However, when it came time to put together a proposal, most of the women who attended the first meeting declined to participate, feeling the arrangement would be too time-consuming and complicated. In her second try, Alma found that the potential members couldn't agree on how much each person would be entitled to charge. The following tips can help you avoid such hurdles and pull together a consortium that works.

1. Treat the consortium like a business, not a networking organization. Many people will show up for an initial consortium meeting if they think they can network and get business for themselves. So make it clear, even before your first meeting, that you're seeking people who will think about and devote their time and energy to participating in a separate business entity that will benefit the entire group, instead of focusing strictly on building their own individual businesses.

2. Operate your consortium with a long-term perspective in mind. It takes time for a consortium to come together as a group of individuals who have learned how to get along, resolve disputes, and work effectively with one another. It may even be useful to ask for a year's commitment from members to allow sufficient time for a cohesive group to develop.

3. Appoint one leader or a team of three leaders. Having a group leader is always important when many people are involved. A leader can organize meetings and agendas, ensure that communications reach all members, and make sure that work gets done. Either select one strong leader who has the time and skills to take on this role, or identify a troika of leaders who can split up the time, duties, and energy required and share in the decision-making authority.

4. Agree up front how you will divide up the work and profits of the consortium. Once you get work to do together, each business has to contribute its share of labor and get paid according to an agreed-upon rate or amount.

However, decisions about who will work on what and get paid how much must be made beforehand. For instance, will each business charge their normal rate, or will each person accept a uniform rate that everyone will be paid? Will the person who brought in the business get any additional fee for doing so? For Alma Lopez's group, it had been planned that whoever found the contract would receive 10 percent of the overall fee, and the remainder would be split among consortium members according to the rate they normally charge. This diversity of fees was based on an assumption that some members' work should be of higher value than others'. The graphic artist, for example, could charge more than the typist, and the writer could charge more than the graphic artist. Whichever way you decide, be sure all parties know their obligations and agree to the decisions for splitting fees.

5. Be sure to respect, appreciate, and acknowledge everyone's contributions. Once you begin working together, there may be so much to do that it will be easy to become focused on responding to problems and challenges, while forgetting how important it is for everyone to feel like a valued part of the team. So, make a concerted effort to demonstrate that everyone's contribution is of value.

Summary—Pros and Cons of Consortiums

Pros

- A consortium allows an individual or small business to participate in large projects they couldn't be part of on their own.
- You can gain many of the advantages of being part of a team or organization while maintaining much of your independence.
- Once the consortium begins getting business, it can bring you a sense of security you can't otherwise attain by having to find and work on one small project after another.
- Sometimes because you are a part of fulfilling larger projects or orders, you will be able to sell products and services through a consortium that you couldn't sell independently.

Cons

- Consortiums can be difficult to put together and keep together.
- Members may remain focused on generating their own work in order to stay in business and thereby prevent the consortium from developing enough momentum.
- When work comes in, it can be a challenge to communicate, mobilize, and coordinate everyone's efforts since each person is operating independently in separate locations.
- A strong leader or leadership team is usually required, but sometimes no one has the time or skills to fulfill this leadership role. At other times, people in the consortium may resent the leader or feel that the team infringes on their independence.
- If not handled well, the group can degenerate into personality conflicts and professional battles that will destroy the team effort.

OPTION 8: FAMILY/SPOUSE COLLABORATION

Family business has a long and rich tradition in most parts of the world. Of course, in the early agrarian years of Western culture, the "First Wave" as Alvin Toffler called it in his classic work, *The Third Wave,* most husbands and wives naturally worked together operating and managing their farm and home. Although the men may have been responsible for the toughest outdoor jobs, many women worked side by side with their husbands in the fields while also taking care of the household and children.

As the Industrial Revolution occurred slowly over the eighteenth and nineteenth centuries, driving millions of rural families into the cities where the jobs were located, the "Second Wave," as Toffler called it, occurred. Here, too, men and women (and children) often worked side by side in the factories. Then, as wages improved in the late nineteenth and early twentieth centuries, husbands generally began to take over the breadwinning role while wives tended to homemaking and child rearing. In the early 1900s, mass education began to take over the job of educating children, and large numbers of women again entered the world of work. Family businesses were especially common in the retail trades, where "Mom and Pop" grocery stores, hardware stores, and pharmacies dotted the streets in most urban areas servicing thousands of neighborhood workers.

The evolution of family businesses took its largest step forward during Toffler's "Third Wave," in which Western society transformed itself from mostly blue-collar, production-oriented factory employment to white-collar, information- and service-oriented economies. Since the 1950s, but mostly in the '70s and '80s, more and more spouse and family collaborations have started up, as couples realized the value of working together and began consciously setting out to do so. In fact, according to the Small Business Administration, husband-and-wife partnerships became the fastest-growing segment of new small-business start-ups. And while some people can't imagine working with their relatives, for others, it's an ideal way for family members to share their goals, their time, and their lives.

We know of many family or spousal collaborations (in addition to our own, Paul and Sarah Edwards). There's Steve and Elisabeth Willey, of Sand Point, Idaho, who operate Backwoods Solar Electric Systems selling solar, wind, and hydro equipment to homeowners and builders who have property lacking power lines. At first the business was a hobby for Steve, but as the workload and client base increased, Steve quit his phone company job and went full-time. When the company grew too big for Steve to handle alone, it was a natural choice for Elisabeth to join him, answering calls from customers, preparing job quotes, and doing the billing and bookkeeping. Today, they also have several employees and produce a glossy mail-order catalogue. They have turned a one-time hobby into an enterprise of national stature which they still run from their home.

Teddi Kessie brought her daughter, Karen, into her seventeen-year-old referral business, the End Result ten years ago when she bought out two partners. While Karen is still technically an employee, Teddi refers to Karen as her partner and expects her daughter to continue the business when she retires. Teddi says, "Having a relative in your business provides an undertone of survival." She trusts Karen like no outsider. "I know she would never steal from me or undermine me." Teddi describes herself as somewhat shy and softhearted, while Karen is more aggressive. Teddi has given her the responsibility for collecting referral fees due from tradespeople. "I need her." Over the ten years they have worked together, their relationship has mellowed and improved so that Teddi can joke when Karen takes an occasional house-sitting job, "Who will I fight with when you're gone?"

Family/Spouse Collaborations Defined

Whereas the traditional family business was usually an enterprise run by the patriarch who provided work for any number of other family members, today's family and spouse collaborations run the gamut from corporations owned by husbands and wives or other family members to an array of more informal arrangements by which a spouse or family member joins in to lend support to a self-employed relative.

Parents lend their son or daughter the money to begin a home business. A wife does the books and answers the phone for her self-employed husband. A brother pitches in to lend a hand whenever his sister has more business than she can handle. A grandparent who lives across the continent edits the manuscripts of her fiction-writer son. A husband loses his job and decides to join in his wife's successful business. All these arrangements are examples of the many ways relatives are teaming up these days.

When to Team Up with Family Members

Family enterprises appear to work best in certain circumstances.

1. When one or more family members are going through a life change such as a layoff, midlife career crisis, or relocation. Crises tend to pull families together to support one another, and it's often a crisis that triggers family members to team up. We've met many husbands and wives who realized over the years that they wanted to work together, for example, but it took a crisis like being laid off to actually act on that desire. For instance, Sharon Crawford was a technical editor at a publishing company when she realized she wanted to take her career in a different direction. Her desire to move on prompted her to propose to her husband, Charlie Russel, who was also a technical writer, that they team up and write a computer book together. That was in 1991. Since then, the two of them have coauthored numerous successful books for a number of well-known publishers, including a series of popular computer books.

2. When a family member buys a business opportunity or franchise. Since business opportunities and franchises can cost from $10,000 to $100,000 and more, it's not surprising that family members often join efforts to purchase such a new business. That's what Virginia-based husband-and-wife team Daniel Lehmann and Patricia Bartello did. They decided to combine their individual backgrounds in health care and business management and bought a business opportunity providing medical billing and electronic claims processing. Although they had not worked together before, they found combining their talents made evaluating their options, purchasing the software, and developing an effective marketing campaign for their new business easier. Their collaboration paid off well. Dan and Pat have built a substantial medical billing business in Annandale, Virginia.

3. When family members have similar strong interests, goals, and talents. Many couples (and even entire families) often share similar interests. As a result, a successful business often grows from combining their mutual hobby or love. David Starkman and his wife, Susan Pinsky, share a passion for 3-D photography. They turned their passion into a business, founding a mail-order catalogue company that specializes in selling all kinds of 3-D photography equipment, paraphernalia, and historic images.

Mauna Eichner and Lee Fukui are also a couple that share talents and interests. Both are graphic artists who met in design school and found that they shared a love of good design and artwork. Each one went on to become a freelance designer, but now that they live together, they team up on many of their business efforts. They go to client interviews together and show a joint portfolio while pointing out the differences in their styles and letting the client choose which one to use. Regardless of which one gets the job, they consult with each other on almost every piece of work that goes through their home-based shop. As Mauna told us, "We are very communicative, despite our different styles, and we promote ourselves together."

4. When family members have complementary skills and talents to help each other. Some husbands and wives or other family members have highly compatible experience and skills that when put together make it possible to be more successful on their own. Tom and Wendy Eidson are a good example. They used their cumulative skills to turn their now famous Mo'Hotta, Mo'Betta hot sauce direct mail catalogue into a storybook success. Wendy was previously a film director and had the artistic flair needed to organize and attractively package a mail-order catalogue. Tom had worked in advertising and used his marketing know-how to put their catalogue into the hands of the right gatekeepers who helped spread the word throughout the gourmet food community. Working together as perhaps no other two people could have done in this situation, they were able to heat up their joint business faster than a chili pepper on a grill.

Medical billers Sheryl Telles and Kathy Allocco in Scottsdale, Arizona, gladly accepted the help of their husbands when they were starting out. While the two women had more than thirty-five years of medical billing experience between them, they didn't have the full range of entrepreneurial skills needed to really make their business fly. But because their husbands had experience, one in marketing and sales and the other in operations management and sales, the synergy between the two couples helped launch the business.

5. When one family member has created more of a demand than he or she can handle on his or her own and others in the family can join in to make the business the success it can be. Often when a family member goes out on his or her own, the business grows beyond what one person can do. Suddenly, the one-person operation must either cut back in order to continue handling everything alone—or find additional help. So if family members with compatible skills are available, such growth provides an ideal opportunity for teaming up. Working with family members instead of hiring employees or teaming up with strangers can spread the good fortune to others in the family, avoid up-front cash outlays, and keep the money in the family.

Lu Howell started Computer Dust Busters in Salt Lake City, Utah. She never realized the pent-up demand for computer maintenance services in her area. Within months, she had far more clients than she could have imagined, so she tapped into her husband's time and brought him onboard, part-time and informally at first, but later more full-time and formally. Her husband's electronics background also allowed them to expand their services from general computer cleaning and maintenance to include repairing broken computers.

A fast-growth curve also forced Virginia Devine to bring her husband onboard. Virginia, whom we mentioned earlier, works with the networking organization Business Network International. As a director of many BNI chapters around southern California, Virginia found that she could not attend to all the administrative duties she had to perform, so she brought in her husband, who was about to retire, for assistance to help her start a slew of new chapters in the San Diego area.

Tips for Effective Family Collaborations

Working with a spouse or family member presents its own unique challenges. Like any partnership, working closely with another person can bring out conflicts and personality differences. But when that partner is your spouse, parent, child, or sibling, the inevitable conflicts can become particularly deep, disruptive, and even destructive. And if you're living with or seeing these relatives day in and day out, every day, these conflicts can be especially difficult to resolve because you're not able to get away from them for even a short while to defuse your feelings. Here are a few tips for making sure your working relationship with a family member goes smoothly.

1. Maintain a perspective that you're a family first. In general, it's more important to preserve your family relationship than your business relationship. Ironically, taking this attitude will usually improve your business relationship, too, because by putting family ties first, your aim will be to preserve your relationship and resolve any conflicts amicably, not wanting to take chances that a dispute will destroy your relationship. Putting family first can help defuse arguments and disruptions and lead to better decision making in the long run.

2. Make sure everyone is participating voluntarily of her or his own free will. Too often family members get pressured, subtly or not so subtly, into working with one another. And sometimes family members volunteer, without pressure, not because they truly want to team up, but out of guilt, duty, obligation, or a sense of responsibility. Usually such motivation spells disaster, jeopardizing not only the business but also the relationship. So provide ample opportunity for family members to fully evaluate and choose whether to team up and allow everyone ample opportunity to change her or his mind if things do not work out as intended.

3. Don't assume anything: have clearly defined goals and responsibilities. Make sure everyone is on the same track, going in the same direction. While this is important for any joint activity, it's especially important among family members where it's all too easy to assume that you intuitively understand and know each other's intentions. Never take agreement for granted. Check out and spell out your joint goals and especially who will be doing what, when. Be up front about financial issues, too; spell out how money will be divided.

4. To avoid conflicts, get agreements in writing and when appropriate make it legal. Because family members know and trust each other, it's tempting to proceed on a handshake or head nod. In some short-term situations, that's satisfactory. But it never hurts and is sometimes crucial to write down your agreements to be sure everyone is actually in agreement. In situations when you would draw up a legal contract or letter agreement with someone outside the family, it's important to do so with family members as well. If your parents lend you money, for example, write down and sign an agreement as to how much you'll owe them, when you'll pay it back, and what role if any they'll have in the business in exchange for their loan.

5. Allow each person to perform his or her own task without interference. Dozens of family member teams have told us that the one rule that preserves their ability to work successfully together is that they allow each other to work independently, respecting and trusting each other to do their own jobs without interference. They might occasionally ask for each other's opinion, but for the most part, family members work best when they let each other have control of whatever tasks he or she does best. Don't be tempted to try getting a family member to perform her or his role in the venture *your* way.

6. Take steps to play down competitiveness. While competitiveness can arise in any collaboration, sometimes family collaborations are even more apt to stir up the competitive juices. But as family-business consultant Robert Caldwell of Le Van Associates points out, competition demands that someone lose. But when someone in a family loses, everyone else loses, too. So to decrease competition, have clearly defined areas of responsibility, mutual expectations, and a win-win plan for how everyone will be compensated.

7. Encourage each other to voice rather than bury dissatisfactions. Nothing will eat away at a family collaboration faster than unresolved resentments. They invariably surface at the worst possible times. So, check regularly to be sure everyone is happy and satisfied.

8. Treat each other with the same respect you would confer on a non-family-member business partner. Sometimes family members are more apt to let it all hang out, exploding, name-calling, or engaging in behavior that they would never display with someone outside the family. Such behavior can be especially vitriolic in a business relationship when money and egos are on the line. So, agree in advance that when conflict occurs, you will step back and ask yourselves how you'd handle this difficult situation if you were working with a respected nonfamily colleague. Then use that answer as your guide in resolving your family business relationship issues.

9. When conflicts occur, take a breather from each other. Conflicts are natural and, practically speaking, unavoidable. There will be times in every business relationship when the parties disagree on a strategy or even a trivial detail. But conflicts among family members tend to be more intense than others, so when tempers flare, it's best for one person to go out for a walk or work in another locale for a while to release some of the tension. Later, once tempers have calmed, concerns and issues can, and should, be addressed.

We'll be examining the details of family collaborations further in later chapters.

Summary—Pros and Cons of Family/Spouse Collaborations

Pros:

- Working together can make balancing work and personal life easier and, with the proper control, make shifting between these aspects of your life a more seamless effort.
- Working with family members can simplify a complex or stressful lifestyle.
- Teaming up with family members can avoid the financial burden of having to pay outside employees and keeps more of the profits within the family.
- Working together can bring family members closer as you jointly overcome adversity and other challenges.
- You can capitalize on the camaraderie, loyalty, and shared spirit that already exist within a family instead of trying to find an outside associate or partner with whom you can build such deep ties.
- You may be able to draw upon similar habits, goals, and work styles based on deeply shared values.
- It's often easier to work with someone you already know and trust than to build such bonds with someone new.

Cons

- Working with family members can amplify everything, the best and the worst in each of us. As the character Douglas Wambaugh said on the TV show *Picket Fences*, "Family members love one another—but they drive each other crazy."
- When business conflicts arise, they can have a deleterious effect on your marriage or family.
- Your business can interfere with family life if boundaries are not respected.
- Your spouse or another family member may not always be the best person for the job.
- It's easy to make assumptions about family members you would never make about someone outside the family. And it's easier to overlook formalities that would protect the rights of those involved. But such assumptions and oversights make you vulnerable to disappointments, resentments, and even ugly and costly lawsuits.
- It's usually harder to end a family business relationship when it doesn't work out.

OPTION 9: PARTNERSHIPS

When people think about teaming up, forming a partnership is usually the first thought that comes to mind. Actually while partnerships are one of the more common ways for people to team up, they're also one of the more challenging options. And while teaming up is on the rise, the number of formal legal partnerships is on the decline. In fact, horror stories or other fears about failed partnerships are one of the most common reasons people don't team up. And it's no wonder. While over 50 percent of all marriages end in divorce these days, business partnerships have an even higher failure rate.

But like marriage, partnerships are an institution that's been around for thousands of years. Many ancient civilizations, from the Babylonians and Hebrews to the Greeks and Romans, have used partnerships in land sharing and business ventures. In the sixteenth century, partnerships were also a popular way of covering the high costs of global trade during the golden age of the great explorers. And to this day, when a partnership is good, it can be very, very good. Partnerships like Ben & Jerry's Ice Cream, Apple Computer's founders Jobs and Wozniak, and Hewlett and Packard illustrate what two partners who are perfect matches can do for a small, home-based (or garage-based) business. Such stories of glory and riches are living proof that partnerships can work wonders when the chemistry is right.

The promise of such glowing successes is what draws many self-employed individuals to the idea of finding the "perfect" partner. But when a partnership turns out to be bad, it can be very, very bad. Over 20 percent of the catastrophes we profiled in our book *Secrets of Self-Employment* involved a bad experience with a partnership! Here are just of few of the devastating partnership experiences we've heard about.

- When one partner had a heart attack and died, the other, unable to run the business alone, ended up in bankruptcy.
- When one partner left to pursue other interests, the remaining partner was surprised to learn she'd been left with a bill of $20,000 for supplies that had to be paid in fifteen days.
- In an effort to expand their business, one partner ran through their entire line of credit, leaving the other to discover they had no funds to fulfill their orders.
- One partner, inexperienced in using computer technology, inadvertently erased all the company's computer records.
- When husband-and-wife partners divorced, the wife learned that the husband's poor accounting practices had run what had seemed like a profitable business into the ground.

Keep in mind, each of these people would have sworn nothing like this could ever happen to them—until it did. Such tales are not meant to scare you away from the benefits of partnering. Quite the contrary. We include them to illustrate why we wholeheartedly advise that you use other more informal, short-term, less legally binding options for teaming up to test the water before formalizing your relationship with a potential partner. Like a good marriage, when carefully selected and wisely handled, a partnership can be the most rewarding of ways to team up.

Partnerships Defined

Throughout time, the basic premise of a partnership has been that two or more individuals (or companies) agree to join forces by sharing in the ownership of a business for the purpose of earning a profit. The modern American legal definition of a partnership is "an association of two or more persons to carry on as co-owners of a business for profit."

SPECIAL CONSIDERATIONS ON FORMING A PARTNERSHIP

Although some people don't realize it, unlike other options for teaming up, a partnership is a specific legal and tax entity. It's one of the three basic types of business ownership: sole proprietorship, partnership, and corporation. (There are variations of these three types of business ownership, which we'll discuss in chapter 4.) Before entering into a partnership, it's therefore important to understand the legal and tax implications of your decision and to be sure you're willing to assume the responsibilities and obligations involved.

First, partnerships are governed by the laws of the Uniform Partnership Act (UPA), a regulatory code that's been adopted by all the states except Louisiana. Although partners can and should draw up a partnership agreement specifying their own rules and decisions, there are also a few legal and financial definitions that always apply to any partnership.

1. If you willingly and openly work with another person and share the ownership of a business, whether or not you use the term partnership, *technically speaking, you* are *in a partnership.* Obviously, many people work together without ever signing an agreement and think, therefore, that they are not really in a partnership. But the truth is, if you work closely with another person in business and your customers and others come to think of your relationship as a partnership, it is possible that you could be declared a legal partnership in the event of a problem such as having a lawsuit against one of you. This means that even if you don't have a partnership agreement, you can still be subject to the conditions specified under the UPA.

2. Under the UPA, each partner can legally perform all acts that are necessary to running the business, including spending or borrowing money, unless otherwise stated in the partnership agreement. This means that unless a partnership agreement so states, one partner may buy supplies or incur debt without letting the other(s) know. And even if an agreement limits a partner's authority, if an outsider thinks the partner is acting on behalf of the other partners in the normal course of doing business, all other partners are responsible for that partner's actions.

3. Under the UPA, each partner is responsible for the business actions and debts of all other partners. This means that each partner is personally liable for any business expenses, damage, fraud, negligence, or malfeasance committed or incurred by the other partners.

4. Partners can share in profits or losses in whatever proportion they agree. However, if there is no written agreement for how profits and losses are to be shared, they are deemed to be shared equally. This means that in the event of a disagreement between the parties, without a written agreement, the profits and losses must be split equally.

5. Partnerships themselves don't pay taxes; profits and losses are passed down to each partner in proportion to her or his individual share in the partnership. Each partner then declares the profit or loss on his or her individual federal and state tax returns.

6. A partnership ends when one partner dies or leaves the business, unless the partnership allows the business to be sold to the remaining partner(s) or to another party. "Leaving the business" usually requires a formal letter of withdrawal and a public notice such as a classified advertisement indicating that your business is no longer operating as a partnership.

When and with Whom to Partner

As you might realize from reviewing the above legal and financial stipulations, forming a partnership should not be taken lightly. Partnerships require those involved to have a great deal of well-earned trust in one another and a good measure of vigilance to boot, because even the most well-meaning partner can inadvertently lead you down an unwanted path. Overlooking the reality that people don't always turn out to do what you expected is the one thing that most often leads a partnership astray. We'll go into more details on the dangers of selecting the wrong partner in later chapters of this book.

Notwithstanding these concerns, there are many situations in which partnerships can be very valuable for a business.

1. When you each can gain more by working together than by working alone. This is the most fundamental reason people enter into partnerships. In certain circumstances, some businesses can rationally and quantitatively assess that they have more to gain by working together than by working alone. For example, when a business is difficult to start up, requires long hours, has simultaneous demands in different geographical areas, or needs twenty-four-hour coverage, joining forces with someone else makes sense because there will be two people who can split the work or the hours.

Mary Herman had an idea to set up an Internet site to handle job searches in the entertainment industry. Recognizing that the effort required to design a Web page and get it up and running, along with marketing such a service, would be enormous, she formed a partnership with a friend, Sam Friedman, to get the work done. By teaming up their company, the Employment Resource Network, was able to get under way within only a few months. We also met the principal of an agricultural export business based in Oregon. The firm specialized in products for the Orient, so it was a logical decision to involve as a partner a man living in Tokyo.

2. *When you each have something the other needs.* Whether it's knowledge, contacts, ideas, or money, self-employed individuals often recognize they can benefit by sharing their strengths with others who can in turn compensate for their weaknesses.

For example, Sheryl Telles and Kathy Allocco, the women mentioned earlier who run a medical billing agency in Scottsdale, Arizona, both had been working for a doctor for almost twenty years when they decided to go into business for themselves. However, each woman knew that she did not have the expertise to do it alone. Sheryl had medical knowledge with a strong background in medical coding, while Kathy was an expert in insurance reimbursement. Sheryl also did medical transcription. By sharing their expertise, they formed their company, Arizona MedLink Provider Resources Inc., and were able to get their first client within just seven weeks. And they were averaging a new client every month thereafter.

3. *When someone with financial resources is seeking to invest in someone else's work.* Money is often a driving force in partnership arrangements. Although money is not always the best tie that binds partners together, it often makes for an appealing package.

4. *To motivate an employee with a share in the business instead of a salary.* Some partnerships originate when a self-employed individual or business owner realizes an employee is contributing so much to an enterprise that it makes sense to offer him or her an ownership stake in the business. For example, Chellie Campbell began as an employee of Cameron Diversified Services, was offered the opportunity to become a partner, and later bought the business in its entirety.

Basic Tips for Effective Partnerships

As you can see, in circumstances like these, a partnership can be an excellent choice for all parties involved. Yet, unfortunately, even if they began with the best of intentions and what seems like the most solid of agreements, it's estimated that more than 50 percent of partnerships fail. Don't let yours be one of them. Here are four basic principles for building a successful partnership.

1. *Be sure you know why you're going into a partnership and that you're doing so for the right reasons.* Many people enter into a partnership without

thinking about why they're doing it. Some people are enticed into joining a friend or a relative in a business because it sounds like such a great idea, but deep inside they know they can't work with this person or in that business. Others get involved in a partnership because they don't believe they have what it takes to succeed on their own. They feel that they need a knight in shining armor, but then they're resentful when their "knight" steps in and wants to be involved in calling the shots. Still others get involved in a partnership because they want to be the knight in shining armor, rescuing someone from undeserved distress. But shouldering so much responsibility can get tiring fast. You can end up resenting your partner for leaving you with what seems like an unfair burden.

To avoid these common traps, spend some time writing down your motivation for wanting to form a partnership. Be sure you're doing it with confidence and from a position of strength, not on a whim or out of desperation. Be sure that as partners you will be able to give and gain equally. A knight's shining armor tarnishes all too easily. The most successful partnerships, like the best marriages, are between fully functioning, effective individuals. So, identify clearly what you need and what you can offer; what you can expect and what will be expected of you.

2. Create a written partnership agreement that specifies your business roles, decision-making authority, financial agreements, and what will happen if and when the partnership dissolves. Many people go into partnerships thinking there's no need to write anything down, believing one's word and a handshake are enough. Sometimes they'd rather play it by ear and see what happens than be tied down to a written contract. Other times they believe they can trust their partner: "After all, she's my best friend." But being in business with another person can bring about the most surprising twists. People don't remember things the same way. Best friends have a way of becoming worst enemies. And playing it by ear can mean playing it in court.

There's no substitute for a written agreement that will protect both you and your partner(s). Make sure you discuss the primary issues of any partnership: who will be doing what, how decisions are to be made, how money will be spent, how profits will be split, and how you will end the business if the time comes to do so.

3. Enter into a partnership only with someone you know well and have come to trust fully. Even with a partnership agreement, much of the success of any partnership will come down to the personal trust and communication between the two parties. It's usually not the legal agreement that causes a business to fail, but rather a clash between the partners' personalities, approach to decision making, or communication habits. So find out about one another's skills, habits, and work style by working together in more informal ways before becoming formal partners.

4. Be vigilant about your communications and your relationship bond. No matter how much you respect and trust your partner, keep abreast of what he or she is doing and make sure you keep your partner(s) informed about what you're doing as well. Neither of you needs to be a criminal to get each other in hot water. It can happen with the best of intentions.

Here are three examples of what can go wrong.

- Two best friends went into business as partners making specialty jewelry. Within a year the partnership had disintegrated into threatening lawsuits. Apparently one partner "borrowed" the other partner's design and began marketing it herself through her own company.
- Two business consultants and former friends created a partnership to expand their business by sharing expertise and jointly developing clients. Three years later, they agreed to end their partnership. It appeared that the one partner was bringing in all the business and resented the other partner for not carrying "his share of the weight."
- Two writers met at a workshop, liked each other's work, and decided to form a partnership to develop corporate training materials and seminars on business writing. Within a year, the partnership dissolved in bitterness. It appears that each partner had a very different vision of what "being in business meant." One partner wanted to aggressively seek clients and expand in many different directions while the other wanted to move slowly and develop a sideline business so he could still work on other projects of his own. A dispute erupted over how much money each partner had invested in the business and who was owed what.

To avoid such misunderstandings, or at least identify them as early as possible so they can be resolved amicably, make sure to keep in touch with each other. Provide each other with regular verbal updates and written summaries on key activities, decisions, and agreements. Review all contracts that either of you negotiates. Look over all financial records regularly. Use the services of outside legal, accounting, and tax professionals who can alert you and your partner(s) to irregularities, be they intentional or unintentional.

We'll elaborate further on many procedures for implementing these principles in later chapters, but keep in mind, whatever your prior relationship with someone—friend, family member, colleague, or former boss—being in a partnership will likely change it. Working very closely with another person will either deepen or strain your relationship. Following these principles can help you preserve what you value most.

Summary—Pros and Cons of Partnerships

Pros

- Unlike corporations which require more paperwork and money to initiate and legally establish, partnerships can be relatively inexpensive and easy to set up. A basic partnership agreement can usually be drawn up within a day or two, assuming the parties have considered the issues and discussed the matters beforehand.
- A partnership generates a certain momentum that can boost a business. When each person knows why he or she is going into a partnership, the merger creates optimism and hope that can energize everyone involved.
- Partnerships can bring added creativity, resources, talents, and skills to an enterprise.
- A formally declared partnership can provide each person with the security of a clear, legally enforceable commitment from the others involved to share in the responsibility of running the business.
- Sharing a workload usually enables people to accomplish more than working alone, and the whole can be greater than the sum of its parts.
- Partnerships can be a good way to finance a business that couldn't otherwise get under way.

Cons

- Complex partnership agreements can take more time and cost a lot more in attorney's fees than a single incorporation.
- You are legally liable for your partner's actions, both good and bad.
- Success depends on a high level of mutual cooperation and planning and time commitment to communicate and work effectively together.
- Expectations for positive results from partnerships are usually high, so the risk of conflicts and disappointments is also high.
- Since the stakes are usually higher, conflicts can be more vitriolic and unpleasant when participants disagree on the strategy or implementation of their business plans.
- Since you're bound to the terms of your agreement, ending a partnership that's not working out can be more difficult. Often you can't just walk out. There may be debts and other customer obligations that must be resolved first. In fact, since the adoption of no-fault divorce, it's easier to end a marriage than to end a business partnership.

OPTION 10: VIRTUAL ORGANIZATIONS

Several years ago, we (Paul and Sarah) flew from California to Chapel Hill, North Carolina, expecting to confer with a roomful of corporate personnel. We'd been hired to consult with a *Fortune* 500 company, and indeed we were met at the reception desk by an employee of the company who assisted us in getting our security name badges and led us to the conference room. But there around the table were twelve to fifteen people, more than half of whom were also sporting security name badges on their lapels. This was our introduction to the virtual organization, and the economic institution of the future.

The meeting was run by outside consultant Deb Watering, owner of Watering & Associates, which she runs from her home in the rural Alabama community of Talladega. Watering was the project leader of a major study to expand the company's customer base. The project team was composed of key in-house personnel and a number of other outside consultants like ourselves. Some had been working on the project for many months; others like ourselves would be involved for only a portion of the study. Still others would join the study at a later date. Some of the consultants were associates of Watering; others like us had separate contracts directly with the *Fortune* 500 company.

This was only the first in what have become many such meetings where we're hired to work with major corporations. It's rare that we meet only with in-house staff. Usually we're part of a team of inside and outside personnel who've been pulled together to work on a specific project. Our most recent meeting was not even in person. It was a telephone conference call among us, one of our consultants, the vice president of another *Fortune* 500 company, two representatives of his PR firm, a second VP of an allied *Fortune* 500 company, and one of their outside consultants. Although as you read about this meeting it may appear confusing, it was not. It's becoming business as usual.

Virtual Corporation Defined

The term *virtual corporation* was probably coined by Jan Hopland, a Digital Equipment Corporation executive who used it to refer to an enterprise that can marshal more resources than it currently has on its own by collaborating with others both inside and outside its boundaries. But to William Davidow and Michael Malone, authors of *The Virtual Corporation,* which came out in 1993, the term is a catch-all phrase used to describe what they and others began observing as an restructuring of the way business is being done and will be done in the future.

In its February 1993 watershed cover story, "The Virtual Corporation," *Newsweek* magazine described the emerging organization of the future as a temporary network of independent companies who come together quickly to exploit fast-changing opportunities and, linked by information technology, share skills, costs, and access to one another's markets. The virtual corporation, they proclaimed, will have neither central office nor organizational chart and no hierarchy.

But as we know firsthand, this phenomenon is by no means limited to employees of corporations. The participants are just as likely to be self-employed individuals operating as sole proprietors or partnerships. So we choose to call this dynamic new way of teaming up the *virtual organization,* referring to any collective of independent individuals or companies of any size who work separately or together to carry out and complete specific time-limited projects.

Unlike a consortium, a virtual organization can come together and disband as needed, with tenuous if not nonexistent ongoing ties among one another when they are between projects. Sometimes participants in a virtual organization never actually meet other participants. Their work is limited to interaction with whoever is running the project. In fact, they may be located in disparate parts of the country or even in other countries, working together electronically via phone, fax, and modem.

As we learned more about this emerging way of doing business, we realized that in essence we have our own virtual organization. Although we have one full-time employee now, we also have a constellation of contingent personnel, some of whom are self-employed themselves, others of whom work for larger companies with whom we are allied. We call upon these individuals in various ways at various times, and they upon us. Our virtual organization consists of our:

- Marketing consultant (who lives in another city)
- On-line publicist (whom we've never met in person)
- Editor
- Freelance writers
- Attorney
- Accountant (whom we've never met in person)
- Researcher
- Graphic designer
- Recording studio
- Product fulfillment houses
- Video production company
- Makeup artist
- Photographer
- Two CompuServe sysops (one of whom we have not met in person)
- Audiotape publisher (out of state)
- Book publisher (out of state)
- CD-ROM publisher (out of state)
- Newsletter publisher (out of state)
- Internet developer
- Television production company

We work with the "departments" of our "organization" as we need them or when they need us. Most of them have never met one another, but others must and do work together often or periodically. Some of them have their own virtual organizations. In fact, we met some of them by having worked on projects with others of them.

Other virtual organizations are more cohesive than ours. Deb Watering's company is a virtual organization composed of independent consultants who are located in various parts of the country. They have regular telephone "staff" conferences and hold an annual "staff" meeting. Several other virtual organizations have developed through the Internet or on-line services like CompuServe. One, called Virtual Fusion, is a collective of over thirty-five people around the world who are more or less led by Michael Daconta. Virtual Fusion uses the talents of its diverse members to produce a shareware database program. They also publish a newsletter for current and prospective members (http://www.electriciti.com:80/~jbalsamo/Virtual_Fusion/vfhome.html).

When and with Whom a Virtual Corporation Makes Sense

Most successful virtual organizations spring up almost spontaneously around an existing need. In other words, a virtual organization usually doesn't come together as an entity in search of work the way a consortium or mutual alliance might. More likely a virtual organization will arise in response to an effort to meet the demands of existing work. This is one of the biggest differences between a virtual organization and the other teaming-up choices we've discussed. They are "pulled together" by someone because there is some work to be done. They may be called into existence by one person, a professional speaker, for example, who decides to produce a video demo. Or two large companies may form a strategic alliance to launch a new product and bring together a virtual organization of others to get the work done. A group of engineers might form a marketing consortium and when they get their first contract, they become a virtual organization in order to carry it out.

In other words a virtual organization doesn't exist until there is something for it to do. That's why virtual organizations may seem so amorphous. They quite literally don't exist until they're needed. Up to that point, they're nothing more than a pool of "possible" teammates, if that. Until this "potential" pool of talent is called into action, there is no leader, no group, no structure, just the possibility of one. Once deployed, however, there is *always* a leader, someone or some company who is spearheading the project that's to be undertaken.

Rob Weller and Gary Grossman, for example, created a production company. They both had strong backgrounds and experience in television: Rob as talent, Gary as a writer. Their partnership, Weller Grossman, was successful from the start, partly because they have a very small full-time staff and deploy a series of virtual organizations to produce whatever TV project they undertake.

We (Paul and Sarah) met Rob and Gary when they were creating a virtual organization to produce a show about working from home for Scripps Howard's cable network, Home and Garden Television (HGTV). When we were selected to be the co-hosts for the show, we became part of the virtual organization that was forming to create what became a series of thirteen thirty-minute shows called *Working from Home with Paul & Sarah*. It was exciting to hear reports about the organization that was taking form. A director was selected, then other production staff were added. Some worked at Weller Grossman, others from their homes, still others had separate offices of their own. While the entire "team" never met together all at once, there was never any doubt about who was "in charge." It was Joel Rizer, our director.

During the three weeks when the shows were actually shot, most of our "team" worked together face-to-face. The crew of fifteen-some people was composed of a collection of individuals who were either Weller Grossman employees, freelancers, or subcontractors. The camera and sound work, for example, was done by Kurt Zell Productions. Kurt's company has only two actual employees, but he deploys camera and sound teams on production shoots all over the country hundreds of times every year. The makeup and wardrobe artist was freelancer Kathryn Merrill, who joined the team at our recommendation. Having worked with Kathryn before, when Weller Grossman needed someone with her talents to be part of the team, we put them in touch with her.

The shooting was exciting and intense. We worked twelve-to-fourteen-hour days. Then it was finished. There was a wrap party, and that was that! The director and some members of the team continued working grueling hours in postproduction. We were called in to do several days of voice-overs. Within weeks, thirteen shows were shipped off to Scripps Howard in Knoxville. And it was all over. The entire "organization" that had swung into action and worked so hard and so well together disbanded. Internal staff at Weller Grossman were assigned to work on other shows. The freelancers and subcontractors went on to other projects.

Then, over a year later, *Working from Home with Paul & Sarah* was renewed. Scripps Howard ordered thirteen more shows, and suddenly a new "organization" began taking form. Working under Joel's supervision, a new director was brought in along with other new freelancers. But many of the people we worked with before rejoined the "team." At times it felt like a reunion. With many of us having worked together before, this project went along more smoothly. And before we knew it, another thirteen episodes were on their way to Knoxville and, once again, we all went our separate ways.

So, as you can see, there is a serendipitous quality to virtual corporations. A project arises, someone calls on someone she or he knows to be part of it, that person calls on another and another. Later, one of those people lands another project and turns to the others and so on and so on, forming and reforming like the "recombinant work teams" we described in chapter 1.

Some fields are quite fertile for virtual organizations because they usually require the input of many people to handle large reoccurring projects. Of course, much of the entertainment industry operates through virtual organizations. You've undoubtedly noticed that movie directors like Woody Allen, David Lynch, and John Cassavettes turn again and again to the same actors, actresses, writers, and lighting and camera people, calling them in on a project-by-project basis. As with so many virtual organizations today, there is no formal agreement that these people will work together again and again, but de facto, they do. And when they do, they're able to function like such a finely-tuned instrument that you'd think they worked full-time for the same company.

Other fields in which virtual organization have become commonplace include:

- Advertising
- Catering
- Computer consulting
- Computer programming
- Event planning
- Executive placement
- Financial planning
- Marketing and public relations
- Media and multimedia production
- On-line seminars
- On-line training courses
- Publishing
- Sales
- Secretarial services
- Temporary agencies

If you're already involved in one of these fields, the easiest route to becoming part of a virtual organization is by generating work for yourself that requires you to pull in other virtual "departments" in order to get the work done. This way, as you start linking with others project by project, you get in the loop, so to speak. Soon, those you've worked with on past projects will start bringing you in on their projects. As you work with various people in this way, those of you who work especially well together may become a "de facto" virtual organization or you may formalize your organization as Watering and Daconta have done.

Tips for Creating Successful Virtual Organizations

When there's paying work to do, creating a virtual organization is a snap! People are always eager to take paying work. But setting out to create a successful virtual organization before there's work lined up can be a challenge. Deborah Dewey, a friend of long standing from CompuServe, describes two efforts she participated in to develop virtual organizations. The first was supposed to be an organization devoted to executive placement. The group originated with about six people from around the country who were sharing laments on a CompuServe message board about the increasing number of highly qualified executives who were losing their corporate jobs. As the participants of the message board exchanged ideas, it dawned on them that perhaps they could link up as a virtual company that could find temporary jobs for these executives. The idea seemed quite plausible, so the group divided up the labor and set out to establish a new company. Each member was supposed to do some preparatory footwork and get back to other members on-line to share their research. Over time, however, the group disintegrated into cyberspace as each member had his or her own agenda to follow.

The second effort Deborah was involved in began when a group of software engineers attempted to start an on-line programming training class that would be marketed to anyone who wanted to learn how to program. Although this group lasted a year and a half, it never became financially viable. As Deborah pointed out, their problem was unstable leadership. Because the group decided to rotate leadership to spread around the chores, and each person had a different style, the group ended up spinning its wheels.

To avoid problems like these:

1. Don't get all dressed up until you have someplace to go. Since virtual corporations form with amazing alacrity when there's paying work to do, don't try to create one until you have a project to work around. If you need to, create a marketing consortium, an independent alliance, or some other teaming-up arrangement to generate the business you need. Your associates in these marketing efforts can serve as the core of your eventual virtual organization. While you're marketing you can also begin identifying other people to pull in once you get your first project.

2. Identify high-quality, reliable people to work with. Through your networking and other teaming-up activities, begin identifying the kind of people you will need to work with you on anticipated projects. Once you find a few good people, one of the best ways to find others is to use their contacts—people they've worked with and know. Proceeding in this way, your "organization" can start out with a track record already under its belt.

For example, when we got a contract to produce our first video, we turned to Kurt Zell since we'd already worked with him at Weller Grossman. Kurt brought in some of the people from the lighting and sound "teams" we'd already worked with, and we drew in another director and makeup artist we had worked with before. This way most of "our" team already had months of experience working together before we came together for our one-day shoot.

3. Select people who have business experience—and potential business. The most common mistake people make in pulling together a virtual organization is to attract a group of other people who are just getting started on their own and therefore have no business or track record as yet. That means everyone involved is hungry and looking for paid work, so they're going to have to take whatever work comes their way first, and finding that work will have to be their primary focus whether it involves opportunities for the others or not.

The best people to have in your organization are those who already have a lot of business and who will be attracted to working with you primarily because you're a peer who can do a good job and secondarily because you have the potential to bring in additional business. By teaming up with people who have a lot going for them, you have a better chance of getting new business and can then pull in your team, rather than the other way around, waiting and hoping for someone to bring you in.

4. Keep in touch. Since your "virtual organization" may be quite amorphous and informal at first, those involved probably won't even know they're part of an "organization." To strengthen your relationships, so that you can call upon them when you need to, stay in touch between projects with everyone you expect to call upon again. Call or E-mail them periodically or set up an occasional dinner or lunch meeting. To build team spirit, sponsor a social or business get-together every few months. It also helps to celebrate at the end of a project with everyone who's around, or to host a party or holiday event to bring people together. Such occasional meetings are important to reinforce the tenuous ties of a "virtual" group. If your team is spread across the country, schedule telephone conference calls or try having an on-line meeting, conference, or party. Or plan a get-together at annual trade or professional conferences that your associates will be attending.

5. Let structure follow function. Don't make your organization more formalized than the work demands. Don't bog the group down with organizational issues like shared goals, policies, and procedures until there is a need for them. Keep the structure as loose and flexible as possible. Operate more like an interdependent alliance until the frequency and size of the incoming work begins to require a more formal structure. At that point, people are more likely to be willing to participate in setting up something more formal, like having a fixed structure or following agreed-upon procedures. But, by nature, a successful virtual organization will always remain highly fluid and flexible.

Summary—Pros and Cons of Virtual Organizations

Pros

- You can keep your overhead significantly lower than if you were running a traditional organization.
- You can remain nimble and flexible, pulling together just the right people on the spur of the moment.
- A virtual corporation is like a "skunk works" in that you can get a project done more quickly and more cost-effectively than a traditional organization could.
- By drawing on the synergy and creative energy of a diverse group of successful people, you can spawn new ideas and better ways of doing a job.
- Like a consortium, you can take on more work and larger projects than would be possible working as a one-person operation or a partnership.
- You can expand into working in other geographic regions.

Cons

- There is so little structure that relationships may dissipate between projects.
- Confusion and miscommunication can occur when people don't meet face-to-face and communicate primarily through a project leader or electronic media like E-mail, fax, and telephone.
- You must be comfortable working in a flexible style and give up old views of structured leadership, loyalty, and project management.
- Whoever is managing a given project will need to commit to a high level of planning and coordination to pull together the abilities of many people who are doing their jobs without supervision.
- Because relationships are often more informal, some individuals may undercut one another, not realizing that this will hinder their success in the future.
- It's difficult to get under way until you and the others involved are established and have business coming in.

THE PROACTIVE STRATEGIC ALLIANCE

In recent years, the term *strategic alliance* has become a popular way to describe the relationships many "big" businesses are making with one another to further their separate strategic goals. It's generally regarded as an alternative to the complexities of undertaking an acquisition or a merger because buyouts take a great deal of time and money, whereas strategic alliances take little time and often cost next to nothing. Therefore, strategic alliances are being heralded as the wave of the future for large corporations.

However, for self-employed individuals or small businesses, making strategic alliances is equally important. Making alliances can help you leverage your limited resources and help you keep up with—or ahead of—your competitors. Alliances have the potential to reduce your risks while increasing your success.

We consider all ten of the teaming-up techniques we've just described to be strategic alliances. Each technique—networking, mutual referrals, cross-promoting, interdependent collaborations, joint ventures, satellite subcontracting, consortiums, family or spousal arrangements, partnerships of all kinds, and a virtual organization—is a matter of joining with others to invest in one another's future success. In other words, strategic alliances are no longer just for large megacorporations; any business can share in the benefits of collaborating to grow and increases its success.

The many benefits of making strategic alliances are open to you right now, but to share in them you will need to be proactive. In today's world especially, you can no longer wait for alliances to come your way. For each moment you wait, observing, evaluating, and reflecting on what to do, someone else somewhere is taking a step forward—one that conceivably allows him or her to achieve the very success you're hoping to achieve for yourself. Don't end up wondering why some people are doing well while you're struggling along. All it takes is for you to jump onto the teaming-up continuum anywhere you feel comfortable so you can start enjoying the surge of energy that comes from linking synergistically with others.

Ultimately, teaming up is a way of working, a habit that can come quite naturally when you shift your thinking from "It's me against the world" to "Together we can all win." The key is to be willing to find win-win ways to work with others. If this idea is new to you, begin exploring possibilities for working with other people in whatever ways you can, focusing on the ideas, leads, and contacts you have. Let each new source of information lead you to others. If you come across something that's not suited to you, refer it to someone else you've met. If you find a job that's too big for you, find a partner with whom you can create a joint venture that allows you to accept it. Join a consortium or become a member of a group. Think of teaming up as a natural progression of activities that allows you to seize many new opportunities while remaining in charge of your future.

RESOURCES

Books

The Best-Known Marketing Secret. Ivan Misner. Austin, TX: Bard & Stephen, 1994.

Business Alliance Guide. Robert Porter Lynch. New York: Wiley, 1993.

The Conversation Piece. Bret Nicholaus and Paul Lowrie. New York: Ballantine, 1996.

Walk Your Talk: Grow Your Business Faster Through Successful Cross-Promotional Partnerships. Kare Anderson. Berkeley, CA: Celestial Arts Press, 1994.

Organizations with Local Chapters or Affiliates

BUSINESS (VARIOUS)

Chamber of Commerce of the U.S.
1615 H Street NW
Washington, DC 20062
202/659-6000

Jaycees
Box 7
Tulsa OK 74121
918/584-2481

Toastmasters International
23182 Arroyo Vista
Rancho Santa Margarita, CA 92688
714/858-8255
714/858-1207 Fax
http://www.toastmasters.org

HOME BUSINESS

American Association of Home-Based Businesses
P.O. Box 10023
Rockville, MD 20849
202/310-3130 or 800/447-9710

Small Office and Home Office Association
1767 Business Center Drive
Reston, VA 22090
703/438-3060
703/438-3049 Fax

A listing of local and state home business associations can be found in Library 17 of the Working from Home Forum on CompuServe Information Service.

WOMEN'S BUSINESS

Business and Professional Women's/USA
2012 Massachusetts Ave NW
Washington, DC 20036
202/293-1100
202/861-0298 Fax

Federation of Organizations for Professional Women
1825 I Street NW, Suite 400
Washington, DC 20006
202/328-1415
202/429-9574 Fax

National Association for Female Executives
30 Irving Place, 5th Floor
New York, NY 10003
212/477-2200
212/477-8215 Fax
http://www.nafe.com

National Association of Women Business Owners
1100 Wayne Avenue
Suite 830
Silver Spring, MD 20910
301/608-2590
301/608-2596 Fax
http://www.alphasports.com/NAWBO/NAWBO.html

LEADS CLUBS

Business Network Intl.
268 S. Bucknell Avenue
Claremont, CA 91711-4907
800/825-8286 (outside So. Calif)
909/624-2227 (inside So. Calif.)

Leads Clubs
P.O. Box 279
Carslbad, CA 92018
800/783-3761 or 619/434-3761
619/729-7797 Fax
http://www.emanate.com/leadsclub

LeTip, International
4907 Marina Blvd., Ste. 13
San Diego, CA 92117
800/255-3847
http://www.letip.com

SERVICE CLUBS

Kiwanis
3636 Woodview Road
Indianopolis, IN 46268
317/875-8755

Lions Club International
300 22nd Street
Oakbrook, IL 60521
708/571-5466
http://www.lions.org/about.htm

Optimists International
4494 Lindell Boulevard
St. Louis, MO 63108
314/371-6000

Rotary International
1560 Sherman Avenue
Evanston, IL 60201
708/866-3000

Professional, Industry, and Trade Associations

Professional, industry, and trade associations, ranging from the American Academy of Actuaries to the World Floor Covering Association, exist by the thousands. A useful multivolume directory for finding potential professional, industry, and trade groups is the *Encyclopedia of Associations* published by Gale Research Company, Book Tower, Detroit, MI 48226. It's available in libraries and on-line on Dialog Information Service.

On-Line Services

On-line services provide Internet access. Hundreds of other national and local providers also make access to the Internet available.

America Online
8619 Westwood Center Drive
Vienna, VA 22182
800/827-5354 or 703/893-6288

CompuServe Information Service, Inc.
P. O. Box 20212
Columbus, OH 43220
800/848-8990, 800/848-8199 (in Ohio), 614/457-8650

Prodigy Information Service
445 Hamilton Avenue
White Plains, NY 10601
800/776-3449

Other

IRS Publication E contains information to help you understand the difference between an independent contractor and an employee.

The Greenberg Group
4029 Westerly Place, Suite 108
Newport Beach, CA. 92660
714/261-8450

Virtual Fusion
On-line Web site and membership organization:
http:// www.electriciti.com/~jbalsamo/Virtual_Fusion/vfinfo.html

3

Finding the Right People
and Making the Right Choices

Scoring champions rarely play for championship teams.
—PHIL JACKSON, BASKETBALL COACH
CHICAGO BULLS

WITH SO MANY OPTIONS for teaming up, where do you start? Which teaming-up option will be best for your business? How do you find the best people to work with? Have you made the right choices? How can you make sure you don't get involved in an unproductive relationship?

Like so many people, you may simply "fall" into a teaming-up relationship in much the same way as people "fall in love." Following your natural instincts and gut feelings, you might decide, for example, to work with an "old friend" in whom you have complete faith and trust. Or perhaps serendipitously, you'll meet someone by chance at a conference or party, and while chitchatting, you realize that you could work well together because your business goals are similar and your personalities seem compatible. Or perhaps a colleague from your past will call and propose that you team up in some way.

In truth, there's usually a bit of serendipity behind all successful relationships. As you may have noticed from some of the teaming-up examples we've given, more often than not, some of the best business relationships arose from a series of coincidences. The same can happen to you. Events that seemingly come out of nowhere can lead to promising new ventures—a sister calls with an idea, you run into a colleague you haven't seen for years, a stranger you meet at a networking event turns out to be working toward similar goals.

But as with romance, even the most wonderful initial relationship doesn't always develop as you originally imagined or hoped it would. The "soul mate" you meet at the conference or party could become an ideal contact and your businesses could both thrive from the connection. Or, on the other hand, the "soul mate" could turn out to have a number of annoying quirks that drive your customers away. Sometimes, a great friendship can lead to a great partnership; at other times, a great friendship can dissolve into anger, bitterness, and a lawsuit once you start working together.

While it's not always apparent which relationships will flourish and which will stumble, there are steps you can take to boost your chances for finding the right people to team up with. By taking the following steps you can find and develop collaborations that will be tailored to your personality, your goals, and your business.

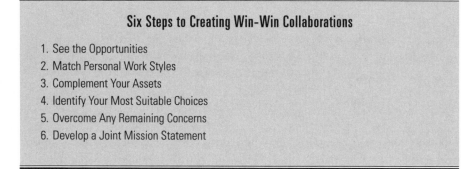

Six Steps to Creating Win-Win Collaborations

1. See the Opportunities
2. Match Personal Work Styles
3. Complement Your Assets
4. Identify Your Most Suitable Choices
5. Overcome Any Remaining Concerns
6. Develop a Joint Mission Statement

Even if you're already involved in or have planned a collaborative arrangement of some kind, reviewing these six steps can be worthwhile. You may have overlooked some valuable options or want to revise some decisions you've made. Regardless of how involved you are in a business relationship, it's rarely too late to clarify, modify, improve, or even call off an arrangement if you discover it's not working as you each intended. If you're already committed to working closely with someone, it could be worthwhile to browse through this chapter together to learn how you could better synchronize your work styles and work habits.

SEEING THE OPPORTUNITIES

The first step to finding workable, mutually rewarding business collaborations is to believe that such relationships are indeed possible and that you can and will be able to establish them. If you develop an open mind and proactively cultivate the possibility of developing such relationships, you'll begin seeing many opportunities for collaboration already around you and they will lead you to still others. But without an open and receptive mind, you run the risk of overlooking such possibilities. You may end up wondering why you never seem to find the promising relationship you'd like to have. So we suggest that you adopt the kind of positive, expectant attitude that will lead you to think that you can find just the right relationships you need to further your goals.

The Power of Positive Thinking

As psychologists and behavioral scientists now know, a positive attitude can have a powerful influence on the outcome of many situations. Sports coaches tell their athletes to think like winners, and it's just as important for you to put yourself into a confident and success-oriented frame of mind. Drop any naysayer attitude you may have about how difficult it is to build rewarding business relationships and start thinking collaboratively rather than competitively. Don't worry at this point about the details of the kind of relationship you might want to establish or how you'll work out the financial and legal aspects. Don't think about the lawyers, accountants, legal documents, meetings, or lost time that could be involved later on in the process. Imagining problems and complications that could arise before you are involved in a situation will prevent you from hearing opportunity when it knocks.

Don't Be Too Eager

When possibilities do appear, don't rush headlong, full-steam-ahead until you've explored the terrain to make sure it's someplace you really want to go. Just as in romance, the early excitement of a newfound relationship may cool or even sour in the face of the bright light of day-to-day realities. If a relationship is right, it won't disappear overnight. The best people for you to affiliate with won't want to be in a pell-mell rush either. No matter how exciting a possibility seems, it's wiser to take some time out to say, "Let's think about this."

Finding the right people to team up with and entering into the right kind of relationship require that you balance your need to be decisive and to keep your business moving forward with a certain amount of reservation and restraint. Many people have told us, for example, that they rushed straight into a business joint venture or partnership with a friend or former colleague, only to discover that their match was by no means made in heaven.

Jill C. discovered too late that her decision to work with a particular person was founded on untested assumptions. Someone who attended one of her management seminars approached her with the idea of becoming partners to market her seminars nationwide. He would sell the seminars, and she would present them. That sounded like a great idea. In fact, she said, it sounded "too good to be true." And indeed it was.

Although her new partner had marketed many real estate seminars, he had never marketed management seminars. Both he and Jill *assumed* that if he could market one, he could market another. But, while his high-pressure, promise-the-sky approach had worked in real estate, it bombed nationwide with corporate executives. They were turned off by both the sales materials and her partner's personal sales pitch. It took some time for Jill to rebuild her reputation in the corporate world. But, rest assured, next time around she tested out any potential partnerships with one-time joint ventures and had several such "trial runs" before finally finding the right partner to help market her seminars.

So don't jump prematurely into more of a relationship than the actual situation warrants. Give yourself time to test your assumptions.

MATCHING PERSONAL WORK STYLES

You've probably heard it said that finding the right business relationship, like finding the right mate, depends largely on chemistry. You can't prepare for it or do anything to make it happen. When it happens, it happens. And you'll intuitively know it.

On the one hand, we agree there is a certain element of truth to the chemistry theory. The good "vibes" you feel when you meet someone you like are actually a physical reaction. They're the result of the endorphins and other physiological responses that are aroused in our bodies when we meet people we like. They literally make you feel good. In this sense, our intuitive responses when we meet someone we trust are based on a reality—not just a vague hunch. So, in general, we believe in "going with your gut." A positive internal feeling toward someone is often a barometer or omen of positive things to come, just as negative feelings can be a warning that all is not as well as it seems.

Being in business with someone, however, isn't exactly the same as falling in love, so to rely solely on good vibes or chemistry in choosing a business associate or partner is not a foolproof gauge of things to come. Finding the right business associates also involves knowing yourself and your business well enough to make an informed choice even when things "feel" great. A good "match" should draw on *both* a positive gut feeling and a certain level of thoughtful analysis of the practical realities of teaming up.

We've heard many stories that prove the value of thoughtful analysis. Every person we talked with who had a failed business relationship told us that, from hindsight, they would have recognized potential problems if they had given more *thought* to the situation before getting involved. In one failed partnership, for example, Arthur and Betsy had worked well together on a professional associate board. They enjoyed each other's company and shared a similar philosophy. But right from the start of their partnership Arthur didn't want to open a joint bank account for their venture. Looking back,

Betsy realized that if she'd given more consideration to Arthur's attitude about this financial matter, she would have realized that their partnership was much less important to him than it was to her. Unfortunately this seemingly insignificant incident turned out to be a sign of things to come. As they worked together, Arthur had little commitment to the partnership and rarely followed through on their joint decisions. By giving more thought to the matter up front, Betsy could have saved herself several thousand dollars and a year lost to trying to salvage their partnership.

In another failed business relationship, Glenn teamed up with Bob, his old boss on a previous job where they'd worked together closely for five years. Their alliance didn't work at all well, however, because Glenn hadn't known before they began working together how much Bob hated marketing. He had no interest in participating in the aggressive speaking campaign Glenn felt was needed to get their venture off the ground. Eventually Glenn bought out Bob's share of the business, but by then they both had endured a year of frustration and disappointment.

So in addition to making sure the chemistry is right, take the time to discover more about what you and those you're thinking about teaming up with bring to a relationship and how well you will actually work together in particular situations. Why enter into an arrangement that will drain your energy, waste your time and money, and essentially lead nowhere? Why not invest some time and energy beforehand to examine yourself and your business in an objective fashion so that you can be sure to team up with people who fit in well with your personality, your goals, your work habits, and the demands of your business?

Assessing Your Motivation

Your personality is the essence of who you are and how other people perceive you. It affects how you treat yourself and how you are treated by others. Your personality is reflected in the way you speak. It shows through in your gestures and body language, your eye contact, the way you respond to situations, and how you feel from moment to moment. It's also apparent in the way you choose to lead your life; your beliefs and attitudes, goals and expectations, hopes and fears; and in how you interpret and understand other people. Given the essential nature of your personality, understanding yourself and your inner drives can significantly affect the way you work, with whom you will work well, and in what fashion.

Psychologists and behavioral scientists have pondered how to measure and understand personality for decades, and they've developed many models and concepts in an attempt to classify personality. They can tell you everything from whether you're introverted or extroverted to whether you're a morning person or a night person, a tidy person or a messy person, a "right brain" intuitive person or a "left brain" analytical person. There are several

books that can help you explore the many different approaches to understanding your personality such as *Who Am I?* compiled by Robert Frager,
and *The Mind Test,* by Rita Aero and Elliot Weiner.

While all such aspects of your personality can affect your work style and
your working relationships, our goal in this chapter is to focus on the specific
aspects of your personality that relate directly to teaming up successfully.
Therefore we've developed a series of surveys that will provide information
about what we've found to be the key elements for understanding with whom
you'll work well and with whom you won't in various teaming-up situations.
The reason it's so important to understand these aspects of yourself is because
teaming-up relationships among self-employed individuals are probably different in several significant ways from most other working relationships
you've had in the past.

1. They are voluntary. When self-employed individuals team up, they
do so by *choice,* not by *chance* or *necessity* as is so often the case on the
job or in other organizational settings. As a result, you and those you work
with will probably have higher expectations, be more demanding, and allow
more things to bother you because you literally don't have to put up with
them.

2. There's no predetermined structure or organizational culture. When
you work with others in an organization, there are many spoken and unspoken rules, regulations, job descriptions, and procedures for how things will
and won't be done. So for the most part many of the stickiest issues and most
difficult problems affecting how you'll work together have already been determined. Not so, when two independent and individuals or companies join
efforts. Potentially anything goes. Nothing can be taken for granted. You
must determine from scratch how everything is to be done.

3. There's no boss. Usually the other teams we've been part of throughout our lives have had a leader. Sports teams have a coach and a team captain.
Work teams on the job have a manager or project leader. Associations have a
president; their committees have chairpersons. But when self-employed individuals team up, as Katie Lachance has discovered in teaming up with her
partner to provide legal scopist training, "No one is the boss." Every individual has 100 percent control over if, when, and how he or she participates.
There's no one person with the final word on how things will be, who will do
what and in what way unless you mutually agree to make it so.

For Katie, sharing responsibility has worked out well. They had both attained success on their own prior to their partnership and they found that
there is a give and take and that both have areas in which they excel. But for

almost everyone it's a new way of working. As Katie remembers, "We didn't know how it would work out."

In other words, affiliations between independent individuals or companies are truly a new breed of "team." They are truly self-determining teams, and this is both their greatest strength and their greatest vulnerability. There are no built-in limits, but there are also no built-in safeguards. There's little to keep an ineffective union going, and there's little that can stop the right one from proceeding.

Team building is challenging enough within more familiar formal structures, so collaborations among independent individuals present both highly interesting and highly promising challenges.

The following surveys are designed to help you understand how you work best so you can know what to look for in others. They will provide insights into:

- Your underlying motivation: the basic needs you want to meet through your work
- Your decision-making style: how you go about interacting with others to get what you need
- Your work habit preferences
- Your quirks and idiosyncrasies
- Your values, ethics, and vision

Each of these aspects of your personality is so integral to who you are and how you work that it's easy to take them for granted and assume that others do too. Yet most of the problems people have with teaming up arise from a mismatch between these highly personal assumptions.

Identifying Your Underlying Motivation: What You Want Most from Your Work

Since collaborations among self-employed individuals and small businesses are voluntary in nature, there's no overriding corporate mission or directive to bind your efforts. Therefore, your personal motivation takes on a far greater significance. While you may share goals, your motivation to attain these goals may be quite different from others you team up with. And those underlying differences can derail an otherwise ideal working relationship.

For example, here are five people, all of whom would like to attain larger contracts to create multimedia software. Conceivably by affiliating with one another they could all achieve this goal; but, as you read the descriptions of each, notice the differences in their motivations.

Person A: This software developer wants to create the best possible multimedia software. He dreams of writing an award-winning product and becoming known for his high-quality work.

Person B: This software developer very much wants to be part of a team of developers that work well together. He wants to win the respect and favor of his colleagues and be included in all facets of their projects.

Person C: This software developer wants to push the envelope of multimedia design, using code to create effects that have never been seen before. He fancies himself a pioneer, leading the field out of the mainstream.

Person D: This software developer is seeking to create a steady, stable flow of work so he can support his growing family by consistently using the proven methods he developed over the years he'd been employed.

Person E: This software developer wants to create a large software association of programmers that by affiliating with one another can bring in ever increasing profits for all involved. To achieve this vision, he wants to take on and quickly complete work for as many projects as possible.

Here we have five people with one shared goal, but five different motivations or reasons for wanting to attain that goal. Will this group be able to work together? Possibly, but as you might imagine, it will be a challenge given their differing motivations. Can you foresee the potential conflicts? Here are a few of the conflicts we would anticipate these individuals might encounter.

- Because producing the best-quality software takes more time and effort, **Person A**'s desire to produce the *best* software could clash with **Person E**'s desire to take on and complete as *many* projects as possible.
- As a maverick, **Person C** could well rock the steady boat **Person D** wants to build.
- **Person B** might get along with everyone, but by going along to get along, he might end up feeling resentful when his ideas and needs are not acknowledged by the others.

Of course, it's possible that these individuals could work compatibly with one another, but only if they clearly understand their individual motivations and work to make sure everyone's needs are taken care of.

All too often, though, we don't know our own basic motivations, let alone those of others. That's where understanding how your motivation affects your work style and that of others can be useful. To help identify your own and others' basic work style motivation, we developed the following survey. To get an objective picture of your motivation, take and score this survey before reading further. It takes no longer than five minutes to complete. Note that this assessment and your scores are not a reflection of your intelligence, aptitude, or ability. This assessment only indicates which needs you're most motivated to attain through your work. As you will see, no one pattern is better or worse than another; all have their strengths and weaknesses, and all can work effectively in a team effort if well matched with other people's motivations.

The PSE Motivation Survey

In each row, choose the word that is most appealing to you and enter a "5." Then choose the next most appealing word, enter a "4." Then give your next choice a "3," etc. The word you give a "1" to is the one that least appeals to you. Do all seven rows in this way. When completed, each row will have a "5," a "4," a "3," a "2," and a "1." Do not create ties. If you find it difficult to make a choice, keep in mind there are no right or wrong answers. *Remember a "5" is high; a "1" is low.*

1A ❑ first class	1B ❑ caring	1C ❑ exciting	1D ❑ conscientious	1E ❑ powerful
2A ❑ in charge	2B ❑ excellent	2C ❑ kind	2D ❑ thrilling	2E ❑ thorough
3A ❑ orderly	3B ❑ forceful	3C ❑ remarkable	3D ❑ helpful	3E ❑ surprising
4A ❑ arousing	4B ❑ systematic	4C ❑ dominant	4D ❑ outstanding	4E ❑ nurturing
5A ❑ reassuring	5B ❑ astonishing	5C ❑ consistent	5D ❑ commanding	5E ❑ exceptional
6A ❑ high quality	6B ❑ affectionate	6C ❑ startling	6D ❑ principled	6E ❑ superior
7A ❑ mighty	7B ❑ extraordinary	7C ❑ appreciative	7D ❑ adventurous	7E ❑ proven

Scoring Your PSE Motivation Survey

Step 1: Get Your Raw Scores

The first step in finding your motivation pattern is to find your raw score for each of five motivation patterns so you can assess which patterns best describe you. Here's how to do that.

To get your Achieving Score—Add the values you gave each of the following words:

1A ____   2B ____   3C ____   4D ____   5E ____   6A ____   7B ____   Total ____

To get your Relating Score—Add the values you gave each of the following words:

1B ____   2C ____   3D ____   4E ____   5A ____   6B ____   7C ____   Total ____

To get your Challenging Score—Add the values you gave each of the following words:

1C ____   2D ____   3E ____   4A ____   5B ____   6C ____   7D ____   Total ____

To get your Conserving Score—Add the values you gave each of the following words:

1D ____   2E ____   3A ____   4B ____   5C ____   6D ____   7E ____   Total ____

To get your Controlling Score—Add the values you gave each of the following words:

1F ____   2A ____   3B ____   4C ____   5D ____   6E ____   7A ____   Total ____

Now put the total score for each motivation pattern in the boxes in the second row under the corresponding title. Then subtract 7 from each row to obtain your profile score for each pattern.

Type	Achieving	Relating	Challenging	Conserving	Controlling
Raw score					
Subtract	-7	-7	-7	-7	-7
Profile Score					

Step 2: To See Your Work Style Profile, Create a Graph of Your Scores

Transfer your raw scores onto the blank grid shown below. First put a dot in each column at the height corresponding to the score you have for each category. To make your scores easier to compare, it is also useful to draw a line from the bottom of each column up to the dot in that column. You now have a visual representation of your personal profile. An example is provided below. Return to reading the test to interpret your profile.

	Achieving	Relating	Challenging	Conserving	Controlling
	15	20	10	19	6

Your Profile

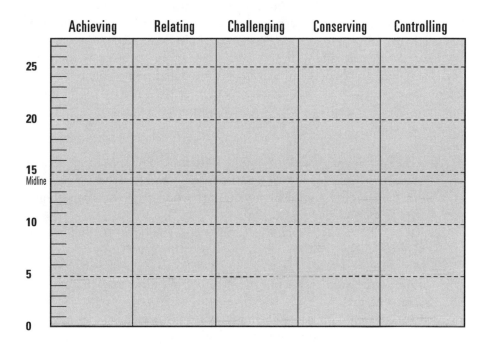

This survey shows the relative importance *for you* of what a wealth of scientific research has found to be an individual's three basic psychological needs.

• *Stimulation:* the need to have or experience sensory pleasure, fantasy, curiosity, creativity, and pushing the limits of personal expression.

• *Recognition:* the need to get attention from others for who you are and what you do. Renowned psychiatrist Eric Berne, author of *Games People Play,* identified attention we get for who we are as *unconditional strokes;* whereas he referred to attention we get for what we do or achieve as *conditional strokes.* Conditional strokes include fame, work achievements, socially worthy activities, heroism, and so on. Unconditional strokes include affection, sharing thoughts or feelings, and being part of shared group rituals and celebrations.

• *Structure:* the need to have a sense of stability, order, and certainty that comes from knowing what's happening and how things will be done. Some people want to create and impose structure on others while others want someone else to provide structure for them. In other words, some people want to be in charge of creating procedures, rules, schedules, and order; while others want to follow procedures, rules, regimes, and schedules established by someone else.

Everyone has all three of these needs at some level, but people vary in how important each of these needs is to them during any period of their life. Some people need and want very little structure; others need a lot. Some people need very few strokes or very little approval from others; others need a lot. Some people need and want very little stimulation, while others want and need a lot. Preferences develop early in childhood and result from our cumulative life experiences as well as from temporary life situations. The dominance of a need generally prompts us to adopt our own particular work style based on a combination of the five following patterns.

1. *Achieving.* If you scored high in this pattern, you have a strong need to be the best you possibly can at what you do and to strive for recognition for your accomplishments. In other words, you want conditional strokes for outstanding work.
2. *Relating.* If you scored high in this pattern, you have a strong need to be emotionally involved with others or to be a part of group effort. You want people to like you and want to work with you. In other words, you want to get unconditional strokes for who you are, not what you do.
3. *Challenging.* If you scored high in this pattern, you have a strong need for stimulation. You want to have new experiences, take risks, and to do things in different, interesting, or unconventional ways.
4. *Conserving.* If you scored high in this pattern, you have a strong need for security and order. You like to do things in a familiar, consistent way. In other words, you like to operate within a structure that imposes order and organization on the chaos or uncertainty of life.
5. *Controlling.* If you scored high in this pattern, you have a strong need for power. You like to direct and influence others. In other words, you like to organize and create structure for others that enables them to work with you to achieve shared goals.

Your scores on the chart on page 123 should give you added perspective on your work style. What do your scores suggest about what's most important to you? Which areas are you dominant in? Where are your lowest scores? What do they suggest is unimportant or even undesirable to you? Do you have areas that motivate you equally? For example, is *Achieving* nearly as important to you as *Controlling*? Or are *Challenging* experiences clearly more important than anything else?

The chart on page 125 highlights what we believe to be the most common characteristics for all five patterns. This table summarizes the needs each motivation style seeks, the typical "slogans" that underlie this style of work, and the most common strengths and weaknesses associated with each style.

Circle the two categories in which you had the highest scores. Do you iden-

WORK STYLE MOTIVATION PATTERNS

	Achieving	Relating	Challenging	Conserving	Controlling
NEEDS	• Recognition for perfomance	• Unconditional recognition	• Stimulation	• To have structure	• To give structure
SEEKS	• Meaningful work • Perfection • Self-development toward inner goals • To prove one's worth	• Acceptance and belonging • To give and get affection, appreciation, and understanding • People, animals projects, or things to care for	• Excitement from risks, sensations, fantasy, ideas • To go beyond the familiar, pushing the limits • To find new and different experiences and ideas	• Order and predictability • Organization: schedules, budgets, rules, policies, and procedures • Safety and security	• To control people, things, information • Results, usually material—the "bottom line" • Autonomy, independence, or to be "number one"
SLOGANS	• "Quality first." • "Make your mark."	• "Two heads are better than one." • "It's better to give than receive."	• "Variety is the spice of life." • "You only live once."	• "Better safe than sorry." • "Dot your *i*s and cross your *t*s."	• "My way." • "Paddle your own canoe."
STRENGTHS	• High standards • Sense of pride • Works hard	• Adaptability • Promotes consensus, bridging differences • Good coach, mentor, or comforter	• Creativity • Energy • Pioneering spirit	• Manages detail and routine • Thoroughness • Sense of duty	• Self-reliant • Self-starting • Takes charge
POSSIBLE WEAKNESSES	• May prefer doing over delegating • May have unrealistic expectations of others • May be dictatorial under the stress of not accomplishing goals	• May say things based on what they think others want to hear • May sit on the fence rather than displease someone with a decision • May exhibit passive-aggressive behavior under stress	• Easily restless and bored • May rebel against authority • May "burn out," burning the candle at both ends	• May get bound by "analysis paralysis" • May seek exactness compulsively, being "penny wise" and "pound foolish." • May be stubborn under the stress of change	• More inclined to tell rather than sell • May discount others' feelings in pursuing "objective" results • May be overly competitive

tify with the list of priorities of those work-style patterns? Can you relate to the slogans listed for your two highest needs or strongest traits? Do the strengths and possible weaknesses listed in the chart on page 125 accurately describe you? To customize your profile, add your own slogans and highlight what you consider to be your own strengths and weaknesses. Armed with this insight into your motivation, you can reflect more consciously on the type of person you are *when working with others.* The better you know your motivation, the better you will understand whom you can work best with and in what ways.

Note, however, that your goal isn't necessarily to find people whose motivational styles are identical to yours. In fact, the odds that someone else would end up with the exact same score as you on each pattern are small. It's unlikely you'll find a person whose profile is exactly like yours. And even if you did, sometimes having the same work style can itself create problems, producing more conflict than compatibility. The key to matching your work style with that of others is to find people who have a work style that complements your own.

Let's say, for example, that your primary work style is *Achieving* in combination with a secondary desire for *Controlling.* If you were to form a partnership with another person who had the same work styles, the two of you might be quite compatible in your desire to succeed and do high-quality work, but you might find yourselves competing for control of the business. Similarly, if your work style is primarily *Relating,* and you were to team up with another person whose primary style is *Relating,* it's possible you would each be so intent on getting along and agreeing that neither of you would have the drive to work through conflicts and make the difficult decisions needed to launch an aggressive campaign and move your venture forward.

Choosing to work with people who have complementary work styles maximizes a person's value in a team effort. Complementary relationships enable everyone to concentrate on contributing his or her strengths while others concentrate on the areas where they perform best. So build relationships that allow you to lead with your strengths—and that let others lead with theirs!

Discovering How You Get What You Need When Working with Others

In the process of growing up, we all learn strategies for how best to interact with others to get what we need. Usually we learn these strategies from our family of origin, and we continue interacting with others in much the same way we learned while we were growing up. These patterns become an integral part of our work style. Usually we're completely unaware of them, until we come into conflict with people who have quite different strategies. Only then do we notice that we don't all approach getting what we want from others in the same way. Yet conflicts like these cause some of the most disruptive problems people face when they try to team up.

For example, Mark, a publicist, thought he'd made a perfect connection when he and another publicist, Andros, began cross-referring clients. Mark

Your Interpersonal Decision-Making Style

According to research originally done by L. L. Constantine, Ph.D., and applied to families with home-based businesses by Alma Owen, Ph.D., there are essentially three "archetypal" family types, each of which has a quite different approach to how family members interact with one another to meet their needs. See which one best describes your household.

- *Ordered Families.* These families prefer to maintain close contact and orient themselves to following predictable roles. There is usually one dominant person in the family whose needs other family members shape their lives and household activities around. This person usually makes the decisions about "big events" in the family's life. This kind of family seeks to maintain stability and traditional values. It engages in activities that often replay the events of the past and the structures of the members' family of origin.

If this describes your family of origin, most likely you'll want to interact with a business associate in a similar way. You'll want to be able to depend on things being done in a particular manner, which you'll consider to be the right or best way. And you'll either spell out how that will be, like Andros, or you'll expect someone else to spell it out for you.

- *Individualized Families.* These families see one another as unique individuals, all with separate personalities, skills, and dreams they should be free to pursue on their own. As a result, individualized families have few rules and little structure. Each person is in charge of his or her own direction and usually does not coordinate his or her activities with others. Family members go their own way each day, although they may share events with one another from time to time. The individualized family enjoys change and variety. Family members are oriented toward the present moment and constant new experiences.

If this describes your family of origin, you will most likely carry this pattern into your work style. Like Mark, you will give those you work with wide latitude to "do their own thing" and expect them to give you such latitude in return.

- *Negotiating Families.* These families combine aspects of both ordered and individualized families. Family members acknowledge ties to family tradition, but they try to introduce change into the family unit when needed to meet members' needs. Other family members' needs are as important as their own in determining the family's goals and actions. Most decisions are made by family members talking over together what needs to be done and then negotiating a choice everyone can agree upon.

If this describes your family of origin, you'll most likely take a democratic approach to your business relationships, wanting all concerned to express their needs, reach consensus, and then follow through on agreements so it's clear what they can count on one another for.

Note: Few families fall exactly into only one of these types. Most are a mixture of types. And, of course, families also change over time. Some families tend toward the ordered type when the children are young, then become more of a negotiating family as the children get older, and eventually end up more individualized as the children reach their teens. In addition, some people will rebel against their family pattern and try to adopt a different one in their own lives. Sometimes this is done successfully but for others the old family patterns creep back into their behavior during times of stress.

worked only with high-tech companies; Andros worked only with publishers and authors. It seemed like an ideal match. As weeks passed, however, Mark found himself increasingly irritated with Andros. It got to the point where he dreaded picking up the phone for fear it would be another call from Andros. While Andros had many leads for Mark, the leads came with specific instructions about what he expected Mark to do, when he was to call, what he was to say, and what type of work he was to offer. Worse yet, Mark discovered that Andros had also told each prospective client detailed expectations for what Mark should and shouldn't do. This was not Mark's idea of how to make a referral. When he made referrals, he would simply be sure the prospective client wanted Andros to call and then turn over the client's name and phone number to Andros to decide how, when, and where he'd handle the referral from that point on.

As it became increasingly clear, Mark and Andros had very different strategies for how to work cooperatively. These previously unconscious strategies were an integral part of their work styles. Neither approach is bad or good per se, but they were clearly not compatible. If you were to trace back how these strategies developed, you'd find that both Andros and Mark were following patterns they had learned in their homes while growing up. Andros was raised in a second-generation immigrant family in which his father was the "dictatorial" head of the household. Because of his family's style, Andros learned that when you wanted to get something done, you took charge and told people precisely how to do what you wanted them to do. Mark, on the other hand, grew up in a seventies "free form" household. His parents, both college professors, had been hippies in their youths. The motto of their family could well have been "Live and let live." Everyone pretty much did his or her own thing as long as it didn't interfere with anyone else.

Such conflicts in how to get things done are common. So what is your decision-making style? How would you handle a situation like the one faced by Mark and Andros?

Whereas in a job most people adapt to whatever situation the organization presents, without the structure of an organization, most people fall into the pattern that's most comfortable for them and they resist teaming up with people who have a different modus operandi. To be compatible, your style doesn't need to be similar, but usually the best people for you to team up with are those who interact with others in much the same way you do.

People who prefer to interact with others as an *ordered* family want to know there is one person who will be making the decisions and acting as the authority; if people disagree with the "leader's" decision and do their own thing, it will likely cause conflict. Those who prefer to interact with others as an *individualized* family will allow all those involved to make their own decisions; this may create chaos for people who expect ordered or negotiated decisions. Those who prefer to relate as a *negotiating* family make decisions by consulting with one another; to people who like individualized or ordered decisions, negotiating takes too long and slows everything down. So to find the best teaming-up relationships, look for people whose interpersonal decision-making styles are as similar to yours as possible.

Evaluating Your Work Habits and Preferences

While your underlying motivation and decision-making styles are the master plan for your relationships, your work habits and preferences are the nuts and bolts of working together. Of course, it's essential to be operating from a compatible master plan, but conflicts over the nitty-gritty details of working together can be as grating as chalk squeaking on a blackboard or as unpleasant as getting too close to someone with bad breath. In teaming up, you often end up dancing cheek to cheek and an unexpected quirk or bad habit, even if you've known the person for years, can get under your skin and erode your ability to work effectively together.

That's what happened to Charles and Marta. Before deciding to become business partners, they'd known each other for over six years. Having worked together on a previous job, they knew that their skills were complementary. Nonetheless, over the course of their first year in business, Marta realized that she and Charles had such different work habits that she no longer wanted to work with him, so she bought out his interest in their partnership. Here's a summary of a few of their differences.

HER	HIM
avid computer user	no interest in computers
morning person	night owl
enjoys using phone	dislikes phone calls
pays bills promptly	doesn't care when bills are paid
enjoys public speaking and networking	dislikes speaking and group activities

As this list shows, what might seem like trivial differences in social situations, or on a job where work protocols are well-defined, can become a significant irritant when working independently with someone day after day. Although some differences in work habits can be overcome, others can be so irritating and annoying that before long you don't even want to be in the same room with someone you once assumed you'd enjoy working with. When work habits become such a thorn in the side, conducting business can get stressful and, worse, even small conflicts can start to feel like the last straw. In fact, a gradual buildup of animosity over what begins as a pet peeve can all too often become the underlying reason a business relationship ultimately fails.

Being aware of your own work habits and even admitting your own quirks can help you avoid such problems. But an honest self-examination of your work habits can be difficult because, after all, they're habits: things you don't pay much attention to. So we've devised a brief questionnaire you can use to identify your work habits. What you learn from exploring this questionnaire can guide you toward the kinds of questions you'll want to ask others before seriously considering working with them.

Identifying Your Work Habits and Preferences

Part I: Preferences

Answer the following questions by putting a checkmark beside the *one* response that best describes how you normally go about your workday in operating your business.

1. Do you honestly like the work you do?
   ___ yes (most of the time)
   ___ no (not really)
   ___ sometimes (some days more than others)

2. What aspects of your work do you like most?
   ___ working with customers
   ___ background work (thinking, strategizing, writing)
   ___ selling/marketing
   ___ other

3. What aspects of your work do you like least?
   ___ working with customers
   ___ background work (thinking, strategizing, writing)
   ___ selling/marketing
   ___ other

4. When do you do your best work?
   ___ morning
   ___ afternoon
   ___ evening

5. Do you get tired or cranky during the day?
   ___ in the morning for a few hours until I've really woken up
   ___ around lunchtime
   ___ in the late afternoon

6. Do you enjoy meeting new people and socializing with business contacts?
   ___ yes
   ___ no
   ___ sometimes

---

7. Do you enjoy public speaking and giving presentations?

____ yes

____ no

____ sometimes

8. Does public speaking make you nervous?

____ yes

____ no

____ sometimes

9. Are you good at presenting your business to customers on the telephone?

____ yes

____ no

10. In the sense that every business has to get clients, what kind of salesperson do you consider yourself to be?

____ very aggressive

____ moderately aggressive

____ somewhat aggressive

____ passive

11. Do you enjoy writing business communications (e.g., press releases, brochures, fliers, letters to suppliers, etc.)?

____ yes

____ no

____ sometimes

12. When a problem comes up and it needs your attention, which do you do?

____ address it immediately

____ finish what you are doing first

____ analyze the situation and figure out how important the problem is relative to your other work

13. What kind of reader are you?

____ I read a lot of business books, magazines, and newspapers each week.

____ I read a few business books, magazines, and newspapers each week.

____ I seldom read business books, magazines, and newspapers.

14. How do you stay abreast of business news and trends in your field?

____ I read about them.

____ I talk to other people to stay informed.

____ I usually don't find out about trends until it's too late.

15. Do you enjoy using computers and learning new software?
    ___ yes
    ___ no
    ___ sometimes

16. Do you know how to function on-line using the Internet and services like CompuServe?
    ___ yes
    ___ no
    ___ not yet, but I want to learn

17. Do you mind devoting a few week nights to your work?
    ___ I usually work into the evening.
    ___ A few weeknights are fine if it helps my business grow.
    ___ No, I need my weeknights to relax and get away from work.
    ___ No, I need my weeknights for my family.

18. Do you mind working weekends? ___Yes ___No
    ___ Saturdays only
    ___ Sundays only
    ___ Both Saturdays and Sundays are okay.
    ___ Part of Saturday or Sunday is okay.

19. Do you enjoy business travel?
    ___ yes, anytime, anyplace
    ___ yes, sometimes; depends on where, when, for how long and what else is going on
        in my work and personal life
    ___ no

20. Do you enjoy business entertaining?
    ___ yes
    ___ no
    ___ sometimes (depends on the client and how long I have to spend with the person)

21. If you disagree with someone, how do you handle it?
    ___ I usually try to convince the other person of my views.
    ___ I usually try to find a compromise or common ground.
    ___ I usually try to listen to the other point of view and am willing to yield to it.

22. If a potential new customer approaches you but cannot afford your prices, what do you do?
    ___ I stick with my pricing; I can't afford to change my profit margins.
    ___ I try to negotiate a price both of us can accept.
    ___ It depends on how much business I already have and what I need.

23. If a supplier underbilled you or a customer overpaid you, what would you do?

____ I would be honest and tell the person about the mistake.

____ It depends on how large the amount.

____ I would keep the money, since I am not the one who made the mistake.

24. If a customer isn't sure he or she wants to buy your product or service, what do you do?

____ I try to close the sale anyway.

____ I give the person the room he or she needs to make a decision.

____ I try to help the person analyze the situation and make a decision.

25. If a customer doesn't like your product or service after you have supplied it, what do you do?

____ I listen to the complaints and try to solve the problem at any cost to me.

____ I listen to the complaints and try to compromise on how to solve the problem so I don't lose too much money.

____ I listen to the complaints but try to get the customer to let it be.

26. Why do you do what you do?

____ I am motivated mostly by a love of what I do.

____ I am motivated mostly by the money I can make doing what I do.

____ I am motivated by both the money and the love of what I do.

27. How do you characterize your ethics?

____ I am a highly ethical person in all circumstances.

____ I am basically an ethical person in most circumstances, but sometimes I disagree with mainstream ideas and need to do what I believe in.

____ I am a freethinker and need to do what I feel is right in all circumstances.

28. How do you feel about working with a person of the opposite gender or a different sexual orientation?

____ I have no problem working with people of the opposite gender or a different sexual orientation.

____ I have no problem, but my spouse would not like it.

____ I prefer to work with people of my own gender and sexual orientation.

29. How do you see the future of your company?

____ I have specific plans to grow my company by increasing clientele or revenues/profits.

____ I just want to make enough to support my family.

____ I have not yet thought about the ultimate plans for my company.

30. Where do you see yourself in five years?

____ I will be doing what I currently do but I will be more successful at it.

____ I may be doing what I do now, but it depends on how successful this venture is.

____ I will most likely be doing something else.

____ I don't know; I haven't really figured out what I want to do.

Part II. Quirks and Idiosyncrasies

Circle as many answers as you need to to answer each question.

1. Let's be honest. What are your quirks or idiosyncrasies? The following is a list of some common quirks and idiosyncrasies that annoy some people who work together. Check the ones that apply to you.

   Note: In and of themselves, the items on this list are not "sins" to be ashamed of or embarrassed to admit. They are simply quirks some people might find hard to live with. So, be as truthful about yourself as you can.

   ___ I think I am perfect, or at least try to be.
   ___ I get angry easily.
   ___ I never get angry or let people know how I feel.
   ___ I argue with others a lot.
   ___ I don't listen to other people very well.
   ___ I listen to other people too much and don't go with my own opinion.
   ___ I like to be in control of every situation.
   ___ I use swearwords a lot, even in front of other people.
   ___ I never use swearwords.
   ___ I am deathly afraid of speaking in public.
   ___ I am technophobic (I don't like to use new technology).
   ___ I don't know how to use a computer.
   ___ I don't know how to use a fax machine.
   ___ I don't know how to communicate on-line via computer.
   ___ I am not good with numbers or money matters (e.g., can't balance my checkbook or keep track of my money).
   ___ I am not a good writer or can't write very well.
   ___ I am not good at understanding legal matters or legal documents.
   ___ I am not good at negotiating.
   ___ I am not a creative person.
   ___ I spend money too easily.
   ___ I love money too much.
   ___ I don't care much about money.
   ___ I am a penny pincher. I don't like spending my money unless I have to.
   ___ I secretly hate working.
   ___ I don't drive.
   ___ I hate flying.
   ___ I don't like some categories of people (men, women, gays, certain nationalities, races).
   ___ I don't like children.

___ I get hungry frequently.

___ I take frequent breaks when I am working.

___ I work morning, noon, and night.

___ I hate to be interrupted for anything when I'm working.

___ I even work at my play.

___ I go to the bathroom a lot.

___ I hate getting dressed up.

___ When I'm working, dressing professionally means dressing up and I expect others working with me up to dress up as well.

___ I talk a lot and often dominate conversations.

___ I get nervous easily.

___ I get embarrassed easily.

___ I often think people don't understand me.

___ I don't enjoy reading business books, magazines, or newspapers.

___ I read slowly.

___ I have a hard time making up my mind.

___ I don't have a vision of what I want to do with my work.

___ My desk and office are very messy.

___ My desk and office are super neat.

___ I am always on time; I hate to be late.

___ Somehow I'm always late.

___ I get impatient easily.

___ Other:

_____

_____

_____

2. Which of the following statements characterizes you?

___ I am from a small town, have small-town values, and intend to stay in a small town because this is where I feel most comfortable.

___ I am from a small town and still have small-town values even though I live in a big city.

___ I am from a small town but I moved away to a bigger city so I could get away from small-town thinking.

___ I am from a city or urban environment and want to move to a small town where I can feel more at ease.

___ I am from a city or urban environment and want to stay here because this is where I feel most comfortable.

3. Which of the following statements characterizes your decision to become self-employed?

____ I am self-employed because I lost my job and couldn't figure out what else to do.

____ I am self-employed because I lost my job, but this is what I'd been wanting to do anyway.

____ I am self-employed because I researched it and intentionally planned to go out on my own.

____ I am self-employed because I always wanted to have my own business.

____ I am self-employed because I needed to find something to create an income for my family.

____ I am self-employed because I had a great idea and wanted to pursue it to the end.

4. Which of the following statements characterizes your business goals?

____ I just want to make a few bucks right now and then I'll see what happens.

____ I want to make a good income this year and learn how to grow my business so it will be even more successful.

____ I want to build my business in whichever way seems to make sense as it develops.

____ I want to grow my company and have employees working for me.

____ I want to turn my company into a major corporation.

____ I want to become a multimillionaire.

____ I want to create a secure economic future for myself and my family.

____ My business is a source of income, but other aspects of my life are what really interest me.

5. What is your attitude toward collaborations and partnerships?

____ I am skeptical of how they can help me.

____ I am open-minded about using a collaboration of some kind, but I don't want to form a partnership with anyone.

____ I am willing to do whatever it takes to make my business more successful.

____ I prefer working in close contact with other people, either through informal or formal partnerships.

Defining Your Ethics, Values, and Vision

Perhaps you realized as you answered the above surveys that many of your work habits reflect your personal ethics, values, and vision. Indeed, it's difficult to separate seemingly simple work habits from what they reflect about your personal beliefs and attitudes. Your ethics reflect how you believe you should feel and behave; your values reflect your priorities in life; and your vision reflects the way you view your work, business, or company. How strongly you feel and how clear you are about your ethics, values, and visions depends upon your upbringing and your conclusions about your current situation in life. Some people adhere strongly to the values from their upbringing; others rebel against the values they were taught as children and adopt new values as they become adults and discover their own beliefs.

In either case, one of the most critical factors in teaming up is to find people whose ethics, values, and visions are similar to yours. According to Professor Jon Goodman, director of the Entrepreneurial program at University of Southern California, having business interests in common with another person is not enough to make a joint enterprise successful. If you intend to team up with another person or other people, particularly in a partnership or some other more formal arrangement, you must know enough about the person—and even about his or her lifestyle—to feel that your values are mutually aligned. Prof. Goodman points out that many people think they know someone well, but once they start working together they learn many truths about each other they were unaware of. As Goodman says, "Knowing someone's general 'public' persona doesn't tell you very much about what they'll be like to work closely with. It's the 'subtle' values that really count."

The contrast between the following two case histories exemplifies how you can save a great deal of time and money by becoming familiar with each other's work habits, ethics, values, and visions before deciding to work together.

CASE STUDY: TINY CRACKS INTO FISSURES GROW

Ray and Vickie decided to form a partnership to conduct seminars together. They had met at a conference and become friends, feeling they shared many mutual interests and skills. Ray had less experience than Vickie in giving seminars and felt that he could benefit from working with someone with Vickie's capabilities. Vickie already had an established career as a business writer but agreed that a seminar business might be "fun" to do with someone else and it could bring in some extra income. As they developed their plans for their seminar business, however, it turned out that Ray and Vickie had distinctly different visions of the kind of partnership they wanted to create.

Ray imagined their having a fancy office, holding lots of meetings, entertaining prospective clients at expensive restaurants, launching aggressive marketing campaigns, and doing a lot of networking to bring in clients. Vickie, on the other hand, foresaw a low-key operation that drew clients largely through word-of-mouth referrals from satisfied clients. She imagined working in a small, homey office part of each week and working from home the rest of the week to continue her writing business. These two partners also had a significant financial dichotomy: Vickie had money to invest; Ray had no funds to contribute, not even a credit card.

Despite these differences, Ray and Vickie became partners. They rented a modestly fancy small office, and in order to get the best price signed a two-year lease. Because Vickie had the good credit rating, she signed the lease alone. This did concern her, but she felt their differences seemed superficial and could easily be negotiated away. In the first few months, they got several clients and made a small profit. But soon after, a lull in the economy hit and their seminar attendance began to decline. As is so often the case, the difficult economic climate amplified their personal differences.

Little by little, they began to have sharp disagreements about their business strategy, and their divergent financial situations became a major bone of contention. Vickie felt she was providing all the financial support while Ray spent money on business and social events she considered to be unnecessary. And she grew increasingly irritated with Ray's messy desk; it became a bone of contention when he couldn't find contracts and key correspondence. Meanwhile Ray was becoming increasingly angry that Vickie wouldn't get out and network. He felt she spent far too much unbillable time "hand-holding" clients who wanted her advice after the seminars were over. To avoid hassles, Vickie began spending more time working at home. Ray was sure she was working on her own projects instead of their business.

As you've probably guessed, this partnership eventually ended in anger. Even dissolving their partnership agreement became contentious because they couldn't agree on how to handle paying for the remaining months left on their lease.

CASE STUDY: WATERS THAT FLOW DEEP ENDURE

Nina, Megan, and Tana met at a church retreat. They had all recently gone through painful divorces that forced them to reevaluate their lives as young single mothers. As Megan said, "Everything I ever believed was torn out from under me. I had to rebuild my life from scratch. But Nina and Tana knew what I was going through. They'd been through it, too, and they'd survived." They formed a strong bond during the church retreat. "We all had dreams," Nina remembers, "but none of us were living them. Instead we were working in dead-end jobs hating the long hours away from our kids and knowing we had so much more to give."

During one of the retreat exercises, they were asked to share their dreams with other participants and discovered their dreams were remarkably similar: they wanted to help single parents who were struggling to raise their children properly. On the final night of the retreat, they pledged to begin working together to make their dream a reality by opening a day-care and single-women's center.

Pursuing this dream was a long, hard road. Their clients had no extra money, so they had to start part-time and raise funds to begin their center. Megan set up a physical fitness program. Tana completed a degree in early childhood education. Nina became the business manager and learned how to use a computer. While they're not making a lot of money yet, they're doing almost as well as they had been before giving up their dead-end jobs. "Money had never been that important to us," Nina recalls. "We want to make a difference for other women and children. That's our shared mission and we've become very close."

Working together isn't always a bed of roses for them. "We have to put up with a lot," Tana points out. "Like I think Megan talks too much and her mind never stops working. Sometimes she drives me crazy, but I love her. We all agree Nina can be very overbearing and bossy at times, but when things get too bad we just start saluting her. And then of course, I'm no saint. Dealing with the kids all day, I get tired easily and I get irritable."

"But we spend a lot of time charting the future of our business," Megan adds, "and that's what really excites us. After our late-night sessions over at Tana's house, we get so charged up with ideas and plans that sometimes I can't sleep. I think we're soul sisters. Each challenge brings us closer and makes us more determined. Together we can do anything."

As you can see, while it's not always essential to work only with those whose ethics, values, or vision are similar to your own, in the long run, it's much wiser to consider all the differences we've discussed as harbingers of things to come instead of trying to gloss over them.

Using Your Work Style Assessments to Make a Good Match

Now that you have a better idea of your work style in terms of your motivation and your preferred ways of working and interacting with others, you're in a good position to start identifying and evaluating who you want to team up with and in what ways. You can begin to see the people you are thinking about working with in a new light and use your understanding to assess how well you think you'd match up. You can do such an assessment either directly or indirectly.

THE DIRECT ROUTE TO ASSESSING OTHERS

You may want to ask the people you're considering working with to fill out the above questionnaires and talk with one another about your work styles. In many situations, your potential collaborators will be interested in exploring areas where you are compatible and where you may conflict.

When six psychotherapists began talking about opening a group practice, they all decided to fill out the questionnaires. They discovered that while they had a similar vision and shared values and ethics, they had varying motivations. Several of them had high *controlling* scores and two had very high *challenging* scores. They also realized that two of them had *ordered* interaction styles for getting what they wanted, two preferred to *negotiate* decisions democratically, and two preferred an *individualized* approach. As a result, the group decided to spend a considerable amount of time discussing how they would handle their varying leadership needs. They decided to rotate the leadership role among the three high *controllers* on a quarterly basis. One person decided he was not interested in joining a group practice because in all honesty he wanted to call the shots on how to operate his practice. The others agreed that their group would not be run on an *ordered* basis; but instead, they would *negotiate* their rules and procedures, and some procedures would be *laissez faire* in nature—i.e., all therapists would set their own hours but would post them for the others to see.

THE INDIRECT ROUTE TO ASSESSING OTHERS

In many teaming-up situations, it's not practical or desirable for those you're thinking of working with to take and discuss the results of any work style surveys. At such times, you'll need to indirectly assess the styles of those you're thinking of working with so you can decide if your work styles are compatible. You'll have to listen to what they say and watch how they operate. Usually people's work styles stand out like a neon sign if you know what to look for. But if they aren't obvious, you can ask questions to uncover what's most important to them and how they prefer working. In preliminary meetings, for example, you can ask people you're thinking of working with what they enjoy most about their work, what other teaming-up experiences they've had, and what they enjoyed and disliked most about those experiences.

Gloria, an image consultant, used an indirect route to assess the work style of a colleague named Louise who approached her with the idea of writing a book together on corporate etiquette. Over a lunch meeting, Gloria observed that Louise was very eager to agree with everything she said. Louise talked a lot about how much she missed the camaraderie of her previous job now that she was on her own. She talked about how this book would enable them both to become well known in their field. From this conversation, Gloria hypothesized that Louise's work style was high in *Relating* and *Achieving* and Gloria thought this would be a fine match with her own *Achieving* and *Controlling* style as long as Louise didn't have conflicting values and opinions about their approach to corporate etiquette.

So to find out more, Gloria suggested that they begin exploring the idea of working together by developing a speech they could offer at a local trade association. They worked together quite well on this joint promotion. Louise was eager to learn from Gloria and essentially worked as her protégé. She handled most of the administrative aspects of presenting the speech and left the content decisions to Gloria. After they presented the speech, Louise pressed even more eagerly to proceed with the book, so Gloria suggested they talk about who would do what in writing the book. Louise wanted to do most of the writing based on Gloria's ideas. She wanted Gloria to do the public appearances while she was happy to handle the follow-up logistics for any seminars that came about through their book promotion. It seemed that Gloria and Louise had made an ideal match, and indeed they had, just as long as Gloria remembered to include Louise in the decision making, recognize her contributions, and involve her in whatever the activities their venture produced.

Whichever route you take, either direct or indirect, using the perspectives of the surveys we've provided, you'll have a better chance of finding people you can work well with. You'll know better how to divide your work activities, identify the likely causes of tension, and resolve conflicts when they develop. If you would like to learn more about evaluating your own and others' work styles, we've listed at the end of this chapter a number of resources that can be helpful.

COMPLEMENTING YOUR ASSETS

Once you understand your inner motivations and work styles, the next step in becoming a winning team is to examine your business strengths and weaknesses so you can best complement each other's assets. Knowing your strengths helps you clarify what you can offer to a business relationship. Knowing your weaknesses points out what abilities you need those you team up with to contribute. Good teamwork requires all involved parties to learn how to share decisions and split responsibilities according to each person's strengths. Like yin and yang, collaborators must intertwine their abilities, filling in for each other where one person is stretched thin. So, it's wise to examine your business weaknesses as honestly as possible, because they will be at the heart of what you hope to gain from teaming up.

As telecommuting consultant Gil Gordon told us,

> My best experiences with teaming up have been when there has been a yin/yang complementarity. When my partners are good at what I'm not good at, or have access to clients that I don't have, or when they have resources that would take me a long time to develop, then we have a good match. But when we're overlapping too much, it's harder to find a continued rationale for teaming up. I've found that the best working relationships are like a good marriage: a combination of strengths, not a pairing of the strong with the weak. After some early disasters, I've stayed away from relationships where I need them much more than they need me or vice versa. That kind of imbalance can easily lead to resentment and other problems.

Assessing Your Business Weaknesses

Here is a list of more than two dozen common weaknesses small-business and home-based-business people experience, and the corresponding business need each one suggests. Check off all those that you feel apply to you. We've also left space for you to include other things you consider to be among your business weaknesses.

WEAKNESS	BUSINESS NEED
❑ I don't have enough business.	You need more clients or contacts to increase your income.
❑ I have plenty of business, but I'm not making enough money.	You need more profitable projects.
❑ I have too much business and not enough time to do it in.	You need to find people to share the workload.
❑ People don't take my business seriously.	You need to project a more substantial business image.
❑ I don't have the manpower to get big contracts.	You need more access to personnel.
❑ I don't have contacts in the field in which I want to do business.	You need to gain entry into a field or industry.
❑ I'm no good at marketing.	You need marketing ideas and assistance.
❑ I don't have time or money for marketing.	You need to free up time to do more marketing.
❑ I don't have enough money to build my business.	You need access to more cash and/or credit.
❑ I'm working too many hours a day.	You need help getting work done.
❑ I miss too many deadlines.	You need assistance getting and staying organized.
❑ I'm losing competitive bids or proposals.	You need new ideas, better proposals, or a more substantial image.
❑ I don't have time to do paperwork and record keeping.	You need administrative help.
❑ I have cash flow problems.	You need assistance collecting from clients on a more timely basis.
❑ My business isn't growing.	You need new services or products to market.
❑ My business is growing too slowly.	You need to find more avenues for distributing your product or service.

❑ I've lost my drive.

You need a new infusion of energy and creativity.

❑ I'm bored with work.

You need to find stimulating and exciting new ideas or ways to work.

❑ I can't keep up with trends in my field.

You need to find time or gain access to key information so you can stay current.

❑ I feel isolated and out of touch with people in my field.

You need personal interaction, support, and encouragement.

❑ I don't know how to grow my business.

You need leadership and strategic advice.

❑ I spend too much time on administrative matters.

You need administrative support.

❑ I keep making bad decisions.

You need feedback and help making better decisions.

❑ I don't have time to develop new projects.

You need help maintaining existing projects.

❑ I have a hard time making decisions.

You need wise counsel to think through decisions and do strategic planning.

❑ I'm not good with money matters.

You need someone to help you price, track, and analyze your financial situation.

Other: _____

Other: _____

Other: _____

From the items you checked off above, select the five that you see as the most critical to your business success over the next year, and write them below. List both your weaknesses and your needs. If you prefer, modify the wording we've used to better describe your situation. Focus your thoughts on what you think your needs will be over the next year to make your business operate in the way you imagine in your dreams.

WEAKNESS	BUSINESS NEED
_____	_____
_____	_____
_____	_____
_____	_____
_____	_____

Now rank the five needs in order of importance to you.

1. _____

2. _____

3. _____

4. _____

5. _____

Keep these five needs in mind as you assess your strengths.

Assessing What You Can Offer: Your Strategic Strengths

While your business weaknesses and needs probably play an important role in why you want to team up with others, your business strengths are what will make working with you attractive to other people. Even if you are newly self-employed, you have qualities that can make you an asset to others. And it's important that they see why and how working with you will be a benefit to them. So it's vital that you not overlook the strengths you bring to future business relationships. Too often people who want to team up will be all too aware of their limitations and what they need from others, but they will discount that they have strengths to offer. Thinking about it though, would you want to team up with someone who has nothing to offer you? Of course not. So be honest, not humble. Any good business relationship brings something of value to each person involved. So, take time to assess the strengths you can bring to a business relationship.

Should you think you don't have much to offer, think again. Your experience, knowledge, skills, and abilities are unique. No one else has amassed precisely the same combination of assets that you've drawn upon to get where you are today. Use the following list of strengths to check off what you can bring to your future business relationships.

❑ An ability to organize, schedule, and coordinate details, materials, and/or events

❑ Financial expertise

- ❏ Legal expertise
- ❏ Money to invest
- ❏ Tangible or intangible assets
- ❏ Leadership to motivate and inspire
- ❏ Extensive contacts in a field
- ❏ Writing/editing capability
- ❏ Design capability
- ❏ Access to high-technology equipment
- ❏ Skills and experience in using special computer and other office technology
- ❏ Ability to close on sales
- ❏ A stable of regular customers
- ❏ A backlog of work to share
- ❏ High energy and creativity
- ❏ A good reputation in a particular field
- ❏ Public-speaking skills and experience
- ❏ A fountain of ideas
- ❏ Contacts with key referral sources and/or potential clients and customers
- ❏ Management experience
- ❏ Typing skills
- ❏ Knowledge of database marketing
- ❏ Marketing expertise in direct mail, advertising, etc.
- ❏ Sales skills
- ❏ PR expertise and contacts
- ❏ Extensive networking capability
- ❏ A unique product or service
- ❏ A knack for strategic planning
- ❏ Willingness to work hard and put in long hours
- ❏ Access to new distribution lines
- ❏ Problem-solving abilities
- ❏ Position as tops in your field
-   Other: _____
-   Other: _____
-   Other: _____

Of course, what will be most valuable to a given company or individual will vary depending on their needs, but review the items you've checked above and select what you consider to be the five most important skills or capabilities you can offer to others.

1. _____

2. _____

3. _____

4. _____

5. _____

Creating Strategic Synergy

The goal of teaming up is always to create some degree of "synergy"—an indefinable extra quality by which people somehow produce more than the sum of their combined efforts, more than anyone expected or imagined. Essentially this kind of synergy is a "synthesis of energies" that occurs when two or more people combine their talents, skills, and resources to achieve a mutual goal. It happens when our needs are filled by the strengths of others, and their needs are met through our strengths. It's this synergy that makes teaming up so powerful it sometimes seems almost magical. The right combination of our mutual strengths overcomes our mutual weaknesses, and each of us becomes more effective in ways we could not even have predicted.

So to complete this step, use your answers from the preceding pages and juxtapose your strengths against your weaknesses and needs on the chart below.

	Strengths	Weaknesses	Needs
1.			
2.			
3.			
4.			
5.			

IDENTIFYING YOUR MOST SUITABLE CHOICES

Having explored your work style and habits and identified your most impressive business strengths and your biggest weaknesses, you should have a fairly detailed understanding of the kind of people you work synergistically with. So now it's time to identify which teaming-up scenarios will best benefit your business.

At this point, the way in which you want to proceed may be absolutely straightforward and clear. For example, Adrienne Weller, a clothing designer and stylist in Los Angeles, knew exactly what she needed to get her business off the ground. She needed to find someone who had experience and key contacts with clothing buyers—people who actually make the purchasing decisions for retailers in the clothing industry. Although she could have continued working to develop these contacts herself and eventually gained the experience she needed, working with the right collaborator would clearly enable her to get her creative designs into stores more quickly. So that became her goal.

With this goal in mind, she eventually teamed up with Teri Bieber, a buyer for a major clothing store chain who wanted to start her own sideline production company. The two women entered into a formal partnership, with Adrienne designing a line of clothing and Teri selling the line to retail stores. Within six months, the two developed nearly $20,000 in business and expect their company to double sales each season.

For others, however, the choice of how to best team up is not so obvious. Sometimes it's not clear whether to try cross-promoting with another business or to launch a joint venture, whether to enter into a formal partnership or create an interdependent alliance. If that's your situation, the question you must answer is which teaming-up option(s) will benefit your business the most? Which will meet your primary business need while making the best use of your professional strengths?

One way to answer this question is to select the teaming-up option that feels most comfortable to you *and* that involves the least risk for your business at this time. In general, we recommend starting with an option at the more informal end of the teaming-up continuum, such as making a mutual referral arrangement or forming an interdependent alliance you can easily disengage from if it doesn't work out. Alternatively, review the pros and cons of the ten options for teaming up and select the method that best matches your business need and presents the least troublesome issues for you financially and administratively. You can use the Pros and Cons Summary on page 148 to review your options. But be selective; don't just jump at the first most readily available choice. Make sure you find a truly good match among your needs, your strengths, and your weaknesses.

Of course, when it comes to teaming up, there's no one guarantee you're making the best choice the first or even the second time around. As in so many other aspects of being self-employed from pricing to marketing, you have to set your goal, select a direction for reaching it, test your choice, and evaluate your results until you find ways to team up that will work for you. Making a commitment to your goal is one of the most important ingredients in finding the best way for you to work with others. To paraphrase Robert Porter Lynch from his book, *Business Alliances Guide,* to implement a strategy you must get excited about it, commit to it, and invest your energy and spirit in it. If a choice you make has no sense of urgency, imagination, or challenge, it won't capture the hearts and souls involved and probably won't lead you where you want to go.

So, take a moment to review your options and identify the teaming-up possibilities that you feel most committed to and energized by and that best meet your strategic needs and strengths. Jot them down here along with your reasoning about why they would be good options for you.

TEAMING-UP CHOICE 1. _____

REASON: _____

TEAMING-UP CHOICE 2. _____

REASON: _____

Summary—Pros and Cons of Your Teaming-Up Options	
Networking	
Pros	*Cons*
• Access to other people's time, information, and advice. • A chance to avoid isolation, keep abreast of new developments, and contribute to your field. • Exposure for your business and the chance to build business-generating contacts. • A low-risk route to explore and test out other possible teaming-up relationships. • Highly flexible as to if, how, and when to relate to a wide variety of people. • Low cost. Most networking groups have no charge or only small membership fees. • High potential to obtain lots of leads and referrals from others.	• Successful networking is time-consuming. You must take time out to attend meetings regularly and you must get involved. Just showing up isn't usually enough. You must follow up on the contacts you make and work at being sure you also reciprocate by helping those you meet. • Not everyone is comfortable promoting themselves directly. Some people don't like mixing business and personal activities. Others feel that networking for leads and referrals is somewhat crass. • There's no guarantee of results from informal networking. Success depends on the quality of contacts you make and your own efforts. You may or may not get worthwhile referrals, and you may not meet people you want to team up with.

Mutual Referrals

Pros	Cons
• Mutual referrals are by far the least time-consuming, most cost-effective way to get steady business. • The majority of successfully self-employed individuals and small businesses get most of their business by word of mouth. • Mutual referrals work so well because they enable you to get business coming to you without your having to spend inordinate amounts of time marketing yourself. • Mutual referral arrangements are flexible, easy to enter into (or get out of), and can be as formal or informal as you feel comfortable negotiating.	• Referrals may or may not be of the nature or quality you are seeking. • You have to make sure the people you refer to will, in fact, provide high-quality services to those you send to them. Your reputation is going to be affected when you make a referral. If a client or customer is disappointed with a referral, they'll become upset or disappointed with you too. • The number and frequency of referrals among you and your associates may end up being lopsided, in which case one of you may start to feel resentful. • By aligning yourself with a particular person, you could cut yourself off from other possible referral sources.

Cross-Promoting

Pros	Cons
• Cross-promotions can be done at whatever scale or level of involvement you feel comfortable with. • Participants can continue or back out after an initial effort if the relationship doesn't work out. • Because those involved are actively putting in time and/or money to help each other get results, you have a better chance of producing a return from your efforts than from more informal relationships that require less investment. • You can often get better results for the same amount of time and money you put into your marketing or advertising independently.	• Cross-promoting requires a higher level of time and energy for planning and coordinating your efforts than more informal teaming-up relationships. • A financial contribution is often necessary to implement a meaningful cross-promotion, and trusting others when money is involved not only increases the risk but also puts added pressures on your relationship. • Increased investment increases expectations among participants, but there is no guarantee of results. Customers still make decisions about whether or not to use your services. Also, one of you may draw a better response than the other(s), thereby creating rivalry. • The higher investment and visibility of a cross-promotion increase potential conflicts.

Interdependent Alliances

Pros	Cons
• You can accept whatever projects come your way at any time, knowing you have backup available to help you. This allows you to expand your business faster or to take it to a higher level with more complex projects.	• Alliances require a high level of mutual trust, cooperation, and planning. Therefore there's a higher risk of conflicts, disappointments, complications, and even problems affecting your reputation if an associate doesn't deliver high-quality work in a timely fashion.
• You can take on larger, more demanding projects that have faster turnaround time knowing you have additional resources available to help you meet a deadline or to fulfill projects with more work than you can handle on your own, thus not having to decline work you might otherwise have to.	• There are tax and legal implications relative to maintaining independent-contractor status that must be taken care of, including filing a 1099 Form for each associate whose services you use.
• You gain the possibility of working on your alliance partner's projects in the event you have no work at hand or some extra time to spare. By increasing your chances of having a steady income, in effect, an interdependent alliance is a like an insurance policy against downtimes and low profitability.	• There is always a risk that in the future, a client or customer will have only enough work for one of you, but will prefer working with your associate although the initial contact was with you. That could mean losing a valued customer or client.
• You can enhance your reputation for being able to handle significant projects.	• You must keep additional records and do increased administrative work to track time and expenses, invoices, and to meet tax obligations.
• Alliances provide an opportunity for building rewarding interpersonal relationships.	

Joint Ventures

Pros	Cons
• A joint venture provides the opportunity to explore a new idea or market you don't have the time or money to undertake on your own.	• Usually you are truly interdependent in a joint venture. You must depend on someone else to accomplish the joint goals. This added vulnerability creates greater potential for conflicts, disappointments, and disagreements.
• You can garner the energy and creativity of others.	• You're legally liable for the actions of your joint venture partner.
• You can boost your reputation by association with your joint venture partner(s).	• To protect your legal and financial interests you need to have all joint venture agreements in writing. These usually should be done or at least reviewed by an attorney.
• A joint venture can open doors not previously available to you alone.	
• You can gain the benefits of a partnership without as many risks.	

• A joint venture can be a productive way to test the waters for a full-scale partnership.	• The joint venture can drain time, energy, and money from your primary business. • It's harder to back out if things don't work out because others are dependent on you and you're legally liable for whatever you've jointly contracted to do.

Satellite Subcontracting

Pros	Cons
• Rainmakers can take on more business than they could do on their own. • Rainmakers can increase their profits by keeping a percentage of the fees they pay to subcontractors. • Rainmakers can grow their business without the costs, risks, and administrative hassles of taking on permanent employees. • Subcontractors can maintain their independence without the time, expense, and frustration of having to market themselves. • Subcontractors can concentrate their time and energy on providing their services or carrying out other responsibilities in their lives instead of having to devote time to marketing themselves. • Subcontractors can bring in an initial income and build experience during what would otherwise be a lean start-up period.	• Satellite subcontracting can be time-consuming for rainmakers who must invest time arranging for, administering, and overseeing subcontractors' work. In fact, your business could grow larger and more complex than you intend or want. • Rainmakers must simultaneously look for good subcontractors as well as for new clients. • The fact that rainmakers are essentially agents for other businesses can lead to a double bind. On the one hand, you must make sure that your subcontractors do a good job for your clients or your business and reputation will suffer. On the other hand, you want to find as much work for your subcontractors as possible to keep them happy working with you. These two issues may lead to conflicts, because you may push your subcontractors to work quickly but at the same time, you expect quality. • Subcontractors may eventually step around you and take your clients as their own. • As a subcontractor, your success is dependent on someone else's ability to get business for you. There's no guarantee you will always have projects to work on, and yet your time may be tied up working on projects you do get. • As a subcontractor your fee will be less than if you had gotten the business yourself.

Consortiums	
Pros	**Cons**
• A consortium allows an individual or small business to participate in large projects they couldn't be part of on their own. • You can gain many of the advantages of being part of a team or organization while maintaining much of your independence. • Once the consortium begins getting business, it can bring you a sense of security you couldn't otherwise attain by having to find and work on one small project after another. • Sometimes because you are a part of fulfilling larger projects or orders, you will be able to sell products and services through a consortium that you couldn't sell independently.	• Consortiums can be difficult to put and hold together. • Members may remain focused on generating their own work in order to stay in business and thereby prevent the consortium from developing enough momentum. • When work comes in, it can be a challenge to communicate, mobilize, and coordinate everyone's efforts since each person is operating independently in separate locations. • A strong leader or leadership team is usually required, but sometimes no one has the time or skills to fulfill this leadership role. At other times, people in the consortium may resent the leader or feel that the team infringes on their independence. • If not handled well, the group can disintegrate into personality conflicts and professional battles that destroy the team effort.

Family/Spouse Collaborations	
Pros	**Cons**
• Working together can make balancing work and personal life easier and, with the proper control, make shifting between these aspects of your life a more seamless effort. • Working with family members can simplify a complex or stressful lifestyle. • Teaming up with family members can avoid the financial burden of having to pay outside employees and keep more of the profits within the family. • Working together can bring family members closer as you jointly overcome adversity and other challenges. • Family collaborations can capitalize on the camaraderie, loyalty, and shared spirit that already exists within a family instead of trying to find an outside associate or partner with whom you can build such deep ties. • You can draw upon similar habits, goals, and work styles based on deep, shared values.	• Working with family members can amplify everything, the best and the worst in each of us. As the character Douglas Wambaugh said on the TV show *Picket Fences,* "Family members love one another—but they drive each other crazy." • When business conflicts arise, they can have a deleterious effect on your marriage and family. • Your business can interfere with family life if boundaries are not respected. • Your spouse or other family members may not always be the best people for the job. • It's easy to make assumptions about family members you would never make about someone outside the family. And it's easier to overlook formalities that protect rights of those involved. But such assumptions and oversights make you vulnerable to disappointments and even disaster.

• It's often easier to work with someone you already know and trust than to build such bonds with someone new.	• It's usually harder to end a family business relationship when it doesn't work out.

Partnerships	
Pros	*Cons*
• Unlike corporations, which require more paperwork and money to initiate and legally establish, partnerships are relatively inexpensive and easy to set up. A basic partnership agreement can usually be drawn up within a day or two, assuming the parties have considered the issues and discussed the matters beforehand. • A partnership generates a certain momentum that can boost a business. When each person knows why he or she is going into partnership, the merger creates a lot of optimism and hope that can energize everyone involved. • Partnerships can bring added creativity, resources, talents, and skills to an enterprise. • A formally declared partnership can provide each person with the security of a clear, legally enforceable commitment from the other people involved to share in the responsibility of running the business. • Sharing a workload usually enables people to accomplish more than they could by working alone, and the whole can be greater than the sum of its parts. • Partnerships can be a good way to finance a business that couldn't otherwise get under way.	• Complex partnership agreements can take more time and cost more in attorney fees than a simple incorporation. • You are legally liable for your partner's actions. • Success depends on a high level of mutual cooperation and planning. • Expectations for positive results from partnerships are usually high, so the risk of conflicts and disappointments is also high. • Since the stakes are usually higher, conflicts can be more vitriolic and unpleasant when participants disagree on the strategy or implementation of their business plans. • Since you're bound to the terms of your agreement, ending a partnership that's not working out can be more difficult. Often you can't just walk out. There may be debts and other customer obligations that must be resolved first. In fact, since the adoption of no-fault divorce, it's easier to end a marriage than to end a business partnership.

Virtual Organization	
Pros	*Cons*
• You can keep your overhead significantly lower than if you were running a traditional corporation.	• There is so little structure that relationships may dissipate between projects.

- You can remain nimble and flexible, pulling together just the right people on the spur of the moment.
- A virtual corporation is like a "skunk works" in that you can get a project done more quickly and more cost-effectively than a traditional organization could.
- By drawing on the synergy and creative energy of a diverse group of successful people, you can spawn new ideas and better ways of doing a job.
- Like a consortium, you can take on more work and larger projects than would be possible working as a one-person operation or a partnership.
- You can expand in working in other regions or other countries.

- Confusion and miscommunication can occur when people don't meet face-to-face, communicating only through a project leader or electronic contact.
- You must be comfortable working in a flexible style and give up old views of leadership, loyalty, and project management.
- Whoever is managing a given project will need to commit to a high level of planning and coordination to pull together the abilities of many people who are doing their job without supervision.
- Because relationships are often more informal, some individuals may undercut one another not realizing how this will hinder their success in the future.
- It's difficult to get under way until you and others involved are established and have business coming in.

Developing Multiple Options

Given the value people get from teaming up, it's not surprising to find that many self-employed individuals become involved in more than one teaming-up effort. Among those we've interviewed for this book, about 20 percent had several simultaneous ventures operating, partly due to the diversity of their interests and partly due to their strong desire to maximize their success. For instance, by teaming up, Wally Bock of Oakland, California, can run his training company, cowrite a book with a friend, and operate a marketing consulting business with a partner. Master marketer and multimillionaire Beryl Wolk's teaming-up activities may qualify him for the *Guinness Book of World Records*. He told us he's involved in 131 simultaneous joint ventures!

As these cases demonstrate, it's quite possible to use teaming up as a way to expand and diversify your business in a variety of ways. Generally, however, we recommend waiting to pursue multiple ventures simultaneously until after you have one venture successfully under way. Like the poker player who can play several hands at once, it helps to have developed a track record of success before dividing your concentration and effort.

Still, it's useful to keep your mind open to the variety of teaming-up options you could pursue. Some choices may not be available to you at this time, but considering various options can put you in the frame of mind to notice "coincidences" of serendipitous events that could lead to opportunities you might otherwise miss. Remember that Jordan Ayan, the business consultant in Chicago, met his collaborator in a most unexpected way. If you recall, he had just lost a bid for a big contract when, while attending a professional conference, he began chatting during a cocktail hour with a woman from Atlanta. It turned out she had won the very contract he'd lost, and she invited him to participate on the project. Since then the two have become ongoing collaborators in a successful alliance that has lasted several years. So always remain open to any possible collaborations that could develop.

Short-Term Versus Long-Term Arrangements

In making a choice about the ways you'd team up, remember, too, that teaming up doesn't have to involve a long-term commitment. You can create a short-term collaboration or association as easily, if not more easily, as one that's intended to last indefinitely. In fact, some alliances like doing a cross-promotion or a particular joint venture are best done as short-term arrangements that allow you to assess your results and decide if and how you want to continue. Both you and those you want to team up with will most likely encounter numerous changes over time, and there's no way you can anticipate all those changes right from the start. So in choosing someone to team up with, it's okay to concentrate on purely short-term needs such as getting more business or finishing a certain contract. You can begin building a track record together before you need to make a long-term commitment.

OVERCOMING ANY REMAINING CONCERNS

Probably the most challenging part of teaming up is finding the right people to team up with. Not connecting with the right people is the number-one reason many of us who would like to team up haven't done it. It's also why some relationships that do get under way don't work out. The fact is, most people experience some anxiety and discomfort at the prospect of making a commitment to work with someone else once a good possibility arises. This is true even if the individuals involved already know each other well, as is the case in deciding to work with a family member or spouse. Some people worry about being let down. Others worry about being tied down. Some people are concerned about how working together will affect what has been a good relationship. Most people don't want to approach their decision to team up with someone like conducting a corporate job interview, yet they may wonder if they can rely on their best judgment and "gut" instincts. Here's how we recommend getting over any remaining concerns so you can proceed knowing you're making good decisions.

Don't base your choices on limited options. Most of us operate in a relatively small world of familiar contacts. We generally talk to and interact with the same circle of people again and again. So to make sure you have considered your best possibilities for teaming up successfully, step outside your familiar circle before you make any final decisions. Meeting new people is one of the best ways to get a fresh perspective on possible teaming-up opportunities; new relationships challenge your ideas of the status quo and your assumptions about what's possible. Seeing how other people conduct their businesses is often an eye-opener that improves your ability to recognize, identify, and evaluate what you want in working with others.

One way to expand your perspective is to participate in new networking groups or professional or trade associations. To find them, in addition to the resources listed in chapter 2, you can consult local organization directories that are available in many communities. Some areas like Orange County, California, have very comprehensive listings of organizations like *Susan Linn's Directory of Orange County Networking Organizations. Power Schmoozing,* by Terri Mandrell, is an additional source of ideas for how and where to meet new people.

Another way to make sure you're not settling for less than would be desirable is by attending the rich array of trade and professional conferences or seminars available through your field, related fields, or adult-education and university-extension programs. For example, Dr. Ann Lastovica, state coordinator for the Home-Based and Micro Business program at the Virginia Cooperative Extension at Virginia State University in Petersburg, tells us her program has linked up many home-based textile and sewing businesses who would not have met one another otherwise. In some cases, they have formed their own support groups that continue beyond the weekend courses, but in other cases people have entered into joint ventures producing crafts or clothing together.

Fran Sexton of Gulsport, Mississippi, could have easily missed out on opportunities to produce a device she invented to catch the fabric that falls off a specialized sewing machine. But by deciding to attend a university extension workshop on "sewing as a business," she met several sewing machine manufacturers, one of whom became interested in her device. As a result, Fran began selling her invention through this one company and eventually through four others. Her device has even been sold to the public on television through the QVC network. Fran's company, Catch It Time, now employs several members of her family and many locals who help her make the device. She also has ideas for other inventions that will eventually come out.

On-line networking is another great way to expose yourself to a wealth of new contacts nationwide. On-line you can meet people you would probably never meet otherwise. So log on to the Internet or on-line services like America Online, CompuServe, or Prodigy and visit the forums, news groups, or interest groups related to your business interests and needs.

When Debbie Dewey decided to leave her banking job and go freelance, she bypassed looking for people to work with in her local area and met two of her most important associates by going on-line on CompuServe. As Debbie points out, both of these contacts live in faraway places and she has yet to meet one of them, although she has been working with him now for seven years. We, Paul and Sarah, met Laura Clampitt Douglas, the coauthor of our book *Getting Business to Come to You*, on-line. We were impressed by the brilliant advice on marketing she provided people and asked her if she wanted to work with us.

Even reading about other people can inspire you to make a connection. For example, Eileen Glick was running a custom picture framing business in Phoenix, Arizona, when she read a magazine article about entrepreneurial women. That's how she learned about Janie Sullivan, a home-based desktop publisher. The article inspired Eileen to call Janie up with the idea of publishing a directory of other people who worked from home in the Phoenix area. The two chatted, met a few days later, and realized that they both yearned to have not just a directory but an association of home-based businesses. They decided right then and there to create the HomeBased Business Association of Arizona, to provide a forum for others like themselves to get together and support one another's businesses. Their profit-making association now has several thousand members throughout Arizona, and not only has Eileen's dream come true for an association but thanks to her decision to expand her own contacts, the association has also become a new business for her.

Also, don't overlook past contacts. For example, when Los Angeles lawyer Hillary Booth decided to leave the large legal firm where she had worked to go out on her own, she believed her chances for success would be greater if she had a partner. So Hillary reviewed her many past contacts, recalling the many people she'd known throughout her career, and decided to contact Jennifer Greenfield, a classmate from law school. It turned out that Jennifer too had recently decided to open an independent law practice, and she was also looking for a partner! The two lawyers spent some time discussing a strategy for working together and ultimately decided to become partners in their own small law firm.

Look with new eyes at those closest to you as well. Jan Caldwell, the home-based lawyer outside of Washington, D.C., began her two additional businesses by exploring various business ideas with her family members. She teamed up with her sister on one business and with her brother-in-law on another. Both of these ventures developed into sideline businesses for Jan. Her sister was a legal secretary, so they pooled their talents to start a demonstrative evidence publishing company to produce courtroom materials. This business has also flourished into a vanity-publishing company through which they help people write and publish their own stories. Jan tapped into her brother-in-law's extensive travel experience and, using his contacts overseas, together they developed a car and truck exporting business which later led to exporting an automotive engine preservative fluid as well.

Build your success upon success. As obvious as it may seem, our research shows that your chances of teaming up successfully will be much greater if you work with people who already have a history of success instead of teaming up with people who are looking for a chance to be successful. Teaming up successfully is not a random happenstance. Those who already have something successful under way do much better at teaming up than those who are hoping that they'll become successful by teaming up. In other words, success breeds success.

Basically teaming up works best from mutual positions of strength. You'll increase your chances for success by becoming successful on your own first, even if it's on a small scale, and then teaming up with others who also have something successful going. In fact, a track record of mutual success is one of the most important predictors of working together successfully. In contrast, too often people who have no track record of working successfully on their own only pull one another down by trying to work together.

Here's a case in point. Jeannette had been trying to get a word-processing service going for eighteen months. But she was busy with her new baby and very little business had come her way. She thought if she could just find a partner, starting her own business would be much easier. Beverly, a friend of her sister's, had just lost her job so Jeanette proposed that they go into business together. At first, the idea of being partners gave them both a boost of energy. Then Beverly landed their first client, who needed a layout done for an annual report on a very tight schedule. Unfortunately, Jeannette's baby became sick and Beverly was left trying to do the project alone. She was late in completing it. The client was unhappy. Beverly was angry. The partnership disintegrated, and each woman went back to trying to build her business on her own. Since neither woman had known what the other could do, they now not only had to build a reputation, they had to repair a damaged one.

We're not suggesting that only already successful people can team up. Consider Robin's situation. Robin wanted to open a small community theater, but she had no funds. Like Jeannette, she thought finding a partner could be the solution. But she didn't want to approach prospective partners without a track record. So she talked a friend into letting her put on a play for one weekend at his theater without having to pay any money up front. She invited her most promising potential investors to come as her guests to see the play. Meanwhile she recruited a volunteer cast who rehearsed for several months in her living room. Then Robin got busy selling tickets to family and friends. She also arranged for local media to review the play. The theater was sold out for the weekend, bringing in plenty of money to pay the cost of renting the theater. The critics reviewed the play positively. The potential investors were impressed. Even though her dream of a community theater was still just a dream, she began creating a track record of success upon which to build future business relationships. She repeated this process several times in the ensuing months before entering into a joint venture with an entertainment lawyer who had the financing to open a permanent theater.

As these stories illustrate, the more you and those you get involved with already have going for you, the better the chances are that you can do even better together. In other words, if you're looking to become more successful, start creating your own success and then join with others who are doing the same.

Do your due diligence. As you identify people you think you'd like to team up with, before proceeding take time to get to know each other's work firsthand so you know if the "chemistry" is right and if your work styles, values, ethics, etc., match. You may be attracted to working with someone based on his or her personality, success, appearance, and business skills and knowledge. Or you may be interested in this person simply because he or she has approached you with an appealing offer. Or, like Jeannette and Beverly, you may be considering teaming up with someone simply because he or she is available and working together would be convenient. Whatever has led you to consider collaborating with someone, don't proceed without doing what's called "due diligence." Take the time to look into a person's or company's background and suitability, because once you become affiliated with someone, her or his reputation and performance will affect your reputation and performance.

Doing a diligent check includes getting a sense of the person's previous track record, financial background, and work quality. If you're considering teaming up with an established company, you can obtain some such information by doing a credit check, contacting the Better Business Bureau in their area, or talking with people in associations or groups to which they belong. But when you're considering working with another self-employed individual, a family member, associate, or friend, performing due diligence will usually need to be done through more informal techniques like:

- Talking with other people who know or have worked with them
- Reviewing their promotional materials
- Discussing with them the kind of projects and work they've done in the past
- Visiting their place of business
- Arranging to see their work and/or observe them at work

If Beverly had done her due diligence before teaming up with Jeannette, for example, she would have learned that Jeannette hadn't had any clients for several months and by talking with her about her goals and priorities, Beverly would have discovered that Jeannette was so busy with her new baby that she didn't have much time or interest in marketing her business. This could have been a clue to Beverly that Jeannette's priorities were not the same as hers at that time in their lives.

As you observe people's work, watch how they treat other people: Are they polite, diplomatic, energetic, courteous, and knowledgeable? Are they aggressive enough for you or too aggressive? Size up their motivation, work style and work habits, quirks and idiosyncrasies. Based on what they tell you about themselves and how they interact with clients and customers, imagine how they would answer the questions on ethics, values, and vision presented earlier in this chapter. Do this type of review even if you've known the person well as a friend or family member. Often when people are doing business they are quite different from the way they are in other roles you've known them in. And vice versa: if you've only known someone professionally, you may not know what they're like on a day-in-day-out basis when they're not putting their best foot forward.

Take time to study and check out thoroughly those you're thinking of working with, particularly if you are thinking of teaming up in a way that involves more of a risk for you, as in the case of a partnership or joint venture. Assess if they can really offer you what you think they have to offer. Determine if your strengths can fill in for their weaknesses and vice versa. Many people feel the pressure to make a decision quickly and get on with the action. But it's better if you can take the time to get to know those you're thinking of teaming up with over a period of several months or more.

Of course, how much time you need to devote to assessing whether someone is a right match for you depends on what's at stake in teaming up. Naturally, if your goal is simply to find a group of people you can network with, occasionally, it needn't take very long. You can attend a few meetings and see if there's a good "fit." If one group doesn't work out, you can always drop out and try another one. But, if you are intending to make an interdependent alliance with someone, you'd be better off spending a few months sizing up those you're considering to be assured of your compatibility and the similarity of your goals.

As you do your due diligence, look for warning signs that might tip you off to potential problems. You want to be sure that your affiliation will be of *mutual* benefit. You don't want to discover that someone is counting on your investment of time, energy, and money to keep their faltering business afloat. Historical facts or anecdotes the person tells you about their business are often tip-offs to potential problems. Unfortunately, too many people overlook blatant signs of future problems. In fact, almost every person we talked with who'd had a disastrous experience teaming up told us something like *"I should have seen it coming." "Looking back, I can see that all the signs were there . . ." "I had a gut feeling something was wrong, but I ignored it."*

For instance, be wary of working with a person who tells you that he or

The Warning Signs of Potential Problems

While everyone has quirks and problems and everyone has made mistakes and failed at times, there are many signs that someone is not in the best position at a particular time in his or her life to work in a mutually beneficial business relationship. So, think twice about teaming up with someone who:

- is in the process of going bankrupt
- is losing clients quickly without a satisfactory explanation
- has an "overdominant" ego (e.g., is highly competitive, prone to one-upsmanship, always needing to be the center of attention, doing all the talking, or not welcoming feedback)
- has had several lawsuits brought against him or her
- has a history of suing other people, especially previous business associates (even if she or he won the suits)
- is having serious financial problems such as a bad credit rating or no credit cards
- asks to use your credit card or borrow money from you without an agreement
- is late for or misses meetings and scheduled appointments
- does not meet deadlines for you or clients
- is not willing to put ideas or agreements into writing
- does not believe in adhering to contracts
- shows disrespect for clients, colleagues, and associates
- interrupts other people all the time
- bad-mouths other people consistently
- tells you he or she didn't say something when you know he or she did
- repeats what you said a few days ago and claims it as her or his idea
- is clearly distracted by and committed to other priorities in his or her life

she has already been involved in several lawsuits, or with someone who bad-mouths other people or who has had a series of previous failed partnerships. Think twice about working with a person with an argumentative personality, someone who always has a story to top yours, or someone who's always talking about the deadlines he or she's behind on. In addition, think ahead about such questions as:

- Is this other person doing anything that conflicts with my values, goals, and mission?
- What opinions will my clients and the public form about me if I work with these people?
- How could my reputation be hurt by working with this business?
- Does the person or business have an image problem they can solve or disguise by affiliating with me?

- How will my association with this business affect other opportunities I might have in the future?

Always base your opinions and decisions on actions instead of words. In forming a business relationship, it's what you do, not what you say you'll do or what you want to do, that counts.

Make a proposal to test the waters. The decision to team up, of course, must be a mutual one. Undoubtedly if you're exploring teaming-up possibilities, while you're checking them out they're probably checking you out, too. In fact, their doing so indicates a serious attitude about your collaboration. Once you feel comfortable with deciding to proceed, take the initiative and propose the idea of working together if you haven't already. Most likely your proposal to work together will be a verbal one, but it helps to write down your ideas and goals in advance so that you can be clear and effective in articulating why and how you want to work together. In proposing the idea of working together, be sure to focus on the benefits that you each can gain from teaming up and why you believe your alliance will be a good match. Again, this is something you may want to spend some time outlining in advance.

Openly and frankly discuss your business strengths, weaknesses, and needs, and invite your potential collaborators to do the same. Notice how they respond; note if they are openly providing the same level of details as you are.

Keep your meeting upbeat and friendly; don't focus on getting a commitment or on hammering out a financial and legal agreement between you. These details should be negotiated later after you and your potential associate have agreed on the idea of working together and have defined the shared goals teaming up could accomplish for both of you. Leave the conversation with each of you considering what you've proposed to determine and agree to talk further.

Document your meeting. It's usually a good idea, and can even be wise from a legal standpoint, to keep a written record of your meetings and preliminary discussions by making notes of your observations and impressions as well as your understanding of any agreements, ideas, concerns, or interests you've each expressed. We recommend, however, that you avoid hiring a lawyer or preparing any formal documents at this point. If you must protect your company secrets, ask your potential collaborator to sign a confidential nondisclosure agreement, such as the one shown in the box on page 163. However, keep in mind that some potential partners will hesitate to sign such agreements and may even decline to talk with you about working together if you ask them to sign any legal agreement up front. It's usually better to structure your conversations more generally at first so that you don't risk divulging sensitive information that could jeopardize either of you.

Sample Nondisclosure Agreements

A nondisclosure agreement is a legal written document in which one or more people agree to keep specified information shared between them confidential. The agreement can be mutual if both parties have proprietary information or ideas to contribute to a potential teaming-up discussion; or the agreement can be one-way if only one person has proprietary information that needs to be protected.

Obtaining a confidentiality or nondisclosure agreement has two goals: (1) to ensure that any confidential information you reveal will not be disclosed to anyone else; and (2) to prohibit the confidential information you share from being used for someone else's gain or in a manner detrimental to you. So to protect yourself adequately, you want your agreement to include a clear definition of what you consider to be confidential and for what period of time. In the case of some trade secret, like the recipe for your own proprietary hot sauce, you may want the agreement to be indefinite. In other situations you may want it only until you yourself make the information public as in the launch of a new product or service. Here are two sample agreements.

Mutual Nondisclosure Agreement

Whereas John Smith and Leslie Jaines are exploring entering into a business relationship together, they recognize that they may disclose confidential information about each other's current business activities, including their business plans, strategies, goals, research, future product or service development, proprietary computer software (whether in source code or object code form), management, personnel, marketing strategies and plans, trade secrets, intellectual property, know-how, financial data, and other proprietary matters relating to their business interests. As a result, both parties agree to keep confidential any information, ideas, plans, outlines, and concepts revealed in the course of their discussions. The parties will maintain all information discussed in confidence with the same standard of care he or she has in safeguarding information about his or her own business, and in no event with less than a reasonable standard of care. Neither party will disclose such information to any person, or use such information for any purpose whatsoever except the evaluation of the viability of the business relationship described above, without the express written consent of the other party. Any written documents, drawings, sketches, illustrations, or outlines shared under this agreement are also covered by this confidentiality agreement. This agreement will remain in force regardless of whether the two parties enter into a business relationship together. If at any time the parties cease their discussions of a potential business relationship, any party receiving confidential information hereunder shall promptly return all confidential information to the other party hereto, or shall destroy all confidential information in his or her possession and shall certify in writing to the other party that all confidential information subject to this agreement has been destroyed. The following categories of information shall not be deemed "confidential information" subject to this agreement: (i) information which is in the public domain through no breach of this contract; (ii) information disclosed to any party by a third party who is under no obligation of confidentiality to the other party hereto; and (iii) information which is required to be disclosed by law, subpoena, or order of a court or administrative agency provided that the party so required to disclose confidential information shall make reasonable effort to ensure the confidentiality of such information in any proceeding in which such party is required to disclose confidential information.

Signed and dated:

_____

One-Way Nondisclosure Agreement

Whereas Jill Roberts Enterprises is exploring a business relationship with Max Maxwell Services, and this relationship may involve presenting information about her current business activities, including her business plans, strategies, goals, research, future product or service development, proprietary computer software (whether in source code or object code form), management, personnel, marketing strategies and plans, trade secrets, intellectual property, know-how, financial data, and other proprietary matters relating to her business interests that Jill Roberts Enterprises has previously obtained. Max Maxwell Services agrees to keep confidential all such information revealed in the course of their discussions. Max Maxwell Services will hold all such information in confidence, and will maintain the same standard of care as it takes for its own business, and in no event with less than a reasonable standard of care. Max Maxwell Services will not disclose such information to any person, or use such information for any purpose whatsoever except the evaluation of the viability of the business relationship described above, without the express written consent of the other party. Any written documents, drawings, sketches, illustrations, or outlines shared under this agreement are also covered by this confidentiality agreement. This agreement will remain in force regardless of whether the two parties enter into a business relationship together. If at any time the parties cease their discussions of a potential business relationship, any party receiving confidential information hereunder shall promptly return all confidential information to the other party hereto, or shall destroy all confidential information in his or her possession and shall certify in writing to the other party that all confidential information subject to this agreement has been destroyed. The following categories of information shall not be deemed "confidential information" subject to this agreement: (i) information which is in the public domain through no breach of this contract; (ii) information disclosed to any party by a third party who is under no obligation of confidentiality to the other party hereto; and (iii) information which is required to be disclosed by law, subpoena or order of a court or administrative agency provided that the party so required to disclose confidential information shall make reasonable effort to ensure the confidentiality of such information in any proceeding in which such party is required to disclose confidential information.

Signed and dated:

_____

_____

Note: Depending on the situation, a confidentiality agreement may also need to contain a provision that the other party will not enter into a competing business or produce a competing product after disclosure of the confidential information.

You will find other types of confidentiality and nondisclosure agreements in books and on software that contain templates for standard legal contracts listed at the end of this chapter. You can also buy preprinted legal documents at many office supply stores. If you are in doubt about what to include in any confidentiality agreements you need to make, consult a lawyer for detailed legal assistance.

If you feel suspicious about a potential collaborator and worried about sharing even the most basic information about your business with her or him, perhaps that's a sign that this isn't the right person for you to be teaming up with. A suspicious beginning sets the wrong tone for preliminary discussions and prevents the kind of honest and frank interaction you need to be able to decide whether or not to work together.

Don't act in haste. After initial discussions, let a few days to a week pass for each of you to reflect on what's been proposed. Over this period of time each of you may have additional ideas that build on your original thoughts and enhance what you could do together, or new doubts and concerns may arise that you'll want to discuss further.

If they decide they don't want to proceed, respect their decision. You seldom gain from working with a reluctant associate or someone you had to talk into working with you. Be grateful that you've identified their lack of interest right from the start so you can get on with finding people who will be as enthusiastic about working with you as you are about working with them. Likewise, if you continue to have nagging doubts, it's best to postpone further plans if and until you feel ready and willing.

Some Caveats About Working with Friends

Because of the way you feel about close friends and acquaintances, you probably don't hesitate to discuss personal matters with them, like your finances, your health, or your romantic life. And so when you have a business idea or problem, you may naturally look to your friends for support, feedback, and even assistance in solving the problem or getting the idea off the ground. If a friend has some skill or experience that you lack, it can seem perfectly natural to propose working fifty-fifty with them on a new venture.

And yes, teaming up with friends can be a wonderful experience. Because of your bond and history together, friends are often more trustworthy, honest, and dedicated to a joint effort than other people might be. And with friends, it seems that there wouldn't be the need to worry about the kind of concerns you'd have when working with a stranger—that they might steal your money or take your ideas or your clients, for example. What better working mate can there be?

Sometimes, however, working with friends can have unexpected drawbacks. Because you're friends, your work styles may be so similar that they aren't complementary. Sue and Gretchen, for example, had been great friends since high school. They were both gregarious, outgoing, and creative. So when Gretchen came up with the idea of creating personalized wedding cakes, as a sideline business, Sue loved the idea and wanted to do it with her.

Gretchen was delighted. She imagined herself selling, designing, and delivering the cakes while Sue would create and bake them. But Sue quickly grew tired of creating and baking. She found the process tiring and tedious. She wanted to be out selling and designing the cakes. In fact, she quickly got even more orders for cakes than Gretchen, but neither of them wanted to actually do the baking. They tried hiring someone else to bake the cakes, but that left too little money for them to split. And they were never happy with the final product. Gradually they drifted into other separate businesses.

Your friendship can also cloud your best business judgment. You may not want to hurt your friend's feelings with honest feedback, for example, or hesitate to cut back his time when business slows. In such cases either your friendship, your business, or both can suffer. In fact, while many people we've talked with have worked successfully with friends, others insist that going into business with a friend was a bad choice for them. Here are some of the problems they've pointed out about mixing business and friendship.

- Tiptoeing around problems rather than bringing them out in the open
- Waiting until the last minute to raise an issue rather than doing it on the spot
- Feeling too embarrassed to talk openly about money concerns and sharing expenses
- Hesitating to disagree on major strategic decisions
- Becoming passive-aggressive (taking little swipes at each other) rather than openly disagreeing
- Nitpicking each other's bad habits
- Worrying about insulting or hurting each other's feelings by disagreeing or discussing problems
- Agreeing to do something out of friendship that you really didn't want to do
- Waiting too long to get out of a partnership or collaboration that isn't working

So in general, we recommend that you ease into working with a friend by taking on short-term or one-time tasks together so you can test out if your friendship weathers any problems or challenges working together presents. And as you do this, it's important to recognize that you'll most likely disagree from time to time and that you need to be able to express your feelings and opinions openly and honestly without worrying about insulting or hurting each other's feelings. You must find out if you can separate your personal friendship from your business relationship and make objective practical decisions. If not, it may be better to find other associates or partners for future ventures instead of trying to turn existing friendships into business relationships.

How Do You Know You're Making the Right Choice?

When you're on your own, it's easy to think the ideal solution to your problems is to team up with someone else, and indeed as we've said, on many occasions it is an excellent decision. Yet, as great as teaming up can be, before proceeding with a joint effort of any kind, be sure you're making the right choice. Here are three key questions you can ask to know if you're ready to commit.

1. Are you willing to adapt the way you do things to accommodate your new associate(s)? No matter how compatible you seem, there will be unforeseen adjustments you'll need to make, but if you're making the right choice, you won't mind finding ways to accommodate for them.
2. Are you willing to spend time managing your relationship with associates: coordinating, motivating, and monitoring the joint efforts you're planning? Even the most informal and short-term of arrangements will involve some degree of management and coordination. You'll need to add these responsibilities onto what you're already doing. But, again, if you're making the right choice, you'll be willing to invest the time and energy.
3. Are you willing to give up some total control over what you'll be doing? Whenever you team up, you lose some degree of control over the task at hand. You will need to involve others in certain decisions, and there will be some new limits on what you can and cannot do. If you're making the right choice, however, you won't mind sharing the reins in whatever ways you've agreed.

If you can honestly answer "yes" to these three questions, chances are you're ready to proceed with your plans to team up and you should be primed for success.

Special Considerations When Teaming with Big Business

Big businesses and small businesses are teaming up as never before. The advantages are many in both directions. The small company or self-employed individual can benefit from gaining access to the vast financial and manpower resources of large companies. Large companies, however, can benefit from the specialized know-how of experts they would not have on their payrolls, as well as the flexibility and innovation of small companies they may not be able to get from departments within their own corporations. In fact, today's enlightened large businesses are as eager to find "business partners" as smaller companies are, and when the fit is right, it doesn't matter how large or small a desirable "partner" company is. Whether the purpose of the relationship is to do cross-promoting or engage in a joint venture, large and small companies are profiting from teaming up.

A self-employed individual's or small business's teaming up with a giant company can be exciting, expanding, and a bit intimidating. Unfortunately, however, without proper safeguards, it can turn into a nightmare instead of a dream come true. Here are several risks and problems you could encounter due to differences in the ways big businesses and small businesses operate, and how to safeguard yourself from running into these problems.

Risk: Sometimes a large company requires a very long time to reach a decision about proceeding with a project. Decisions may need to go through multiple departments and layers of approval, and contracts may go through time-consuming legal review. The decision-making process can take months, even years. But once the decision is made to proceed and the contracts are drawn, they often expect their "partners" to act very quickly, sometimes overnight.

Safeguard: Never assume that you will actually be working with a large company until you have a signed agreement or contract. Definitely do not do work or expend funds related to the project until you have signed proof that the company will actually be proceeding. Most certainly do not turn down other business based on the possibility of a teaming-up venture with a large company. If other business comes your way, either discuss it with the prospective company in hopes of speeding up a definite commitment to you, or line up other people who can step in to handle possible overflow of work and be sure your "partners" know they may be working with your associates and not just you.

Risk: It's easy to think that well-established, highly profitable large companies are excellent credit risks. In fact, large companies can be very slow payers. They have specific accounting procedures and cash management strategies that could hold up your expected payments and reimbursements well past the standard 30 to 90 days, 120 days, or six months or more.

Safeguard: Make the method, process, and time frame for how you will be paid explicitly clear in a written contract. Since your account may be a small one for them, add an interest clause for past-due payments. Get expenses and partial payments up front whenever possible. Follow up on past-due bills immediately. Account for possible slow payment when planning how you'll manage your own cash flow.

Risk: Large companies often reassign or turn over personnel frequently, so your contact person may change from week to week or month to month. When this happens, you will probably need to begin again in establishing a relationship, reviewing the parameters of your agreement, and discovering the details of how you can best work together.

Safeguard: Avoid limiting the company contact you'll be working with to only one person. Establish as many relationships within the company as you possibly can. Account for possible turnovers when estimating costs and setting your fees. Don't assume a new contact person will know the history or nature of your agreement or even have much of a commitment to your project. Set aside time to meet with them; establish rapport, review your understanding of the work you'll be doing, and be primed to resell the project. Be prepared for each new person to have his or her own preferred ways of working, and remain flexible.

Risk: Out of necessity, large companies protect themselves by having their attorneys develop contracts that cover all kinds of contingencies and government requirements. Sometimes they require coventurers to carry large insurance policies that would wipe out or significantly reduce any profit for a small company. You may also find that their contracts contain wording that would require you to treat the corporation better than it will treat you with respect to important matters like cancellation and penalties for noncompliance. And their standard contract clauses for how and where disputes will be settled may be disadvantageous to you.

Safeguards: First, read contracts carefully, and if they are not absolutely clear and reasonable, have them reviewed by an attorney experienced in contract law. Second, don't assume because a contract looks "standard" and ominously large that you can't negotiate changes in it to protect your needs and interests. You may do such negotiations yourself, perhaps after having your attorney prepare a memo for you, which outlines problems in the contract and suggests changes. Or you may find it to your advantage to have an attorney carry out negotiations for you. This can be expensive, but living with the consequences of an unfair contract can be even more costly.

Risk: Despite well negotiated contracts, giant companies still can change direction suddenly, e.g., Microsoft's and AT&T's decisions to move their on-line networks to the World Wide Web after their business partners (both large and small) had invested tens of thousands of dollars in developing their on-line sites. What may be a minor change in focus for a large company can be a monumental setback for a small company. For example, when a $250,000 joint venture between a professional engineer working solo and a *Fortune* 500 company gets canceled, it's probably no big deal for the large company, but it could be disastrous for the solo professional.

Safeguards: One way to protect yourself from such disasters is to include a cancellation fee in your agreements. Another is to require payments for expenses up front whenever possible, or to expend funds only on those portions of a project that actually are under way, reserving judgment as to if and when you will proceed to the next level of expenditure.

By building such safeguards into your business relationships with large companies, you can make your association as rewarding and profitable as possible for both of you.

DEVELOPING A JOINT MISSION STATEMENT

Once you agree that there's a strong mutual interest in teaming up, it's time to focus together on defining your specific joint goals. This is the point when you can actually start planning the details of what you'll do and how you'll

---

Sample Mission Statement for a Cross-Promotion

Dear George:

I very much enjoyed our lunch yesterday, and I'm especially glad we'll be developing a promotional newsletter together on pet care. With your knowledge of dog training and my experience in grooming we'll be able to provide valuable information to both our clients and many prospective new ones, too.

I agree that a quarterly newsletter will be most practical. We can both provide this through column articles for each issue and since we'll both be using Microsoft Publisher we can design the basic layout together next week.

We can split the cost of printing 1,000 copies of every issue and each distribute 500 of them to past, present, and prospective clients. Hopefully we'll be able to scan pictures of some of our clients' pets. I've been wanting to buy a scanner anyway. I could go ahead and invest in one, especially since you're planning to get a postage meter for us. I'm so glad we agree that the newsletter should be educational in nature rather than a blatant sales piece. As you said, the more information we provide, the more people will respect our expertise. We both hope that eventually people will find it so valuable that they'll subscribe to it on an annual basis.

So instead of having ads, we can each have a one-column update of new things we're doing and how people can reach us.

Let's take Monday to find a time to start designing our masthead.

Warmest regards,

Beverly Green

do it. By taking the time to define your joint mission, you can begin building your relationship and developing the mutual trust that will make it work once you get under way. Sitting down to define your joint mission also helps to make sure you're both on the same page of the same book. As you brainstorm your goals and the ways you want to accomplish them, you'll develop stronger personal ties. All in all, concentrating on formulating a mission before you start will lay the groundwork for a win-win agreement and future success.

Depending on the teaming-up option you'll be pursuing, your "mission statement" can be as formal or informal as you wish. On the one hand, a joint mission for a mutual referral agreement, for example, will most likely be quite simple and informal in nature. On the other hand, a mission statement between partners or members of a new networking group or consortium could involve having several meetings or even a weekend retreat followed by a formal written statement everyone can read and modify until all agree.

You don't need to call the shared statement you develop a mission statement if that sounds too formal, but you should have a clear understanding between or among you as to what your joint goals are and you should write it down. The process of writing down your goals or mission, be it in a casual letter or a formal treatise, translates your verbal agreements into a preliminary *nonbinding* document that outlines your intentions. Such a mission statement is sometimes called a Statement of Principle, and it affirms the essential nature of your association by identifying and codifying the following.

- Your strategic objectives and goals
- The time frame for the association
- What roles and contributions each of you wants to make
- How you'd like to work together

Keep your mission statement upbeat and positive. Make developing it exciting and fun. Avoid the temptation to get into "negotiating" details—if a formal contract or legal agreement is called for, this will come later. Now is the time to get down in writing why you're excited about working together and what you're committed to accomplishing. Write in simple, clear language, without resorting to legalese, or worse, "pseudolegalese." Think of the statement as a road map to your destination; you and your associate simply want to draw a line from here to there.

Your statement doesn't need to be very long; a few paragraphs or a page or two will suffice. When we, Paul and Sarah, decided to work together, our mission statement was one sentence we still use today, sixteen years later: to provide information resources and support to help people make the transition from an Industrial era when everyone has a job to a time when more people will be able to create their own jobs and work for themselves from home. Everyone involved should get a copy of whatever statement you develop to keep in their records. In a more informal relationship, you could consider this document to be a follow-up letter summarizing your discussion at a luncheon meeting.

We urge you to write up such a mission statement even if you'll be working with family or friends. Don't assume that because you already have a close relationship, you don't need to set and define goals. Developing and agreeing in writing to what you want to accomplish together can help avoid future misunderstandings that might jeopardize your business or personal relationship. The box on page 171 shows an example of an informal mission statement in the form of a letter between two professionals who will be referring business to each other.

Beware: Do not call whatever written document you create a Statement of Intent. This term has legal implications in some states and can be considered a form of a contract, so it is not suitable at this stage of your relationship.

GETTING ON THE PATH TO SUCCESS

The steps outlined in this chapter can put you on the path to an effective teaming up venture. There's no need to struggle with pursuing relationships that end up leading nowhere. If you take these steps, you'll have a greater chance of finding potential alliances that complement your personal style and whose skills most closely match your needs.

Ultimately, a business relationship is usually only as good as the time and effort that went into assuring its success. So avoid the temptation to get involved in business alliances—formal or informal—without taking the time to think through what you can realistically expect from everyone involved.

Sometimes you will need to move quickly in making a decision to work with someone and you won't have the time to carry out the level of due diligence we've suggested. You might want to share a booth at a trade show, for example, and need to scramble quickly to find someone with whom to share expenses. Such a cross-promotion is limited in its duration and the risks are minimal, so even if you end up sharing a booth with a less-than-stellar companion, it won't be disastrous. But if you're a new business seeking a partner to help finance your start-up costs, or if you are seeking to establish an alliance to expand your territory for a local service, there's much more at stake—so it will be in your best interest to take the time to follow these steps as closely and thoroughly as possible. The more you do, the better your chances of success.

RESOURCES

The Mind Test: 37 Classical Psychological Tests You Can Now Score and Analyze Yourself. Rita Aero and Elliot Weiner. New York: Morrow, 1981.

Power Schmoozing, The New Etiquette for Social and Business Success. Terri Mandell. New York: McGraw-Hill, 1996.

Who Am I: Personality Types for Self-Discovery. Robert Frager. New York: Tarcher/Putnam, 1994.

See the Resources at the end of chapter 4 for books and disks containing legal forms.

4

Taking Care of Business:
Legal and Financial Issues

Don't expect what you don't inspect. —JODIE FOSTER

ONCE YOU'VE IDENTIFIED a compatible individual or company to team up with and you've agreed on your mutual goals, it's time to get down to business—not doing business, but taking care of business. In other words, it's time to address the appropriate legal and financial aspects of your relationship. It's vital that these issues be addressed up front, before you proceed with any joint activities. Unfortunately, for most people, talking about money and legal concerns is the most uncomfortable aspect of teaming up. But, if you've taken the steps we discussed in the last chapter, it need not be the difficult or unpleasant process you might fear. In fact, if you've taken the time to define your mutual goals and test your compatibility, legal and financial negotiations usually proceed more quickly and easily.

When Diane Ratliff and Debbie Bellmer decided to team up to create *The Home Business Directory* in Columbia, Missouri, they didn't actually think about formalizing their partnership. But to launch their venture, they consulted with their Small Business Development Center where it was suggested to them that they legalize their partnership. "I'm very glad we did," Diane told us. "It was not as difficult as you might imagine, and it has helped us clarify our plans and approach our business more seriously." Already their circulation has grown to over ten thousand copies in print, and each addition is larger than the last.

So don't be tempted to let the technical, legal, and financial aspects of your relationship "work themselves out." Once you've agreed on goals and on how you envision proceeding, it's time to iron out the nitty-gritty details that can trip you up if you don't get them straightened out before getting under way. Depending on which teaming-up option you want to pursue, you may be able to handle all these details yourself in a simple, informal manner. Or, at some point, it may be useful and vital to your self-interests to involve an accountant and/or lawyer to advise you. Either way, it's important to know and understand the legal and financial issues you need to address. But, as you'll see, these issues need not be formidably complex. While you won't want to launch a million-dollar enterprise on a handshake, you also needn't spend thousands of dollars in legal fees on an agreement you could create with an inexpensive off-the-shelf software program. Neither underdoing nor overdoing financial and legal planning makes sense.

TWELVE PRINCIPLES FOR NEGOTIATING HONEST, FAIR, AND LASTING FINANCIAL AGREEMENTS

Financial disputes are no doubt the most common reason for alliances to fall apart. It doesn't seem to matter whether there's too little money or too much money, people in business relationships all too frequently argue about how to split up profits and losses. In some cases, the dispute originates from the fact that those involved don't have a written agreement and so they end up arguing about what each person claims he or she agreed to months or years ago. In other cases, the dispute is related to the fact that the parties didn't reach a fair financial agreement in their initial negotiations. In still other cases, business circumstances change but the parties involved aren't willing to modify their agreement to fit new realities. There seems to be a myriad of reasons why people fight over money.

But you need not fall prey to them. The following twelve guidelines will help you develop honest, fair, and lasting financial agreements that prevent needless financial disputes. They're based on our own experiences as well as those of the hundreds of others who've enjoyed successful business relationships. Some of these principles are common sense, but they're all too often overlooked or ignored in the midst of hammering out a touchy financial agreement. Others are based on the philosophy of win-win negotiation, a term that's often espoused but less often followed. But adhering to these principles can go a long way toward making sure your financial agreements are made in the best interests of you and all other parties involved.

1. Make Negotiating Fun

While it may sound overly optimistic to think of negotiating as fun, our experience shows that unless people enjoy the negotiations and believe they will get personal satisfaction from the final agreement, their willingness to work hard to find workable compromises dissipates. Too often people think negotiating requires adopting an austere, hard-edged demeanor to convey that you can't be pushed around. But actually, when negotiations are approached with a defensive or adversarial attitude they tend to turn into a winner-take-all game of one-upsmanship and the atmosphere turns angry, tense, and combative. Instead of approaching your negotiating in this way, bring along your sense of humor. Work to approach each other with an open, friendly, positive regard. Avoid comments that will polarize and antagonize, like "You can't get everything you want," "I don't see how I could ever agree to that," or "We're miles apart." Rely instead on unifying comments that bring you closer together in spite of differences you need to resolve, like "I think we're getting closer to an agreement," or "I'm sure we can find a way that will work for both of us."

As you enter into negotiation, imagine that you and your associate or partner are taking an interesting and important journey together and that you both must cooperate if you're to find your way. If you begin disagreeing and the atmosphere starts to grow tense, stop for a moment. Take a breath and remind yourselves that everything you're doing is voluntary and your goal is to find a way to proceed so you can both enjoy your trip and arrive at your journey's end together.

2. Let the "51% Rule" Prevail

Whether they know it or not, the people involved in every successful business relationship we've encountered have been following what we call the 51% Rule: the willingness of each party to contribute a little more than their 50% share of the effort if need be. The willingness to put in this extra 1 percent of effort is what creates the "synergy" that enables a team to produce far more than the sum of its parts. Translated into practical terms, the "51% Rule" reminds each party to take as much initiative as possible to find ways to make the agreement work, including brainstorming, thinking creatively, and compromising. In fact, when negotiations appear to stall, it's often a sign that you're both holding back to make sure you won't have to put in any more than your 50%.

3. Don't Procrastinate About Key Points

During many negotiations, the parties involved reach an impasse. They seem to be unable to come to terms on a key issue, so rather than settle it, they often gloss over the issue and allow it to remain unresolved in the hope that it will work itself out at some later date. But, unless lack of agreement is due to a missing piece of information that must be obtained later, it's generally inadvisable to let key issues go unresolved. While you may want to temporarily table an issue until later in the discussion, proceeding with a joint activity with key issues unresolved all too often leads to conflicts later. Without having actually reached an agreement, each party tends to assume the matter has been resolved as she or he would want, whether that's feasible or not, and ultimately everyone ends up unhappy. At the same time, beginning with the smaller issues on which agreement can be easily reached develops a momentum to carry you through the more difficult issues.

4. Work Toward Flexible Agreements

While it's important to reach agreement on key issues, the best agreements are also flexible enough to accommodate the possibilities for changing conditions. Unfortunately, this concept is counterintuitive to what most of us have been taught. As Robert Porter Lynch points out in his book *Business Alliances Guide,* our legal system grew from Old English roots that date back to medieval times when contracts were literally "carved in stone." It was also a time when the world was a more stable place. Change was measured across centuries—not in days or hours, as it is today. In the Middle Ages, an agreement didn't need to be flexible. As a result of this history, even to this day in this country, our expectations for agreements tend to be more rigid than in other countries like Japan, where agreements are often more fluid and general rather than specific.

A more fluid approach is more realistic today when major change can take place overnight and often we have no control over it. Furthermore, being flexible in your negotiations is also more in the spirit of working together as a team. There is little chance for collaborating and assuring that both parties can benefit from the arrangement unless there can be cooperation and accommodation instead of competition. So it's best to reach initial agreement on details and then provide for how changes can evolve to everyone's satisfaction when necessary.

Of course, the challenge of living by this principle is that people can disagree as to which changing conditions justify changing your agreement; e.g., the general marketplace, a drop in the stock market, a loss of more than a certain number of customers, a personal or family crisis, the declining size of each party's bank account, or what? In actuality, in the long run, it doesn't matter how you define what calls for flexibility, as long as you agree on the principle that each person involved will honestly take into account the changing conditions that are important to both.

Think of it this way: If an associate tells you he or she needs to revise your mutual agreement because of a problem in his or her life, but you don't agree that the change is serious enough to warrant a modification, you may be able to win the point legally or technically, but you now have an associate who's less committed to your joint venture and is most likely holding a grudge against you. So, truly, what have you won? In the long term, it's in your best interest to at least discuss any condition an associate believes to be a major change in her or his life circumstances and try to find some way to be flexible enough to find a way to accommodate it. Sometimes your accommodation can be the occasion for negotiating a modification you've been wanting too.

5. Think Long-Term, Not Short-Term

Perhaps it's a characteristic of our fast-paced culture to think first and only about immediate financial results for teaming-up relationships; however, it's far wiser to view your financial negotiations from a longer-term perspective because that helps all parties focus on building a relationship rather than simply "using" one another to make money. When you and your teaming-up associates develop a sincere rapport, it's far easier to be honest, frank, and open about your financial needs. And honesty builds trust, the touchstone of a true business alliance.

A long-term view ⟶ builds a strong relationship ⟶ that leads to honesty and frankness ⟶ that leads to trust needed for a true alliance.

This principle applies to any teaming-up arrangement you might make. If you are joining a networking group, make your membership decisions as if you'll be part of that organization for ten years, not just one. If you're working out an arrangement to cross-promote with another business, do so as if the relationship will become one of your best sources of business, not just this one time, but in the coming years. If you are setting up an interdependent alliance or a partnership, take the position that you're developing what will become a long-term relationship that puts you both in the major leagues.

Although you need not actually be making a long-term commitment, taking a long-term perspective during negotiations will help prevent you from getting hung up on unimportant details. Many details that seem important in the moment are truly insignificant when you like working with someone over time. For example, assume you are trying to negotiate how to split the fee from a joint project you each intend to put in roughly an equal amount of time on. Suppose your associate suggests splitting the fee 60/40 since she brought in the client but you'd prefer to split fees 50/50, because you'll be putting in half the effort. To negotiate hard for a 55/45 split to appease her would be a somewhat silly stance. After all, if your associate found the contract and has the potential to bring you additional business in the coming years, your bargaining for an extra 5 percent could be myopic when compared with the future potential benefits the relationship could bring. In fact, stalling your negotiation for an additional 5 percent could make her think that you have a greedy streak that could lead to future problems between you. And, of course, if you agree to 60/40 now, it sets a precedent for a 60/40 split later when you bring in a contract.

In finance, it's often said that a dollar today is worth more than a dollar tomorrow. However, in reality, such mottoes can steer you in the wrong direction when you are trying to negotiate a *meaningful* business relationship.

It's wiser to live by the adage that today's major crises are tomorrow's trivial events. In short, don't waste your energy holding out for a small sum of money today when your teaming-up alliance could generate a large sum of money in the future.

6. Aim for Financial Equality

Despite the fact that some business relationships can work with other than an equal financial arrangement, negotiating financial equality is usually the best way for a teaming-up arrangement *to work with the least amount of conflict.* Generally if people don't feel like financial equals, they won't put forth their best. They'll hold back.

Unfortunately, achieving *equality* can be quite subjective. So negotiations will usually go most smoothly when equality is defined in the simplest and clearest of terms instead of according to some complicated scheme or formula that varies depending on many different options, circumstances, what-ifs, and maybes. It is easiest if the agreements simply divide income to be gained equally among the participants, that is 50/50 between two people, 33.3/33.3/33.3 among three people, 25/25/25/25 among four people, and so on.

Obviously, such simple equality is not always possible or appropriate because what people invest in capital, time, expertise, and other factors may vary considerably. What's most important is that all participants feel that they're getting an equitable return on their investment. So depending on what each person will be putting into a relationship, there will be occasions when a 80/20, 70/30, 60/40 or another split will be perceived as perfectly equitable.

But our point is that, as a general principle, simple equality makes for better teaming-up relationships that have a greater chance of long-term survival with fewer chances of discord. Here are the two reasons we found this to be true.

A. Equality avoids future complications. Agreements with lots of variables or contingency clauses become difficult to follow and even to remember just what they originally represented. Too often variables and contingencies end up with people feeling confused and sometimes hurt, bitter, or dissatisfied. And as time goes by in an unequal agreement, the person with the lesser share may begin to question the fairness or wisdom of his or her decision and begin participating less and less wholeheartedly.

For example, when a person we'll call Bill teamed up with two other people, they decided to share profits and losses using a complicated formula that reflected how much money each member put in, how many hours each one worked, and the source of the projects. So on one kind of project, Bill was entitled to 33.3 percent, while on another project, he was entitled to only 15 percent; on others, he was entitled to nothing because his associates defined these clients as their own. Within no time, Bill came to feel that the rewards

he was receiving were not equal to the efforts he needed to make to participate in any of the projects, and the collaboration dissolved soon afterward.

   B. Equality affects the degree of commitment and dedication given to a
relationship. It's human nature that if we don't feel like equal participants in
an activity, we tend to give it less attention and care less about what happens.
We increasingly feel insignificant, excluded, and powerless so we act accordingly. But when we share and share alike we feel important, included, and responsible and will put forth the effort to prove it.

   Here's a case in point. One partner agreed to contribute about $8,000 to
a joint venture while the other partner contributed only a few hundred dollars. Although the two agreed to this imbalance in order to get the business
off the ground, a bitter rift developed between them later when the partners
began having cash flow problems. As generous as the moneyed partner may
have felt in the beginning, it became difficult to sustain those feelings of gen-
erosity when adversity struck and began to further deplete her funds.

   The point of this example is not that the partner who put in the $8,000
should have somehow maintained her commitment. The point is that it would
have been wiser for the partners to have contributed equally or nearly equally
in the beginning, even if that meant starting more slowly. By making an equal
financial commitment, they would have been taking an equal risk, and thereby
been equally invested in making the company succeed and equally willing to
share any pain when times got rough. Having made an equal contribution, even
if the company didn't succeed, the two partners could have parted on better
terms because neither one would have felt shortchanged or taken advantage of.

   So we recommend that you should always negotiate to achieve a simple
financial equality among all parties that makes each person's contribution of
time and money equal to her share of profits and losses.

7. Account for Nonfinancial Contributions, Too

Of course, it's unrealistic to think that it will always be possible or desirable for
everyone who works together to invest and profit equally from every joint effort.
Often the parties involved bring varying resources to the table. So, sometimes it's
necessary to create equality by having parties make different types of investments in order to negotiate a mutually rewarding agreement. But when unequal
financial contributions are involved, given human nature, it's still vital that all
parties believe that a fair relationship exists between contributions made, risks
undertaken, and potential benefits to be received. When someone either contributes less or takes more than her share of the rewards, it usually breeds resentment—and the resulting conflict can eventually destroy the relationship.

   So if at any time you begin to feel that you're getting the short end of the
stick or that you're being taken advantage of, pay attention to those feelings.
When those you're talking with express similar dissatisfaction or concern, lis-

ten carefully. Don't be tempted to dismiss such concerns or let them slide. They're all too likely to come back to bite you. It's far better to sort through such feelings during negotiations and find creative solutions that leave everyone feeling equally satisfied. Such discussions are worthwhile even if they take longer or result in your not proceeding. Sometimes when it gets down to specific details, there just isn't a match, and no one needs to feel bad about discovering this up front. It's discovering it later, after the investments have been made, that justifiably leads to bad feelings.

So during negotiations it's important for everyone involved to recognize the value of reaching an equitable agreement. Some people seem to believe they deserve to contribute less than others while deserving the same rewards. Others seem to think that if they contribute more at the outset, they deserve more *forever*, even though their associates are working just as hard as, or harder than, they are. Unfortunately, usually neither view leads to productive business relationships because at some point the others involved end up feeling cheated, unrewarded, or manipulated, so it's best not to proceed unless an equitable agreement can be reached right from the start.

One way to help find balance and parity when not everyone can make an equal financial contribution is to take nonfinancial contributions and benefits into account. In almost every teaming-up alliance, there are many noncash contributions each party can make or noncash benefits each party can get from an arrangement. Consider the following ideas for how to equalize a negotiation between participants who want to do business together but must balance their differing contributions and desires for rewards.

Give credit for extra time worked. When two people can't contribute equal amounts of cash to an endeavor, one solution is to have the person making a lesser financial investment compensate by working extra time and to assign a specific monetary value to that time contribution. The time = money approach works especially well when the disparity between contributions is small and the missing amount can easily be made up by working over the course of a few months or perhaps even a year. To implement such an arrangement, it's important to agree on a specific dollar value (per hour, per day, per week, or whatever) for the extra time to be worked and calculate how many hours are needed to equal the cash investment. Once this extra time has been factored in, the person is deemed to have been an equal contributor.

For example, assume Bob and Al want to do a cross-promotional campaign but Bob can invest $2,000 to pay for advertising fliers and brochures while Al can only afford to chip in $1,000. In this situation, they might agree that Al will do most of the work to get the materials designed and printed and they will value his time at, say, $25 an hour (or any other amount they agree upon). After Al has put in forty hours, he will have made an investment on a par with Bob's and they can split the profits from their efforts 50/50—simple equality.

Admittedly, many people still think cold cash is more valuable than do-ing extra work, and it's certainly true that if an enterprise fails, the party who has invested the cash has more to lose. This is especially true when the gap be-tween how much each person can invest is large. The most common solution to this dilemma is to decide that the person who invests more will get a greater share of the profits *forever.* The problem with this solution is that if both parties work equally hard over time to make the enterprise successful, the person getting the lesser financial reward will probably begin to feel short-changed, particularly after he or she has been working equally hard for sev-eral years. So, we recommend that if the gap between the contributions or investments is substantial, it may be wiser to find other ways to balance long-term contributions. For example, one person may begin investing more cash later or both parties may contribute cash equally from a certain point for-ward. This is often referred to as a *deferred contribution,* and it can be included in your agreement by stipulating how much each person will con-tribute and when. Another solution is to have one person continue working extra time according to a progressive profit-sharing schedule that leads to-ward parity in a future year.

For example, assume Susan and Rita are establishing a partnership, and Susan can invest $20,000 but Rita has only $5,000. They expect to put equal amounts of time into their enterprise. So, should Susan receive 80 percent of the partnership profits while Rita gets only 20 percent? That would seem un-fair and most likely lead to problems in no time. A better solution would be to have Rita invest additional money from her profits after taxes so they can reach parity within a reasonable amount of time.

Give credit for donated or loaned property. Another way to equalize contributions is to trade donated property in lieu of cash. *Property* can be any tangible item, not just real estate or land. It could include business equipment, a car, a truck, furniture, materials, collectibles, jewelry, and so on. For exam-ple, if your collaborators in a joint venture invest $4,000 each and you can't contribute that much, you might contribute your computer and laser printer valued at $4,000 to the venture. Alternatively, you and your collaborators could agree that your property need not actually be donated, but simply bor-rowed or loaned to the joint effort.

Give credit for goodwill or reputation or existing business. Another way to help equalize contributions to a teaming-up effort is to give credit for some-one's reputation in a field or for his or her established client base or contacts. For example, assume six people want to form a consortium. Ideally, it would be best if they all could invest the same amount of cash to get the consortium going, but if that's not possible, a member who is reputation rich but cash poor might be given credit for his or her reputation or ability to attract valued customers. Such recognition would also be important or even expected if one or more members are bringing in a significant amount of existing business.

Give credit for initiating the idea. Collaborations are often formed when one person originates an idea and shares it with others who help to develop and implement it. In such situations the inventor or creator might contribute less cash for having developed the idea or get a larger share of the rewards. But again, if the enterprise is successful, those getting a lesser share of the profits may begin to feel dissatisfied after having worked equally hard for several years, so the parties involved might want to negotiate right from the start a specific time when profits would be shared equally.

Sometimes the amount of work a person has done to get an idea to the stage where it is when negotiations begin can also serve to offset a financial contribution. If you've already spent several years and several hundreds or thousands of dollars developing a prototype for a product, for example, this investment of time and money can be valued as equal to the cash investment an investor or new partner contributes for taking the idea to the next step. A rough measure of the value to place on development efforts may be obtained by estimating what it would cost to have a consultant do comparable work.

Admittedly, the difficulty with all such nonfinancial contributions and rewards is how to value them in a way all participants can agree upon. A cash contribution is still clearly the easiest way to measure equality. But when this is not possible, if teaming up is still sufficiently desirable, parties can negotiate honestly and fairly to find noncash substitutes to offset imbalances in initial cash contributions. And if equity can't be achieved at the outset, it's truly worthwhile to work toward it over a period of time by giving credit for other contributions. In sum, equality, be it cash or otherwise, is the most effective glue for holding an alliance together; so it's worth the effort to make sure your negotiations result in an agreement that everyone truly believes to be equitable.

Tax Issues in Making Contributions to a Partnership

When you make a capital contribution to a partnership, there are tax consequences you should be aware of. Accountants and tax lawyers agree that partnership taxation is one of the most difficult and complex areas of the Internal Revenue Code, so it's easy to make mistakes if you don't get assistance from an accountant or lawyer who specializes in this area. Here are four things to keep in mind.

1. If you and your partners will be contributing cash, you should to do so in proportion to your percent of interest in the partnership. For example, let's say you and two other people are contributing $50,000 in cash each to a partnership that will have total capital of

$150,000 ($50,000 × 3). The best way to structure the investment would be for each of the three partners to take a one-third (33.33 percent) interest in the partnership.

2. If, for whatever reason, you and your partners decide to vary your interest in the partnership, e.g., 50–25–25, the Internal Revenue Service (IRS) would call this a "special allocation," and as such, your partnership may be open to an audit or examination. A "special allocation" is potentially any situation in which partners contribute cash to a partnership but divide profits and losses in a way that is disproportionate to their cash investment. Under the IRS regulations for partnerships, a special allocation is okay as long as it has a "substantial economic effect"—in other words, if there is a good business reason for the disproportionate share of profits and losses. Let's say, for example, that you and your two partners put in $50,000 each and you each take back one-third (33.33 percent) interest in the partnership, but you decide that because you are contributing all the equipment the partnership will be using you want to take 100 percent of the depreciation deductions on that equipment (in other words, each partner will not be taking one-third of the deduction). This is a special allocation but one that will probably have substantial economic effect because it reflects your actual contribution of the equipment. If the equipment had been contributed by all three partners, and you still wanted to take 100 percent of the depreciation deduction, that would be a special allocation that would probably not have any substantial economic effect.

3. Contributing property in lieu of cash to a partnership is also risky. To avoid adverse tax consequences, you will need to prove that the property you contribute has a value approximately equal to the value of the partnership interest you receive in return. For example, if a partnership has a total value of $100,000 and the three partners split profits and losses equally, and your contribution consisted entirely of equipment, you would have to show that the equipment had a value of $33,333 at the time you made the contribution. So, you will need to have the equipment appraised by a competent expert. Moreover, when you contribute property to a partnership, you must ask yourself the question, "Do I want the property back if the partnership breaks up or dissolves?" When property is contributed to a partnership, it is no longer owned by the partner who contributed it; rather, each partner owns a fractional share of each piece of equipment contributed, such that to get it back, you will have to buy out your partners' shares of the equipment. If you want the partnership to use the property but you will want it back when the partnership breaks up or dissolves, do not contribute the property to the partnership; instead, lease the property to the partnership for a period of years.

4. Finally, if your contribution to the partnership takes the form of "services rendered" or hours of work, instead of cash or property, be sure to consult your accountant or tax lawyer before signing on the dotted line. Under certain circumstances, the IRS will treat your partnership interest as current income and require you to pay taxes on this "phantom income" even though you received no cash from the partnership. In such situations, your lawyer should make sure the partnership is required to distribute funds to you each year in an amount at least sufficient to cover your tax liability from the phantom income.

8. Be Creative and Open in Your Negotiating Position

Many people approach a negotiation as if it were a cut-and-dried, all-or-nothing proposition. Good negotiations, however, are actually very creative processes that require the parties to brainstorm possibilities and new ideas that address the needs of everyone involved. The fact is, there is never one all-purpose "right" agreement. The best agreement always comes down to the best ideas those involved can invent to achieve their mutual goals. When all parties keep an open mind and work creatively toward their goals, there are usually many solutions to what would otherwise be irresolvable differences.

One way to make sure you approach negotiations with an open mind is to remain uncommitted to any particular position or financial demand, except that of finding some way to achieve an equitable agreement. It is wise to define beforehand any issues you believe to be nonnegotiable, but then set those aside and be attentive and listen carefully to the essential needs of the other party(ies). Someone else may present a solution you would never have thought of. Together you may come up with better solutions than you could have imagined on your own. If, at any time, you get stuck trying to hassle out the details of an agreement, take a step back and ask yourself, "What would be a creative solution to this problem?" Thinking of negotiating as a creative problem-solving process can often prevent endless hours of arguing about what may actually be trivial distinctions.

Remaining open also means being realistic about an ever-changing, fast-paced world in which today's agreement may not be worth the paper it is written on tomorrow. Business situations change rapidly, and so, unless you're at serious peril of losing a considerable investment, it's important to recognize that in the future it may be necessary to renegotiate your agreement. So throughout the negotiations, be willing to listen to your associate's needs and determine how much of a strain it would be—in the long term—for you to give him or her a break or find some way to balance giving up one thing here in exchange for getting something else there.

Adrienne Weller, the Los Angeles clothing designer we mentioned in the previous chapter, faced a serious dilemma when her partner decided she wanted to leave the partnership and pull out her investment in order to pay for her upcoming wedding. Rather than reacting harshly or precipitously, Adrienne and her partner talked over the situation for a few weeks and agreed that Adrienne would get all the profits for one season in exchange for doing all the work, while her partner would remain with the company "on leave." Meanwhile, her partner would get a loan from the partnership which she would pay back at current interest rates over the next year from her own future profits. This solution fulfilled the needs of both partners and saved the partnership from a premature breakup.

9. Agree That the Party Who Loses Any Ensuing Lawsuit Pays All Court Costs

There's no more effective way to avoid litigation than to agree up front that in the event of a lawsuit, the person who loses will be required to pay all court costs. Although this may sound harsh, the burden of paying court costs can weigh heavily on the hearts and minds of people who cannot settle their differences amicably. This agreement is also a preventive against frivolous or useless lawsuits. In the long run, it's better to recognize that most disputes are best settled privately, by agreement, rather than in public in front of a judge. Going to court consumes enormous amounts of time and money, and in many cases, neither party really wins as much as the lawyers.

This principle also reinforces once again the importance of teaming up in a cooperative, rather than in a competitive, spirit. Whereas competition usually engenders a punitive attitude that requires whoever failed or did wrong to pay for his or her mistakes, cooperation means everyone is willing to compromise even when things don't work out.

10. Don't Just Say It: Ink It

Always put financial agreements in writing. Your financial agreement should be part of whatever contract or letter agreement you develop. Such a written document, as we'll discuss next, is necessary for legal purposes, for your own documentation in the event of problems, and/or in order to fulfill government regulatory and tax requirements. So make sure that you and your teaming-up associates put into writing all the details you've agreed to for handling contributions of time, money, and/or property, your understanding of how you'll pay for any expenses and how you'll split any profits and losses. As we said in the last chapter, even the best of friends should have a contract or written record of whatever business agreements they make—especially their financial agreements, because as time passes people often remember things quite differently.

11. Don't Negotiate with Someone Who Won't Negotiate

Don't ever enter into a negotiation wanting it to work out so much that you'll do anything to reach agreement. In other words, don't get so invested in reaching an agreement that you give away the store. When you get into the trenches to negotiate a deal, you may find that someone wants to dominate, not negotiate. Some people bully, bluster, stonewall, manipulate, lie, and even hire fast-talking, mean-spirited lawyers to get what they want. If this happens, don't allow yourself to get swept up in the promise of whatever riches or rewards the joint effort could produce. Realistically, why would you want to team up with someone like this? If those you're negotiating with won't think long-term, won't strive for equality, won't give credit where credit is due, won't try to be creative and flexible, won't put it in writing, or won't agree to pay court costs for a lawsuit, well, it's time to recognize that they won't negotiate either.

In the event negotiations break down, the best solution is to back off and let the arrangement die a natural death. If your gut assessment is correct, you don't want to work with such people anyway. And if by chance your assessment is wrong and you've completely misunderstood your counterparts and mishandled the negotiations, you still probably wouldn't want to work with them because the chances of more such misunderstandings are quite high.

12. Cut Your Losses—FAST!

If, after you've reached agreement and been involved for a while, you should start feeling that your agreement isn't being and will not be lived up to, we recommend cutting your losses as fast as you can before you lose more time and money. Just as your gut feeling can guide you in picking the best people to work with, when the feeling you consistently get is that a relationship isn't working, it's likely a strong indication that it's time to end your relationship. And the sooner you do so, the more likely it can be done on a friendly note. On the other hand, the longer a negative relationship continues, the more likely it is that it will deteriorate further.

We know of many alliances in which one partner or member experienced a growing problem, but due to the momentum of their activity, they kept going and refrained from terminating the relationship. For example, a programmer set up in a partnership with a colleague who owned a small specialized software company. He thought he would own 25 percent of the business after two years of work based on the initial conversations he'd had with his partner, but he never got the promise in writing. Although he began feeling uncomfortable with the situation, he overlooked his concern, not wanting to cause trouble. Later, as the company became successful, his partner began backpedaling on their agreement while slowly transferring the assets of the company to a new one he was starting. By the end of the whole process, our friend ended up owning essentially nothing.

In another instance, a designer of custom-made pottery and quilts formed a partnership with a woman who agreed to market the business. Although the designer's partner kept balking at signing a partnership agreement, the designer proceeded to make the crafts, trusting, despite her nagging doubts, that the partnership agreement was simply a formality they'd get to eventually. Within six months, however, the two women started to disagree on how to run the business. Still, the designer kept faith that the partnership would eventually work out. Finally, after a year had passed, the marketing partner suddenly decided to form her own company, found another partner who used similar designs, and set about marketing them to the same clients.

In chapters 5 and 6, we'll discuss in more detail how to resolve the inevitable conflicts and disagreements that can arise when you team up with other people. At this point, however, it is worthwhile noting that if the legal and financial negotiations with potential associates are marred by disagreements, unpleasantness, one-upsmanship, or egocentric behavior, your relationship is only likely to get worse, not better, over time. So it's best to back out as soon as your intuition tells you to.

In fact, it seems that the experience you have with others as you go through the negotiations will closely predict the type of experience you will have working together. If a person is flexible, understanding, and willing to compromise during the negotiation phase of your business relationship, he or she will likely remain the same when tough times occur later on in business together. But if your potential partner argues, nitpicks, or plays a tough hand when the two of you are negotiating your own agreement, it is likely a harbinger of how you will be treated later on.

The 12 Principles for Negotiating Honest, Fair, and Lasting Financial Agreements

1. Make Negotiating Fun.
2. Let the "51% Rule" Prevail.
3. Don't Procrastinate About Key Points.
4. Work Toward Flexible Agreements.
5. Think Long-Term, Not Short-Term.
6. Aim for Financial Equality.
7. Account for Nonfinancial Contributions, Too.
8. Be Creative and Open in Your Negotiating Position.
9. Agree That the Party Who Loses Any Ensuing Lawsuit Pays All Court Costs.
10. Don't Just Say It: Ink It.
11. Don't Negotiate with Someone Who Won't Negotiate.
12. Cut Your Losses—FAST!

MAKING IT LEGAL:
PUTTING YOUR HANDSHAKE INTO WRITING

Many people have a fear and loathing of entering into a written contract or legal agreement of any kind. Some people don't like feeling pinned down. Others worry about having the agreement challenged at a later date. Still others feel uneasy or embarrassed about having to commit to writing what they expect from a business relationship and what seems like a simple meeting. Many people believe that if they're working with "friends" or family members, a simple handshake or a hug is sufficient to seal their bond. And finally, some people just don't want to get involved with anything that might require a lawyer or legal fees.

But if you intend to enter into a business relationship with someone—regardless of which teaming-up option you choose or for how long—you will be best served to create some type of written statement spelling out what you've agreed to. Even a simple one-sentence summary or a letter agreement is better than none at all, and often that's all that's needed. Whatever reservations or reluctance you might have about making your agreement legal, keep in mind that doing so is only truly difficult when the parties involved don't trust each other fully or don't intend to function cooperatively. When people trust one another and want to work cooperatively, it's only natural for them to want to document what they'll be counting on one another for and how they'll be proceeding.

Even if the person you're working with is your best friend or a family member, writing down your basic agreements demonstrates that you're on the same wavelength with your business association. In today's age of prenuptial and marital agreements, having a written business agreement with a spouse you'll be working with professionally may serve you well. Of course, state laws may preempt any written business agreements you may have with a spouse in the event of divorce, death, or just plain disagreement. So if you are or will be working with your spouse, you may want to consult an attorney and accountant regarding the specific laws and tax implications in your state affecting couples working in a business together.

Three Legal Reasons for Formalizing Your Agreement in Writing

Whether or not you like the idea of developing a written contract of some kind, you should be aware of three facts that could have consequences for your business if you don't.

1. *In some states, contracts are legally required for certain business situations, particularly in regard to partnerships (including general partnerships, joint ventures, limited partnerships, and limited liability companies [LLCs]).* New York, for example, requires general partnerships and LLCs to have a written partnership agreement when the partnership is intended to last for more than a year, if real property is involved, or if there are any guaranteed payments to partners. And of course, the various forms of corporations (C corporations and S corporations) all require extensive written documentation and legal submissions that effectively become a contract.

2. *Verbal agreements can be enforceable, so if you ever make a verbal commitment to do something and then you do not perform it as stated, you could be held in breach of contract.* A written contract can therefore help to

limit your liability for verbal statements you may have made thoughtlessly or unintentionally without actually realizing you'd have to live up to them.

3. Disputes among business partners seldom take place when there is nothing to fight over. The expectations people have when a business is just getting started can and usually do change when the business either takes off and becomes successful or dive-bombs into failure. The time to write the blueprint that will keep the partnership together for the long term or help you dissolve it amicably is during the "salad days," before anyone has a reason to want to enhance or diminish his or her role in the business or squeeze anyone else out.

In view of these three considerations, it's best to make the effort to consolidate your teaming-up arrangements in some type of document all parties can agree to and sign.

The Purpose of Having a Written Contract

In essence, having a written contract serves two purposes.

1. A contract is first and foremost a written record of your agreements. As much faith and trust as you might have in someone, experience shows that written records can be crucial simply because people forget what they've said, or in some cases, imagine that they've said something different from what they actually did say. Without a written agreement, each party may remember the discussions a little differently, and you can end up with a "We said this, not that!" standoff. The fact is, our memory is usually quite selective about what we think we said at an earlier time, and we tend to recall only those facts we want to recall. Even if you can't agree on an issue, you can at least agree on the larger principle you will follow and write down, or make notes on, exactly what options you were negotiating. For instance, if you are attempting to create an agreement with your associate on how to split the cost of buying an expensive computer but you don't know the actual price, you should at least write down the principle of how you both agree to split the cost. In this way, written agreements give you a reference point for future discussions and negotiations.

2. Your contract is a legal document that protects you in the event of serious disputes. As much as we try to avoid them, there are situations in which the harm caused by a collaborator can only be rectified through the legal system, and if you lack a written contract, it's usually more difficult to prove your case. With that said, however, be aware that, in the majority of cases, when parties find themselves in disagreement on issues, they terminate their teaming-up arrangement without resorting to litigation. Going to court is both expensive and time-consuming, and in many small-business matters, the potential gain is offset by the costs. Nevertheless, as any lawyer will attest, if you have to go to court, you might as well go with some evidence that supports your position.

Choosing the Form for Your Agreement

Formalizing an agreement can actually be quite straightforward, especially if you have thoroughly and openly negotiated all the pertinent details. After all, in most cases, it involves simply creating a written version of what you've presumably already agreed to verbally. So, depending on the teaming-up option you're pursuing, it can be a more or less formal document ranging from a simple letter of agreement to an official contract. Of course, at times a verbal agreement is all that's necessary.

Networking agreements, for example, are often flexible enough for a verbal agreement to be sufficient. I, Sarah, am part of a four-person networking and support group. We have no written agreement because everything we do is voluntary and there are no negative repercussions if someone doesn't participate as agreed. Similarly, mutual-referral agreements also are often verbal, but we recommend solidifying them with a confirming letter that spells out in a friendly, but clear and professional way, what you understand the agreement to be. For the reasons discussed above, all other options, including family collaborations, work best with some form of a written and signed agreement.

Your written agreement can take the form of a simple letter, a one- or two-page summary of your discussions that you create on your computer, or even a handwritten note. Although many people feel more comfortable referring to a contract as an "agreement," any legally binding agreement is a contract. Whatever form your written agreement takes, it does not need to be in complex legal language or "legalese" to be binding; normal English sentences work fine, as long as they are clearly written and unambiguous. For example, for many teaming-up options like cross-promoting, mutual referrals, interdependent alliances, satellite contracting, and consortiums, a simple short-form contract needs to contain only whatever portions of the following information are pertinent to your situation.

SHORT-FORM WRITTEN AGREEMENTS

Check off the information that's relevant to your situation.

___ Names of the parties and their independent business names
___ Date
___ General statement of what is being agreed to
___ Significant details such as:
    ___ Responsibilities each party agrees to perform
    ___ Amount of any contributions made by each party (time, money, labor, goods)
    ___ How profits/losses will be split or moneys paid
    ___ Who will manage and decide what
___ Contingencies and provisions, including:
    ___ Duration of the agreement

___ Criteria for quality of the work and how problems will be resolved
___ Why and how the agreement may be terminated
___ Whether the parties to the agreement intend to form a legal partnership or will be acting "at arm's length"
___ Whether, and to what extent, the parties may engage in other related activities

Here's a sample agreement between two independent consultants who agreed to form an interdependent alliance in which they will hire each other as much as possible for a set amount of money in an effort to further develop both of their businesses. This contract reflects the terms to which they've agreed and is a model of how you might create your own short-form agreement for a similar situation.

Agreement

John Surmack, owner of Expert Marketing International, and Sally Rafael, owner of Rafael Marketing Consultants, agree as follows.

1. That as of January 1, 199x, they are establishing an interdependent alliance in which each party will provide subcontracting work to the other on an "ad hoc" basis. Neither party makes any guarantee of the frequency or amount of such subcontracting. The relationship created by this agreement is not exclusive, and the parties are free to enter into similar business relationships with other persons.

2. That when subcontracting occurs, John will pay Sally $45 per hour or Sally will pay John $40 per hour, and time may be billed to the nearest quarter-hour increment. All bills for subcontracting work under this agreement will be paid within thirty (30) days of the invoice date. Receipts are required for miscellaneous expenses related to the project which will be reimbursed by the customer directly. Each party is responsible for its own normal cost of business (paper, printing, office supplies, etc.).

3. That each party agrees to perform the work within the time frame estimated and bill for only those hours. If a party knows the work will require additional time or will incur a delay, he or she will notify the other as soon as possible in the event contingency plans must be made with the client.

4. That each party will try to perform the work at the level of quality he or she performs all such work in his or her own business.

5. That decisions will be made by the party which obtained the contract with the customer.

6. That the alliance may terminate at any time on two weeks' notice by either party to the other.

7. That each party will not contact or solicit for business the other's clients for a period of six months following termination of this contract.

8. The parties shall act at all times as independent contractors, not as employees, and there is no intent to form a partnership, joint venture, or other legal entity.

Signature _____ Date: _____

Signature _____ Date: _____

As you can see, short-form agreements do not have to be obtuse or voluminous. In fact, the clearer and more straightforward they are, the better. This simple agreement clarifies exactly what John and Sally have decided to do through their teaming-up effort. It serves both as a record of their agreement and, if needed, as a legal document in the event of a serious lapse of cooperation between the two people that cannot be solved amicably or by simple termination of their collaboration.

Template for Agreements

Teaming-up arrangements for mutual referrals, interdependent alliances, and satellite contracting don't need to follow the detailed procedures or customs required in establishing a partnership or joint venture. Such agreements are usually tailor-made to reflect your specific situation and needs. Therefore you can create a draft of your own contract for these agreements and, if you feel you need the extra protection, have it reviewed by a lawyer.

You can find many standard business contracts, however, in template form on commercially available software programs for less than $100. Such programs contain boilerplate contractual wording for a variety of common business situations such as:

- nondisclosure
- confidentiality
- loans
- leases
- rentals
- buy and sell agreements

- employment contracts
- partnerships and joint ventures

and many others. Using these templates is usually quite easy. You simply import a document into your word processor and then fill in the blanks with the specific information for your situation, such as the names of the parties, addresses, dates, dollar amounts, and so on. These documents are generally considered legally valid in most states. However, because templates are general forms that are not tailored to the legal requirements of a particular state or to a particular business situation, be careful about using such "off the shelf" agreements without having them reviewed by a competent lawyer who specializes in small-business agreements. Attorney Cliff Ennico of Connecticut tells us that in fifteen years of drafting contracts for small-business clients, he has never been able to take a template form, fill in the blanks, and present it to a client as a finished product. Each template usually requires modifications tailored to your state or your specific needs.

AGREEMENTS FOR PARTNERSHIPS AND JOINT VENTURES

If you're forming a partnership or entering into a joint venture, having a written agreement is not only a good idea, it's absolutely essential for several reasons. First, on the practical level, partnerships and joint ventures are more complex than other ways of teaming up. Each party is making a more binding and interdependent commitment, often including an investment of money and extensive time. They take us beyond simply supporting or enhancing each other's independent activities. In essence a "wedding" is taking place between the partners, in which they share in the profits and losses of the business regardless of their individual contribution to those profits and losses. If you and your partner agree to split profits and losses 50/50, and you bring in 90 percent of the partnership's business during the first year, you still split that year's profits 50/50. Whereas in more informal relationships if your efforts don't succeed, there's usually not much lost and dissolving them is easy, if a partnership or joint venture doesn't work out, it can be quite disruptive to all involved and dissolving it takes time and sometimes money.

Second, a partnership is actually a specific form of business ownership that has binding legal and financial consequences, just as a sole proprietorship or a corporation does, in the eyes of the legal system and the IRS. These legal and tax consequences are largely ruled by the Uniform Partnership Act (UPA), a general code that has been adopted with small modifications in nearly all states (except Louisiana). In the absence of a written partnership

agreement, the UPA dictates much about how partnerships function. For example, the UPA obligates each participant in a partnership to certain rights
and responsibilities, such as:

- Each partner is personally liable for all debts and legal obligations of
  the partnership. If the partnership cannot pay, each partner must pay
  out of his or her own pocket. In addition, the partner's liability is not
  limited to his or her percentage share of the profits and losses, and it
  extends to his or her personal assets (such as his or her house, bank accounts, and investment portfolios) as well as to business assets.
- Each partner has the power to represent and bind the entire partnership in normal business matters.
- Each partner owes loyalty to the partnership and, technically speaking,
  cannot engage in any activity that conflicts with the partnership's business.

Furthermore, the IRS also requires partnerships to follow certain regulations in their accounting and tax-reporting procedures, such as:

- The partnership must obtain an EIN (Employer Identification Number)
  from the IRS (Form SS-4), or use the social security number of one of
  the participants.
- The partnership must file its own "information" tax return (Form 1065)
  showing income, deductions, and other information, and each partner
  must report his or her own percentage share of the profit or loss on his
  or her own tax return. Since a partnership itself does not pay taxes on
  its earnings, the partnership tax return (Form 1065) is strictly to inform
  the IRS about the partnership's business activities and how expenses,
  profits, losses, and other deductions are proportioned among the partners. Each partner must then report on his or her own tax return the
  amount of earnings, losses, and deductions he or she has from the partnership. The partnership must deliver to each partner a statement on
  Form K-1 of the partner's percentage share of profit and loss, against
  which the IRS will compare the partner's statement on his or her Form
  1040.
- For tax purposes, the partnership must track all contributions of cash,
  equipment, or property by each partner, as well as the payment of expenses, charitable contributions, and many other business deductions
  that can only be taken by each individual partner.

In view of these legal and tax ramifications, not having a written partnership agreement is a risky proposition that can jeopardize your personal
and financial well-being. Without a written partnership document, any verbal

agreements you have made may be overridden by the standard provisions of the Uniform Partnership Act, and if you did not have an agreement covering everything that you needed to, such as how losses would be divided, you could be jeopardizing more than you bargained for.

Your own agreement can spell out clearly what you and your partners have determined about the financing and management of your enterprise. You can use the following checklist to identify which of these decisions might apply to you.

___ Division of profits and losses
___ Authority of each partner to borrow
___ Authority of each partner to make decisions
___ Management duties of each partner
___ Ability and timing of partners to withdraw profits
___ Methods in which disputes will be resolved
___ Method for termination or buyout of a partner

Note that your own partnership agreement cannot negate the personal liability requirements of a partnership—since this fact is an implicit aspect of being a partnership as opposed to a corporation—but you can agree that if one partner pays more than his or her fair share of the partnership's debts and obligations at any time, the other partners will reimburse the partner's over-payment so that each partner ends up paying only his percentage share. Lawyers call this a "contribution and indemnity clause," and it's a good idea.

These are all matters you need to resolve in negotiating your partnership agreement, but writing them down provides a tangible manifestation of your agreements and becomes the means of amicably resolving disputes, misunderstandings, or difficulties that arise. You can either write your own agreement or you can use one of the many standard partnership agreements that are available in template form in books or on software. (See Resources at the end of this chapter for references.)

If you prefer to use a template, the basic clauses are all set up for you and you simply fill in the details for your partnership, print it out, and have each participant sign the document. Be sure each person gets an original copy of the agreement. Such documents developed from software are usually legal and binding in every state, but as mentioned above, they are not necessarily tailored to the legal requirements of a particular state. To be sure that a template form will work in your particular situation, it is best to have it reviewed by a competent lawyer before you show it to your prospective partner(s).

On the other hand, writing your own partnership agreement is not as complicated as it may seem. Preparing your own tailor-made agreement can sometimes serve you better and requires developing a deeper understanding of what you and your partners must comply with for the proper operation of your business. If you do write your own agreement, you should have a draft reviewed by a lawyer. The fee you pay for this may be less because you've already done the work to cover most of the fundamental issues.

Here's an overview of seventeen major elements of a partnership agreement with standard clauses that you can modify to suit your situation.

Standard Elements of a Partnership Agreement

Opening: The title on your contract, centered at the top of the page, should read, *"Partnership Agreement,"* followed by the following opening clause:

"This Partnership Agreement is entered into and effective as of [date] by [names of partners], the partners."

This statement indicates who will be the parties to the agreement and if you are acting individually or as a business or corporation. If you are doing business under a trade name and you are a sole proprietor, you should fill in your name as follows: "Your Name d/b/a Your Business Name." For example, John Doe who operates as On-Target Consulting would fill in "John Doe d/b/a On-Target Consulting" ("d/b/a" stands for "doing business as").

The agreement should then consist of the following numbered items:

I. Name Clause
Example: The name of the partnership shall be: _____
The agreement needs to state the name of the partnership entity. If a partner is being added to an existing business, you may very well continue to use the existing business's name. If you are using a new name, don't forget to check on the legal availability of your business name to be sure you are not encroaching on any previously taken trademark or business name in your county or state. A name may be trademarked on the national level, too, so be sure to do a thorough search to make sure you have the right to use the name you've selected. Note that a partnership cannot use the term "Inc." or "Ltd.," as if to suggest it is incorporated or operating as a corporation. You must file your name with your state's secretary of state and/or county government if it is a "fictitious" business name, that is, a name that differs from your own real names.

II. Term Clause
Example: The partnership shall last until it is dissolved by all partners, or a partner leaves for any reason, including death [or your own wording].
Unless your contract specifically states how long your agreement lasts, the partnership will continue until a partner leaves or dies. So, if you're creating a short-term partnership or joint venture, your clause should include a specific final date when the partnership will end.

III. The Purpose Clause
Example: The purpose of our partnership is to provide high-quality [fill

in whatever your business is, such as consulting, marketing, writing, etc.] services to companies primarily in southern California but also nationally as we are able to obtain contracts.

The purpose of this clause is to state simply the main business of your partnership. This statement can be brief, but its value is to be sure you and your partners agree on what your true mission or focus is. Not surprisingly, many partnerships actually have difficulty describing their main business because each partner conceives of it somewhat differently. This clause is therefore an opportunity, like your mission statement, to be sure you are all on the same wavelength as to what your business is established to provide.

IV. Contributions Clause

Example: The initial capital contribution of each partner shall consist of cash in the following amounts:

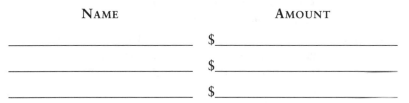

NAME	AMOUNT
_____	$_____
_____	$_____
_____	$_____

In most simple partnerships, each partner contributes an equal amount of cash to "capitalize" (fund) the start-up costs of the partnership. These contributions become what is called a "capital account." Each partner has a capital account reflecting his or her investment in the partnership (which could also be, in addition to cash, real property, personal property, or intangible "intellectual" property such as patents, trademarks, or copyrights). As the partnership earns profits, each partner's capital account increases by the dollar amount he or she gets from the profits (whether or not they are actually distributed). If the partnership incurs losses, each partner's share is subtracted from his or her account. When the partnership files its "information" tax return for the year, the IRS then knows how much income each partner will report on his or her personal tax return.

As we discussed, in some partnerships, the partners do not contribute equally. One partner may contribute more cash than others, or someone may contribute goods or labor rather than money. (Loans made by a partner to the partnership, which are repaid with interest over time, are not generally considered contributions to a partnership's capital.) When these arrangements are made, the agreement must include additional clauses that recognize these contributions, such as:

Example of contribution of labor: To equalize the contributions, [name] shall contribute [#] of additional hours of labor valued at $_ per hour until the amount equals the cash contributions of the other partners.

Example of contribution of goods or property: [Name of partner] shall contribute property valued at $_____ and consisting of _____ by [date].

These special arrangements can have tax consequences for you, so you will want to consult an accountant before finalizing them.

V. Sharing of Profits/Losses Clause

Example: The partners shall share profits and losses as follows:

NAME	PERCENTAGE
_____	%_____
_____	%_____
_____	%_____

Profits shall be distributed in cash to the partners, in proportion to their respective percentages in the partnership 's profits shown above, and are to be paid monthly [or whatever time period you desire].

In many partnerships, the partners make equal contributions to the partnership and share equally in profits or losses. In others, they make different contributions of capital and share in profits and losses in the same percentage as their capital contribution. For example, if one person supplies $30,000 and another supplies $10,000, they would share 75/25.

Important note: Unless it's otherwise stated in your partnership agreement, the Uniform Partnership Act provides that all partners share profits and losses *equally.* If your agreement only refers to how you will share profits, but fails to mention how you will share losses, the UPA requires that you share losses in the same percentage as you share profits. This could come as a surprise to you if, in your agreement, you accidentally forgot to cover both profits *and* losses. It is therefore worthwhile to include a specific clause regarding the sharing of profits and losses in your agreement. If you and your partner(s) decide to share profits one way and losses another way (assuming your tax accountant also agrees), your agreement must express the exact percentage each person will share in, e.g., profits are shared 60/40, losses are shared 50/50. Many partnerships agree to share losses equally if they all work the same amount in the enterprise, even though they may have agreed to share profits unequally to reflect their different contributions of capital.

VI. Salary Clause

Example: No partners will be entitled to a salary, except by unanimous written consent of all partners.

Note that a salary means that one partner will get paid regardless of whether the business is profitable. When all partners work equally in the enterprise and share profits either equally or in the percentages established, there is usually no need to pay salaries if the business profits are paid out regularly. In some cases, however, the partners decide that one partner will receive a salary while the others don't, usually because that person works more hours than the other partners. If so, the salary must be reasonable relative to your industry, so the IRS won't question whether the salary is actually a withdrawal of profits. If a salary is paid, the clause might read:

Example: Partner [name] will be entitled to a salary of [amount] to be paid [weekly, monthly, etc.]

If paying a partner a salary creates a loss, the loss will be shared by all the partners. Another approach is to agree to a "draw" by one of the partners. Because a draw is an advance against future distributions of a partnership's profits, if earnings do not cover the amount of the draw, it is a debt owed to the partnership.

VII. Management Clause

Example: All partners will participate in management decisions, which must be made by unanimous agreement.

The simplest way to handle management in a partnership is to allow all partners to be involved in management decisions. Alternatively, some partnerships make a distinction between major and minor decisions based on the dollar amount to be spent or the substance of the decision. (For example, "Joe will make all marketing and product development decisions for the Partnership, while Carole will be responsible for all financial, tax, and accounting matters.") However, when such distinctions are made, the agreement must specify clearly the definition of major versus minor decisions and who is entitled to make each category of decisions.

Note that a partner who is not truly involved in the business or management decisions may be considered by the IRS to be not materially participating in the partnership or a *passive* partner. As a result, his or her income from the partnership will be considered passive (investment) income, which is subject to different tax regulations than active income. If your partnership involves a person who is essentially an investor, consult an accountant and a lawyer. You may want to organize your partnership as a "limited" partnership instead of a "general" partnership.

VIII. Responsibilities Clause

Example: Each partner shall participate in the business by working in the manner stated below:

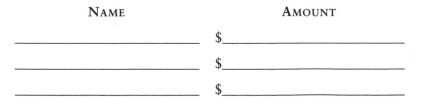

NAME	AMOUNT
_____	$_____
_____	$_____
_____	$_____

If the partners intend to function independently and perform different tasks, the partnership agreement should specify what each partner's general responsibility will be. Alternatively, if the partners intend to have everyone involved in all aspects of the business, the clause might read:

Example: All partners shall be involved and participate in the operation of the business.

IX. Working Hours, Vacations, and Holidays Clause

Example: Each partner shall work [#] hours per week, and be entitled to [#] weeks [paid/unpaid] vacation per year and [#] holidays.

While this clause may seem unnecessary among trusting partners, it's not uncommon as the years go by for one partner to believe another is not working as long or hard as he or she is. Such a perception can erode the trust and friendship needed to keep a partnership functioning smoothly. Although including a clause like this can't help with the perceptions of how hard someone is or isn't working, at least it does lay out the number of hours each person is expected to work. The clause also identifies how many vacation weeks and holidays each person is entitled to.

X. Accounting Clause

Example: Proper and complete books of account shall be kept at the partnership's principal place of business and shall be open for inspection by any partner during regular business hours.

In addition, the partnership's profit or loss for each fiscal year shall be determined by a public accountant, [specify who, if you know what accountant you will use], who will prepare federal, state, and local returns, including but not limited to sales and use tax returns.

These clauses are useful to include so that it's clear among the partners that proper and open accounting is required out of fairness to all partners. Having an independent professional accountant oversee your books and prepare your taxes is also an important safeguard against any partner tampering with the books, purposely or inadvertently.

XI. Expenses Clause

Example: The partners shall individually and personally assume and pay all expenses associated with the normal business activities of the partnership, except for out-of-town travel including airfare, hotels, and meals, which expenses shall be reimbursable by the partnership.

The partnership may choose to reimburse or not reimburse normal business expenses in any way the partners decide. Reimbursed expenses may be deducted by the partnership as business expenses, assuming proper documentation, such as receipts, are provided. Expenses not reimbursed to a partner may be deducted by the partner on his or her personal tax return. However, there are a number of specific conditions and regulations that the

IRS applies to the deductibility of business expenses, so you may wish to consult an accountant to clarify the best choice for your partnership to make on reimbursing business expenses.

XII. Check-Signing Authority Clause
Example: No partner shall disburse funds or sign checks for an amount greater than [$ amount] without prior approval by all partners.

Most partnership agreements indicate that either all partners must sign checks (particularly if there are only two partners) or that checks may be signed by any partner up to a given amount, above which more than one signature is required. You can modify this clause to best suit your needs, but agreeing upon it in advance is one way to protect yourself from having to assume responsibility for debts that you did not and would not assume. Note, however, you will still be legally liable for unauthorized expenditures incurred by your partner(s).

XIII. Borrowing Clause
Example: No partner may borrow money on behalf of the partnership without prior written consent of all partners.

The purpose and value of this clause is self-evident. It does happen! But, once again, you will still be legally liable even for unauthorized loans obtained by your partner(s) ostensibly for the partnership.

XIV: Meetings Clause
Example: To discuss matters of general and specific interest to the partnership, the partners shall meet [specify time period such as weekly, monthly, etc.] or at such times as agreed to by the partners.

This clause specifies that the partnership will have a regular schedule of meetings. The clause can be useful in the event of a recalcitrant partner who never seems to have time to meet with others to discuss the business of the partnership. Such regularly scheduled meetings can also serve the purpose of providing for the progress meetings we suggest in chapter 6 on page 309.

XV. Ownership of Business Assets Clause
Example: All trade secrets used by or developed by the partnership, as well as any ideas pertaining to partnership business or copyrights in the partnership name shall remain the property of the partnership. The partnership business name [identify name] shall also be partnership property. In the event that a partner departs for any reason whatsoever, the control and ownership of the business name shall remain with the partnership.

This clause is important to protect you and your partner(s) from a problem like that of one person we know whose partner took the concepts developed from their partnership and used them to start her own training business. In other words, this clause protects the assets of the partnership in a continuous manner. Of course, you can also modify the example used above if you agree that one partner will retain ownership of the business name or any ideas, copyrights, etc. This would be important when one partner, more than the others, has developed, already owns, or founded the partnership and conceived of the business name and proprietary material. All such ownership issues, of course, should be discussed thoroughly in negotiating the partnership agreement, so that no confusion develops later as to who owns what, or who can take what assets with them should the partnership end.

This clause applies to tangible assets as well and can prevent problems like those one dog breeder experienced when her new partner was tragically killed in an auto accident en route from a dog show. Because they had no business asset clause, all assets of the partnership including several dozen dogs were frozen in probate and the remaining partner could not sell a litter of puppies until probate closed, after which the dogs were too old to obtain a profitable price. The untimely death of the partner forestalled the continuation of the breeder's business for over a year.

XVI. Dissolution or Buyout Clause

Example: If any partner leaves the partnership for any reason, he or she (or his or her estate) shall be obligated to sell his or her interest in the partnership to the remaining partner (partners), who may buy that interest at a price determined by [specify method such as adjusted book value, appraisal by an independent third party (if possible, name this party), a formula that might be a multiple of sales, net income, gross revenue, or the death benefit payable from life insurance to the partnership].

Most partnerships end in an unexpected manner for any number of reasons. Sometimes the partners don't get along; other times, a partner moves, wants to start a different business, is involved in an accident, or dies. So, preplanning for the dissolution of your partnership is an important element of the contract. But unfortunately this step is often overlooked, and how to end the partnership becomes a matter of contention when someone wants out or everyone agrees to dissolve the relationship.

A dissolution clause serves two purposes: First, it protects the remaining partners from not knowing what to do with the business or whom they might end up working with if a partner dies and leaves her or his share of the partnership to an estate. A clear buyout provision is particularly crucial when there are only two partners and the partnership essentially ends when one partner decides to leave. Second, it also helps the departing partner by clearly indicating how much money he or she is entitled to upon leaving, or at least by what method the company's value will be determined. As with many financial matters, you may wish to consult an accountant in creating this clause to reflect common valuation methods and tax issues. Each valuation method is based on a different concept of how much a business is worth, and so getting professional advice in this area is strongly suggested if you have no background in such financial concepts.

Keep in mind that when a partner dies, files for bankruptcy protection, or otherwise withdraws from the partnership, the partnership technically dissolves and ceases to exist as a matter of law. The dissolution clause should contain a mechanism by which the surviving or remaining partners can "revive" the partnership and continue in business by formal vote within a specified number of days after the partnership's dissolution. Whether a revived partnership can continue to use the name of the deceased or withdrawn partner varies from state to state.

A Formula for a Good Buyout Clause

Los Angeles Attorney Les Klinger urged us to stress the importance of incorporating a buy-out mechanism into partnership agreements. Often there are situations in which the parties don't get along but both want to keep the business. Some agreements will provide that the partner willing to pay the most—the highest bidder—gets to buy out the other. Les suggested that a fairer mechanism is that one partner be allowed to make an offer to buy the business from the other, but the other partner can then either accept the offer or buy the first partner out for the same price he or she was offered.

However you write your clause, be sure you have a way to resolve a buyout stalemate in the event you cannot settle your personal differences.

XVII. General Provisions
Examples:

   1. The partners have formed this agreement under the laws of the State of _____.

   2. This agreement contains the entire understanding of the partners regarding their rights and duties in the partnership. Any alleged oral representations or modifications shall be of no effect unless contained in a subsequent written modification to this agreement signed by all partners.

   3. Any attached sheet or document shall be regarded as fully contained in this Agreement.

   4. This Agreement shall be binding on and for the benefit of the respective successors, inheritors, assigns, and personal representatives of the partners, except to the extent of any contrary provision in this Agreement.

   5. If any term, provision, or condition of this Agreement is held by a court to be invalid, void, or unenforceable, the rest of the Agreement shall re-

main in full force and effect and shall in no way be affected, impaired, and invalidated.

Most contracts end with a number of boilerplate clauses such as the five listed above. You can either use these clauses or modify them as needed for your situation.

The seventeen clauses discussed can serve as the basis for you to create a solid partnership agreement for a partnership involving from two to five people. The box that follows shows a hypothetical partnership agreement using these clauses or modifications of them suited to two people who are forming a desktop publishing partnership. As with all template forms, after making your best effort to tailor the following hypothetical agreement to your business situation, it is still worthwhile to engage an attorney to assist you in finalizing your agreement.

Sample Partnership Agreement

Partnership Agreement

"This Partnership Agreement is entered into and effective as of———, 199x, by Jack Hogan and Ron Goldsman, the partners."

I. Name

The name of the partnership shall be "Lightning Publishing Services."

II. Term

The partnership shall last until it is dissolved by both partners, or a partner leaves for any reason, including death.

III. Purpose

The purpose of the partnership is to provide high-quality desktop publishing services including typesetting, graphic design, scanning, and printing to companies primarily in western Massachusetts but also statewide or nationally as the partners are able to obtain contracts.

IV. Contributions

    Example: The initial capital contribution of each partner shall consist of cash in the following amounts:

Name	Amount
Jack Hogan	$7,000
Ron Goldsman	$12,000

In addition, Jack Hogan shall contribute property valued at $5,000 consisting of a computer and laser printer by ———, 199x.

V. Sharing of Profits/Losses

The partners shall share profits and losses equally. The partners are entitled to draw from expected partnership profits, the amount of which will be determined by a vote of the partners on the first business day of each month based on the prior month's sales vs. expenses.

VI. Salary

No partners will be entitled to a salary, except by unanimous written consent of all partners.

VII. Management

Both partners will participate in management decisions, which must be made by unanimous agreement.

VIII. Responsibilities

Each partner shall participate in the business by working in the manner stated below:

Name	Type of Work
Jack Hogan	Sales/marketing and graphic design work
Ron Goldsman	Typesetting, proofing, scanning

IX. Working Hours, Vacations, and Holidays

Each partner shall work 45 hours per week, and be entitled to 3 weeks unpaid vacation per year and 10 holidays.

X. Accounting

Proper and complete books of account shall be kept at the partnership's principal place of business and shall be open for inspection by any partner during regular business hours.

In addition, the partnership's profit or loss for each fiscal year shall be determined by a certified public accountant, who, in accordance with generally accepted accounting principles, will prepare a federal income tax return and state return to be filed by the partnership for that year.

XI. Expenses

The partners shall individually and personally assume and pay all expenses associated with the normal business activities of the partnership, except for out-of-town travel including airfare, hotels, and meals, which expenses shall be reimbursable by the partnership with proper receipts.

XII. Check-Signing Authority

Neither partner shall disburse funds or sign checks for an amount greater than $200 without prior approval by the other partner. Only checks for amounts less than $200 made out to a third party may be signed by either partner alone.

XIII. Borrowing

Neither partner may borrow money on behalf of the partnership without prior written consent of the other partner.

XIV. Meetings

To discuss matters of general and specific interest to the partnership, the partners shall meet on the first business day of each month and at such other times as agreed to by the partners.

XV. Ownership of Business Assets

All trade secrets used by or developed by the partnership, as well as any ideas pertaining to partnership business or copyrights in the partnership name shall remain property of the partnership. The partnership business name, Lightning Publishing Services, shall also be partnership property. In the event that either partner departs for any reason whatsoever, the control and ownership of the business name shall belong to Jack Hogan.

XVI. Dissolution or Buyout

If any partner leaves the partnership for any reason, he (or his estate) shall be obligated to sell his interest in the partnership to the remaining partner), who may buy that interest at a price determined by one-half the prior fiscal year's net profit.

XVII. General Provisions

[This section contains the usual boilerplate clauses shown above.]

Additional Partnership Agreement Issues

Depending on your situation, you may need to substantially modify the seventeen major clauses in your partnership agreement or add more clauses to cover other issues regarding the capitalization and management of your partnership. Some partnership agreements grow to dozens of pages, taking into account more complicated arrangements between the partners such as:

- Contributions of appreciated property
- Deferred contributions

- Loans made by a partner to the partnership
- Interest to be paid on a loan to the partnership
- Contributions of intellectual property
- Failure of a partner to make a contribution
- Additional contribution requirements
- Partner draws and complex formulas for salaries
- Unequal sharing of profits versus losses
- Required retention of profits for reinvestment
- Unequal management powers
- Authority to borrow money
- Record keeping
- Sick leave
- Permitted outside business activities
- Authority of a managing partner
- Addition of a new partner
- Amending the partnership agreement
- Notices of withdrawal
- Conflicts regarding buyouts
- Varying buyout methods
- Insurance
- Effect of a divorce on the partnership agreement
- Payments to departing partners
- Expulsion of a partner
- Estate-planning issues

If you have few additions to the standard partnership agreement, you're better off creating your own draft of an agreement either by using a commercial template, or by consulting books such as *The Partnership Book* from Nolo Press, which contains extensive advice about writing your own agreements. Then you can have a lawyer review your draft document and you may be able to save several hundred dollars in legal fees.

But if your partnership is anything more complicated than an arrangement between two or three people in which each person will fully participate in the business and contribute and share equally in profits/losses, you'll probably want to seek the counsel of a lawyer and an accountant in developing your agreement. In addition, if your partnership includes members who are themselves companies, partnerships, or corporations, the level of complexity and liability increases and so professional advice is also recommended.

AGREEMENTS FOR LIMITED PARTNERSHIPS, CORPORATIONS, LLCs, AND LLPs

Most of the teaming-up arrangements discussed in this book involve two or more sole proprietorships working together in an informal or formal manner, or people involved in a legally established partnership arrangement. However, there are four other options that you may wish to explore in developing an alliance with other people or companies: limited partnerships, C corporations, S corporations, Limited Liability Companies (LLCs), and Limited Liability Partnerships (LLPs). The following is a description of these options and how to pursue them.

Limited Partnerships

A limited partnership is one in which there are two classes of participants: general partners and limited partners. A general partner actually runs the business and technically can be a single individual, two people, a partnership, or even a corporation. As with a general partnership like those described above, the general partners have unlimited liability for business losses and debts, even extending to their personal property if the partnership cannot pay off the debts.

Limited partners are basically investors. They're liable for business debts and losses only to the extent of their investment. Limited partners cannot be involved in the management or day-to-day operation of the business, however. Their income is strictly passive and is treated differently for tax purposes, particularly in regard to the deductibility of business losses on their personal tax returns. Typically, limited partners are offered a specific return on their investment, such as a fixed amount each year or a percentage of the profits.

Limited partnerships are useful when a sole proprietor or partnership needs capital but doesn't want to share the decision-making authority with investors or when an investor has cash to contribute but no time to participate as a general partner. Because they can't participate in the management of the company, limited partners are only willing to invest their money in a partnership when they have a high level of faith in the business acumen of the general partner(s).

Note, however, that limited partnerships involve a greater degree of legal complexity. They are essentially offering the equivalent of a stock or security for sale, and so sales of interest in limited partnerships are governed by a number of federal and state securities laws. In addition, limited partnerships may be required to file a registration certificate listing the names and addresses of all general partners, particularly in regulated businesses such as those involving a liquor license.

An alternative to starting a limited partnership would be to create a general partnership in which the investor plays an active, although small, role in the operation of the business while receiving a larger share of the profits for a fixed term. Of course, with this arrangement, the investing partner's liability is not limited, which makes his or her participation more risky. But such an arrangement does avoid the legal hassles of forming a limited partnership.

We discuss limited partnerships in greater detail in chapter 8 in the context of finding investors and getting money *after* your business has become established and already has some level of success.

C Corporations

Sometimes forming a C corporation can be a better alternative for working than a partnership, particularly if your business involves a high-risk activity that might subject you to many lawsuits or claims. Unlike a partnership in which the partners have unlimited personal liability, an adequately capitalized corporation is considered a separate legal entity from its owners. This means that the owners are protected in their liability from debts and obligations, as long as the corporation was created with a relatively reasonable amount of cash (capital) to operate as a bona fide business. If not, in the event of a lawsuit, a court could declare the corporation insufficiently capitalized to cover reasonable liabilities, and the "corporate veil" can be pierced, making the owners personally liable for the corporation's debts.

Becoming a C corporation is not necessarily a good choice for every business for several reasons. First, incorporation can be more expensive to create than a simple partnership and usually involves much more paperwork. In every state, you must file articles of incorporation with your secretary of state or a corporations commissioner. You must then choose your directors who are responsible for the overall supervision of the business and your officers (CEO, president, vice president, treasurer, and secretary) who are responsible for the day-to-day operations. Finally, you must also create corporate bylaws, which cover the same types of detailed provisions found in a partnership agreement. Of course, if your corporation involves just one or two people, these steps are easy, but filing all the documents usually involves paying a fee to the state government that can range from a few hundred dollars to more than $1,000, plus legal fees that can range from $1,000 to $2,500, depending on the "bells and whistles" you choose to build into your incorporation documents. Many lawyers charge flat fees for preparing basic incorporation documents, but lawyers may be reluctant to fix their fees for preparing agreements that may require time-consuming negotiation and multiple drafts (such as "shareholders' agreements" or buy-sell agreements by which the shareholders of a closely held corporation agree to restrict the transfer of their stock to third parties).

Although incorporation kits are available that allow you to perform the paperwork of incorporating yourself and you can even incorporate from your home using a service offered on the Internet, CompuServe, and other on-line services, it is nonetheless advisable that you also hire a lawyer experienced in small-business law to be sure you are making the best choices for your situation. All in all, your fees to incorporate can mount up to $2,000 to $5,000 depending on which state you live in. Contrary to popular belief, it is not necessarily wise to incorporate in Delaware or Nevada. You may still need to pay corporate taxes in your own state, and you will likely need to hire a service company to maintain an office and file papers for you in Delaware or Nevada, which can cost several hundred dollars a year.

Second, incorporating no longer offers some of the tax advantages it did in the past. In fact, some corporate tax rates, particularly for personal service corporations, are higher than individual tax rates. Furthermore, profits from C corporations are taxed twice: the corporation is taxed first on its profits, and stockholders are then taxed again on their personal tax returns. The double-taxation drawback is moot, however, for many small corporations in which the owners are effectively the employees. The IRS allows corporations to pay out their profits as salaries to employee/owners, rather than as stock dividends, as long as the salaries are reasonable in that industry. These salary payouts therefore become deductible corporate expenses against profits on the corporation's tax return, and so all owner/employees effectively pay taxes only once on their salaries, just as any salaried person does.

Despite these two drawbacks, incorporating can still be useful in some teaming-up situations, especially when the new enterprise is expected to grow to a considerable size. By incorporating, you and your teaming-up partner gain the following benefits.

- A corporation has an "eternal" life beyond those of its shareholders. If an owner departs or dies, the corporate entity continues to exist. In contrast, a general partnership theoretically ends when a partner leaves or dies.
- Corporate ownership is more easily transferable through the sale of stock than by selling an interest in a partnership. This means new shareholders can be added if your company grows.
- Finally, being incorporated adds a certain feeling of substance to a small business. Some people feel that they're taken more seriously when they have the term "Inc." after their name.

S Corporations

An S corporation is in some ways like a C corporation but is taxed like a partnership. While a C corporation as an entity must pay taxes on its profits, an S corporation is generally not liable for federal income tax. Instead, like a partnership, profits from an S corporation "flow through" to the owners and are taxed only on the owners' personal income tax returns along with their other income.

The value of forming an S corporation instead of a partnership is that, like a C corporation, an S corporation offers advantages not available to partnerships. First, owners of an S corporation may limit their personal liability, which many people prefer over the unlimited personal liability of a partnership. Second, losses from an S corporation are deductible on your personal return but only to the extent you have invested in the S corporation and have personally guaranteed its debts. This can be helpful if the S corporation is expected to lose money for a few years before making a profit. Third, owners of an S corporation can establish tax-deductible pension plans or profit-sharing plans for themselves, whereas partnerships can only deduct these plans for employees, not for owners.

As the popular saying goes, however, there is no "free lunch." S corporations must follow many specific government and IRS regulations, and setting up one correctly will cost as much or more as setting up a C corporation. You need to file incorporation papers, select a board of directors and officers, write your bylaws, and so on.

S corporations are subject to a number of legal restrictions that, if not complied with strictly, can cause you to lose the benefit of "flow through" taxation. For example, the shareholders of an S corporation must be natural persons (i.e., not partnerships or corporations) and either U.S. citizens or permanent resident aliens (holders of the "green card"), an S corporation cannot have more than thirty-five shareholders, an S corporation can have only one class of stock (so, for example, you cannot have an S corporation with preferred and common stock), and so forth. These restrictions can be traps for the unwary, so you may be required to work closely with a legal expert in order to operate an S corporation.

Furthermore, some states, such as California, tax corporate income of an S corporation just like that of a C corporation. Of course, state tax rates are lower than federal rates. There are also many intricate tax laws regarding the transfer of profits from a C corporation to an S corporation, so if you do decide upon incorporating, be sure to decide from the outset which type of corporation, C or S, you wish to organize.

LLCs

Limited Liability Companies (LLCs) are a relatively new form of business that more or less merges the benefits of general partnerships and S corporations. LLCs have been accepted as legal business forms in virtually all states as of this writing. The advantages of an LLC are that they offer limited liability for all participants while allowing for the flow through of income and deductions to the owners rather than facing the double taxation of C corporations. Similarly LLCs are easy to operate, requiring only that the partners (called "members" in LLC language) sign a simple "operating agreement," which is similar to a partnership agreement. In fact, many partnerships that convert to LLC status simply change the name on their existing agreement from "partnership agreement" to "operating agreement," and this can work in many states. However, LLCs must follow many federal and state-specific legal and tax regulations, most of which require the assistance of an accountant and a lawyer to correctly understand and apply to your situation.

Like other options, LLCs have both benefits and drawbacks for a closely held small or home-based business. On the positive side, LLCs can be a good alternative to a limited partnership. The person who would have been the "general partner" gains because he or she has limited liability, and the "limited partner" (i.e., passive investor) gains because he or she may participate in the day-to-day management of the company. This means that a small business that becomes an LLC instead of a limited partnership can conceivably attract the capital and expertise of an investor while offering limited liability for all participants. On the negative side, LLCs must involve at least two members, whereas corporations can be formed by a single individual. LLCs may not be available for certain types of businesses (such as in California where professionals and people who are licensed by the Business and Professions Code are not eligible). LLCs may also be subject to high state taxes and registration fees. All in all, as Los Angeles CPA Steve Salant says, depending on the state you live in, forming an LLC can be more trouble than it's worth.

LLPs

In a growing number of states, there is a fifth alternative called the limited liability partnership or LLP. This is an entity designed primarily for professional service firms that cannot become LLCs or that have offices in several states. In general, an LLP is a partnership in which the partners have unlimited liability for the debts and obligations of the partnership (as in a general partnership) but enjoy some limited liability for the negligence or professional malpractice of the other partners of the partnership. In virtually all states, a professional such as a doctor, lawyer, or accountant is prohibited from limiting liability for his or her own professional malpractice.

Obviously we cannot cover all the intricacies of forming a limited partnership, a C or S corporation, or an LLC or LLP here, so if you're interested in pursuing any one of these options further, please see the Resources section at the end of the chapter and be sure to consult a lawyer and accountant.

WHICH BUSINESS FORM IS BEST FOR HUSBAND/WIFE OR FAMILY BUSINESSES?

If you're working with your spouse or a family member, you might be wondering if you should go through the trouble and expense of forming a partnership or a corporation. The answer to this question depends on your own needs, the tax implications, and the laws in the state where you live. Here are the issues you may want to consider.

Your Own Needs

If your business started as a sole proprietorship and your spouse or a family member has decided to join your already ongoing concern, the easiest solution may be to simply hire your relative as an employee. Any salary you pay may be deductible as a business expense to you. In fact, hiring your children can prove to be a tax bonus, since their salaries are a deductible business expense to you while their earnings will in most cases be taxed at a lower rate than your own. However, the salary must be reasonable and your children must actually render services that add value to your business.

When hiring an employee, however, you will need to comply with many federal and state regulations on employees. This means two things.

1. If your business is home based and your city has a zoning code forbidding employees to work in your home, you could run into a problem if the employee is a family member other than your spouse or children.
2. When you become an employer, you must maintain payroll records and file and pay many tax items. You must withhold federal income, social security, and Medicare taxes, as well as state income and possibly state disability taxes. You must prepare quarterly and year-end payroll tax returns, pay the employee's portion of social security taxes and federal and state unemployment taxes, usually purchase worker's compensation insurance, and prepare year-end earnings statements for each employee. (You do not have to pay social security taxes, however, on your own children under eighteen if they perform services in your trade or business.)

All this record keeping can be a headache for some people, and if that's the case for you, it might be easier to have your spouse or family member work on a volunteer basis—without pay. Naturally, this works fine if the person is your spouse or your own child because they receive the benefits from your income indirectly anyway. It probably won't work so well, however, if the person is a parent, brother, sister, or cousin, who needs to receive income from their work.

In some cases, however, the better choice is to make your spouse or family member a co-owner (partner) in your business, complete with a written partnership agreement along with a handshake, hug, or kiss. A partnership agreement and the Uniform Partnership Act provide both you and your relative with some form of protection in the event of a disagreement or dispute that might eventually force you to divide up the business. Although it's unusual, some couples are able to keep their business affairs separated from their personal affairs, and so can find themselves selling their interest in their partnership to another party without animosity or threat of divorce.

Of course, if you've decided to form a C corporation, S corporation, or LLC for reasons related to the risk factors of your business or to obtain the various tax benefits they afford, you won't have any choice about how you handle your spouse or family members who co-own the company with you. In using these forms of business, regardless of who your co-owners are, you still need to file papers with your state listing them as directors or officers of the company. These documents are required to be updated annually, or whenever there are changes in the corporation's directors or officers. You also need to determine whether you will pay them a salary and benefits because these financial issues have specific tax consequences when employee/owners are family members.

Tax Implications

There are specific tax implications to be aware of when a partnership or corporation is owned by members of the same family. For example, if you try to include your child as a partner in your family partnership with the intention of transferring a portion of the partnership income to him or her (thereby reducing all the partners' shares of income and hence their taxes), the current income tax laws dealing with children and earned income make this option less worthwhile. Such an outright transfer of partnership income to a child may arouse IRS scrutiny.

However, hiring your child is feasible and has some advantages as long as you pay him or her a "reasonable" wage for actual work done. In this way, your child's wages are deductible business expenses to your partnership, and the child's earnings will likely be taxed at a lower rate than your own. In addition, if your child becomes an employee in your business, he or she is entitled to open an IRA and put up to $2,000 in earned income per year toward his or her retirement. However, no business deduction is allowed to the partnership or a partner for any contribution you make toward your child's IRA.

There are also ways of setting up a limited partnership or LLC in such a way that your children, by working for the family business over a number of years, increase their percentage ownership by means of nontaxable "gifts" each year from parents, who continue to receive a steady stream of income until they formally retire from the business. The documents necessary to create such entities must comply strictly with the estate-planning provisions of the Internal Revenue Code and can be quite complex; usually you will need the assistance of a tax attorney who specializes in "succession planning" for small businesses.

Be aware that there are many special IRS regulations affecting family members who are owners/employees of a C or S corporation. These regulations are intended to prevent families from shifting expenses among family members to create losses such as through making sales of corporate assets to one another at a so-called loss, or from taking a loan from their corporation at "special low" rates. For tax purposes, family members who own more than a certain percentage of stock in a corporation are considered "related parties" to the corporation.

Furthermore, under a provision of the IRS code called the "family attribution rule," an individual is considered to own as much stock as is owned by any of the following members of his or her family: spouse, siblings, direct descendants (children and grandchildren) and direct ancestors (parents and grandparents). This means that if two brothers each own 30 percent of a corporation's stock with an unrelated party who owns 40 percent, each brother is actually considered to own 60 percent of the stock for purposes of determining whether or not he is a "related party" to the corporation. This is important because tax rules are different for "related parties" when it comes to determining the deductibility of certain expenses, interest charges on loans, and losses on the sale of assets. The IRS maintains such rules to prevent family members from manipulating the books to reduce a corporation's earnings in order to pay fewer taxes. In short, if you are choosing to start a C or S corporation that includes your spouse or other family members, be sure to see an accountant so you can properly plan how to best divide the ownership of the company.

Your State Laws

Spouses have a legal interest in the business matters of their mates. This is especially true in the "community property states" of Arizona, California, Idaho, Nevada, New Mexico, Texas, Washington, and Wisconsin, where each spouse automatically owns one-half of all community property. In effect, this means that it makes no difference if you're a sole proprietor and your spouse is or is not involved in your business as a partner or otherwise if you began the business after you married, in general, he or she is still entitled to 50 percent of your property in the event of a divorce. This is also true in those common-law states in which divorce proceedings require an equitable division of property. In some states, personal agreements between spouses as to how they will divide their interests in a family business upon divorce or separation are not enforceable, and the family court is required to divide the business ownership based on the state's rules of equitable distribution. This does not preclude you from writing a partnership agreement with your spouse to use as the basis for your working relationship, however, if you desire. In fact, we think it can be a good idea.

OTHER LEGAL AND FINANCIAL ISSUES

Whatever form of business you and your associates choose, in addition to creating an agreement or contract formalizing your relationships, there may be additional legal and financial issues for you to comply with or resolve. For example, your teaming-up alliance may require you to get a separate business license, to register or trademark your name or service, or simply get a federal tax ID number (IRS Form SS-4). You may need to make choices as to which accounting method you'll be using, how you'll handle expenses and receipts, whether you want to purchase business insurance, and other financial matters. This section highlights some of the issues involved in handling these additional legal and administrative matters.

Permits and Licenses

Most cities and counties require business licenses to operate a business. If you have been a home-based business and failed to get a license in the past, your new teaming-up alliance may increase your visibility, so you should not delay any further in obtaining the proper license for yourself or your collaboration if it's a partnership or joint venture. The fees for obtaining a business license are often minimal.

Note that if your teaming-up relationship is a legal partnership, it's advisable to put your license in the name of the partnership. This suggestion is a preventive measure in the event that you and your partner(s) have a falling out and one party attempts to take control of the business without following whatever agreements you have made concerning the dissolution of your company.

If you are in the business of selling goods or certain types of services, you will need to obtain a sales tax permit from your state taxing authority. These are discussed below under Sales Tax Permits.

Zoning Laws

Most cities and counties also have zoning ordinances relating to the operation of a business in a residential or commercial area. If your teaming-up arrangement causes you to move into a small office or commercial district, be sure you are aware of the specific applicable zoning laws that might affect your business. This is particularly important if your business will be noisy or produce chemical fumes.

Similarly, if you are a home-based business and your teaming-up relationship will result in people visiting your home for business purposes, you should make sure that your local zoning code doesn't preclude having business guests in your home. Many zoning laws are out of step with the realities of the 1990s when millions of people are working from their homes, many of whom are technically doing so illegally because their zoning codes forbid doing business in residential neighborhoods. While you might escape notice as a one-person home-based business, when you begin having collaborators and customers drop by on a regular basis, or if the neighborhood children cannot play in the streets during the day because they would be dodging UPS trucks making deliveries to your home office, you could draw unwelcome attention to your business.

Fictitious Business Name Statement and Trademarks

If you will be creating a new business using a name other than your own or those of your associates, you must file and publish a "d.b.a." (doing business as) statement in the county of your principal place of business and usually in each other county where you maintain a physical office for your business. To be sure you have the right to use the name you select, you should also visit your county clerk's office to determine if the name is already in use. If not, you can register your business name for a modest fee. The process of filing a d.b.a. may include having your business name published in a local newspaper announcing the creation of your company and the names of the people involved. Most people choose to do this filing through a smaller community paper where it is least expensive to have their name published.

If your teaming-up enterprise is going to sell a product or service that you want to name in a unique fashion, you should consider trademarking it. A trademark or service mark is a distinctive name, symbol, or combination of the two used to distinguish your product or service from those of competitors. While putting a ^{TM} or ^{SM} symbol next to your name offers an initial degree of protection against others taking it from you, you are not truly protected until you register your mark with your state (if your state offers this service) when you are doing business locally, or with the U.S. Patent and Trademark Office when you are using or intend to use the mark throughout the nation. Registering with the U.S. Patent and Trademark Office gives you the right to put the ® symbol after your product or service name. For trademark information and applications, you can phone (703) 557-3158 or write the U.S. Patent and Trademark Office, Washington, DC 20231.

Copyrights

If your teaming-up alliance will be creating intellectual property such as manuscripts, books, music, software, training materials, or lyrics, you should be sure to register a copyright for it with the U.S. Copyright Office. You are initially protected by putting a copyright notice as follows: "© [date] by [your name]" but as with a trademark, your rights to claim the material as your own for a period of time are preserved only if you register your copyright. For copyright information, call the Information Line at (202) 707-3000 and ask for General Information Packet #118, or write Copyright Office, Library of Congress, Washington DC 20559.

Federal and State Tax ID

Technically speaking, business partnerships must obtain a separate Federal Employer Identification Number (EIN), essentially a tax ID number, from the

IRS. This is easily accomplished by filing Form SS-4 with the IRS and any other needed forms with your state tax agency.

If you're wondering why you can't simply use your existing tax ID or social security number, the answer is, a separate EIN is not only required for each separate business entity, it also helps you in administering your alliance. In fact, the need to file separate taxes often provides the major impetus for moving an informal collaboration toward a legal partnership. Without a separate tax ID number, any customer who pays you will probably need to write the check in the name of just one partner, which itself is not a good policy. Furthermore, in situations requiring customers to report payments to outside freelancers or providers of services using an IRS Form 1099, not having a separate Federal Tax ID number will result in their reporting the payment in the name of the one partner only. This means that this partner would have to turn around and file 1099s for the other partners to show their share of earned income and to make sure that he or she is not solely responsible for paying taxes on the entire income earned by the partnership. In short, your administrative tasks are much easier and your business relationship clearer to everyone involved if you formalize an ongoing collaboration with a legal partnership complete with a partnership agreement and a separate tax ID number.

Sales and Use Tax Permits

If your teaming-up arrangement involves the sale of any goods or certain types of services, you will need to obtain a tax permit or license to sell the goods and collect the state sales tax. All states except Alaska, Delaware, Montana, New Hampshire, and Oregon impose a sales and use tax. As a business, you must collect the sales tax and reimburse the state according to a schedule, usually on a quarterly or annual basis. At the present time, most states charge a sales tax only on your sales to in-state customers; you will not normally be required to charge the sales tax unless your business maintains an office in their state. The law in this area is changing rapidly, however, as revenue-hungry state governments come up with ever more creative ways to levy taxes on out-of-state businesses.

A "use" tax is the inverse of a sales tax; when you purchase goods or services from an out-of-state vendor that will be consumed in your business (i.e., not resold by you to your customers), you will need to pay a use tax to your state government, usually at the same rate as the state's sales tax. What services are subject to sales and use taxes? The answer is not easy and varies widely from state to state. In some states, for example, tax-consulting services by accountants are not subject to sales and use taxes, while the accountant's preparation of tax returns based on his consulting advice is subject to sales and use taxes.

Sales and use tax is not normally charged on your purchases of raw materials, inventory, and other goods and services that you process and resell to customers. To avoid paying sales and use tax on these goods and services, it is a good idea to obtain your state's "resale exemption certificate" or deliver it to each vendor from which you purchase these goods and services. Before starting up in business, you and your partners should consult with a tax accountant and describe your business in detail to ensure that you will not underwithhold nor underpay sales and use taxes in your state.

To obtain a tax permit, you usually need to file a form with your state taxing agency, estimate the amount of sales you will make each quarter, and post a "deposit" for the first payment. Your deposit is usually refundable at a later date. It's often recommended that you make your initial estimate of your sales volume on the low side to reduce the amount of your deposit.

A corollary to obtaining a permit is that you and your associates must also keep accurate records of your sales tax collected, as well as make your payments on time. Without good records, if your state's tax agency audits you to be sure you are paying the full amount due to the state, you could be charged a severe penalty. So be sure to decide together how you will carry out these requirements.

Transferring an Existing Business to a Partnership

If you're transferring an existing sole proprietorship to a partnership, you may need to close state and federal tax returns, licenses, permits, and bank accounts on the existing business and obtain new permits and licenses for the new partnership. Furthermore, if you're transferring inventory from an existing business to a new partnership, your state may have a "bulk sales" law that requires you to notify certain creditors or suppliers about the termination of the existing business and that the partnership will be assuming its debts. These laws are intended to prevent the manipulation of inventory to avoid payment of debts.

Employee Records and Taxes

If your new teaming-up relationship involves hiring any employees (as a partnership, consortium, or satellite subcontracting might), you need to be familiar with your obligations as an employer to keep records and pay federal taxes, state taxes, and social security on their behalf. In brief, at the federal level, each employee must fill out a Form W-4 for you indicating her or his status for purposes of withholding income taxes. You must then file quarterly federal tax returns and payments to report and remit federal income and social security taxes withheld, as well as your share of the social security tax.

You will also need to file and remit federal unemployment taxes (FUTA). If you hire freelancers/independent contractors, you must also file IRS 1099 forms for each person paid more than $600 in a calendar year. The 1099s are sent to the contractors with copies to the IRS and your state tax agency. At the state level, you generally must file state income tax records and remit your payments, as well as state unemployment insurance and, in some states, state disability insurance payments.

As with state sales and use taxes, in most states the shareholders of a closely held corporation and the members of an LLC, notwithstanding their limited liability in other areas, are personally liable for the business's failure to pay employment taxes.

While the details of procedures for filing these forms and remittances are beyond the scope of this book, see the Resources at the end of this chapter for where to get additional information. You may want to hire a payroll service or consult your accountant or bookkeeper about how to perform the required paperwork and payments yourself.

Bank Accounts and Credit Card Capability

In some cases, teaming up will mean that you should consider opening a joint bank account or a new business bank account. If your arrangement is a partnership, a joint account is highly recommended to maintain the integrity of your financial affairs. Your new teaming-up alliance might also benefit from being able to accept credit cards from your customers. Some banks are reluctant to give home-based businesses and some types of small businesses a credit card merchant account, or will charge much more for doing so. If you encounter such difficulty, we suggest that you keep looking to find a bank that wants to work with small enterprises. Having the proper business licenses and a tax ID can help to facilitate your banking relationship. Other sources of merchant accounts are Independent Service Organizations and small business associations. The Small Office Home Office Association, for example, has a merchant account program for its members (see the Resource list at the end of this chapter). Do shop around for the best rates for any monthly fees that will be charged for a terminal as well as for the percentage the bank will charge you on each transaction.

Insurance

Many small and home-based businesses overlook purchasing insurance to cover potential liabilities and risks. However, in teaming up, you should give careful consideration to your insurance needs, particularly if you're involved in a high-risk industry and/or could be included in a suit against a teaming-up associate by virtue of working together or even being perceived as working in association with one another. Whether the suit is a nuisance suit or a legitimate one, you are best protected by making sure you have the proper insurance coverage for liability, errors and omissions, auto-related accidents, and so on.

You also may want to increase your insurance protection simply because your teaming-up relationship involves carrying out activities you previously didn't perform or creates new circumstances for doing business. For example, you may find yourself needing fire and casualty insurance to cover inventory you've never had on hand before. You may need business property/small-business insurance to cover new equipment you've added, or business automobile insurance if your vehicle will be driven by others for business purposes. Similarly, if you hire an employee as a result of your teaming-up alliance, you'll need to have workers' compensation insurance and possibly provide for medical insurance. Finally, if you're involved in a partnership, you may want to consider obtaining partnership insurance to protect yourself in the event of a lawsuit arising from the actions of any of your business partners.

Accounting Methods and Money Management

You and those you're teaming up with should discuss how you plan to keep your financial records, even if you're not merging any money as in a formal partnership. You should consider issues such as whether each person will use cash-basis or accrual-basis accounting. In cash-basis accounting, income and expenses are recognized when cash is received or paid, respectively. In accrual-basis accounting, income is recognized when a bill is sent, not when it is paid; similarly, expenses are recognized when they are incurred, not when they are paid for. Cash-basis accounting is most often used in small, non-inventory-based businesses; accrual-basis accounting is usually used for businesses with inventories. Accrual basis accounting is also required for LLCs. Whichever method you choose, it's best if you and your collaborators are coordinating how you operate. If you're involved in a partnership or corporation, you must choose only one method.

How any fees received from shared work will be paid to those involved should also be clearly defined. For instance, if you're expecting to receive 33 percent of a contract's fees plus your expenses, unless it's been clearly stated beforehand, you'll likely feel upset if, when the contract is done, the client pays your associate who deposits the checks and then tells you he or she will send your share of the fee ten days after the client's check has cleared the bank. As we pointed out above, you should also be sure you agree on all such rules for handling business expenses, including telephone costs, office supplies, gas, insurance, and even whether you can charge for travel time.

Not surprisingly, a mutual understanding of how each person thinks about and handles money is crucial to an honest, long-lasting relationship. Different perceptions of money matters can cause more strain than any other issue when teaming up. Some people, for example, feel that buying only the best equipment and paying top dollar for outside consulting and supplies is the way to prove to the world that your business venture is professional. Others feel that a business must trim every expense possible to the barest bones, and that to buy a new piece of equipment or even a simple piece of office furniture, you must prove beyond a reasonable doubt that the business desperately needs to purchase it.

Another situation that frequently creates problems is the belief some associates have that they should pay others for services used only when and if they get paid for something they do. In other words, they expect their associates to take the risk with them. On the other hand, without an explicit understanding, those who don't have a primary relationship with a client would usually expect to be paid when their services are rendered or within a matter of days. Naturally, such diverging views can cause conflict between collaborators. Money issues have a way of raising tensions between people beyond the true value of the disagreement. Here are a few cases to illustrate what can happen.

Case A: One partner had a habit of spending hours on the phone with customers, costing the joint venture a few extra hundred dollars in phone bills every month. Because the business was new and money was at a premium, the other partners were not pleased to share this extra cost.

Case B: One partner consistently caved in quickly when clients called and tried to negotiate for lower fees for the partnership's consulting services. The other partner felt that his colleague was "giving away" their services, encouraging all clients to ask for reduced fees, and even developing "their" reputation as a discount operation.

Case C: The leader of a satellite subcontracting group asked his various subcontractors to estimate their fees for a contract he was bidding on. The members all estimated rather conservatively, but the leader of the group was able to win the contract price and kept the difference for himself. The members then complained that the leader was not paying them fairly.

In sum, we quote an old French saying, *"Les bons comptes font les bons amis."*/"Good accounts make good friends."

The Use of Professional Advice

Finally, regardless of the teaming-up method you pursue—from cross-promotion to virtual corporation—you and your associates should also share your views about seeking professional advice from lawyers, accountants, and business consultants of all kinds, professional organizers, information researcher, marketing consultants, management consultants, etc. Some people view such outside services as "money well spent," while others see it as "money down the tubes." For this reason, we recommend that you and those you're teaming up with spend time discussing how comfortable you each feel about hiring outside expertise, the amounts you're willing to commit for such services, and when you believe they're necessary.

A word of warning, however, about using the services of professional consultants who are family members or friends. Clearly, having family or close relations help you with your business decisions can be useful and sometimes less expensive than hiring an outsider. However, in some cases, relying on people with whom you have a close personal relationship can turn into an awkward situation. What if you or your teaming-up colleague disagree with the person's advice, for example? What if the person's advice leads to problems or expenses you weren't counting on? What if you're sued because you follow that advice? What if, instead of being objective, a relative of your teaming-up associate offers advice that is skewed toward his or her self-interest? Be sure to consider issues like these in determining how much you might actually save or gain by hiring a family member or friend.

One partnership we interviewed used free legal advice from one partner's brother. The brother, although an attorney, wasn't experienced in the areas of business law that this partnership needed. Consequently his "free" advice led the partners to formulate an unacceptable proposal that lost them the business they'd hoped to win. In another situation, a husband/wife team was advised by a lawyer relative to form an S corporation. The incorporation cost them a few thousand dollars, but they later heard that given the nature of their business, the S corporation was not needed or desirable.

This is not to suggest that professional advice is seldom worthwhile. Many alliances, collaborations, and partnerships can benefit greatly from professional advice at points during their planning, start-up, and growth stages. A good accountant can be invaluable in minimizing your tax burden completely by legal means; a good marketing consultant can help augment your client list; a good PR agent can tap you into sources of free publicity you could not have gotten yourself; and the right lawyer can save you from unethical competitors or deadbeat customers.

We've covered each legal and financial issue above with only the briefest of explanations to orient you to the issues you need to consider. If you need specific accounting or legal advice concerning your obligations to the Internal Revenue Service, your state, or your partners, it can be well worth a few hours of your time to consult a lawyer or an accountant about your specific situation. In addition, you should consult current business literature and recent books such as those we've listed in the Resources at the end of this chapter for more in-depth explanations and advice on each topic.

PLANNING FOR CONTINGENCIES

To conclude our discussion of legal and financial matters, we want to emphasize the value of planning for contingencies. A *contingency* is an event that may or may not occur, and every human activity holds the possibility for many such events. But in particular there are three contingencies you should plan a way to address in case they arise. Whatever formal agreements you reach with those you will be working with, you should include either specific clauses to address these contingencies or an "arbitration" clause that places any disagreement into the hands of an outside objective third party who can help you resolve these matters. The three contingencies you should plan for are: failure, catastrophe, and unexpected success. The following suggests a few questions to ponder for each.

Contingency 1: The Unheralded Failure

As hopeful as we are that our business ventures will succeed, there are many events beyond our control that sometimes interfere with our ability to achieve the results we want. Whether it's an inability to get along with one another, cash-flow problems, having too few clients or too much competition, or bankruptcy, any number of things can result in wanting to abandon a joint enterprise. In some cases, though, you can improve the outcome of such events through diligent efforts, mediation to work out differences with associates; or by learning new ways to do things. In other cases, alas, there are market forces or personality issues that cannot or will not be resolved.

Whatever the situation, you should be prepared both psychologically and professionally for the "F-word" contingency: Failure. From the psychological viewpoint, it helps to see your venture as an experiment whose outcome is always unknown. As disappointing or upsetting as a failure may be, after time you will be able to go back to working solo until you can move on to other more successful teaming-up ventures. As talk show host Oprah Winfrey has said, "I haven't made many mistakes in my life; but I've learned many lessons." We think that's an excellent way to approach any teaming-up venture that doesn't work out the way you had hoped and expected it would.

From a professional viewpoint, you want to make sure your agreements provide for how you and your associates will dissolve your teaming-up arrangement in the event of a failure. You can do this by making sure your written agreement specifies how you intend to dissolve or terminate your association. In fact, you may also want to consult a lawyer or accountant about the specific clauses you may need to cover your situation. You should address such questions as:

- Who will own any shared assets? How will they be divided?
- Who gets the rights to any trademarks, copyrights, or patents?
- Who can continue to use the company name?
- Can a substitute be found to take over for someone leaving?
- Who will settle the dispute if no agreement about dissolution can be made?

Mediation and Arbitration Agreements

Mediation and arbitration are two common ways to settle disputes among business associates. Mediation is the use of a third party who has no authority to impose a solution but whose goal is to help the involved persons come to their own mutually satisfactory agreement. Arbitration, on the other hand, gives the arbitrator the power to make a final decision based on each side's presentation of the case. Mediation is useful if you believe that you and your associates will have a continuing relationship and are not likely to remain adversarial. Arbitration is most often used when the parties can no longer communicate and their chances of finding a mutually satisfactory resolution are practically zero.

Here's a sample mediation clause you can include in your agreements.

The parties (partners) agree that any dispute arising out of this Agreement or their business shall first be resolved by mediation, if possible. The parties are aware that mediation is a voluntary process and so pledge themselves to cooperate fully with the mediator in an attempt to reach a satisfactory settlement. The cost of the mediation shall be split equally by the parties.

Here's a sample arbitration clause you can use.

The parties (partners) agree that any dispute arising out of this Agreement or their business shall be arbitrated under the rules of the American Arbitration Association. The cost of the arbitration shall be borne by the parties as the arbitrator shall direct.

Many lawyers contend that even if you believe mediation is sufficient for your purposes, you should also include an arbitration clause because you can never be sure all parties will agree to mediate.

Contingency 2: Catastrophic Events

Although many people would classify any failure as a catastrophic event, we're referring here to feats of nature that are completely outside of your control—like a fire, earthquake, flood, car accident, health problems, divorce, family crisis, and so on. Many collaborations and partnerships speed along nicely toward success until suddenly halted by a catastrophe that completely alters their game plan. Perhaps one partner or party dies, perhaps someone gets a divorce and moves out of state, perhaps someone's child develops a life-threatening illness and the partner must take a six-month leave of absence, or perhaps one partner's spouse takes a job in another location and the partner moves, leaving you in the lurch.

When such unexpected events occur, there's usually nothing you can do except work around them. In the face of a catastrophic event, whatever your agreement says, your best course of action is to muster as much compassion and sympathy as you can for the person you're working with and do your best either to take control yourself or to work out a new agreement with the person or his or her family to do their best to hold up their part until you can find someone else to step in.

Often there are situations in which both parties want the business. In such cases, see the formula for a buyout clause on page 204.

Contingency 3: Success Beyond Your Dreams

It does happen! Some enterprises become far more successful than planned. So when thinking about the future of your venture, consider how you'll handle unexpected success. Will you retire from the company and withdraw all your profits? Will you continue to manage it but from afar? Will you stick with it—challenges and all?

Wendy and Tom Eidson, founders of the Mo'Hotta, Mo'Betta condiment food catalogue, never imagined that their catalogue company would catapult them so quickly to the level of success they achieved. They did know that someday they wanted to move from Los Angeles to a quieter community and raise a family. However, as the stress of handling their extraordinary success mounted and more and more decisions needed to be made about their growing company, they found that the fun they'd wanted to get from having their own business was missing. As a result, they consciously began slowing down their success until they regained their balance by helping each other remember their original goal: to enjoy their work. At that point, they decided to hire an operations manager to help them run the day-to-day operations of their business. Now, they're not only enjoying their work again, they're able to take time away from work to spend part of each day with their children.

Not all success stories end so neatly, however. Collaborators or partners can often find themselves divided over a variety of issues such as:

- What direction to take the company in after its surge to success
- Who will manage the company if an owner decides to scale back his or her personal day-to-day involvement
- How to divide up profits if an owner decides to retire or sell out
- Whom to sell to if outside buyers become interested

The secret to dealing with success is to imagine that you must make the same decisions you're faced with but without the abundance of money or other resources success has brought you. In other words, ask yourself, "Without the bank account I have now, what would my choice be?" In most cases,

Finding a Lawyer to Review Agreements Drafted by You

Attorneys Denis Clifford and Ralph Warner, founders of Nolo Press and authors of *The Partnership Book,* point out that when you draft your own contracts and partnership agreements, you may have a hard time finding a lawyer who's willing to review them and apply his or her stamp of approval to your contract. In part, they say, this is because lawyers bill by the hour and it may not be to their advantage to take on such a minimal project. Another part of the problem, however, is that like other professionals these days, lawyers are worried about malpractice claims and difficult clients who *ex post facto* blame the lawyer for their business problems and try to sue the lawyer for causing them. As a result, a lawyer may feel that their risk is too great for the money involved to simply review a predrafted or standard-clause agreement without rewriting it in his or her own language, custom-tailored to the situation.

Nonetheless, Clifford and Warner recommend that in most cases, if you keep looking, you can eventually find a lawyer who's sympathetic to your need to minimize your legal costs. They suggest letting the lawyer know you will likely be bringing in additional business at a later date once your enterprise gets off the ground.

In fact, Clifford and Warner advise that establishing a long-term relationship with a lawyer you like and respect makes sense in this era of knee-jerk litigation. Sooner or later, nearly all businesses will need legal advice to handle a disgruntled employee, a deadbeat client, a patent or copyright infringement, a breach of contract, or any number of other issues that accompany success. In some cases, a lawyer can also help resolve a personality conflict in a partnership dispute especially when the conflict centers on struggles over what constitutes the best business and legal decisions.

To find a lawyer for your business needs, Clifford and Warner recommend that you locate someone who deals with small-business issues, preferably one who specializes in the same field as your work. Avoid lawyers who seem to be desperately seeking new clients. Finally, they also suggest that you talk to more than one lawyer initially and determine which one seems most knowledgeable about your business needs and with which one you feel the most rapport. In doing this, however, be sure to ask in advance of the meeting how much your initial consultation will cost so there will be no surprises.

---

taking this perspective will help you to focus on your priorities and the true desires beneath the sense of wealth or security success has brought you.

Here's how one business training company handled their success when it became too overwhelming. Run from a home office by a husband and wife, the company was a virtual organization of freelancers who were creating marketing documents and sales and customer training materials for many well-known high-tech companies. At one point, the company was billing over $1 million in receivables and had more than thirty freelancers reporting to them. From the outside it looked like a storybook success. But one day, after a particularly frenetic morning, the wife turned to the husband and announced, "I want out." Through this crisis, the couple realized that their marriage was more important than having a million-dollar business, so they decided to begin turning away some contracts until they had cut back their business to the point where they could reclaim their lives. They now run a more low-key, stress-free business which brings in less income but provides them with a more fulfilling and satisfying lifestyle.

Alternatively, success like this might be an opportune time to seek the advice of a professional consultant who specializes in helping small-business owners deal with growth issues. A professional consultant versed in these issues can guide you toward the best decisions—decisions that will have a positive effect on your business, your tax situation, and your personal life.

ACHIEVING LEGAL AND FINANCIAL SECURITY

When it comes to dealing with legal and financial affairs, the ultimate goal is the peace of mind that comes from creating satisfying business relationships. Fortunately, we each have a choice in terms of how we approach the matters that most effect our working together. People take one of three approaches in their efforts to create the security and control they need.

1. Expect the worst. Some people are extremely aggressive when it comes to asserting their legal and financial rights. At the first hint of exploring a teaming-up relationship, these individuals are ready to meet with their lawyers, ask you to sign five different confidentiality agreements, and expect you to commit all your assets if you make a mistake or deviate from their expectations. They believe this aggressive posture helps protect them from future problems.

2. Hope for the best. Other people go to great lengths to avoid dealing with any hassles from legal or financial issues. They don't want to upset others. They don't want to discuss touchy issues. They don't want to get involved with lawyers or the court system. They don't want to pay money for professional advice from CPAs or lawyers. These people often won't get involved in a formal teaming-up relationship at all, or if they do, they want to do everything on a casual, see-how-it-goes basis.

3. Prepare for the possible. These people recognize that teaming up will further their business interests, so they want to make sure their teaming-up effort works for both their long-term interests *and* those of their collaborators or partners. They believe that a teaming-up effort that is cooperative and mutually beneficial is one that will last, so they willingly invest in negotiating the legal and financial agreements that will make that possible.

Do we need to ask which of these types of people you'd rather do business with? Or which one you would rather be? We hope this chapter has laid the groundwork for you to proceed with confidence in creating written agreements that will preserve and protect your best professional and financial interests. Obviously, we could not cover all the legal and tax intricacies you may need to take into account and for that reason, we encourage you to make an effort to learn more about these issues as they affect you so you can draft any needed documents of your own and discuss them in detail with a competent professional lawyer and financial advisor or CPA as appropriate to your needs.

In the next chapter, we will turn our attention to how you can build a teaming-up relationship that works, so all the effort you've put into identifying the right people to work with and creating a satisfying agreement will pay off.

RESOURCES

Articles

"Finding the Right Lawyer for Your Home-Based Business: Ten Questions You Should Ask." Cliff Ennico, Esq. *Home Office Computing Magazine,* November 1990.

Books

Basic Legal Forms. Clifford Ennico, ed. Boston: Warren, Gorham & Lamont, updated annually. This book contains many standard legal forms you can use in your business; the book also includes the forms on diskette.

Forming Corporations and Partnerships. John C. Howell. Blue Ridge Summit, PA: Liberty Hall Press, 1991.

How to Run a Family Business. Michael Friedman and Scott Friedman. Cincinnati: Betterway Books, 1994.

Inc. Yourself. Judith H. McGowan. New York: HarperCollins, 1992.

The Partnership Book. Denis Clifford and Ralph E. Warner. Berkeley, CA: Nolo Press, 1981–1996. 510/549-1976; 800/992-6656. Nolo publishes other titles that may be pertinent, such as:

   How to Form a Nonprofit Corporation

   How to Mediate a Dispute

   The Legal Guide for Starting and Running a Small Business

   How to Form Your Own Limited Liability Company

   Tax Savvy for Small Business

Software

The Desktop Lawyer
The Open University
P.O. Box 1511
Orlando, FL 32802
800/874-0388

It's Legal
Parsons Technologies
One Parsons Drive
Hiawatha, IA 52233
319/395-9626 or 800/223-6925

Kiplinger's Small Business Attorney
Block Financial Corp.
4435 Main St.
Kansas City, MO 64111
800/813-7940 or 816/751-6000
816/751-6020 Fax

Legal Point
The Teneron Corporation
7300 West 110th Street
Overland Park, KA 66210
800/529-5669

Partnership Maker
Nolo Press
950 Parker Street
Berkeley, CA 94710
510/549-1976 or 800/992-6656

Quicken Family Lawyer
Parsons Technology (An Intuit Company)
One Parsons Drive
Hiawatha, IA 52233
800/223-6925 or 319/395-9626

Legal Forms Available On-line

Electronic Legal Source
http://www.e-legal.com

Legaldocs
http://www.law.net/usalaw/index.htm

5

The Psychology of Making
Your Relationships Work

*From one small seed of our first encounter has
come many harvests.*
—RUSTY BERKUS

WHEN HAROLD FIRST approached Geneen about teaming up, she was elated. She'd
been running a successful word-processing service for many years and to help
keep her business thriving she'd formed an informal networking group. Over
several years, the group had grown unexpectedly into a profitable sideline
business, but as membership continued to grow, managing the group's many
volunteer activities had begun to detract from Geneen's word-processing
business. Harold was the head of a growing national business networking organization, and he wanted to establish a chapter in Geneen's city. Having gotten her name from a colleague, he called to propose that they meet about
forming a joint venture.

It seemed like a perfect solution for both of them. Harold could add a
fully functioning chapter to his national organization, and Geneen would be
relieved of the time-consuming aspects of administering the group. Early
meetings in person and by phone went well, as did contract negotiations. But
when they began working together, the problems began almost immediately.
In talking with others, Harold kept referring to their venture as an acquisition, and he wrote frequent memos directing Geneen on how to carry out the
simplest of details. Having always considered their venture to be a partnership between equals, she felt as if the thriving organization she'd created had
been consumed by a large, impersonal entity. And her ego was a bit bruised
as well. She began to fear she'd made a dreadful mistake, so to assert her au-

thority she began submitting larger invoices to cover Harold's newly required administrative activities. Her requests angered Harold, who felt Geneen had grown greedy after realizing how successful his national organization was becoming. They both began searching for ways out of their venture.

Claude was a career counselor. For some time, he'd been wanting to leave the agency where he worked to open a holistic counseling center. Through the local Chamber of Commerce he met three other professionals who shared his dream: a psychotherapist, a psychologist, and a pastoral counselor. They began talking among themselves, and before long they formed a consortium to develop the center Claude had dreamed about. They created a board of directors, took all the necessary legal steps, and the center opened on the first day of spring the following year. Two years later, however, the center closed and the consortium members were hassling over who would pay their outstanding debts. Claude felt he'd been betrayed by two of the members who had taken new jobs when the consortium didn't generate enough clients to provide them with a full-time income. Since they then were only seeing clients periodically, they decided they owed only a fraction of their monthly payments to the consortium's costs. When serious financial problems ensued, the third professional blamed Claude for not doing a better job of marketing the center. As the weeks passed, their administrative meetings grew increasingly tense and finally boiled over into hostile accusations. To free themselves of all debts, the consortium members were about to sue Claude for breach of contract.

What had gone wrong in these situations? Both had begun with such promise but turned sour despite successful negotiations and harmonious beginnings. Why is it that some collaborations fall apart despite what seem like the best of efforts, while others thrive?

Ironically, in most cases, all the people involved in a failure will say that the problems weren't their fault. They will blame one another, their business problems, the economy, and so on. Often, however, lurking beneath the surface lies a more fundamental explanation for why joint enterprises fail: not understanding the psychology of working successfully as a group. In fact, it's not an exaggeration to say that the success of all teaming-up ventures ultimately depends on building a healthy group and a strong team relationship. With a healthy working relationship, any group of two or more can function well in good times or bad. In such a group differences of opinion can be resolved and problems overcome as they arise. But when the group relationship isn't healthy, a newly formed team can end up bickering, arguing, or smoldering silently over any number of matters—significant and insignificant—in both good times and bad, and the failure to settle even petty differences will take its toll on the venture.

This chapter is about understanding the underlying dynamics of building healthy group relationships. We'll start by discussing the natural stages any group of individuals will go through as they begin working together. We'll also present the six communications steps that we believe a group needs to take to solidify their bond and interact positively through the best and worst of times. Even if your collaborator or partner is a good friend, a family member, or your spouse, you'll find that the ideas discussed in this chapter can provide a new perspective on your business interactions and be helpful in understanding why things happen the way they do once you've teamed up.

THE FOUR STAGES OF BUILDING A WORKING RELATIONSHIP

Organizational psychologists who study group behavior agree that groups—be they of two or ten or more individuals, formal or informal, and regardless of size—take on a life of their own once formed. They develop their own personality, their own temperament, and their own dynamics. So if once your venture begins you sometimes feel as if you've lost control, in a very real sense you have because you're now operating as part of a team that literally has a life of its own.

More importantly, organizational psychologists also know that groups go through four phases of development. Just as a child must go from infancy through adolescence en route to adulthood, so every team effort or group must pass through these phases before it begins truly to function efficiently and successfully on its own. We mentioned these four phases in chapter 2 when we discussed the problems of forming your own networking group, but we'll describe each of them again here in greater detail because they are inevitable in the formation of any type of teaming-up enterprise when two or more people decide to work together.

As you read through the stages, keep in mind three things.

1. You will likely go through some of these stages several times, beginning even during the negotiation and contract phases of setting up your teaming-up effort. You will also go through them when you begin to actually work together on your business, focusing specifically on the jobs and tasks that must get done. In fact, most long-term relationships will "recycle" through these stages many times over as circumstances and needs change.
2. People are complex. A group may not go through the stages precisely in a one-two-three-four lockstep order, nor will it necessarily complete any one stage in the same amount of time as another team or group of people would. Some groups may find themselves zipping through one or more stages only to get stuck for an inordinately long time in another. Other groups will appear to skip a stage, only to find that it emerges later. Even if you negotiated these stages smoothly

while forming your relationship, there is no guarantee that you will go through them smoothly again when you actually get down to work. However, any business relationship that doesn't navigate these stages successfully once the venture has begun will probably not survive, and certainly won't thrive.

3. Directly discussing the four stages may not be useful to your team members. Just as most teenagers don't like parents telling them they're "just going through a stage," many adults don't like to discuss the psychology of their own interactions. For the most part, these stages take place organically and unconsciously. So while it's not always helpful to point them out or call the attention of others in your group to them, it can be valuable for you to know that what your group is experiencing is part of a natural process all groups go through. When your group gets stuck, remind yourself of these stages by asking yourself, "What's going on here? What issues are occurring in my group?" Then, by recognizing what might be happening, you may be able to help the process along through your own interactions with others.

Here are the four stages of group development.

Stage 1: Forming. This stage of developing a working relationship could also be called the honeymoon period. It's a time when everyone is excited, optimistic, and enthusiastic about what they'll be doing together. You've gotten past the hurdle of finding someone to work with or the pain of the negotiations, and now it's time to get more acquainted with your new relationships. It often involves talking eagerly about the ideas that brought you together and the goals you are looking forward to implementing. In this stage, your discussions will typically focus on what activities you're going to do together and how each person will go about doing them. However, in this stage, there is often a good amount of joking around and socializing before people really get down to work, and so often decisions don't actually get made or remain more or less general.

This means that if you're a highly goal-oriented person, you may end up feeling that nothing is being accomplished during this stage. Don't be fooled, however, into thinking that you're wasting your time during this period of getting acquainted. What's actually happening is that everyone involved is testing out the basic ground rules and seeing how they can fit in and how everyone will eventually best interact.

Stage 2: Storming. You know you're in this stage the moment you begin to feel as if "the honeymoon's over." Whatever discord remains among you will begin to emerge. It may take the form of open conflicts and disagreements, or just mild squabbling and bickering. Suddenly it may even appear that there is no way you can work together, after all. You may wonder if you made the wrong decision and start to doubt whether you want to continue. Power struggles may emerge. Egos may get hurt. Unanimous decisions may seem impossible. In fact, decisions that are made may not be followed through on and must be discussed again and again. And you or another team member may start looking for ways to get out.

Needless to say, this is the most vulnerable stage in any new business relationship. Sometimes one or more parties do back out and the venture dies before you have a chance to find out if it could have been successful. That's what Geneen was about to do when she called us to say how disappointed she was with her new relationship with Harold. But the stormy nature of this stage is not a definite sign that the relationship can't become a good one. The disagreements are not necessarily evidence that you will ultimately fail. They are more like a test—the first real test. If this stage doesn't kill a relationship, you come through this period feeling even better about yourselves and your relationship. A deeper bond will have formed between or among you and you will have built a strong foundation for a productive and healthy future working relationship.

For example, once Geneen realized that the misunderstandings she and Harold were encountering were a natural stage in their developing relationship, she began to view the events from a broader perspective. She clarified her expectations that their venture was a merger, not an acquisition. She withdrew her demands for additional funds. Harold began to respect her as a partner and peer. Their venture went on to be profitable and satisfying for both of them.

So, just as we suggested before, don't try to sweep this stage under the carpet. That's how Claude and his consortium got off the track. Being highly congenial individuals who disliked discord, they skipped over this stage both during negotiations and again as they began working together. They tried to bury their concerns and irritations. But of course, like all such dissatisfactions, theirs began to fester months later. Even then, however, they tried to keep them from surfacing and their meetings grew increasingly cold and tense. Finally, consortium members began cutting back, looking for other opportunities, and eventually dropping out. And by that time, the relationships had become so gangrenous in nature that a court battle ensued. It was only years later that Claude realized what had happened to his dream for a holistic career center. From hindsight he could see that the group never allowed the necessary storming process to take place that could have solidified their relationship.

While living through this stage may be rather unpleasant, it's vital. It's a chance to find out just how much each person wants to be involved and if and how you can reach accord about how you'll actually work together. As a rule of thumb, the smoother this stage goes during your negotiations, the more surprisingly intense it may be when you get under way. Be it only mild showers or a violent thunderstorm, however, you can draw once again upon the basic negotiation principles discussed in the previous chapter and the communications techniques that follow later in this chapter to help your group return to sunnier times.

Stage 3: Norming. As the disagreements and dissatisfactions that have emerged get resolved, during this third phase everyone begins to act cohesively. The "norms" for how you'll work together evolve. Each person recognizes and accepts his or her role, and a true "relationship" emerges. There's now a feeling of affinity and unity. You've become a "team." You begin treating one another with newfound respect. When someone violates the newly accepted procedures and behaviors that are emerging, there may be temporary regressions to the storming stage, but you usually will find ways to resolve concerns more rationally than emotionally, without focusing on personality clashes. The team is also much better at making decisions during this stage. Decisions are now reached more congenially after debate and discussion. In addition, once decisions have been reached, everyone adheres to them voluntarily.

Stage 4: Performing. At this stage, the basic structure of the relationship has become clear. Those involved understand each person's role and suddenly everyone is able to get down to business. Interactions proceed productively. Decisions are made quickly and easily. Problems are solved effectively.

Again it should be emphasized that each teaming-up venture will pass through these stages in its own manner and time frame, depending on how easily the members get acquainted and the amount of time and effort that has been required to establish the relationship in the first place. How quickly you'll get to the performing stage will also depend on the leadership and decision-making skills of those involved. The key to survival is learning how to manage the relationship, not just the output of the joint effort. As Edgar Schein, a renowned author and professor of organizational behavior, wrote in his classic textbook, *Organizational Psychology,* probably the most important factor influencing the success of your joint effort will be the degree to which you and those you're involved with develop a sensitivity and skill for managing your relationships and your group "process." You need to learn how to listen and empathize with one another. Lack of respect and mistrust can arise if you don't.

Early in the venture you may be preoccupied with your individual needs for identity, security, attention, and status, and so fail to pay attention to the needs of others. Preoccupation with such emotional needs makes it difficult to work constructively on the tasks at hand. However, imposing or forcing a

Recognizing the Stage You're In

Forming

1. You're spending a lot of time reviewing previous meetings and catching up.
2. You're spending a lot of time socializing and joking around.
3. You feel that nothing has been decided after you've had a meeting.

Helpful interaction: Facilitate getting acquainted.

Storming

1. You or others constantly feel the need to assert yourselves over one another.
2. You or others lock horns over decisions and appear to not hear one another.
3. Decisions are either not made or not followed.

Helpful interaction: Facilitate productive ventilating and accommodating of concerns.

Norming

1. People tend to treat one another's ideas with respect.
2. When a conflict or disagreement erupts, the team finds a way to resolve the issue without becoming focused on personality or emotional issues.
3. Decisions are made by consensus after debate, and then followed by team members.

Helpful interaction: Acknowledge and enjoy your progress.

Performing

1. You get right down to business.
2. You follow one another's thought processes and eagerly join in brainstorming and sharing new ideas, regardless of who originated them. Ego is not a question.
3. Decisions are easily made and tasks get completed as planned.
4. You're successful in all problem solving and decision making.

Helpful interaction: Return again and again to what's working.

structure on your relationship prematurely just to get down to business, or pressing for immediate output, can lead to shallow or hasty solutions because the group is not psychologically prepared to work together on its tasks. For a venture to function optimally, you must find a balance between your desire to get work done and making sure each team member is happy with the way things are proceeding. The team as a whole must be satisfied with how decision making is carried out and with how consensus is reached. These are, in fact, the issues that need to be resolved as you recycle through these four stages.

Think about a group you've joined in the past or a relationship you've built, including the one or ones you are now in. Can you recognize having gone through any of these stages? Usually it's easier to notice them in looking back on previous group relationships, because from hindsight you can see the patterns of behavior, the trouble spots, and your own role in the process.

When you're still building a team relationship, sometimes it can be difficult to notice the stages you're in because you're so personally involved in the events that you may lose your objectivity. But as Geneen discovered, when you make the effort to understand the psychological stages of a teaming-up venture, you can usually find the right perspective to help the process along.

If at any point after all agreements have been reached you begin having difficulties getting your relationship under way, remember that your problems could be related to the stage of development you're in. Reflect on where you are in the process of teaming up and what events are occurring. Use the box on page 239 to check out the types of problems or issues that are usually associated with each stage.

Recognizing which stage you are in and taking the lead to interact in helpful ways can often circumvent problems and help your group move on to the next stage. You may be able to defuse frustration or tensions during the forming and storming stages by recognizing that two people (including yourself) may be jockeying for authority and leadership or that both of you are unable to make decisions because you don't understand one another's style of thinking. But once the problem is identified, you can usually make a conscious commitment to resolving your difficulties through honest and frank discussions that lead to fruitful negotiation and/or compromise. By recognizing that what you're going through is a natural stage of developing a working relationship, you can often increase your patience and make a renewed commitment to working together until you can find your way to the norming and performing stages.

The Four Main Issues to Resolve in Moving Through the Four Stages

In more informal teaming-up efforts such as networking or a mutual-referral agreement, there's less to lose if relationships don't work out. This means that people are usually more patient about allowing these four stages to work themselves out naturally, even if the resolution is that those involved decide not to work together. But the more formal your teaming-up relationship is, the more important it is to work through these stages as quickly and as effectively as possible. In the most formal relationships like a consortium, a satellite subcontracting arrangement, a partnership, or a joint venture, there may be considerable time, money, and even risk at stake, so it's often critical for those who've teamed up to work through these four stages and begin performing the activities that brought them together. Usually progressing smoothly through the stages of group development centers on resolving *four main issues* that any group must address before the members of it can work well together. Here they are, along with some ideas that can help you resolve them.

1. Where do I fit in? Before people in a new business relationship can function effectively, they need to know how each of them fits into the "team"—that is, what role they'll play not just in terms of the work that's to be done, but within the relationship itself. One person might be the idea generator, for example, while another is the initiator or doer, and another is the arbitrator or caretaker who makes sure everyone stays on board. In a relationship among only two or three people, each person will actually play several roles in maintaining the relationship. But since no one likes stepping on anyone else's toes or having her or his toes stepped on, much testing and exploration need to take place during the four stages of developing a workable team relationship so you can discover who will be doing what.

Given the complexity of human nature, as a group develops and passes through the four stages, the roles each person plays may also change until a good fit develops. However, in some cases, *role ambiguity* occurs, meaning that a person may never truly understand what others expect him or her to do or just what he or she can expect from others. In other cases, *role conflicts* arise in which people have very different ideas about what they each should and shouldn't do. In still other cases, *role overload* develops, meaning that someone feels pressed to take on too much responsibility within the relationship. In all three situations, the team must resolve the role dynamics through clear communication and consistent expectations before they will be able to work well together. When the role dynamics remain fuzzy or conflicted, the relationship tends to disintegrate.

In one three-person consulting company we interviewed, the first six months of working together were marked by a tremendous amount of conflict as the partners experimented to find their roles. The three had joined together after working for the same company for several years, but now they wanted to run their own consulting agency. Each of them had different skills. One partner, John, considered himself to be the "idea man" whose creative skills would drive the group's ability to help their clients. Another partner, Tim, thought he was the best man for handling the marketing of the company because of his ability to articulate the company's purpose and capabilities to potential clients. The third partner, Sally, had an extensive background in research and information retrieval, and she was proud to be the behind-the-scenes backbone of the company in obtaining good information and being the "analyst."

Unfortunately, as the business began, Sally's exceptional analytical skills led her to want to take part in all aspects of the company. And soon the other two partners began to feel that Sally was stepping on their territories. After a few months, the three partners found themselves in bitter disputes over who was doing what, and they realized that they had to sit down to discuss what their roles would be. Fortunately, through this process, Sally learned that the other partners were not averse to her suggestions and participation in their functions, as long as she agreed that her main task would be doing the research and analytical thinking they so admired of her. In addition, after this frank discussion, all three partners became slightly more flexible in their roles and allowed one another greater leeway to make suggestions that benefited everyone.

   2. What's acceptable and what isn't? While going through the four stages of developing a new relationship, everyone is seeking to define its behavioral norms—that is, the behaviors that will be acceptable to the group and the ones that won't be. Every group relationship, even those between only two people, will evolve its own group norms. These norms are usually unspoken rules for how things are to be done, such as who gets to talk when, how late people can be for meetings, even what people will be expected to wear. Without such norms, the group never gels, because people don't know what to expect of one another. On the other hand, when one person becomes dictatorial or authoritarian about setting the norms in accord with his or her own personal beliefs at the expense of others' needs and desires, the others in the relationship usually rebel and reject or combat any norms they feel are being forced upon them. This can create conflict and prevent productive work from getting done.

   For example, when Susan, Nicole, and Juanita decided to do joint promotions for their respective businesses, it soon became clear that Susan expected to call all the shots. She set the meeting times around her schedule and expected everyone to be there. She laid out the agendas and led the meetings. Meanwhile, Nicole was having serious marital problems and wanted to talk with Juanita and Susan about these problems whenever they got together. She even began calling them for advice during the business day to discuss particularly pressing personal concerns. However, Susan and Juanita were both quite busy with their businesses, so Nicole soon found her calls to them went unreturned. Eventually the three women could find fewer and fewer dates when they could agree to meet, and nothing was being accomplished to get their joint promotional plans under way.

   Usually teams that encounter normative conflicts like these simply drift apart. That's what happened in this situation. Each of the women let the idea of doing joint promotions slide and thought about it later as a good idea that never panned out. "We just got too busy," Susan said to explain why their venture petered out. As is so often the case, no one recognized they were having trouble defining their group norms. Had they thought about it, however, they could have discussed the issues and perhaps found a way to resolve them, or at least they would have known why their plans didn't work out.

   3. Is there enough to hold us together? The main reason Susan, Nicole, and Juanita didn't go to the trouble to work out their normative difficulties was probably that they didn't have sufficient motivation to resolve the issues that arose. For a relationship to develop, there needs to be sufficient ties that bind. The ties that bind people together in a team effort are referred to as *group cohesion.* High cohesiveness makes people want to be part of the group and compels them to work together to resolve whatever issues arise; in relationships with low cohesiveness, however, people tend to lose interest in the group instead of investing whatever time and energy is needed to make things work. Some groups are cohesive to the point that they would go through hell and high water together. Others dissolve at the first sign of inconvenience.

There are several key factors that increase group cohesiveness: personal attraction, agreement on shared goals, positive interactions, and favorable results. Similarly, there are factors that tend to reduce group cohesiveness: disagreement on goals, intragroup competition, domination by one member, and unpleasant experiences. You can greatly increase the success of your joint efforts by working to foster the following behaviors that will make the group more cohesive.

- Limit your joint ventures to people you enjoy, admire, and respect.
- Keep activities and interaction focused on shared goals. Leave other aspects of your lives or businesses for other arenas.
- Don't let any one member dominate conversations or decisions. Consider everyone's needs equally.
- View one another as collaborators; play down and avoid competition.
- Enjoy one another's successes and victories.
- Set smaller, attainable goals you can achieve together to build a history of joint success.
- Take a positive, problem-solving approach especially to overcome unavoidable difficulties that arise.

4. Is someone taking charge? There are many things to attend to in forming any new team effort. Many of those things have to do with achieving the goals of the relationship, but an equal number of things need to be done to get the relationship itself worked out. So one final issue a group is working out as it develops is who will do what. Someone must be willing to assume responsibility for making sure the work gets done in the right way, doing such things as calling to set up meetings, leading the meetings, following through on decisions, and so forth. Someone also has to take responsibility for maintaining the cohesiveness of the group, doing such things as making sure everyone can attend, that everyone gets to express her or his views, that meetings don't go on too long or occur too often.

Of course, in more informal relationships like mutual referrals and interdependent alliances, these tasks may virtually take care of themselves. But not always. Many a mutual-referral relationship has died on the vine because no one took the initiative to stay in contact in between referrals and keep the lines of communication open even when no referrals were flowing through them. In more involved relationships like joint ventures and consortiums, these tasks can become very time-consuming, so there must be sufficient investment in the joint effort that someone takes on these chores.

While one person can assume the leadership role and perform all these functions, most business relationships work best when those involved divide up the work so that not all the responsibility falls on any one person.

THREE WAYS TO DIVIDE UP THE WORKLOAD

The number-one concern people express about teaming up is that they could end up with a disproportionate share of the workload. They worry that the joint effort will take away too much time from their own goals and take them off course. So as you begin working with others, often the most important housekeeping issue will be how you're going to divide up whatever work is to be done, so things can get done without anyone's feeling overburdened. This means deciding clearly who will do what and why. In some cases, of course, this decision is quite straightforward. Each person has a specific expertise to contribute or the task requires a specific division of labor. But in other cases, people who want to team up can struggle mightily with who's going to do what. And even when you make a decision to parcel out tasks in a certain manner, you may end up disagreeing later if someone decides he or she doesn't want to perform the particular tasks they've already agreed to take on.

Basically there are three ways a team can divide its workload in order to achieve its goals.

1. Pool the results like a gymnastics team. One way of organizing the workload is to operate like a gymnastics team. On a gymnastics team, each gymnast does his or her best on each apparatus and all individual scores are pooled to achieve the team score. Bowling teams also operate this way; each player bowls his or her best and the team's score is the sum of all their individual scores. Of course, no team member wants to let his or her teammates down, so all are motivated to perform as best they can. And, in the process, team members provide one another with moral support, help out when needed, and commiserate or celebrate together.

So in using this approach to dividing up the workload, all participants essentially work on their own, presumably performing to the best of their ability and then individual efforts are pooled so everyone can share in the benefits from the collective results. In his seminal book on teams, *Organizations in Action,* business analyst and professor J. D. Thompson refers to such teams as *pooled teams.*

In business, when a team uses a pooled approach to dividing the workload, everyone has a common goal, but each person essentially works on his or her own, and success is attained through the combined results of everyone's output. What matters is that all the participants perform to the best of their ability, achieving their highest potential so everyone can win.

Example: Carol Ann, Michael, and Richard operate a desktop publishing service. Each of them is responsible for getting and working with his or her own clients, but they pool their earnings each month to pay for their office space, an administrative assistant, an after-hours answering and paging service, and to pay themselves. This association works well, Carol Ann told us. "Essentially we're each in business on our own but by sharing expenses we're able to afford a more professional office setting and administrative support. And, of course, we help one another out if a job is too big for one of us to handle alone."

A pooled relationship works much like three children building their own sand castle on the beach; each castle stands alone, but together they make a village.

2. Sequence the tasks like a relay team. Another way to organize workload is to operate like a relay team with each runner carrying the baton for his or her portion of the race and passing it on to the next team member. Each person has his or her part in achieving the overall goal, but they do their parts sequentially, one after another. One person's output becomes the input for the next person, and so forth. J. D. Thompson refers to teams that work this way as *sequential interdependent teams.* As with the pooled approach, each person does his or her best in order not to let the team down, and no one wins unless all do the best they possibly can.

The most traditional business example of a sequenced team is the manufacturing assembly line, but sequential teams can also exist in small-business alliances where, for example, one does the marketing that produces the leads for the salesperson who makes the sale and then passes the clients along to the person who actually provides the product or service. What matters when you take this approach is that each person produce the highest-quality output for the next person. The success of the team depends on the quality of whatever number of successive "handoffs" occur from the first person to the last.

Example: Susan, a medical doctor, Bufford, a clinical social worker, and Art, a physical therapist, met when they worked for a rehabilitation center. Susan already had a medical practice specializing in workers' compensation injuries, so when Bufford and Art decided to go into private practice they each rented office space in the same medical building where Susan had her office, and the three of them set up a mutual-referral arrangement. No matter who initiates contact with patients, they are referred first to Susan, who does a complete medical workup. She then refers the client to Bufford, who helps them deal with the psychological and practical aspects of coping with their injuries. They then begin physical rehabilitative therapy with Art. The clients' insurance is billed through Susan's office.

"This is an ideal arrangement for us," Susan reports. "None of us has the responsibility or expense of putting full-time professional staff on the payroll, but we can count on each other to provide our patients with the full range of treatment they need."

Returning to our earlier metaphor of three children building sand castles on the beach, in working sequentially one child might build the foundation for each castle they create, another would add the doors, windows, and turrets, after which the third child would create the surrounding walls and gates and moat.

3. Act as one like a basketball team. A third way to divide up the work is put the whole task in the collective hands of those involved and operate like a basketball or football team. All participants have their own roles, but they act as a unit and nothing gets done unless everyone works together at the same time. J. D. Thompson refers to this type of team effort as a *reciprocal team.* In working this way there's no acknowledgment of who originates an idea or who creates a solution. Working reciprocally requires being highly synchronized and contributing to one another's work by brainstorming and creative problem solving.

A hospital surgery team is another example of a team that acts as one unit. Everyone in the room is performing his or her individual role as they work together to keep the patient alive. A development team works this way as well, with all members contributing their ideas and expertise to creating the best possible new product.

Example: Pete, Denise, and Linda met through their work with children who have Attention Deficit Disorder (ADD). Pete is a pediatrician, Denise is an educational psychologist, and Linda is a marriage and family counselor. Together they established Reach Out, Inc., an ADD treatment center. All the families coming into the center are clients of Reach Out. They will meet and be evaluated by all three professionals, one of whom will become the case leader and coordinate a client's overall treatment plan. Together they assess each client's needs, develop a treatment plan, and then each professional works with the child and his or her family in accordance with that plan.

"Sometimes we bring in other specialists who are affiliated with the center," Pete explains. "We may involve an audiologist, or a math or reading tutor. We consider the child's teacher and school principal to be a part of the team, too, and work as closely with them as possible. Sometimes we prescribe medication. Sometimes we don't. The most exciting thing for us is that by working as a team, we can work with the whole child and his or her family and hopefully contribute what we learn to the field of knowledge on how to best treat this disorder." The Reach Out staff have presented numerous professional workshops and papers together on their work with ADD.

Returning again to our metaphor of three children building sand castles on the beach, working reciprocally as one unit they would jointly build one grand masterpiece, embellishing one wing after another with everyone's contributions.

As you can see, each of these approaches to dividing the workload can be effective; no one is better or worse *per se* than the other. Each could be useful to small businesses or self-employed individuals who want to work in a joint alliance or collaboration of some kind. The method you choose—or unconsciously fall into using—should depend on the nature of your business, your personal style, and how you and your collaborators interact best.

What's important is that you clarify how you prefer to handle the workload with your associates. Collaborations can get into difficulties when, for example, one person is expecting everyone will be working independently as on a gymnastics team, while the others are expecting everyone to function like members of a basketball team.

For example, when Claude took the initiative to recruit and form a career counseling center, he expected the counselors would operate much like members of a gymnastics team with each person carrying his or her own weight by keeping his or her calendar filled with client appointments. From Claude's point of view, the success of the center would be the sum of four financially successful individual practices. His colleagues, however, thought they were signing on to work together more like a basketball team and would be getting their clients through a collective marketing effort. The partners also thought everyone would be participating in all the decisions about how the center would operate, while Claude expected they would make decisions about their own practices independently with the common goal of having a successful center in mind. So, when Claude went off on his own and filled his own practice, instead of feeling pleased, the other partners felt angry and abandoned. From their perspective, Claude was taking all the clients for himself. But Claude felt angry, too. From his perspective, his colleagues weren't doing their part to make their joint venture work, expecting instead that he'd do all the work.

Clearly, how you define "doing your part" will vary considerably depending on how you expect the work will be divided. Bill and Matthew experienced a similar misunderstanding when they formed a partnership to create a multimedia Web page design firm. Although they never explicitly discussed how they would divide the workload, they were working more or less like a relay team. Bill took responsibility for the sales and marketing to bring in their clients, and Matthew did the creative work of actually developing the Web pages. Bill was willing to do cold-calling and sales presentations because he was good at that, but he did expect Matthew to network among his colleagues and business associates because he already had many business contacts and a good reputation as a designer from his prior job in the computer industry. Unfortunately Matthew hated networking; that's why he needed Bill. But Bill became quite annoyed with Matthew's unwillingness to "do his share" and before long he decided to end the partnership.

Here are a few rules you can follow to avoid such misunderstandings by clarifying what "teamwork" actually means to each of you and deciding how you'll divide your workload.

1. Recognize that you are a TEAM. In the beginning of this book, we stated that teaming up is a conscious process in which small and home-based businesses intentionally choose to work with others for their mutual benefit. So even though you are self-employed or in your own business, think of those you work with as your "teammates." Think of yourselves much as you would if you were on a sports team together or working on a team for the same employer. Think of yourselves as being there for one another. Seek ways to help one another. Make a commitment to act responsibly and honestly toward one another. Don't patronize one another. Never put one another down in front of others . . . even jokingly. When clients or acquaintances see that kind of behavior, it's only natural for them to question the quality of your relationship and question doing business with you. Even if your teaming-up relationship is an informal one, you should always aim to think about it as a "team" effort if you want to accomplish your goals by working together.

2. Divide the workload to best fit your situation and your needs—and then make it explicit. Decide what type of team you want to be and make sure you're playing the same game. Each of the three ways teams divide their workload has its own specific advantages, as follows.

- **The Gymnastics Team Approach.** Pooling results of individual efforts is the best approach when the same work can be performed simultaneously by several people and each person has relatively the same capabilities and expertise to get the work done well. It provides the greatest degree of autonomy and the least administrative responsibility. Using this approach, you get most of the benefits of remaining on your own, along with the many of benefits of being part of a team.
- **The Relay Team Approach.** Sequencing the tasks that need to be done and parceling them out to various participants is the best approach when the work involved can be divided easily and distinctly into sequential steps or when differing levels or types of expertise are needed at different times. This approach allows all involved to continue working autonomously in the areas they're most suited for while someone else does the work they cannot or would rather not do. But when anyone falls, everyone falls.

- **The Basketball Team Approach.** Performing as a unit is the best approach when the work that needs to be done is constantly changing or requires the unique talents of all team members working simultaneously in order to achieve the desired results. It's also useful when creating something new when everyone's specialized expertise or opinions are needed. While this approach allows less autonomy and requires more coordination, it provides the greatest sense of feeling that you are truly part of a team.

Note that the decision as to which way to divide your workload depends in large part on how you assess each other's capability and expertise. If your team is made up of people who trust each other's shared expertise, and your business can be carried out in full by any of those involved, working independently and pooling results can work well. For example, two equally experienced and qualified computer consultants can each handle the full range of a client's needs without assistance from the other. Similarly, two medical transcriptionists in a partnership could each have their own clients and work independently while sharing overhead costs.

However, if your teammates don't have equal capabilities and shared expertise, and therefore wouldn't feel confident in one another's ability to carry out the entire work process independently, trying to pool results like a gymnastic team can lead to trouble. For example, if a seasoned computer consultant decides to team up with a novice consultant, the novice may have difficulty living up to the challenge of carrying the full responsibility for a client. The seasoned expert may have doubts about her inexperienced colleague's ability to provide the quality of work she would want to be associated with. Also, the novice might resent having his more seasoned colleague constantly checking his work and looking over his shoulder to point out "mistakes" or making helpful "suggestions." Such a team might better choose to sequence their workload as a relay team would, with the novice doing certain tasks such as setting up or maintaining a client's computer systems while the seasoned expert comes in to work on the more complex problems, do the detailed training, and handle systemwide troubleshooting.

On the other hand, if your alliance is trying to operate like a relay team and one person can't perform his particular tasks well enough, everyone else's success will suffer. In such cases, it would be better to work on projects together more the way a basketball team would so whoever is best qualified to handle each task can pick up the ball when needed.

To prevent misunderstandings, discuss your views and assumptions about each other's expertise and ability to handle the various tasks and situations required in your business. Then you can consciously and openly decide the best way to divide your workload. Encourage everyone to be honest and straightforward about what they can and cannot do. By making your strengths and limitations known to others right from the start, you can clarify not only which way to divide your work, but what each person can actually be expected to contribute.

When marketing consultants Claire and Marcia formed an interdependent alliance, for instance, they were already close friends, so they began mutual marketing and subcontracting work to each other. Because of their friendship, however, they never discussed their perceptions of each other's capabilities. When Claire began asserting that she wanted to handle all the "creative work" and leave the "grunt work" to her friend, Marcia naturally felt insulted and hurt. After an emotional evening session, however, they both realized that Claire actually was better at coming up with ideas for innovative and creative marketing campaigns, but Marcia was better at writing proposals and presenting the campaign options to prospective clients. While Claire had taken that to be "grunt work," during their discussion, she realized that it was equally important and vital to their success. From that point on, they began to respect each other's strengths and could think of themselves more like a relay team and could proudly divide their work so that each could do what she does best.

For further guidelines on how to divide up your responsibilities, see the box below.

Which Division of Labor Is Best for Your Team?

To determine whether you're best suited to divide your work up more like a gymnastics team, a relay team, or a basketball team, answer the following questions about yourself, those you'll be working with, and the nature of your work. Select the approach that best fits how you can work optimally. Then, use the secrets that follow for maximizing your success.

Pooling Your Results Like a Gymnastics Team
- Is the work that needs to be done distinct in that each project or job can be easily defined and identified?
- Can each person handle the work to be done with a client in its entirety and take full responsibility for working with that client without relying on other team members?
- Do team members prefer to work more independently?
- Does each team member have roughly the same level of expertise?
- If team members need to consult one another for ideas or solutions, are such consultations limited in terms of the level of creative or problem-solving input required?
- Can the costs of team activities be easily divided among team members according to an equal investment in time and effort?

If you can answer "Yes" to all these questions, pooling results can work for you. If you answered "No" to any question above, go on to consider working more like a basketball or relay team.

Secrets to Successfully Pooling Results

1. Respect one another's abilities and decisions. Support one another's projects without interference, unless invited to discuss them.
2. Expect that each person will pull his or her own weight in all phases of business, from marketing and sales to billing (unless you arrange for support services or staff to handle such functions).
3. Divide profits equally.

Acting As a Unit Like a Basketball Team

- Is each project different and distinct, requiring separate analysis, planning, and implementation?
- Is each project an integrated whole, unable to be divided into clear-cut phases or specific sequences of tasks?
- Does each project benefit by having several team members participate in the analysis, planning, and implementation?
- Do team members have roughly equal levels of expertise either in the same field or in different fields that are necessary to a project?
- Do customers feel better knowing that more than one person with different skills and expertise will be working together with them at the same time?
- Can team members coordinate their schedules and handle the logistics of working together productively?
- Do team members prefer working on tasks with others?

If you can answer "Yes" to all these questions, acting as a unit can work for you. If the levels of expertise among team members vary, working like a basketball team can still be viable if there is a team leader or mentor to assist those with less expertise. If you answered "No" to any question above, go on to consider working together more like a relay team.

Secrets to Successfully Acting As a Unit

1. Make sure team members recognize that each person's input is needed and valuable. Opinions should be willingly solicited and considered.
2. Everyone needs to willingly join in carrying out all aspects of the work jointly, including support functions such as secretarial services, billing, and customer support (unless you have staff or outside support services to handle these functions).
3. Make all major decisions collectively or under the guidance of one appointed leader.

4. Consistently share all pertinent information with all team members.

5. Divide profits equally or, if not equally, according to agreed-upon percentages reflecting each person's effort in a project.

Sequencing Tasks Like a Relay Team

- Can each project be segmented into phases with a clear beginning and ending point?
- Do the phases occur in a clear sequence, chronologically; i.e., one after the other, with little overlap?
- Can one person be held responsible for each phase?
- Does each person have the capability to specialize in her or his given phase?
- Do team members like being part of a team while still doing their own thing?

If you can answer "Yes" to all these questions, operating like a relay team can work for you. If you answered "No" to any question, you may need to consider working more like a basketball team where tasks can be shared among all team members.

Secrets to Successfully Sequencing Your Work Tasks

1. Let each person handle his or her phase of the work without interference from others. However, it usually does help to appoint a team leader or someone to oversee the various operations and assure that the final product is acceptable.

2. Count on each person to contribute to the best of his or her ability. Then make the most of what you are given.

3. Profits can be split in any manner desired, as long as they are agreed upon in advance.

Note that these suggestions are not cut-and-dried. To handle some situations or solve special problems, you may want or need to operate using one approach while later adopting another approach under differing circumstances. Your preferred way of dividing up your workload may change over time, as well. When we, Paul and Sarah, first began working on our own we worked strictly like a gymnastics team, pooling our results. We each had our own sole-proprietorship and operated our own business autonomously, but shared our home-business overhead and household expenses. Occasionally we would bring each other in on a project as a sub-contractor, in which case we would divide the tasks involved sequentially, with the subcontractor stepping in to do his or her portion of a particular project at the designated time. When we formed our formal partnership to specialize in providing information on self-employment and working from home, we continued working primarily on a pooled basis at first. Paul would write certain chapters or portions of an article and Sarah would write others which we would pool into the final product.

Over time we began working more like a relay team. Paul would do the research for a book, speech or article, for example, Sarah would write the first draft, Paul would then edit that draft and Sarah would put the final polish on it. Our presentations and even our interviews were also more sequential in nature at first. Paul would cover certain areas; Sarah others. Our early attempts at working as a unit were rocky as we tended to bump heads and step on toes too often. Now, although we still write sequentially, we've come to speak and broadcast as a unit, literally passing the ball back and forth between us and building on each other's efforts as the situation demands.

Of late, as our business continues to grow, we're finding that we need to use all three ways of dividing our workload depending on the demands of the projects we're working on. The only challenge is being sure that we're on the same game plan so that if one of us is to assume full responsibility for a project we each know that and no one is waiting for the other to do some task he or she doesn't realize is expected. And if we're going to be passing the baton or the ball to one another on a particular project, we need to be sure we've arranged with each other to be standing by in position to take over when that moment arrives.

3. Be flexible and willing to modify your workload divisions if needed.
At any time in a business relationship, a change of circumstances or crisis situation can arise that will affect your workload and require that you find a different way to divide up who does what. You may have a customer with a critical turnaround time that demands you all pitch in and work as a unit, or you may need to break up your sequential approach and work independently to make sure the job gets done on time. You may hear about an opportunity to bid on a new proposal that demands the creative input of everyone on your team, and so you'll want to switch from your customary gymnastic approach and act like a basketball team to get the benefit from everyone's input.

The ability to be flexible in your approach to your work is actually one of the strengths you gain by teaming up. Whenever circumstances change, you can take advantage of the resources your relationships provide and reconfigure the division of labor in whatever way meets the demands of the situation. Here's an example of the benefits such flexibility can offer. Mary Beth Mason, owner of WordMason, a desktop publishing service in Silver Spring, Maryland, acts as a satellite subcontractor providing work for many other sole proprietors of word-processing services. Normally Mary Beth divides work tasks up sequentially with her subcontractors handling various stages of a job that she eventually assembles and publishes at her place of business. However, when a large job comes to Mary Beth needing a fast turnaround time, she reverts to a "crisis" mode and asks each of her subcontractors to handle additional aspects of a job and holds them responsible for total quality output. Mary Beth points out that she can do this because she has enough confidence in her subcontractors to know that, if necessary, they will put in the extra work to make sure the job is done right. "My subcontractors have saved me many a time," Mary Beth told us. "I am really lucky to have found people I can trust and who know what I consider 'quality' work."

In general, these three rules governing the successful dividing up of your workload apply to any alliance of small and home-based businesses. Whether you're teaming up with one person or ten people, there's no escaping the fact that you'll need to clarify how you will divide up the tasks so you can function together most effectively.

USING GOOD COMMUNICATION
TO BUILD YOUR RELATIONSHIP

When all is said and done, the success of your teaming-up relationship depends greatly on your ability to communicate with one another. Good communication is the foundation of your relationship. From the simple banter at a friendly networking meeting to the complex negotiations and management of a multiperson joint venture, people who work together need to communicate effectively in order to:

- Transmit pertinent facts about their businesses to one another
- Express their views and opinions
- Make joint decisions
- Resolve any problems or disagreements

In general, the closer peoples' goals and values are to one another, the smoother their communications will be. This is one reason many people prefer to establish business relationships with friends or family members with whom they already feel they share common goals and values. It's also why we suggest that in considering a teaming-up relationship with anyone you don't know, you should put in as much effort as you can to become acquainted with their personal values and ethics before working together in any formal capacity. Getting to know people personally before working with them professionally enables you to discover the extent to which you actually share values and goals, and thereby determine how easy or difficult your future communications will be.

Generally speaking, the more you agree on the following topics, the smoother your communications will be. Conversely, the more disagreement you have on these topics, the more time-consuming and difficult your communications can become no matter what the specific business tasks might involve:

- Honesty
- Fairness
- Personal integrity
- Timeliness and punctuality
- Manners and the treatment of other people
- Aesthetics and etiquette
- Attitudes about family
- Educational level
- Attitudes about the profession or business you are involved in
- Money and financial matters

In fact, for many people, good communication with other people and sharing values on issues like these are almost synonymous. When people share values, they usually feel a bond with one another that's so strong that no matter what each person says, they understand one another perfectly. You may occasionally have "miscommunications," but in general you'll give one another the benefit of the doubt because you know you're on the same wavelength. This makes it possible to resolve problems more quickly and easily.

But no matter how great your personal rapport, you still need to foster good communication habits. Having a good rapport with someone will make communication infinitely easier, but everyone can benefit by following several basic rules of good communication because sooner or later, we all will run into situations where even the strongest personal bond doesn't assure that we'll understand one another. When working with colleagues or business associates, even a natural-born communicator needs to keep good basic communication habits in mind to prevent communication breakdowns. And the same good habits are equally important for people who are partnering with a spouse or best friend.

Every teaming-up relationship can expect to have communication difficulties from time to time, but with the right tools, such difficulties need not become a problem. As we've suggested earlier in this book, the world is changing rapidly and this fast pace of change strains the limits of our communication. As in the popular television commercial where the overnight delivery service spokesperson has to talk at what seems like ten thousand words per minute, most of us feel pressured to get our messages over quickly, to be understood without question, and to make the right decisions right here and right NOW. And as self-employed individuals and small-business people, we're often working with a wide variety of clients (domestically or even abroad), interacting with clients whose values and attitudes differ tremendously from our own and working under tighter deadlines and on more complex projects than ever before. Such new situations and competitive pressures can tax your communication skills to the limit, sometimes presenting you with disagreements or conflicts that you have never encountered before (and never expected to encounter).

Fortunately, there are many sources of information available today to help us develop our ability to speak articulately, clearly, and persuasively and to listen effectively to what others are saying. For purposes of teaming up, however, the many theories of communication and models for improving communication skills can be distilled down to six fundamental principles, which we call the VELCRO approach to good communication. VELCRO is an acronym for six key characteristics that can keep communication flowing in a teaming-up relationship.

1. Viewpoint—respect each other's viewpoint
2. Evident—make your communications evident, not tacit
3. Listening—engage in interactive listening
4. Constructive/Creative—keep problem solving constructive and creative
5. Rational—use rational decision making
6. Organized—organize your communication

Like Velcro, the material that enables fabrics and other surfaces to stick together, the VELCRO approach for good communication can make your teaming-up relationships stronger and more durable. Before we explain each principle of the strategy, however, we need to emphasize two overriding points about the VELCRO approach to communication: it will help you become more *proactive* and keep you focused on *business,* not personal issues.

Becoming a More Proactive Communicator

Using the VELCRO principles will help you become more *proactive* in your communications and thereby prevent communication problems from developing in the first place. This is not to suggest that you and those you work with will always agree and never have differences of opinion when following this approach. That would be unrealistic. No one *always* shares opinions to the point that they will always agree. But proactive communication prevents problems from becoming divisive and interfering with the reasons you've decided to work with one another. By following the VELCRO principles, a potential conflict can usually be resolved amicably and need not develop into a full-blown conflict, but can turn instead into a useful business dialogue. In other words, by following this strategy everyone involved can stay on the track.

If you aren't proactive, when conflict occurs, your efforts usually get off the track and you have to resort to *reactive* communication to overcome your differences and get back on the track. There's nothing wrong with reactive communication *per se,* but often by the time it's needed, you've already sunk into a communications quagmire that you must then struggle to extricate yourselves from. The more quagmires a relationship has to struggle through, the less you'll enjoy working together and the more likely you'll be to decide you cannot communicate with one another. Each successive quagmire damages your relationship a little more until it becomes difficult, if not impossible, to work together.

Distinguishing Between Business and Personal Communications

The VELCRO principles of communication are designed specifically for business, not personal relationships. Communicating effectively with someone you're working with is not the same as communicating with your family, children, or with friends over the dinner table or on the tennis court. Even if you are working with family and friends, your business communications will need to be more goal oriented and structured than your informal personal conversations. Your job in working together is to obtain information, analyze situations, negotiate with one another, solve problems, provide a product or service, and please your clients and customers.

This distinction is crucial because it will help you focus on the business aspect of your relationship even if you and your teaming-up associates have been or are in the process of developing a personal relationship. Many of the most problematical communications problems people have in teaming up arise from blurring personal and business communication. In personal relationships, many things are assumed that would otherwise need to be negotiated and made explicit in a business relationship. Ida, for example, assumed her friend Bill would pay her for providing the background music for the weekend seminars he gave as part of his business. After all, he knew full well how difficult it had been for her to get established as a professional musician. She had discussed it with him many times, and he had always been sympathetic and understanding. Bill, on other hand, assumed that Ida would play at his seminars for free, after all, she was his friend and knew how difficult it had been to get his seminar business off the ground. He had talked with her about it often, and she had always been sympathetic and understanding. In this case, their personal relationship had interfered with their having clear business communications.

Something that's funny or cute in a personal relationship can be dead serious or embarrassing in a business relationship. Mark, for example, habitually called his wife "sweetie" in their personal relationship and she enjoyed this term of endearment, so when he joined her management consulting business as a partner, he repeatedly called her "sweetie" during client meetings. His wife was understandingly embarrassed, and this habit led to more than one argument before Mark resolved to modify his communication in the business setting. Likewise John loved it when his girlfriend tricked him with outrageous practical jokes until they started a home-based mail order business from his apartment. The pranks that delighted him after hours irritated him while at work. On the other hand, as one couple pointed out, applying the VELCRO principles to your friendships or your love life would take away much of the romance, spontaneity, and surprise that make personal relationships so special. But in a business relationship, they can literally mean business.

Making the distinction between business and personal communication is also particularly important when you encounter a difficult time in a teaming-up relationship. The VELCRO principles will help you stay focused on talking about issues that keep your enterprise afloat instead of letting profits disappear amidst smoldering personal animosities. Not surprisingly, in most cases, when profits go up, relationships have a way of improving rather than deteriorating. In addition, making a distinct separation between business and personal communications can also make it easier to pull the plug amicably on a business relationship with friends or family members that isn't working out.

With these thoughts in mind, the following six principles can help keep your business communications on track.

SIX PRINCIPLES FOR BUILDING TIES THAT BIND: THE *VELCRO* APPROACH TO COMMUNICATION

1. VIEWPOINT—Respect Each Other's Viewpoint

Although most of us profess to know that everyone has her or his own viewpoint on nearly everything, we often fail to apply this knowledge to our business communications. We inadvertently go into meetings with our own preconceived ideas and suggestions, overlooking the possibility that others may see things quite differently. We therefore can end up arguing, protesting, or putting forth our own ideas as the right ones instead of listening to others.

In a teaming-up situation, however, it's always best to start out from the outset recognizing that each of you will have your own perception and analysis of events. The unique perceptions each of you brings to a situation are based on your differing life experiences, education, values, and insights. Often it's intentionally exploring your differences that will make each of you more successful than you would be by relying on your own perceptions and ideas alone.

Mike Hakimi is one of four partners in the Chicago Internet service provider American Information Systems. He admits that he and his partners have had many cantankerous meetings during which each person steadfastly held to the position he or she thought was best for the future growth of their company. Mike told us,

> I've learned that the more partners there are, the more complicated it
> gets; you can no longer make the decisions you alone think are best,

but that's what has helped us so much. We all trust each other and know that each partner wants what's best for the company. So we all understand that when we disagree on an issue, we can't let it get personal. We've had our share of, shall we say, "heated" debates but at the end, all is forgotten and we are friends. We all spend a lot of time together and when it comes to making decisions for the company; it's the respect for each other and our willingness to listen to each other's ideas, and not letting your ego get in the way that's been our strength.

Mike was right on target in our view. As he points out, to communicate effectively with associates and develop a good rapport, you have to be willing to *understand* their viewpoints and *respect* them.

Understanding requires that we set aside our perceptions and get to know the other person's frame of reference in as much depth as possible. It means not speeding through the conversation, pretending we get someone's point after just a word or two so we can get our own ideas on the table. At times, it may mean having to probe deeper and peel away the layers of what someone's trying to say, getting deeper and deeper into the person's thinking and truly discovering the origins of her or his viewpoint and its ramifications.

For example, consider this scenario: James and Elaine are planning their business strategy. Each has a different perspective on how to spend his or her limited marketing funds. James wants to invest in a newsletter to be distributed via the Internet. Elaine wants to stick with creating and sending out a periodic direct mail piece. In many partnerships, such divergent views could lead to a disagreement and possibly even a conflict between the partners. However, if James and Elaine can stop for a moment and, instead of jumping into a combative stance arguing to convince the other that his or her point of view is the best, can ask each other several probing questions, they'll undoubtedly gain new insights into the why each one thinks his or her idea is the best one. In most cases, there's a useful insight behind each person's point of view that isn't fully communicated at first glance.

In this case, it turns out James knows of another company that received an excellent response from a Web page they created, but he had never mentioned this story to Eileen before. Based on the other firm's success, he believed they too could get customers by marketing on-line. Meanwhile, Eileen had been reading about how many companies advertising on the Internet were disappointed with the response they were getting, and she was afraid that only a small number of their customers would be surfing the Web. Understanding their two perspectives in greater detail helped them develop the best solution for their firm. They decided to share a Web page with another company as a way to test out that market, while continuing their plans for the direct mail piece Elaine had planned.

Understanding someone else's point of view, as this example illustrates, is only half the equation. *Respecting* her or his viewpoint is also necessary. To demonstrate respect for each person's point of view, you must be willing to start a conversation or discussion from the premise that there is no fixed right or wrong approach to any problem and that each person is not only entitled to present his or her ideas and suggestions, but that every contribution can be of value to the path you will follow or the decision you will pursue. Of course, this is more difficult when you're teaming up with people who have an area of expertise that's quite different from yours. But often the best solutions come from spicing up your area of expertise with a dash of fresh perspective.

Maintaining an understanding and respectful attitude is especially important for getting through the forming and storming phases of your endeavor. Many teams literally fall apart at the beginning of their relationship because they either don't take the time to explore each person's viewpoint in depth or they don't respect one another's perspectives. Failing to understand and respect each person's viewpoint is particularly common when team members don't know one another very well yet. This lack of understanding often sows seeds of miscommunication and conflict right from the start, that can lead to problems later.

Mutual respect and understanding also foster a ripe environment group synergy. When people understand and appreciate each member's point of view, they gain access to a multiplicity of new ideas and perspectives, from which a synthesis can arise that goes beyond what any one person would have contributed. In James and Elaine's situation, they eventually benefited because after their initial foray onto the Web through sharing a page, they ultimately applied Elaine's targeted direct mail list to marketing on the Internet. She developed the list criteria and James used his knowledge of the Web to target news groups and sites that met those criteria. They both ended up feeling great about this strategy and immediately began implementing it with enthusiasm.

2. EVIDENT—Make Your Communications Evident, Not Tacit

No one can understand and respect someone else's viewpoint unless it gets communicated clearly, so this second principle is a corollary to the first: your communication must be evident, not tacit. When a working relationship seems good, we often take it for granted that we understand each other. We assume that someone already knows what we need, want, expect, and value. There's a tendency to leave portions of our verbal and written communications unstated, relying on assumptions or on what we imagine someone wants rather than asking about it directly. Sometimes our expectations and feelings remain below the surface because we think people already know them or because we simply don't have time to go into the necessary detail to explain our views in depth. As a result, only half of our message gets communicated clearly leaving the other half vague or missing altogether.

Making sure we understand one another, however, requires communicating in sufficient detail that our messages can be acknowledged and confirmed or denied. In other words, communication is not a one-way street. We can never assume that the message sent is the message that was received. Communication is actually a three-step process.

message sent ⟶ *message received* ⟶ *message confirmed*

Unless you make sure important communications include all three steps, your relationship and your work together can suffer from never truly knowing what each other is thinking or feeling. Consider these two typical examples.

Case 1:

Situation: Betty and Jim have agreed to bid on a big project together, and they discuss the bid at length in a meeting on Monday. Jim agrees to write the proposal, and Betty will do the market research. On Friday, Jim calls Betty asking for the market research results. Betty replies that she's been waiting for Jim to send her the proposal first so she will know what to research. Jim is annoyed. He thought it was understood that they would both begin working on their tasks immediately so they could get the job done as quickly as possible. Betty is surprised. She claims they never clarified this process and so she assumed that Jim understood she needed to see the proposal before she could begin doing the research.

Background and Analysis: After analyzing the situation, these two collaborators realized this is a classic case of tacit assumptions and expectations. Miscommunication occurred despite the fact that they both thought they'd been very clear about their expectations during their first meeting. As it turned out, in her past corporate position, Betty always wrote as much of a proposal as she could first, and then filled in the holes by doing research on the facts she was missing, so she assumed Jim worked according to this pattern too. Meanwhile Jim thought he'd made it clear that this was a rush job, so there was no time to waste; from his perspective, the two tasks had to be accomplished simultaneously. As a result, these two collaborators ended up working the entire weekend to complete their proposal on time, and both were disappointed with their miscommunication. Although they resolved their problem this time, they agreed to be more careful the next time to spell out just how they expected to proceed on joint projects.

Case 2:

Situation: Justine and Elliot agree to provide mutual referrals to one another of their existing customers. In the first month of operation, Justine made it a practice to ask *every* customer if he or she needed Elliot's services, and she spent some time chatting with each of them about the high quality of Elliot's work. At the end of the month, she had referred ten people to Elliot, but Elliot only sent her two referrals. When she called to ask if he'd been making an effort to refer people to her, he assured her that he indeed had. But he pointed out that he was only discussing her services with a few select customers because, after all, he didn't want to send "just anyone" to her. He wanted to prescreen clients to be sure they truly needed her services and thereby never waste her time with inappropriate referrals.

Background and Analysis: As in the first case, the two people came to realize their disagreement resulted from tacit expectations. Although they both thought they had clearly discussed how their mutual referrals were going to work, each person's perception of how the process would work was different based on their previous experiences and expectations. Justine believed that the whole point of making mutual referrals was to drum up as much business as possible for each other. That's how she had done it before with another colleague, and it had been very successful. Meanwhile, Elliot, not knowing about her previous success, had never mentioned to her that he dislikes it when someone he's doing business with "accosts" him with a referral. In his mind, he believes that the best referrals are carefully targeted ones he can approach in a very low-key, professional manner. That's why he only mentioned Justine's services to customers who expressed a need or appeared to clearly be in need of what she could offer.

Once it became clear how differently these two people approached making referrals, Justine began cutting back her efforts. Over time, they gradually referred fewer and fewer people to each other and made referral arrangements with others who worked more as they did. Their arrangement got off on the wrong foot because of tacit communications.

In addition to making assumptions and failing to overtly express expectations, many people also fall into the trap of thinking that if you act a certain way toward others, they in turn will understand that you want them to act the same way toward you. This process is called "modeling." It means that instead of stating what you want or need, you "model" or show others through your actions how you want them to act or behave. For example, if you're always apologetic whenever you've created a problem, you might expect other people to be equally apologetic when they cause a problem. In *Getting Together: Building Relationship As We Negotiate,* authors Roger Fisher and Scott Brown point out that people fall into the modeling trap because they're following the Golden Rule idea: "Do unto others as you would have them do unto you." As a result, they think that if they treat someone well, he or she will actually treat them well too. But as Fisher and Scott remind us, modeling can create many communication problems.

The Golden Rule is a useful rule of thumb in helping me understand how my behavior is likely to affect you and how you might want me to behave. But the Golden Rule is *not* based on the premise that if I behave as you would like, I can safely predict that you will behave the same way. If I try to build a strong working relationship based on such an optimistic view—that you will reciprocate my actions—I will make dangerous mistakes. This is particularly true when partisan perceptions are taken into account.

Modeling is an inefficient, if not counterproductive, method for assuring clear communication in a business relationship because there's no guarantee that the other person understands your expectations, agrees with you, or is willing to do things the way you're doing them. Expecting someone to act as you act is no more reliable than assuming an associate will pick up on unstated expectations. In both cases, to be understood, you must make clear what you want and expect from each other by specifically communicating it. You can't expect that others will get your point by making a point of treating them the way you want to be treated.

Consider this situation: A woman was having a problem with her business partner. She very much wanted them both to work as hard as possible to reach their financial goals within the first year of their formal partnership. Although she showed up at the office at 9:00 A.M. sharp every morning, he continually arrived around an hour later. She didn't want to express her disapproval directly, but she did think he should get to work earlier if they were going to succeed. So she began coming in even earlier, 8:30 A.M., and then 8:00 A.M. Each morning she'd let him know how early she had arrived by dropping little comments here and there. Still he showed up at 10:00 A.M. Finally, she became so frustrated that she vented her feelings about his "lazy attitude," and they promptly got into an argument. Once their conversation calmed down, he pointed out that he regularly stayed at the office long after she left, and she realized they were putting forth an equal effort after all. However, if she had *proactively* brought up the issue when it first began annoying her, they would have avoided this unpleasant episode.

In short, making your communications evident is an important key to proactive communication. Whether you're talking about how you'll run your collaboration or how you'll relate to your customers, each person needs to communicate her or his desires and expectations clearly in order to avoid the frustration, wasted energy, and even lost business from miscommunications.

3. LISTENING—Engage in Interactive Listening

As we said earlier, communication is a three-step process: sending a clear message, getting the message, and making sure the message you got was the message intended. This third principle focuses on making sure what you're *hearing* is what your associates are actually trying to say. We call this process "interactive listening." It incorporates what many communication books refer to as "active listening," along with other techniques that are helpful in a business setting.

Listening "interactively" instead of passively prevents several communication problems that can dampen any business relationship. You've probably experienced them all and hope never to again.

- One person talks too much
- One person talks at the other
- One person talks too little (doesn't express his or her thoughts and feelings)
- One person talks on a different level than the other person
- One person talks indirectly rather than directly
- One person sends mixed messages
- One person continues to talk without knowing if the other understands

The goal of interactive listening is to make sure that every conversation is a two-way process in which all take responsibility for the quality of their communication to be sure they've heard and been heard correctly. Here are several guidelines for becoming an interactive listener.

1. Think of yourself as a partner in the conversation. Be attentive and interested; have a desire to listen and to understand what others are saying. Don't be distracted by your own ideas and thoughts or by the activities going on around you when you're listening to others speak. Your attentiveness contributes energy to the conversation and makes you a partner in the process. Show your energy by using appropriate nods, smiles, supportive comments, and encouragement.

2. Show empathy. Put yourself in the other person's place to identify with what he or she is saying (the content of his or her message), how he or she is feeling (the emotions involved in the message), and what the situation means to him or her (the values underlying the message). Having an empathic attitude toward what a speaker is saying usually helps draw out the message in greater detail than if you appear to be distracted or disapproving of what you're hearing.

3. Engage in "repartee." Repartee is a critical ingredient in interactive listening and refers to making comments and responding to what you're hearing. Repartee shows that you are participating in the conversation; it lets people know that you are hearing them.

Ironically, people who talk too much often do so only because their audience does not participate in the conversation through repartee. By becoming engaged in the conversation, you can preempt someone who might otherwise talk on and on and take over in your absence. To engage in repartee with someone who's doing too much of the talking, use the phrase, "Let me share something with you before you go on." This alerts the person to the fact that you wish to participate in the conversation too.

4. Listen actively. As you listen, particularly when you are unclear about the message or if you sense a possible disagreement arising, provide feedback on what you are hearing by paraphrasing what you understand the speaker to be saying. Active listening is often described as repeating back to the speaker what you think you heard them say, as in "So, you are saying that . . ." By doing this, you are able to double-check if your understanding of what the speaker has said is accurate. If you've misperceived the message, the speaker will most likely correct your interpretation by restating the message in a different way or by elucidating in greater detail what he or she was trying to convey.

5. Look between the lines for not only what is said but also what isn't being said. As discussed above, buried within many conversations are hidden assumptions, expectations, and feelings. As you listen to other speakers, try to determine if there are incomplete or unstated messages beneath what's being said. Ask questions to be sure that you understand the assumptions or premise behind what's being suggested and that you've heard their viewpoint correctly. To get at buried assumptions, for example, Justine could have asked Elliot to give her an example of his best and worst referral experience. Had she done this, she would have known right from the start they had different perspectives on making referrals.

6. Clarify mixed messages. People are often ambivalent about their opinions and feelings on a topic, and so their conversations may be inconsistent. Sometimes we want to be accommodating, for example, despite the fact that we're not fully in agreement, so we try to straddle the fence on an issue. Whenever you detect a mixed message, it's wise to diplomatically interject for the sake of clarification a statement such as, "A while ago I thought you were saying _____. So I'm confused by what you just said. Would you mind clarifying?" In doing this, your goal isn't to antagonize the speaker but to make sure that you're understanding one another.

7. Use criticism sparingly. Criticism can be a stumbling block in many relationships. It's usually wise to avoid criticizing a business associate unless the person is seeking or otherwise ready and willing to listen to your feedback. If you see people doing things that appear to be against their self-interest, you may want to check out if they're interested in your feedback and, if so, share your evaluation of the situation. But having done so, then leave it at that.

"Constructive" criticism is only constructive when the person perceives it to be helpful. So accept that your feedback may or may not be useful and don't expect people to use it unless they find it valuable. You may even be right about your concerns or reactions, but if the person isn't in a place to hear and use it, it's better to drop your comments in the interest of developing your overall relationship.

Avoiding criticism, however, doesn't mean you can't disagree. Disagreement and criticism are two quite different things. In disagreeing, you're saying that your views are not the same. In criticizing, you're saying there's something wrong with the other person's viewpoint or behavior.

Should a situation arise in which you need to express your criticism because an associate is doing something that directly affects your well-being, do so by focusing on facts and stating your observations, concerns, and reactions—not your opinions or judgments. Provide reasons for your comments. It also helps whenever you need to make a negative criticism to balance your comments with positive feedback. Point out what you think is working well as well as what you think isn't. Whenever possible, provide the alternatives or changes that would correct or eliminate your concerns.

Following these guidelines for interactive listening can go a long way to improve your communication and your teaming-up relationship. When people both listen and *feel* listened to, they're usually more willing to be team players and work for the benefit of all.

4. CONSTRUCTIVE/CREATIVE—Keep Problem Solving Constructive and Creative

This fourth principle is a proactive antidote to the most common source of all communication difficulties—*problems, problems, problems.* Most people don't have much difficulty with normal, everyday communication because the routine issues we handle day in and day out without thinking about them don't usually engender communication breakdown. Usually it's when a problem develops, when a crisis occurs, or when a misunderstanding arises that communication becomes challenging. In fact, it's been said that a good business is one with interesting problems. However, challenges and problems also present many opportunities to splinter a business relationship by putting pressure on your communications.

Facing a problem or crisis together can be an opportunity to strengthen and deepen a business relationship. Therefore, it's of great benefit to approach whatever problems develop with a constructive and creative attitude, instead of falling prey to blaming, shaming, or competing with one another. Approaching problems with a positive attitude can help reduce the tensions that can otherwise turn a challenging situation into a communication problem. Here are three key principles for constructive and creative problem solving.

1. Focus on defining and solving the problem, not on finding who's to blame or at fault. Tracing the origins of a problem for the purpose of discovering who's at fault is usually counterproductive. In today's business environment, many problems are, in fact, complex, and the fault can't be placed on a single individual's shoulders. In fact, sometimes problems occur as a result of incomplete communication to which everyone unknowingly contributed. So it helps if you all focus your efforts on clarifying the nature of the problem, its ramifications on your business, and how you can best respond instead of spending your time trying to find out who caused it in the first place. In other words, the goal of problem-solving discussions should be to figure out how to solve the problem.

2. Use creative brainstorming techniques. Creative brainstorming is an excellent problem-solving tool for many reasons. First, it increases the energy in a group because it invites each person to freely contribute his or her ideas and suggestions. Second, it eliminates criticism and competitiveness because, under the rules of brainstorming, all ideas—good, bad, brilliant, and awful—are equally welcome. No idea is too ridiculous or stupid to discount.

Creative brainstorming is essentially a four-step process.

- **Phase 1: Orienting Everyone to the Challenge at Hand.** Creative brainstorming begins with someone explaining the situation and focusing attention on a clear description of the desired outcome—this is the positive result you want to achieve. Everyone and anyone can ask questions at this point until they fully understand the specific situation and the desired results.
- **Phase 2: Generating Ideas.** Everyone involved then begins generating ideas for possible solutions. *Any* contribution is acceptable. No idea is too absurd or too silly to discount at this point in a brainstorming session. Every idea should be written down on a large easel in front of the room if several people are involved or on a notepad if there are just a few of you around a table. This list of ideas will usually spark additional ideas, so write clearly and make sure everyone can see all the items on the list to review as you brainstorm. In addition, be sure to write ideas down exactly as stated by whoever suggested them. There should be no editing, rewording, discussion, or evaluation of the ideas during this phase. It may well be tempting to jump in and say, "But we already tried that" or "We can't do that because . . ." or to explain why a certain idea won't work, but remind each other to hold off on all such evaluations until later. They interfere with the creative process.
- **Phase 3: Evaluating Your Ideas.** Before moving into this part of the process, it helps to pat yourselves on the back for generating so many ideas and possibilities. This reinforces the fact that your joint efforts are

appreciated and that each person's contributions are valued and helpful. During this phase, then, the team begins to discuss the pros and cons of the various ideas you've generated, explaining objectively why they may or may not work. Don't spend time trying to remember who contributed which idea or giving credit to anyone. Instead, stay focused on making the evaluation process a team effort.

Also, keep an open mind during this phase. Look for overlapping ideas and places where parts of several solutions might work in combination. Often the best solutions to complex problems are a synthesis of multiple ideas and approaches: a little of this idea and a little of that. These solutions often arise from the synergy that's created when two or more people pool their creative thinking. This is one of the real benefits of teaming up. It can be easier to get your mind around a problem together than having to figure it out alone. The best solution is often the result of successive contributions of ideas, each one building on the previous ones, until the problem is "surrounded," "captured," and "surmounted." At other times, the solution comes as a sudden insight from a single person who draws on the collective experience to come up with an "ah-hah!" for everyone. But even then, that person would probably not have had the grand "ah-hah!" without everyone else's previous contributions.

- **Phase 4: Reaching and Implementing a Decision.** The last stage of brainstorming is obviously to select the best solutions from those you've been generating and develop a plan to implement them. In most cases, the process of brainstorming will have stimulated a unanimous decision because everyone's been involved in the process and part of the chain of thinking that has produced the best answer. In some cases, however, several ideas may seem to have equal validity; if so, if there are several of you involved in the process, you may need to vote to arrive at one alternative over another. If you do decide to vote, however, be sure that everyone agrees in advance to support the most popular idea, because a successful joint effort usually needs everyone's full support.

3. Keep your problem-solving energy and momentum moving forward. Another key to keeping problem solving constructive and creative is to prevent the process from bogging down or getting stuck in apparent impossibilities. Instead, stay focused on your goal and continue to tap into the positive energy and momentum that can be generated when people work together for a goal. Most of us can identify with the special feeling we get when we are working productively with other people: there's a sense of enthusiasm, a vitality and fervor that make us all feel we can achieve any goal we set our minds to.

Take a minute to think of a situation in which you were working at "peak" energy with someone else. Remember what happened to your energy if someone started complaining, protesting, or arguing. Most of us know quite well when an effort has lost its energy and momentum. We can recognize when negative energy arises and feel how it stops creativity in its tracks. So whenever you sense negative energy developing in your group discussions, suggest that you stop and refocus your attention on your goals. Here are some common triggers that block the flow of positive, creative problem solving.

- Naysaying, putting down, or berating ideas
- Arguing over every point
- Criticizing each other's ideas or role in the process
- Changing the subject to unrelated topics instead of staying focused on the goal
- One person dominating the conversation and not letting others speak
- Interjecting too many jokes and not taking the problem-solving effort seriously
- Constant interruption to handle other business or personal matters
- Nitpicking an idea to death
- Holding grudges from past sessions or discussions

Whenever the negative energy of such behaviors saps your joint efforts and halts your momentum, take action to recapture a positive team spirit. To do this, you may need to take a break or candidly talk about the behavior that's blocking your momentum. Whoever is engaging in such behaviors may not be aware of it (and it could even be you). So it's useful to point out when your team's problem-solving energy seems to have dissipated so that all present can take a breather and refocus their efforts on achieving your joint goals.

5. RATIONAL—Use Rational Decision Making

In general, making rational decisions asks that we place reason above emotion and objective factors over subjective perceptions. Of course, it's never wise to ignore our feelings in making important decisions. In fact, it's impossible. But aiming to balance our emotions with reason enables us to better understand most situations and to make more consistent decisions. As Roger Fisher and Scott Brown write in *Getting Together*:

> Every problem, large or small, has an emotional aspect. Two people should be able to think clearly about their differences while they feel and cope with emotions of different kinds and intensities. Their emotions should not cause them to lose the ability to consider the pros and cons of a range of options before making a decision—whether the issue is sharing a family car, settling a lawsuit, working out a divorce, [or] reworking a contract in light of changed market conditions. In every case, emotions and reason should each be informed, but not overwhelmed, by the other.

Of course, in matters that affect our livelihood, financial survival, and self-image, it can be difficult to keep an objective point of view. This is especially true when you're working with family or friends with whom you're already emotionally involved. But here are several guidelines you can use to keep your problem-solving efforts focused on reaching objective decisions.

1. Avoid emotional extremes. We all have feelings and become emotional under stress, and we may deal with our emotions in different ways. Some people become very excited, exuberant, and even overwhelmed by their emotions. Other people put emotions on the back burner, close down, and present a cold, distant exterior to the world.

The truth is neither of these approaches is helpful in a teaming-up effort. Too much emotion shrouds reasoning and interferes with communication. One person we interviewed told us that she and her partner in a joint venture frequently had knock-down, drag-out screaming matches over their business strategy. Little was resolved any time they tried to discuss their problems and come to a decision. This pattern persisted until one day when they were attending a convention where several potential new customers had come to visit their booth. That evening, back in their hotel room, they had a bitter feud over how the afternoon had gone and the woman realized that being in business with this partner was not worth the constant emotional drain on her energy. She ended the partnership shortly thereafter.

On the other hand, ignoring your emotions can be equally detrimental to developing a healthy business relationship. If someone you work with remains cold and distant, you feel that you must "read between the lines" to guess what the person is really thinking or feeling. People who show no emotion also appear to be uninterested and unmotivated. This leaves others feeling as if they must take responsibility for holding up the relationship's team spirit. Eventually this becomes a chore, and you can lose interest in working with such people.

The best path is to balance emotions and rational thinking so that you can communicate in a meaningful, clear, and sensitive way that lets others know what you're feeling without their having to resent it or guess at it. Use your emotional responses to a situation to enhance, not hinder, decision making. Use your intuition to alert you to the consequences a decision might have. If you feel suspicious about someone's motives, angry about how you have been treated, or frustrated by a customer's constant requests for information, use your feelings to spur creative rational solutions. Such emotions can guide you to the right decision with your teaming-up associates.

In short, emotional extremes are more often destructive than constructive. So avoid emotional flair-ups and don't avoid your feelings; channel them into effective communication that will solve your problems, not create more of them. For more information on using your emotions effectively in business, see the Emotional Road Map in our book *Secrets of Self-Employment,* listed in the Resources at the end of this chapter.

2. Focus on "needs," not "wants." In decision-making situations, you and your associates are usually trying to determine the best course of action for your business. What frequently happens, however, is that our reasoning can be clouded by our "wants" instead of our "needs." Wants are based on emotional desires such as power, prestige, influence, and approval. Needs, on the other hand, arise from an appraisal of actual situations, and the pros and cons of the options you're faced with. By focusing on the needs of your teaming-up relationship, you can usually exercise better judgment and arrive at more satisfying decisions.

Consider this common scenario. Jim and Dave are invited to bid on a large consulting contract with a well-known company. Their eyes light up with dollar signs as they begin fantasizing about how much they could charge this potential client. Jim wants to charge $25,000 because he figures a contract like this will take three months and he wants to make sure the firm believes that he and Dave are top-notch consultants. Dave, however, feels they should charge only $15,000, because he doesn't want to risk losing the contract and he feels certain $15,000 will be an irresistible price.

Their debate over what to charge heats up until they realize that their "wants" are not really based on a sound assessment of the facts of the situation. Instead of continuing to argue about how much to charge, the collaborators sit down and begin to project how much time they'll need to complete the project, how many additional freelancers they might need to bring on board to supplement their own work, the cost of materials, and the amount they can reasonably add for overhead and profit. Based on this calculation of their actual needs, they agree to bid $18,500, an amount they can clearly justify to their prospective client.

Examining your needs instead of acting on the basis of your wants can be helpful in making many kinds of decisions teaming-up associates commonly face, such as:

- Whether or not to buy a piece of new office equipment or furniture
- Whether or not to attend a conference or trade show
- Whether or not to take on a new customer
- Whether or not to invest in developing a proposal for a project
- How much of the profits to keep personally versus how much to reinvest in the business

3. Focus on building each other's self-esteem. When people are blamed, chastised, yelled at, cursed, attacked, threatened, or called names, their feelings about themselves can be damaged at the core. And such personal damage can damage the relationship to its core as well. Sometimes the effects from such exchanges can be repaired but often they can never be undone. When their self-esteem suffers in a relationship, some people lash back, get angry and bitter. Others simply withdraw from such situations, feeling rejected, hurt, or angry, closing the door to future interactions. So whatever problems arise, always avoid behavior that will damage others' self-esteem and foster behavior that will build their self-confidence and belief in themselves and their abilities. No matter what circumstances develop, the aim should be to increase others' feelings of acceptance, confidence, hope, joy, optimism, and self-respect.

That doesn't mean that you have to swallow your feelings or ignore negative behavior or problems. Quite the contrary. The goal is to express your needs and feelings and solve problems in a way that leaves all parties feeling good about themselves. Think of it this way: Do you want to work with someone who is always berating you or making you feel your opinions are unwanted, silly, or stupid? When you are in a relationship with someone who treats you in this manner, it's usually difficult to make joint decisions because you end up either asserting your counteropinion, which sets off a fight, or remaining silent and feeling bad because your needs are not being heard.

Going back to the analogy that a partnership is like a marriage, it is important to realize that people who work closely together in a business relationship need to demonstrate their respect for one another every day. Respect can never simply be assumed or taken for granted. This means accepting and complimenting one another's ideas and opinions and respectfully holding one another to commitments and agreements. If you disagree on a point, negotiate over it in an affirmative way. Don't knock down the other person's idea, uphold its value, while showing how you believe another idea carries more value in a given situation.

In short, many conflicts can be avoided even in times of difficulty when people remember to focus on building one another's self-esteem instead of tearing it down.

4. Persuade, don't coerce. Coercion usually arises from needing to convince someone that you're right. Persuasion, on the other hand, involves reaching a meeting of the minds in which you acknowledge someone else's point of view while trying to show the person why you believe that yours will work better. Coercion usually involves personal attacks, blame, insults, scare tactics, exaggeration (using words like *never, always, forever,* etc.), and threats to win an argument, while persuasion requires focusing on the issue at hand and using logic and reason to debate the best possible solution. As a result, if you want to reach rational decisions, persuasion will work much better than coercion.

After coercing someone to adopt your viewpoint, you may have won the battle, but you've usually lost the war because someone who has been coerced is rarely enthusiastic about following through on the resulting decision. But when you use persuasion, there is no battle and everyone wins because everyone is truly convinced that the resulting decision is the best one to follow and therefore follows through enthusiastically to implement it.

Consider the difference in the box below between comments made by someone who's coercing versus someone who's attempting to persuade, and note the difference in your own reaction to each.

Coercion	*Persuasion*
• Your position is ridiculous (silly, absurd, etc.).	• I understand the benefits of your opinion, but I think this other position will gain more for us because . . .
• You're crazy; you don't know what you're talking about!	• I hear what you are saying, but I disagree; the facts and research show that this option will work better for us. Here's how . . .
• I'm not budging on my position. I don't care what you say.	• Let's listen to one another again and see what merits each approach has. I think we can come to a consensus.
• That will never work; I've never heard such a preposterous idea.	• Your idea has some advantages, but overall I think it has several disadvantages and we need to consider those. The ones I see are . . .
• Where did you get such a stupid idea?	• Your suggestion is creative, but right now we need to stick to the target we've already agreed upon.
• If you don't agree with me on this, our relationship is over.	• Each of us is right sometimes. Let's try to find a place where we can both agree.

Coercive comments usually alienate others and drive you further apart. The issue becomes an emotional battle instead of a discussion of what could achieve the best possible results. Persuasion reaches for commonality. It's a search for solutions, so it brings people together.

5. Take a break when emotions erupt nonproductively. A last guideline for reaching rational creative solutions is to disengage temporarily from conversations when negative emotions flare up. Many emotional exchanges are productive because they help people understand how and why issues are so important to them but when an emotional interchange is leading nowhere, it's time to pull back and cool off. Instead of locking in and battling it out to the bitter end, when it's evident that neither party wants to compromise or recognize the other side's position, take a break. Provide one another with a chance for your tempers to cool down and regain your perspective. Step out of discussions so all those involved can regain their composure, calm down, and reconnect with their goals.

Here are several ways you can take such a break, listed in order from shorter to longer intervals.

- Suggest that you each take a minute to gain a fresh perspective. Close your eyes and count to ten, taking a deep breath between each count. In most cases, counting and breathing will relax you and allow you to reapproach your discussion more calmly, objectively, and with greater clarity.
- Suggest that you stop all your discussion for a few minutes to allow each person to go somewhere else in the room to think about the situation and come back with some fresh ideas.
- Suggest that everyone take a break for refreshments so people can leave the room for a while to reflect separately on the situation, perhaps taking a walk or engaging in some other form of physical exercise. Often a half hour of physical exercise will replenish the body, mind, and spirit with fresh thoughts and new perspectives.

If the issue isn't pressing, you might postpone your discussions for several days or even a few weeks, then invite everyone involved to think about the situation and try developing new ideas and solutions you can consider when you come together next time. Instead of pressing on to make a hasty decision based on a forced compromise, taking such an extended break can allow time to develop more satisfactory resolutions to complex situations. In general, the more time allocated to a decision, the more ideas team members can develop, but be sure to set a specific time to reconvene your decision making, or the level of commitment may begin to dissipate and your alliance could simply drift apart.

Overall taking such steps to insure rational decision making will significantly improve the quality of your communications, your relationship, and the results of your work together.

6. ORGANIZED—Organize Your Communication

The sixth and final principle of the VELCRO approach to communication is a reminder that infrequent, haphazard communication generally increases your chances for *miscommunication*. So make it a policy to communicate regularly and systematically. Here are several guidelines you can follow.

1. Share information openly and frequently. Some of the major problems between people who work together arise from a one-sided flow of information. In today's information age especially, keeping up with the events in your business or industry is usually essential for success. It's important that whatever information each of you has that the others need or could benefit from be shared quickly and consistently.

For example, a common cause of miscommunication among associates is when one person has information and unconsciously forgets or intentionally neglects to provide it to others. The information might be an article that appeared in a journal or magazine that affects your business. It might be a message from a client who wants something done or a decision you made that affects your venture. Unfortunately, whatever the uncommunicated information is, its value is diminished if each of you can't act upon it in a timely way. In essence, when any one of you fails to transmit key information to the other, the team suffers. Without the right information any one of you may take an embarrassing or ill-advised action and then chances are you'll waste time arguing over what happened. And, of course, if customers or clients consistently see that a team fails to communicate key information, their confidence in your effectiveness will be undermined. Your efforts can appear incompetent or, at the very least, uncoordinated.

So when you initiate a teaming-up effort, it's worthwhile discussing among yourselves what information will be important to convey regularly to one another. Often it turns out that what one person thinks is important and needs to have shared, another person would have considered to be trivial. So, find out what each person wants and needs to know for you to work well together. For example, find out which of the following anyone needs or wants to know about:

- Customer calls and faxes
- Customer complaints
- Customer inquiries
- When payment checks are received
- When invoices are sent out
- New projects on the horizon
- Articles of general interest to the team
- The status of each project

Also try to cover the information that's specific to your business and agree which items everyone needs to know about versus which ones are trivial and not worth the time sending back and forth. Also, agree how quickly each of you needs to be informed about these issues, e.g., every day, once a week, once a month. Depending on how often you need to keep each other updated, determine the best format and interval for sharing the information. See the box on page 276 for tips on using today's technology to keep each other up-to-date as quickly and easily as possible. Also consider scheduling regular progress meetings as described on page 309.

Selecting the Best Way to Share Key Information

Thanks to today's sophisticated communications technology, sharing information and facilitating communication between associates has never been easier. Indeed, most people would be hard-pressed to come up with an excuse for why they can't communicate easily and consistently with one another. Here is a list of the many ways business affiliates can communicate with each other, organized from the least to the most technical. Each method is described along with its pros and cons.

Method: In-Person Meetings

Pros	Cons	Other considerations
• Face-to-face conversation is best for building personal rapport, handling complex situations, and when disagreements need to be solved. • In-person meetings allow parties to see each other's emotions, body language, and reactions; a definite advantage over phone calls, fax, and E-mail communication.	• If team members are located at different sites, in-person meetings on a regular basis can be difficult to arrange. • In-person meetings often take longer than phone calls or faxes. • You may need to meet in a neutral location such as a restaurant or hotel lobby if having someone to your home or office is awkward.	• If parties are located at different sites, it can help to set up regular face-to-face meetings on a weekly, monthly, or even quarterly basis.

Method: Phoning

Pros	Cons	Other considerations
• A most convenient way to get in touch and discuss issues quickly with an associate or partner. • You can arrange for conference calling if more than one person needs to be involved in a conversation. • With cellular phones, pagers, and 500 numbers, you can virtually be in touch with one another whenever and wherever you need to be.	• You risk wasting time playing phone tag when people are busy. • Coordinating calls can be frustrating if you and your associates are located in different time zones, such as East and West Coasts. • Long-distance or cellular calls get to be expensive.	• If you have more than one collaborator or partner, it's worth the investment to purchase conferencing capability from your local phone company.

Method: Voice Mail

Pros	Cons	Other considerations
• A good way to avoid playing phone tag: each party simply leaves message of whatever length is needed for others and waits for a reply whenever that person is available. • Associates can assign one another their own private voice mail boxes to leave and retrieve personal messages when they want.	• Not useful when a dialogue is required on the spot.	• Voice mail can be purchased either as part of your telephone set (e.g., the Sony model), from most local phone companies as a premium service, or as a board in your computer.

Method: Faxing

Pros	Cons	Other considerations
• A good solution when written communication is needed to think out a problem or confirm a decision involving much detail. • A quick alternative for handling situations that require a signature. • The process can be automated so all team members get exactly the same fax simultaneously.	• Requires buying, learning to use, and maintaining additional technology. • Requires writing out your ideas and thoughts first, which some people don't like or don't want to do.	• If you can afford it, get a plain-paper fax machine, or at least one with an automatic paper cutter.

Method: E-Mail Messages

Pros	Cons	Other considerations
• An excellent and inexpensive way to maintain frequent contact anytime day or night regardless of each other's schedule or time zone.	• Requires additional software and hardware as well as the time and expense of joining and logging onto the Internet or an on-line service.	• Overall the most efficient method for communicating regularly with others. It's faster and costs less than mail, phone, or fax.

Pros	Cons
• The process can be automated so all team members get exactly same E-mail message simultaneously. • E-mail is very cost-effective.	• It takes time to type out your message.

Method: Direct Modem Transfer

Pros	Cons	Other considerations
• An excellent way to send lengthy files. • Cheaper than using postal service to send disks back and forth.	• It requires file transfer software, compatibility among users, and knowledge of using a modem.	• It's easy enough to learn and can be very useful when you are dealing with lengthy documents that must be seen by each team member.

Method: Application Sharing

Pros	Cons	Other considerations
• An excellent way to hook up your computers together so that two people can work on a document at the same time.	• Requires some additional computer savvy, but today's software is becoming easier to use.	• Look into buying software products such as LiveShare Plus that are designed for collaborative computing.

Method: Videophone

Pros	Cons	Other considerations
• Excellent idea for people who can't see one another regularly (such as those living in different cities). • Ideal when people located at a distance must see and work on physical materials together.	• Videophone equipment is still relatively expensive.	• Check into this method if you team up with someone in another city and would benefit by seeing him or her regularly.

Method: Teleconferencing		
Pros	*Cons*	*Other considerations*
• An excellent choice when many people at a distance need to talk together.	• Requires arranging to rent specially equipped rooms from a phone company. • People must travel to the teleconferencing site.	

Method: Direct Videoconferencing		
Pros	*Cons*	*Other considerations*
• An excellent choice when many people in distant locations need to meet periodically.	• It's expensive to rent video-conferencing facilities in each location. • People must travel to the videoconferencing site.	• Kinko's offers videoconfer-encing facilities in many locations.

When Bud began working with Pauline and Stan, many communication problems developed. Bud lived in Connecticut, while Pauline and Stan were based in Alexandria, Virginia. Pauline and Stan organized art exhibits for corporate promotions; Bud's role was to locate corporate sponsors for the events. Bud quickly set out contacting companies and scheduling phone conferences for them all but rarely informed Pauline and Stan of the details beforehand. The results were often embarrassing phone conversations that left the distinct impression this team was working at cross purposes. Fortunately, they recognized their problem promptly and solved it as follows.

Each time Bud made a client contact he kept notes of the meeting using Lotus *Organizer* and using the broadcasting capability of his fax, he promptly faxed a copy of the contact notes to Pauline and Stan. Also, before each phone conference, the three held their own three-way conference call to set the goals and the agenda for the upcoming call as well as to clarify any questions anyone had about previous contact with the client.

Bud, Pauline, and Stan also decided to hold monthly progress meetings by phone, and when a project got to the proposal or contract stage they agreed to E-mail drafts for review and editing to and from one another so nothing ever went out in writing to a sponsor or client without all three having approved its content. With this "communication" system in place, they were able to work quite effectively together.

2. Make your communications a consistent habit. Establishing a regular time, place, and procedure for communicating with those you're working with is a matter of courtesy and respect. It's also a sound business policy.

We've noticed a common pattern in what happens when one person in a collaboration is inconsistent in sharing information or discussing issues with the others they've teamed up with. Lack of communication or inconsistent communication fosters suspicion, lack of interest, or distrust, even when there has been no ill will intended. Consistent communication, however, makes other people feel that you are thinking about them and that you are responsible. Having a dependable and consistent way of communicating builds interest, greater commitment and trust.

3. When faced with a difficult decision or a conflict, give yourselves the time and place to talk about it. In a hurried world, we often feel forced to make decisions on the spur of the moment and under duress. Don't let this happen unless you absolutely can't avoid it. Too often we rush into a decision when in actuality it doesn't need to be made immediately. You've probably noticed that pressures to hurry up and decide usually come to a screeching halt once your decision is made while people try to gear up for implementing it. So why not take the time you need up front. Put the decision on hold, briefly, until you can arrange and plan for a meeting at least by phone with those who might be affected by it.

Sensitive conversations concerning a conflict, or potential conflict, in particular, should be planned and scheduled, not caught on the fly. If you and your associate or partner are having a disagreement, it's often counterproductive to blow up or blurt out your anger at the moment. It's wiser to take the time to collect and organize your thoughts and set up a specific meeting where you can each allocate enough time to clear the air, talk out the issues, and resolve any real or perceived differences. To plan ahead for this meeting, think about where you want to meet and what you want to say. If you expect to have a frank exchange of words to iron out a serious dilemma, don't plan to meet in a location like a hotel lobby or a restaurant, where other people could overhear what should be a private conversation.

Holding a Retreat to Develop Your Teaming-Up Enterprise

Just as many large corporations hold "retreats" so executives can get away from the daily routine of their work and spark their creativity, you too might want to give some thought to holding a periodic retreat with your collaborators or partners. Of course, the nature of your retreat should depend on the scope of your teaming-up relationship. Two businesses that will be doing cross-promoting together might make do perhaps with a Saturday morning meeting followed by a recreational afternoon, while several people launching a formal partnership might want to consider scheduling an entire weekend away at a resort or country house. For example, Patricia McGinnis and her partner took a week-long trip to Hawaii, where they devoted time to aligning their business strategy, discussing potential customers, and devising a marketing campaign.

A business retreat of whatever length can serve many purposes. First, it contributes to developing personal bonds of friendship and affiliation among the members of your team. Many studies show that people work more closely and effectively when they know one another personally. Second, being away from your regular routine can improve your ability to think more analytically and creatively. Finally, being away at a resort, an outdoor setting, or a quiet seminar room can also help team members relax and concentrate on a crisis or complex decision without the usual distractions.

The kinds of things to do and issues to tackle while you are "on retreat" include:

- Review your mission statement, goals, and objectives; be sure you are aligned on them.
- Write, clarify, or review your business plan.
- Plan or discuss the effectiveness of how to divide responsibilities and tasks.
- Develop marketing and sales strategies.
- Calculate, evaluate, or revise your pricing.
- Create marketing sales and PR materials.
- Identify potential new customers or markets.
- Develop contingency plans for problem situations.
- Work on key projects that require everyone's input and skills.

You might even plan to read sections of this book together and share passages that pique your mutual interest. The more you and your teaming up partner can agree on your goals, objectives, values, strategies, and needs, the more successful you're likely be. One of the most common problems collaborators experience is becoming confused about goals, unresolved roles, or cluttered objectives. So periodically taking the time to discuss and synchronize your visions can help ensure that you and your associate continue to see eye to eye.

Note that some expenses for your business retreat may be tax deductible. However, check with your accountant to verify if you qualify for such a deduction and which costs you can write off as business expenses.

Summary of the VELCRO Strategy

The six principles of the VELCRO approach to communication can go a long way to help your teaming-up relationship stay healthy and effective. Disagreements, arguments, and miscommunications can gradually take a toll on any relationship, so it's best to be proactive and avoid them as often as possible. To test the quality of your communication habits, ask yourself these questions.

Viewpoint
1. Do I truly understand and respect my associate's or partner's viewpoint?
2. Do I acknowledge and credit my collaborators for what they have to say and what they offer to our conversations?

Evident
1. Do I state what I have to say to others clearly and directly?
2. Do I speak in concrete terms when I present my opinions, being sure not to leave my real message unstated?
3. Do I expect people to follow my lead based on what I say?

Listening
1. Do I engage in interactive listening with others?
2. Do I show empathy and support for other people when they speak?
3. Do I speak clearly and articulately when others listen to me?

Constructive and Creative
1. Do I look for the constructive, positive aspects of others' comments even if I don't agree with them?
2. Am I creative in my problem solving, searching for solutions, not trying to establish blame?
3. Do I help others find creative solutions by inspiring them to think about new options and ways of doing things?
4. Am I flexible about possible solutions to problems instead of making up my mind early and sticking with my decision no matter what?

Rational Decision Making
1. Do I employ logic and reason when I'm trying to make decisions with other people?
2. Do I avoid coercion and emotional tactics when I want to persuade others to adopt my opinion or approach?
3. Do I take a break when emotions begin to run high during disagreements?

Organization and Planning
1. Do I consistently share information with others?
2. Do I let others know what I consider to be important information I want to be informed about?
3. Do I plan my sensitive conversations to occur at the right time and place?

If you can answer "Yes" to most of these questions, you're well on your way to good communications with your teaming-up associates. However, if you honestly answered "No" to more than a few questions, you'd be best served to become more conscious of your communication habits. Notice which ones are counterproductive to your teaming-up goals. Notice which ones bring you closer to your goal.

How Men and Women Talk About Business

In the past few years there has been considerable research that suggests that men and women approach business from different perspectives and that these perspectives are reflected in the way they talk about their businesses. In the 1990 best-seller *You Just Don't Understand,* researcher and linguist Deborah Tannen identified a variety of differences in how men and women communicate. Later she also wrote about other studies that identified how these differences are reflected in the way men and women communicate in the workplace in her book *Talking from 9 to 5.* More recently, researchers at the Universities of Minnesota and of Wisconsin have studied how self-employed men and women who work together in family businesses communicate and again have found that there are specific gender differences. Here are some of the results.

Surprisingly, both men and women tend to discuss their businesses in emotional terms (i.e., strongly held opinions and feelings), although men talk about the management of their business in more practical terms than women, who tend to address the same issues in more emotional terms. And while both men and women tend to focus their communication most often on issues related to managing the business, achieving success is the next most important focus of conversation to men while business issues related to customer satisfaction and personal and family life are next most important to women.

Sometimes subtle differences in perspective and communication styles between men and women can lead to unnecessary misunderstandings and conflict. If each sex becomes aware of these differences, however, these misunderstandings can be avoided. For example, Deborah Tannen and other researchers have found that:

- Men tend to seek freedom and independence, while women look for interconnectedness and interdependence.
- Women tend to want to talk over, share, network, and connect with the others they're talking to; men, on the other hand, tend to want to talk about how to solve problems and get on with the actions of business. This can leave men feeling "pestered" by female associates who want to discuss and talk things over, while women can feel that their male associates are uncaring and uninterested in communicating in depth.
- Women tend to talk more about a given subject and are better at sharing feelings about problems, while men tend to be more succinct in covering a particular subject

and are less interested in sharing feelings about problems. This difference leaves many men feeling that a woman partner constantly wants to focus on problems; while the women feel that their male partners want to gloss over and avoid problems.

Such differences explain in part why many women who get involved in teaming up tell us they think women make better collaborators because they are more interested in networking, sharing feelings, discussing problems, and avoiding competitiveness. These differences also explain why some of the men who are involved in collaborations tell us they'd rather not team up with women because it's too difficult to communicate with them about practical business issues. Some men we've talked to say that they tend to be more confrontational with other men but they prefer it that way.

Of course, people always will prefer working with those they feel most comfortable and compatible with, but by becoming aware of subtle differences that arise in how men and women communicate, those who wish to do so can enrich their business by learning to work as effectively in male/female teams as in same-sex teams. Many successful male and female teams, for example, tell us they're infinitely more effective as a team because they can approach their business from a more holistic perspective. By reaching out to understand and respect each other's point of view and communication styles, they say they can work more successfully and with a wider variety of clients and customers.

SPECIAL TIPS FOR SPOUSES AND FAMILY MEMBERS WORKING TOGETHER

As you might surmise, working with family members or a spouse adds an extra dimension to the group dynamics and communication issues raised in this chapter. When you start working with a spouse or family member, you already have a strong personal relationship that has its own well-established patterns of communication. So while your goal isn't to build a relationship, you must focus on preserving and enhancing the one you have. You also have to enlarge a relationship that's been focused on personal issues into one that's focused on work-related needs as well. In general, we find that the transition from a personal relationship to a business one usually puts an initial strain on the relationship, similar to the *storming* phase we described earlier in this chapter as something all groups go through. The good news, however, is that every couple we interviewed in researching this book agreed that once they got past this initial adjustment period, working together turned out to have an enriching and positive effect on their relationship.

Here are several important guidelines that can facilitate working with your spouse or other family members. These guidelines reflect the comments other couples have shared with us as well as our own experiences (we, Paul and Sarah, are a couple, and I, Rick, have worked in partnerships and joint ventures with couples). While these guidelines are phrased primarily for couples working together, they can be equally useful in working with any family member and even in working with very close friends. (Also, see the box on page 127 for additional insights into family dynamics.)

1. Recognize that even families can have business disagreements and problems too. Many couples or other family members who team up in business activities think that because they're "family" they'll be immune to the kinds of problems they might have in working with people outside their family. They don't expect that family members could also be subject to strong differences of opinion, in-fighting, politicking, distrust, betrayal, and so on. But this is not necessarily true. Every family has its own set of interpersonal dynamics for how members relate to one another, and no matter how good your family relationship seems, working together can bring out many differences and tensions that would otherwise remain below the surface.

It's not unusual for a wife who once thought of her husband as "a little stubborn" to decide, after working with him, that he's "pigheaded." A husband who once thought his wife was somewhat "emotional" may suddenly consider her to be "irrational" when he's working with her. In actuality, a spouse's "annoying" personality traits—whatever they may be—existed before he or she entered into a working relationship. But when working together in close proximity day-to-day, what was only annoying may become aggravating.

By recognizing and preparing for such potential tensions, however, couples can get through these snags and learn to work productively and lovingly together. As we said above, most spousal teams go through a period of conflict akin to the *forming* and *storming* phases of any group. The key to reestablishing harmony in your new working relationship lies in accepting and respecting each other fully and unconditionally without the expectation that you'll never have disagreements or conflicts. Once you realize that you can have both love and respect in the midst of a disagreement, when conflicts occur, you can "reframe" them so they don't need to become a major threat to your relationship. Conflicts can be seen instead as events that will occur between any two people who work together.

It also helps to get to know one another's *business persona*. Most of us act differently in business situations than we do with friends and family. We may be more or less understanding, distant, curt, formal, subservient, cunning, or manipulative. Many people are surprised by this "new" persona when they first begin working with their spouses or family members. "Why are you acting like that?" they may wonder. For instance, many couples told us that they found working with their spouses "strange" at first. "It was as if I didn't know him anymore," one woman said. Another man related that when he first began working in his grandfather's business, he was shocked to discover a cold, calculating, stubborn side to his grandfather that he'd never seen before. Whatever new traits you discover in your family members, keep in mind that you're simply getting to see another side of the same person. You don't need to "get back the person you knew before"; he or she is still there. You just need to learn how to relate to the additional aspects of that person. In other words, you're actually getting to know him or her better.

2. Whether you're starting a new business together or bringing a family member into an existing business, make it clear who will be running the business. In many cases, one family member who's running a successful business will eventually bring other family members into the business, either to save the costs of hiring an employee or simply to share the joys and the wealth of a successful venture. In other cases, however, a family may go through a life transition, as in the case of a husband who loses his job and decides to move to a new state, and in the process, he and his wife realize they want to start their own business together. In either situation, it's crucial that the couple make a clear decision about who owns the business and what roles each will play in it.

For example when Fred Gladney sold his computer consulting business and decided to join his wife, Wendy, in her event-planning business, the couple had many discussions to clarify what role Fred would play in the business. Although Wendy had already been in business on her own for several years, she was positive she wanted to share it equally in every way with Fred because his experience would be an excellent complement to her skills. On the other hand, when another couple we know went into business together after their marriage, the husband, who had already been running the business on his own, made it clear that he was still the president and CEO of his company, and their marriage did not automatically make her a partner.

In addition, family members need to define roles clearly for financial and tax reasons. Family members must decide, for example, whether to operate as a sole proprietorship, a partnership, a C or S corporation, or an LLC. The major impetus for clarifying roles, however, is to make sure that you understand the psychological boundaries of the business relationship once you begin working together. Katlin and Mike, for example, were newlyweds. She had quit her job as an advertising account executive and moved from Atlanta where she'd lived when they met at a conference. The intention was that after the wedding she would join Mike in running his software company. She was shocked, however, when in addition to running the company's advertising and marketing campaigns, Mike also expected her to take phone messages for him, do his filing, and make coffee for him and his business associates.

"He's treating me like a secretary!" Katlin complained. "But, I thought she wanted to help me out in my business," Mike remarked. "Now, I come to find out, she only wants to do the things she enjoys. I don't get to do that. I have to do it all."

Cheryl and Steve had a similar conflict. Steve had been a prominent lecturer, traveling from coast to coast to present his theories to fellow professionals. He met and fell in love with Cheryl at one of these presentations. She loved his theories and had done many professional presentations herself. So after the wedding, they decided they would speak and travel together. Their first presentation, however, was a disaster. Only Steve's name appeared on the official program. He was introduced as the speaker and then invited Cheryl onto the stage to add in her comments at times he specified. At the close of the seminar, Steve thought the program had gone well until he discovered that Cheryl was no longer speaking to him.

"I was humiliated," she told us. "I don't know why she's so upset," Steve admitted. "Surely she didn't expect to join me on the platform as an equal, considering our respective experience and reputations."

Like these couples, anyone teaming up with family members must ask themselves: "Who's running this business?" "Whose business is this?" "Are we going to run the business together and share equally in the decision making—or is one person the leader, the boss, whom the other supports and assists?" Unfortunately, such issues are all too often left undecided until a problem develops. This is especially true in husband/wife teams. And the results are predictable. Each person feels let down and taken advantage of. In situations like Mike and Katlin's and Steve and Cheryl's no one is right or wrong. Everyone is simply uncertain as to what their roles are vis-à-vis the business.

Ironically, one reason this happens so often is that our social norms used to implicitly and automatically grant the leadership and authority role to the husband in any joint enterprise, but in today's business times, this can no longer be assumed. First, with more women in the workforce, the wife is often the founder of a successful enterprise—not the husband. Sarah Stambler, for example, founded her company, TechProse, Inc., in 1983 to specialize in electronic marketing consulting. In building her business, Sarah developed a highly successful monthly fax newsletter, *Marketing with Technology News*. When she got married in 1990, she brought her husband into her business, but they agreed right from the start that Sarah was the "boss."

Second, as more women have attained a level of education and experience equal to their husbands', some of today's couples are choosing right from the start to operate with a "two heads are better than one" leadership style. Tom and Wendy Eidson, founders of the Mo'Hotta, Mo'Betta condiments catalogue, recognized that they each had skills to contribute to getting their business off the ground. So they consider themselves equals, sharing in all major decisions and the overall workload. About working together as a married couple, Tom told us, "You should be getting along well together first before you go into business; don't look at your business as being able to put a relationship back together. Our feeling is that it's the two of us against the world, and that's what keeps us working as a team. But when the marriage isn't already like that, that's when combining a marriage and a business goes wrong."

Whatever the initial agreement, however, most family members will still go through an initial period of trial and error in which they dance around and test out the "control issue" in order to iron out precisely what their psychological role boundaries will be. The conflict appears to be the most difficult when a spouse joins an existing business owned by the other spouse. Even if the couple agrees to operate on 50/50 basis, the new person may nevertheless end up *feeling* that she or he isn't being treated equally. The mate who founded the business is used to being the boss and so may continue to act that way, even unintentionally. Clients and customers are used to relating to one person, not two. So they, too, may unintentionally turn to the original partner for decisions. It can take some time to develop new patterns for sharing authority.

Debra Goldentyre, for example, a lawyer who joined her husband's video and multimedia production company, told us, "We started out working together for an initial trial period, but we never had to look back. It did take me a year or so before I really felt psychologically that I was a full-fledged partner. For the most part, we divide up the work and don't step on one another's toes. We jokingly call one another department heads, but it's serious, too. We respect one another's territory."

In another situation, a husband we'll call Wayne told us about the mistakes he made in bringing his wife into his already established consulting business.

> What I found was that our relationship changed when we became husband and wife business partners. I had been running my company for five years, and I had a way of running it that was my own. When she came in, she wanted to make changes and do things differently, but I didn't like the changes she made. I felt that I was the CEO and that she shouldn't start restructuring things without telling me first. And if I made a decision like hiring someone without consulting her, she would get annoyed. So if I had it to do all over again, now that I see what happened, I would clearly tell her from the beginning that I was still going to be in charge and we were not going to be equal partners. I should have told her that she was always welcome to contribute ideas but not to implement them without consulting me first.

Deena wrote to us saying that her brother-in-law invited her to partner with him in starting a mobile disk jockey service. She designed flyers, had them printed, and began promoting their new business. After she did the first weekend gig, she discovered that her brother-in-law, who's employed full-time during the week, wanted to spend weekends with his children and expected her to do all the work of the business until his wife changed her weekend work hours. "Why should I share the money that's coming in, if I'm doing all the work?" she asks.

Given the potential for conflicting expectations and hurt feelings, it's tremendously useful to sit down with your spouse or family member and honestly discuss how each of you views the ownership and control of the business venture once you start working together. Don't wait for a conflict to erupt before making it clear who, if anyone, will be the president and who will be the vice president. Furthermore, make this clarification explicit regardless of how obvious it might be to you based on your backgrounds, interests, and experience because once you start working together, unstated assumptions can easily lead to disappointment and anger.

For instance, Tony and Susan Camas work together in a computer consulting and programming enterprise, Boston Automation, which Tony founded several years ago. Later Susan joined him in the business. Because of Tony's background as a programmer and consultant, he handles the heart of the business while Susan uses her bookkeeping and administrative background to handle invoicing, billing, and personnel matters. Although their lines of authority appeared obvious, nonetheless Tony and Susan experienced several months of difficulty that strained their marriage as they tried to work out their feelings about how to share control of the business. Ultimately, Tony decided that he wanted to maintain final authority on all matters and asked Susan if she would be willing to continue working with him under the condition that he would consult her sometimes but not always on business issues. Susan agreed to this role, and their personal and business relationship is working smoothly now.

In the long run, it doesn't matter how you divide up the business—other than how such decisions might affect your legal and tax status—as long as you truly agree on a specific plan to account for the leadership and decision-making tasks each person will be responsible for. As in any collaboration or partnership, your goal is to reduce the chances of conflict and stress and make your work together more productive and rewarding. This effectively means you have two choices—you can either share responsibilities 50/50 or let one spouse make all final decisions—and then live with your choice.

Having clarity on such matters is important to your clients and customers and your business image. If clients feel confused about your roles, your business reputation can suffer, as one mother-and-daughter team discovered. The daughter told us,

> At first, everyone assumed I was a secretary and that Mom was the boss. They assumed that I passed on everything they told me to her

and so they'd be angry if she didn't know about a discussion or decision I'd made with them. Often they wouldn't even take my word for a decision until they spoke to her. Fortunately, my mother brought me into this business as a full partner and over the first few months she was great about saying to customers, "Oh, I'm sorry, you'll have to speak with Lenore about that; she handles all the publicity." Eventually, everyone got the idea that we're two fully functioning professionals with distinct responsibilities like in any other organization and I know our company's stature has grown over the years we've been working together.

Of course, also keep in mind that your decision about who runs the business can change over time. One person might tire of having the full responsibility of running the company and want the other to take on more responsibilities. For example, Todd Elision and his wife, Judy, have run their consulting business, the Quadrant Group, for nearly fifteen years focusing on helping hospitals plan their growth strategies. Although in the past, they both shared equal authority for running and consulting with clients, in recent years, they've agreed that Todd will take a backseat in the business, with Judy handling the consulting contracts while he handles the administrative aspects of their business. Indeed, one of the values of working with your spouse or other family member is feeling that you can trust the other person to step in for you if you need to take a break or shift your responsibilities.

When James Craighton opened a picture frame shop, for example, he hoped it would be a stepping-stone to having his own art gallery. His wife, Carolyn, helped out at the shop and over the years took on more and more of the responsibilities, freeing James to begin painting. Eventually he opened the gallery, first in the back of the frame shop and later in a space next door. Carolyn now runs the frame shop nearly full-time, but each helps the other out in the two businesses whenever needed.

3. Divide responsibilities clearly, then don't interfere. Regardless of who's ultimately in charge, it's also important to define who will carry out what day-to-day tasks. Nearly every family business relationship we talked with told us that the most important factor in their success at maintaining a good relationship as both associates and family members was that they clearly divided up the work to be done and let each person take full responsibility and perform his or her work without interference. This meant no meddling, no coaching, no kvetching, no Monday-morning quarterbacking, backseat driving, or peeking over anyone's shoulder.

Agreement on this point was virtually unanimous. Just as we don't want an outside partner or collaborator criticizing our work or second-guessing our decisions, most of us equally resent it when a spouse or family member acts in this way. Unfortunately, however, it's ever so much more likely that a family member will jump into criticizing and advising. While we might be more hesitant to be critical or bossy with a colleague, we may have no such compunctions when it comes to letting our relatives know what we think. It's easy to feel that since you're so close and have such a long-term relationship, you can say or do whatever comes to mind. A wife, for example, may think that because she and her husband have been married for ten years they understand each other so well that she's entitled to criticize her husband's work and that he won't mind. Even worse, she may feel comfortable taking over a task entirely if it appears to her that it's been mishandled.

But marriage, or any family relationship, is never a justification for acting any less respectfully or considerately than you would when interacting with any other colleague. One-upsmanship, rudeness, arrogance, or an air of superiority doesn't work any better among family members than it does with any partner. Couples can't maintain a business and personal relationship if each spouse doesn't give the other the respect, independence, and autonomy needed to perform his or her work in the way he or she pleases.

For example, Steve Willey and his wife, Elizabeth, operate Back Woods Solar Electric Systems in Sand Point, Idaho. Their company sells solar power equipment to rural homeowners and businesses. Steve and Elizabeth have agreed to a specific division of labor. They both answer questions from prospective clients and explain the systems they sell, but Steve handles the technical installations while his wife handles the accounts and invoicing. Through the years, they've nevertheless had a running battle about the use of an answering machine to handle client phone calls. Steve prefers to use the answering machine, thinking people will leave a message and can be called back. Elizabeth doesn't want to use the machine because she thinks that people often don't leave messages, so it's best to let the phone ring until they hang up. That way, people will call back at another time. Steve finally gave in to Elizabeth's system, however, even though he doesn't agree, because their business was booming and there was no need to let this disagreement erode their relationship.

As Elizabeth explained,

> Part of our success is that we have different specialties. Steve doesn't criticize me for the way I do things. He answers letters and handles the technical issues, and I acknowledge that he's better at that than I am. We both talk to customers, but if there is a technical question, I call him to provide the answer. There is simply a need to acknowledge that someone is more capable in certain areas and then to decide which person should handle which job.

Even when couples respect one another's territory, a nagging question often arises: "What do I do when I think my spouse is not doing a good job and the business is suffering as a result? Should I step in and take over on that task or what?" The fact is, this question in and of itself is a trap. First, if a business isn't doing well, it's easy for one spouse to blame the other and to see the way their partner is performing as the cause of all problems. In actuality there are many other likely causes for business problems—market conditions, a faulty product, the wrong pricing policy, or any number of other factors. So the couple should examine all the possible explanations before erroneously blaming each other. Second, if one spouse tends to blame the other whenever something goes wrong, it may be there are other motives involved. One spouse may be jealous of or feel competitive with the other. Or one spouse may be a perfectionist and no matter what her or his mate does, it's never going to be good enough. So avoid the temptation to blame each other for problems and focus instead on working together to solve whatever problems arise.

For example, Susan thought her husband, Carl, should be more diplomatic with potential clients. She thought they were losing business because he wouldn't discount their fees, took calls on his own time schedule, and worked only with clients he felt would boost their reputation. Carl had been a CEO of a *Fortune* 1,000 company and had lots of experience handling potential customers, and since they'd agreed that marketing the business was Carl's job, Susan kept her mouth shut. She let him do things his way. When business slowed to a mere crawl, however, she proposed that they take a day off to brainstorm new marketing ideas. He agreed and together they generated many new ideas that ultimately brought in the new client base they needed. Carl still continued running things his way and Susan still thought he should be more diplomatic, but she knew that, together, they had been able to make their business thrive again.

We (Paul and Sarah) find that being able to get feedback from one another has made each of us so much more effective. An outsider might not share an observation about how a partner could improve, but we want to. It's how we do it, though, that makes it possible to learn from each other's observations. If Paul thinks there's an area I (Sarah) could improve in, he asks if I would like to hear his feedback, and vice versa. Usually now we're eager to hear feedback from each other because we've learned how valuable each other's perceptions can be. But truthfully, we don't always want to hear observations at the time they're offered. So we let each other know that and save our feedback until later when we're open to hearing it.

And, of course, there are areas we don't want feedback on. For example, we each organize our computer hard drive differently and we both think the other should adopt our "superior" method, but neither of us is interested in doing so. In other words, "My drive is just fine, thank you."

The feeling that *someone else's performance* needs improvement can arise in any collaboration or partnership, but when the people involved are spouses or family members, sharing feedback in the form of criticism and blame is potentially even more disastrous because the discomfort affects not only your working relationship but also your marriage or family relationship and the entire family unit (children, parents, in-laws, etc.). Therefore the solution to this dilemma is for both spouses or family members to commit to working as a *team*. Everyone involved should grant the others full autonomy and independence to perform their own jobs to the best of their ability. And, on the other hand, they should welcome one another's ideas, feedback; and comments especially when problems arise. But even then any criticism should be offered respectfully, constructively, and politely. In essence, the couple should think of themselves as participating in a balancing act that aims to preserve both the marriage and the business at the same time.

As one husband in a spousal partnership told us, "Although the chemistry is better working with my spouse than with a stranger, it's easier to hurt your partner's feelings, and you can carry this hurt home with you, so you risk losing the positive side of your marriage." Don't let this happen to you and, if it does, act quickly to repair the damage. For example, when graphic designer Geena first joined her husband, Peter's, architectural firm, she really blew it. She inadvertently revealed proprietary information about one client to another over the phone. Peter was furious. He would have been furious had any partner committed such a transgression, but that Geena, his spouse, lover, and life partner would do such a thing made him all the more furious! And because she was his wife, he let his uncensored feelings hang out, which he admits he wouldn't have done had she been a fellow architect.

Geena was already feeling devastated about having made such a terrible mistake, but Peter's rage cut her even more deeply. She felt so bad that she couldn't return home that night. Instead she stayed in a hotel. At that point, Peter realized how seriously he'd overreacted. He quickly sent flowers to her room and had room service deliver her favorite meal with a note that read, "What champion hasn't had one disastrous performance. There's no one I'd rather have on my team than you. Love, Peter." Needless to say, they both learned a great deal from the experience. Geena never made the same mistake again, and both their personal and business relationships grew stronger from having weathered their mistakes.

4. Give yourselves time for a private life—individually and as a family or couple. When family members work together, it's easy to allow your work to consume your entire relationship. When working with a spouse, for example, as soon as the alarm goes off in the morning, it's tempting to jump right into a discussion of your plans for the workday and, when you sit down for dinner at night, to round out your day with a quick review of all pending business issues so you can be prepared for the next day. If you're both working from home, it may seem as though you never escape from your work mentality. Your personal and professional life can meld into one amorphous twenty-four-hour workday. As one man related, "I didn't realize how intertwined our personal lives had become with our work until one night when I leaned over, somewhat romantically, to kiss my wife good night in bed; instead of kissing me back, she rolled over and asked, 'Did you remember to send that express package to that customer in Ohio?' "

Despite the many advantages of having immediate access to your business partner, you need a healthy personal life to have a healthy professional life. So, we adamantly recommend that you make it a priority to preserve time each week—and preferably each day—for your personal lives.

If you don't allow time to enjoy your private life as an *individual,* you're more susceptible to stress, anxiety, and mood swings, and you can lose touch with your individual values and goals.

If you have no private life as a *couple or family,* you may begin to lose the personal relationship you once valued so highly and begin relating to each other strictly as business associates. With each passing day of lost intimacy and the sharing of nonwork-related thoughts and feelings, you could slowly lose a little more heart and soul from your relationship. In the process of losing this, your marriage or family ties may lose their grounding and the many added advantages that come from working with someone special.

If family members don't respect their private lives, they begin treating each other more like employees than lifelong mates or relatives. So, to preserve your relationship, you have to invest in it day in and day out, from week to week and month to month. You can never take your personal relationship for granted just because you work together.

Don and Paige Marrs, who work together as marketing consultants in their company, Marketing Partners, Inc., have put a specific time limit on their business discussions: no shop talk before 9:00 A.M. or after 5:00 P.M. Don admits that this is sometimes hard to do and that it takes discipline to enforce, but on the other hand, he knows neither he nor Paige enjoys spending their dinner hour together wondering if the other sent out a certain report, completed a certain project, talked with such and such client, etc. As a result, they make every effort to discuss all their business in their home office, not in the kitchen.

Many couples or families who work together say it's hard to find the time for themselves outside their work. This is especially true when you're starting a new business that seems to require a twenty-hour workday from each of you. As one spouse told us: "I found myself thinking, 'Oh, I'll see Mom tomorrow at work so there's no need to get the family together for a picnic this weekend.'" Or as someone else said, "We realized we hadn't taken a vacation in five years because we kept thinking that since we'd added on a couple of days here and there to business trips, we'd had all the vacation we needed."

To create a more balanced life, here are a few suggestions for how to make sure you don't forget to include your own needs and your needs for each other in your daily schedule. We've organized them from simple, spontaneous things you can do to more carefully planned activities.

- Take a walk alone or together for half an hour at lunchtime.
- Join a health club and go swimming or jogging in the morning or early evening, alone or together.
- Send each other flowers or a special gift periodically.
- Take an hour off every afternoon to go out for coffee, for a drive in the country, or to just sit in the park watching the people pass by.
- Take a class from a local adult-education program—choose a topic that is nonbusiness related that motivates either you alone or both of you.
- Set aside one night each week for a "date" or "family night" when you go to a concert, a movie, ball game, dinner, or whatever you'd enjoy. Pencil your "date" into your weekly calendar and make it a standing commitment you can't postpone or change. Even when you're stressed and pressed, you'll find that after about an hour of such free time, your mind will begin to release some of the day's tensions and the two of you can focus on each other at least for the evening.
- Take a Saturday night away each month or every couple of months. Go to a nearby resort or hotel. Many hotels or B&Bs have special Saturday night rates for couples or families to draw in nonbusiness travelers.
- Take a two-to-three-day or weeklong vacation at a romantic inn or family retreat by the seashore or in the mountains where you can forget business and indulge in nature.

Engaging in sports activities or simply being in nature has a powerful rejuvenating effect on anyone who's suffering from stress. But whatever method you choose for reducing your stress and enjoying your lives together, be sure you do it consistently and without feeling guilty about it. Think of it as an important investment in your health, your partnership, your family, and your business—because it is. We know it's easy to let personal and family time slip off the agenda. We, too, get so busy that it's hard to make the time for our private lives. But actually the more balanced your life is, the more relaxed and focused you will be in your work together. Elizabeth Willey of Back Woods Solar attributes her ability to work so well with her husband for so many years to the single fact that each of them has managed to get out of their home office one afternoon per week alone to do something special he or she needs or wants to do. So make a commitment to yourselves to have a healthy private life, and you'll see a positive difference in your work habits.

5. Discuss special family business issues with an accountant and a lawyer. Many couples and families in business together experience strife over

handling financial and legal affairs because they don't know the full implications of the various choices they have and the decisions they're making.
Sometimes it's months or years before you realize you should have taken a
different financial or legal approach. Don't put yourself through such frustration and risk. Obtain the counsel of a CPA and a lawyer when you decide
to work together in business.

For example, if you're a sole proprietor, you may wish to determine the
best way to "hire" your spouse or family member, or you may want to explore the value of forming a partnership or corporation of some type. And, as
mentioned in chapter 4, if you are forming a corporation, you need to take
into account many specific IRS codes that impact on the business dealings between a corporation and people who are considered "related parties"—i.e.,
anyone who owns more than a certain percentage of stock in the company,
including what direct relatives (spouse, brother, sister, mother, father, etc.)
own. Without considering these tax laws, you may be surprised by an unexpected tax bill if you decide to transfer assets or make a loan to a family member at favorable rates.

6. Seek the help of a professional business or family counselor if needed.
Not surprisingly, with more and more couples and family members going into
business together, an entirely new field of professional consultants is emerging who specialize in working with family-run businesses. These advisors usually have strong business backgrounds as well as a clear understanding of the
unique problems that arise when spouses or family members work together.

Unfortunately, many couples or families are reticent about turning to
professional advisors when they encounter difficulties. For some people, the
primary concern is financial, but with the right planning, fees for professional
counseling may be deductible as management-consulting fees. A more common reason people avoid professional counseling is doubting that an advisor
could help them. It's easy to think that your problems will eventually iron
themselves out through sheer persistence or that the conflicts will magically
disappear if you don't talk about them.

The truth is, a professional advisor or therapist *cannot* force people to
change; that must come from you and your partner working together to make
a positive change. But, the right advisor can help you understand more clearly
than a board member, friend, or other relative where the problems lie and
how you can best proceed to address them successfully. In reality, there's seldom a situation in which one person is at fault for all the woes of a relationship. Each person contributes something to the quality of a relationship, so
righting a problem usually requires both people to reflect on what they're doing and change their behavior in some way. A professional advisor is trained
to help both parties examine their motives and feelings so that they can learn
to live and work in sync with one another.

TAKE THE INITIATIVE

Applying the concepts presented in this chapter can help you and your teaming-up associates create more cooperative and "synergistic" ways of working together. As we've emphasized, the key to building a good working relationship between team members is to seek a mutual understanding of your goals and how you want to work together and then make sure right from the start that you interact with each other in healthy ways that will promote a team approach. By paying attention to the dynamics of your relationship in addition to going through the four stages involved in developing any team, dividing up your responsibilities in meaningful ways and pursuing proactive business communications, you can eliminate many of the difficulties that would otherwise occur in business collaborations or partnerships.

But in the event you encounter obstacles in making your business relationships work, the next chapter provides a "teaming-up troubleshooting guide" for how to handle the most common difficult situations and prevent them from turning into serious problems that sour your relationship and cause you to abandon working together.

RESOURCES

Books

The Eight Essential Steps to Conflict Resolution: Preserving Relationships at Work, at Home, and in the Community. Dudley Weeks, Ph.D. New York: Tarcher/Putnam, 1994.

Getting Together: Building Relationships As We Negotiate. Roger Fisher and Scott Brown. New York: Penguin, 1988.

Getting to Yes. Roger Fisher and William Ury. Boston: Houghton Mifflin, 1992.

Home-Based Businesses and Their Families. Report by Alma J. Owen. Ithaca, New York: Cornell Cooperative Extension In-Service Education, 1994.

Honey, I Want to Start My Own Business, Azriela Jaffe. New York.: Harper Business, 1996.

Organizations in Action. J. D. Thompson. New York: McGraw-Hill, 1967.

Secrets of Self-Employment. Paul and Sarah Edwards. New York: Tarcher/Putnam, 1996.

Working from Home. Paul and Sarah Edwards. New York: Tarcher/Putnam, 1995.

Work with the One You Love. Cameron and Donna Partow. Minneapolis: Bethany House, 1995.

Support Group

TEC, 5469 Kearny Villa Road, Suite 101, San Diego, CA 92123. 800/274-2367 FAX: 800/934-4540. An international organization of CEOs. The minimum size for membership is $3 million in sales and 25 employees.

6

A Teaming-Up
Troubleshooting Guide

The world breaks everyone, then some become strong at the broken places.
—ERNEST HEMINGWAY

IT'S UNREALISTIC TO EXPECT that even people who work together well will get along all
the time. You can expect disagreements, conflicts, and misunderstandings in
the healthiest of relationships. In fact, it is through resolving the inevitable
disagreement, conflict, and misunderstanding that people become increasingly better over time at working together. As the weeks, months, and years
of resolving issues pass by, you can expect your relationships to grow increasingly effective and satisfying. Certain kinds of disagreements, however,
are more difficult to resolve than others, and some have the potential to escalate into divisive rather than helpful conflicts. Sometimes the most challenging disagreements arise from highly emotionally charged issues like financial
decisions or business strategy, while at other times, clashes arise over seemingly trivial issues that actually mask a more serious underlying power
struggle.

This troubleshooting guide is organized around the fifteen most common
complaints we hear from people working together in collaborations of all
kinds, including those with family members. Each is presented in the words
people most often use to describe them and analyzed with the goal of helping
you understand the underlying issues that cause them, along with specific suggestions for resolving them. You'll notice that sometimes the problem can be
solved by changing *your* behavior. Whenever possible, this will usually be the
easiest, quickest way to resolve problems. It's always easier to change our

own behavior than to try to get others to change theirs. At other times, however, you'll need to bring up the issue directly and discuss it openly right at the time it is occurring. And in other situations, to find the best solutions, you will need to set aside a separate time to work through issues with your associates.

Several of the problems posed may seem to be related or similar, and indeed there are often overlapping issues. However, each problem discussed here reflects a specific element of the issues that cause the most trouble in business relationships.

The Top Fifteen Teaming-Up Problems

1. My associate* and I can never seem to agree on anything.
2. My associate is a difficult person to work with.
3. My associate and I have different views of our venture's strategy and direction.
4. My associate is constantly bossing me around and making decisions without considering my opinion.
5. My associate is noncommunicative. He/she never tells me what's going on and always acts without consulting me.
6. My associate doesn't trust me or take what I do seriously.
7. My associate always bickers, argues, and insists on doing things his/her way.
8. My associate is always criticizing me, whatever I do.
9. My associate doesn't seem to understand what to do, and I end up having to make all the decisions.
10. My associate never follows through on what he/she has agreed to do.
11. My associate keeps making bad decisions.
12. My associate doesn't seem to have the same interest in making money that I do.
13. My associate is always busy working on some other project or business and doesn't devote the same energy to our venture that I do.
14. My associate keeps involving his/her spouse or other people in our business.
15. I'm fed up and want out.

*We use the term *associate* to mean any type of teaming up colleague, from an informal collaborator to a formal partner.

All suggestions we make in addressing these top fifteen problems assume that you have a sincere interest in preserving a working relationship and are willing to try to resolve your conflicts. At times, some of these problems could provide ample grounds for abandoning your teaming-up venture, but in presenting the suggestions provided here, our goal is to help you put your enterprise back on track if at all possible.

Of course, the time may come when you'll need to look honestly at the level of conflict in your venture and admit that the energy required to keep your team effort afloat is simply not worth the return. The candle may not be worth the flame. Making this decision and delivering the news to your collaborators in the most productive possible way is covered in the next chapter, "When Breaking Up Is Best."

WIN-WIN CONFLICT RESOLUTION

When business partners or associates are no longer able to get along, for whatever reason, it's a sign that there is an underlying conflict of some kind going on. In truth, conflict is not in and of itself bad in a good relationship. In many cases, disagreements can lead to new, more creative and useful ideas and better ways of working together. The key is to be able to manage the conflicts that arise in ways that prevent them from turning into futile arguments, personal attacks, or meaningless compromises of benefit to no one. Here's how to recognize whether you're in the midst of a constructive or destructive conflict.

• *Constructive* conflicts are characterized by a high level of team spirit. The focus is on particular topics rather than on personalities. Conversations address what to do rather than who's to blame. Attention is on overall goals, not insignificant details. You can spot a constructive conflict by the way those involved make efforts to understand one another clearly. They summarize one another's views, take note of where discussions lead, and avoid personal attacks when debating issues.

• *Destructive* conflicts are characterized by personal attacks, haggling over insignificant details, and arguing about what happened when, why, and who's to blame. One warning sign of a destructive conflict is when communication becomes a series of increasingly sharp "attacks" followed by a defensive response and counterattack. The same statements and emotions arise again and again, only they become progressively more heated. Those involved are defending or attacking instead of listening to one another's responses.

Constructive problem solving de-escalates discord; destructive conflict escalates it. As concerns escalate, things go from bad to worse; dissatisfaction becomes anger, concerns become threats, threats become lawsuits, and so forth. Preventing such escalation is one of the primary goals of constructive problem solving, which aims to turn anger and threats into interest and concern, dissatisfaction into curiosity about possible solutions, or talk of lawsuits into an amicable dissolution.

Here are several things you can do to de-escalate discord and turn conflicts into productive solutions.

1. Stalling. Sometimes putting a discussion on hold will allow all parties time to collect their thoughts, get hold of their emotions, gather better information, and gain perspective so that problem solving can proceed later. But stalling may not help when the parties involved are indifferent to one another's opinions or like things the way they are and want to avoid making a decision.

2. Smoothing. A second solution is to recognize your differences and "agree to disagree." Such an effort to smooth things over can be useful when it's important to maintain harmony in the group at any cost, such as when you're in the midst of an important project with a tight deadline. It won't work well, however, when the issue at hand needs to be resolved in order for work to proceed. And it won't ever be a permanent solution unless people can truly accept their differences.

3. Confronting. Sometimes the best way to address a problem that's going from bad to worse is to confront what's happening head-on. Often this will cause people to stop in their tracks and reevaluate their actions. Confronting is particularly useful in times of crisis. It's not especially helpful, however, if the confrontation is viewed as a power play itself instead of an effort to improve a mutually unpleasant situation.

4. Bridging. A fourth option is to communicate from the premise that everyone's needs can be met; reach for similarities of interest, intention, or desired outcome; and use these shared goals as a bridge to finding a mutually desirable solution. This approach will probably take longer, but the results will last longer, too.

No single strategy will work with every person. Some people will keep escalating the conflict until you assert yourself; others will de-escalate only if you do so first. So the key is not to rely only on the approach that is most comfortable or familiar to you but on what will work best in the situation with your colleague.

As Thomas A. Kayser points out in his book *Building Team Power: How to Unleash the Collaborative Genius of Work Teams,*

> Collaboration is usually the most effective way to resolve conflicts when you want to continue working with those involved. Collaboration addresses differences directly, confronting them openly and using the synergy of the relationship to solve problems permanently. Those involved join forces to work through their differences. They channel their energies to defeat their differences rather than defeat each other. In taking a collaborative approach to conflict, each person entangled in the conflict actively seeks to satisfy his or her own

goals while also striving to accommodate the goals of the others. Instead of dividing up the pie so everyone gets a little less than they want as you would do in compromising, by collaborating, each party looks for ways to expand the pie so there are ample servings for everyone.

Talking about win-win problem solving and actually doing it are two quite different things. Using a win-win philosophy means all parties are sincerely seeking to find a solution that satisfies each of their *fundamental interests,* even if it does not reflect anyone's *original* position. In short, a win-win resolution leaves all parties feeling good about themselves and the relationship for having encountered, faced, and resolved a conflict. It enables everyone to wholeheartedly support the results with 100 percent of his or her energy.

As you'll see, such a collaborative win-win approach is at the heart of what we'll be recommending throughout this chapter and serves as a foundation for resolving the fifteen most common conflicts that arise in teaming-up activities.

RESOLVING THE TOP FIFTEEN TEAMING-UP CONFLICTS

1. My Associate and I Can Never Seem to Agree on Anything

Having successfully formed a business relationship, discovering that you just can't agree on anything can be most dismaying. When you begin debating and arguing about almost everything, you'll most likely start to wonder if you made a mistake by participating in the venture. However, feeling as though you can never agree it is often a reflection that you are still going through or recycling the forming and storming phases described in chapter 5 (p. 236) now that you've gotten to know each other better or your business situation is changing.

If you recall, during these phases, you often seem to be talking right past each other because each of you wants to have your opinion heard and respected first. In essence, real communication—the exchange of ideas and acknowledgment of others' opinions—is not happening yet, so you're left with a general feeling of disagreement.

If this is your situation, the key word in this complaint is *anything.* When people say they don't agree on *anything,* it indicates that those involved have closed minds and don't want to find agreement because they're too concerned that their own needs aren't being or won't be met. So, as we stated in chapter 5, it's an indication that you need to spend some time asking each other what you want and need from your business venture and getting to know each other's thinking in more detail. Such a discussion will help you reestablish and strengthen your rapport as well as uncover any actions or unstated assumptions that are triggering your disagreements. Undoubtedly you'll discover one or two key points on which you do agree that can serve as a foundation for proceeding.

Then you can reexamine remaining issues of contention, narrowing down little by little the specific points on which you don't agree. In doing this, you may discover that you agree on a concept or principle but disagree on details of the implementation. At this point, you can begin working toward finding a win-win solution.

For example, if you're at odds over a decision about whether to spend your money to attend a particular trade show, see if you can find one point on which you both agree, such as "We both agree that going to *some* trade shows would be worthwhile." Once you can say this, you can narrow your disagreement down to the fact that you don't see eye to eye on the *specific* show being discussed. Then you can each present the reasons for your opinion. If you still cannot achieve consensus, you'll need to find a compromise. Perhaps you could settle this issue by agreeing to go to the show but not to spend more than a certain amount of money. Or you might agree to skip the show this year but reserve a spot for next year at the early-registration price.

If you have been working together well for quite a while and suddenly start feeling as if you can't agree on *anything,* your disagreements probably indicate that at some time in the past you diverged on an important issue, and now one of you is withholding agreement on all other matters. Perhaps you had a conflict that was never settled so one of you or both of you were left feeling bitter or hurt. In this situation, the key to realigning your relationship is to think back over your interactions and identify the event(s) that caused you to stop feeling like a team. What happened that led you to feel like adversaries? When did you stop *hearing* one another? One or both of you may need to apologize. Or explanations may be called for so you can recapture your former synergy and start working in sync as a team once again.

It may also mean that the situations that brought you together have changed and you must rethink your relationship. In one partnership two women who did medical transcription had started working together to develop a formal partnership agreement. They spent several hours on the phone discussing how they would set up their partnership, and each had faxed the other various ideas. One of the women then got a very large contract with a clinic, and suddenly her need to be in a partnership was no longer as strong as it had been. She considered dropping the idea of partnership completely. However, the more she discussed her business goals and objectives with her partner-to-be, the more she realized that there could still be value in working together at least in an interdependent alliance. She discussed her new ideas with her friend, and the two agreed to pursue that arrangement instead of a formal partnership.

At whatever point you begin to feel as if *"We never agree on anything,"* beware. Such gross generalizations are rarely true and almost always escalate whatever conflict has developed. So take this feeling as a sign that somewhere along the way, a conflict of more limited scope has developed and use the following five-step approach to release whatever specific differences or conflicts have occurred.

Five Steps to Managing Conflict

In *Building Team Power: How to Unleash the Collaborative Genius of Work Teams,* Thomas A. Kayser outlines five steps for managing conflict in situations when you feel *"We never agree on anything."* As we've pointed out, you most likely do agree on some points but have lost sight of the areas where you agree because of an unresolved conflict that's developed about a specific important area of concern. These five steps are particularly helpful when your conflict seems impossible to resolve and your emotions are running high. The first three steps allow you to define more clearly where you do and where you do not agree; the last two steps help transform your differences into a constructive joint effort to find solutions. The five steps are as follows.

Step 1

Clarify existing positions and associated interests: The goal of this first step is to make sure that you and everyone involved fully understands one another's positions and interests in an friendly, nonthreatening "informational" exchange. All present should state or write down their point of view as to what they consider the problem to be and the solution they have to offer for resolving the conflict.

Example: *"I think our problem started when we started talking about offering our services on the World Wide Web instead of remaining a local business. And I think the solution would be to get back to our basic business here in this community."*

Example: *"I think our problem started when the last client we had turned in a negative evaluation. And I think the solution would be to send an official letter of apology and offer to cut our fee in half to compensate for the client's dissatisfaction."*

Following this discussion, all should state or write down their "interest" in the position they've taken. This will uncover the deeper desire or concern that needs to be addressed before everyone can feel that he or she is part of a "team" again.

Example: *"My favorite part of doing business is networking face-to-face here in this community. I don't like computers. And my success has always come from offering a personal hands-on service."*

Example: *"I've never had a negative evaluation from a client before, and I'm afraid it will tarnish the reputation I've worked so hard to build over the past five years."*

Step 2

Define areas of agreement: It's easy to overlook this step and jump automatically into comparing positions and focusing on your differences. However it's much easier to resolve differences while standing on a foundation of agreement no matter how general or broad that argument may need to be. Identifying broad areas of agreement like shared goals or outcomes reenergizes your relationship and creates a hopeful expectation that you can resolve your differences.

Example: *"We both want the business to expand."*

Example: *"We all feel bad about what happened on the last project and want to be sure it doesn't happen again."*

Step 3

Define areas of difference: At this point, you can define, often more objectively than when you began, the specific areas in which your interests and positions differ. Again, the goal of defining these differences should be to share information rather than to reassert personal positions and interests.

Example: *"So we agree that we want to expand, but I want to serve more local clients, and you want to start offering our services nationally on the Internet."*

Example: *"So we agree that something went wrong and we should do something about it. But I think the solution is to reduce our fee for this client to regain our reputation, and you think it's best to leave the past alone and just make sure we don't make the same mistakes with any future clients."*

Step 4

Jointly search for options: The goal of this step is for everyone to generate as many options as possible that would reconcile the various positions and interests expressed in the previous steps. This step is more or less a brainstorming activity (as described on p. 263) in which everyone uses his or her creativity to develop new ideas and original thoughts about how to resolve the conflict.

Example: *"Let's just advertise on the Internet but keep our local focus." "Why don't I handle growing the local business and you expand the on-line business." "Why not offer consulting locally and sell our products on-line nationally."*

Example: *"Let's take off an afternoon and do a postmortem of what went wrong." "Let's admit we ran into a problem but avoid blaming one another." "Let's offer to redo the work for this client for free and that way we won't lose any more money." "Let's ask the client how they think we could take care of their concerns."*

Step 5

Joint evaluation and selection of a win-win option: In this final step, you jointly evaluate and select the options that have been generated to find a solution that everyone can fully support. Each person should reflect on the options and present his or her opinion as to

a) what he or she likes about the various options
b) any concerns he or she has about a particular option

In most cases, one option will emerge as the best, most acceptable one for all concerned. When this occurs, everyone will feel energized and pleased with the process. In case no single acceptable option arises, those involved will need to agree upon one that most closely meets their joint needs.

2. My Associate Is a Difficult Person to Work With

There are people who can truly be classified as "difficult" by nature. Unless they're extraordinarily talented, connected, or gifted, however, such "difficult" people rarely become successfully self-employed because to make it on your own these days you need to work reasonably well with others. If, by some chance you have hooked up with such a truly "difficult" person, chances are you knew about their "difficult" personality before you teamed up and decided to proceed for some specific reason. Part of the solution in this case is to recognize that you were aware of the situation and have already agreed to work with this person despite her or his personality.

More likely than not, however, your associate is not truly a "difficult" person; *you're* having difficulty working with him or her. In most cases labeling your associate as a "difficult" person isn't particularly helpful. It would be better to clarify specifically exactly what aspects of the person's behavior are making it "difficult" for you to work together. Ask yourself, for example:

- Is the person a perfectionist who tries to impose unrealistic standards on me?
- Does the person have an irritating work habit I wasn't aware of when we agreed to work together; e.g., taking several days to return phone calls or write a proposal?
- Does the person have personal habits I don't like, such as smoking or chewing gum?
- Does the person lack communication skills I think are important, like listening or acknowledging feelings?
- Is the person alienating our customers?
- Is the person "difficult" because he or she disagrees with me?
- Does the person bicker and argue over small details?

Once you can identify more clearly what specific aspects of the person you find difficult, it will be easier to choose a course of action to improve your work together. There are three possibilities to consider.

1. Could you be part of the difficulty? One of the most common reasons people have difficulty working with others is because we tend to "externalize" our problems; that is, we tend to believe that the other person is the sole cause of whatever problem has developed, and that we have no role in it. It's a natural tendency to see the sins of others, but not our own. So if you think your associate is "difficult," it's a good idea to spend some time thinking about how you might be contributing to the problem too. Is it possible that your associate is difficult to work with because you, too, are difficult? Is the simple fact that you disagree on many issues the reason you believe he or she is difficult? Are you overvaluing your contribution to the venture while undervaluing your associate's? Are you wanting him or her to think and act just like you?

After working together for six months, for example, Shana began to feel that Claire was a difficult person. They both ran their design business out of Shana's loft apartment, and as Shana examined the problem more closely she identified what was really bothering her. Claire was leaving her things strung out all over the apartment. She found Claire's honey on her kitchen sink, half-drunk cups of coffee here and there, half-eaten sandwiches left in the fridge, and umbrellas and raincoats tossed about. Although she had never raised these issues, Shana felt like she didn't have her own home anymore. The atmosphere had become quite tense, however, and it seemed as if Claire wasn't cooperating on anything. Upon reflection though, Shana realized that the housekeeping issues were at the crux of her difficulty. Once she understood this, she was able to quickly solve the problem on her own initiative, without ever having to talk about it directly. The next morning she told Claire the following.

> I've been concerned that you don't you have any place to call your own here in my apartment, so I've set aside a space in the kitchen cabinets for you, your own shelf in the fridge and this area of the guest closet is for you. What do you think?

Claire loved having her own space, and almost by magic the air cleared between them.

Of course, it can be challenging to examine your own actions to learn what role you might be playing in a particular situation. So you might want to ask an objective third party to give you some honest feedback about whether you're being a "difficult" person, too. In short, try to assess if you both have some role in the difficulty before you assume that your associate alone is the cause of your conflict.

2. Could you be more accepting? A second possibility is that there's some way you can be more accepting of your associate's "difficult" nature. In many instances, especially if you and your associate don't know one another well, it can take time for you to learn to appreciate one another's differences in thinking style and professional or personal habits. Many initial conflicts actually disappear once people get to know each other and are willing to accept each other's personalities—flaws and all. In short, no one is perfect: so just as you want your associate to accept you, try making an effort to be more accepting of him or her.

3. Can you bring the problem into the open and resolve it? If you haven't done so already, make your associate aware of the specific behaviors you find difficult to work with. But be sure to do so in a way that doesn't make matters worse. Focus your objection on a very specific incident, behavior, or event

Holding a Progress Meeting

A progress meeting is similar to the meetings psychologists have recommended for families who are having difficulty getting along. Rather than holding in resentments or blurting them out haphazardly at inappropriate times, associates or team members can agree to set aside a specific time to discuss the status of their business relationship for the purpose of identifying any decisions that need to be made or problems that need to be resolved. The basic rules for running a progress meeting are as follows.

1. Anyone can express the need for a progress meeting. And when someone does, it's best to schedule one as soon as possible. Don't let more than three days go by without holding a meeting whenever someone requests one. A delay in holding the meeting can defeat the purpose, which is clearing up any problems before they turn into bigger ones.
2. The meeting should be scheduled to last no more than twenty to thirty minutes, so everyone will get to the point, address the issues at hand and resolve them without unduly disrupting the regular course of business.
3. Whoever called the meeting should take five to ten minutes to introduce the topics for the meeting and express his or her view of the decisions or problems at hand—without interruption. Then others should express their perceptions.
4. As in the five-step conflict management process (on page 305), the goal of the discussion should be to identify the interests you share in common, isolate your differences, and seek to find a harmonious solution that takes each person's long-term interests into account.
5. Sarcasm, insults, personal attacks, threats, or making fun of someone's ideas and emotions should be off-limits during these meetings.
6. Devote equal time to identifying what's working well and going smoothly so such meetings don't become a dreaded event but a way to identify and reinforce the positive aspects of your efforts, too.

The success of a progress meeting will ride on each person's taking the process seriously and recognizing that everyone is entitled to express his or her feelings about the situations at hand without fears of recrimination or mockery.

rather than generalizing with abstract terms like "I find you difficult to work with" or "You're a perfectionist" or "You're too critical." Instead say something like "Please don't criticize the way I've organized the proposal. Just tell me what you want added" or "I really don't like it when you arrive late for appointments."

Being specific helps limit your discussion to what you would have liked to see handled differently rather than blaming or labeling, which usually just makes people defensive or antagonistic.

When such open conversations don't work and working together continues to be chronically difficult, we suggest setting up a progress meeting (see box on page 309) instead of unexpectedly blurting out weeks' and months' worth of pent-up feelings. Arrange to meet in a private location on neutral territory so your associate won't feel threatened or backed into a corner. Then before presenting your side of the case, reaffirm that you want to spend some time talking about ways to improve your working relationship. Present your analysis of the situation and explain how you'd like to see it handled. Be open to having your associate explain why he or she handles such situations differently. Don't fight to become the one who presents the "winning" solution. Seek a constructive, creative resolution you can both support and claim ownership of. People are much more willing to change their behavior when they think it's been their own idea to do so.

3. My Associate and I Have Different Views of What Our Strategy and Direction Should Be

Collaborations often falter when those involved don't agree on their strategy. The conflict might be over the vision each person has for the venture. One associate might want to take the company in one direction, while the other sees a different course as more desirable. Or the conflict might concern differing attitudes toward the way a venture should be managed. Disagreements may arise over priorities, how to handle money, or when to hire employees. Whatever the cause, when the associates have conflicts on key issues about the purpose and direction of the venture, it's time to reassess the relationship, because it's difficult to proceed when those involved are heading in different directions.

Here are several steps you can take to get headed back in the same direction.

Write or rewrite your business plan and mission statement. In many cases, disagreements over strategy or management arise because no one took the time to write out a business plan or mission statement in the beginning. Or sometimes the initial plan was too superficial. Other times, the plans you made initially have grown outdated by changing conditions. So if a conflict has developed, propose that you outline a new business plan together and begin by having each person spend a week or a weekend drafting her or his version. Then you can exchange drafts and identify areas where you agree and where you don't. Finally, hopefully, you can create a single document that reflects a consensus of your views. If you can't arrive at a shared plan, you'll know that further exploration will be needed if you are to get headed back in the same direction.

Research your viewpoints. If your strategic views continue to be considerably different, it probably means that you're operating from different information and/or assumptions. So you need to discuss your assumptions together and review the factual evidence behind your perceptions. You might turn to such sources as your bank statements, any market research you've done, news reports, the results of polls and surveys and financial projections—so that both of you can operate from the same knowledge base. Unsupported personal opinions are difficult to negotiate and plan from, so the more you can find concrete data to support your own beliefs and hunches the easier it will be to make a case for your respective viewpoints.

Hire an outside consultant. If you simply can't resolve a conflict and you want to continue doing business together, consider hiring a knowledgeable business consultant. First, the right consultant may be able to provide information about your industry that can break through your deadlocked views. Second, a consultant can be an informed third party who can help guide your discussions and provide you with feedback on what others in your field are doing and what companies in other industries do when struggling with similar strategic decisions. Examining your dispute in this light also can eliminate any of the impasses that can develop when egos get involved in proving that one person is "right."

4. My Associate Is Constantly Bossing Me Around and Making Decisions Without Considering My Opinions

It's not unusual for one person to want to take charge and impose his management style on the others. Sometimes this works out fine. But more often than not, independent individuals don't like being bossed around. That's usually a large part of why they became self-employed.

However, the truth is, it's difficult in any relationship to maintain absolute equality at all times, even if you're supposed to be equals. In many situations, one person has more expertise than another or is more assertive about making decisions. It's important to look at your relationship and determine why your associate is "bossing" you around and making decisions without considering your opinion. Ask yourself these questions.

- Does my associate have more knowledge about this aspect of our business than I do?
- Do I actually have as much knowledge about our business as my associate, but I am not letting it be known that I too am knowledgeable?
- Do I have more knowledge than my associate, but I am not asserting my expertise?
- Does neither of us have more knowledge than the other, but my associate is simply more aggressive about decision making?
- Does my associate come from a corporate or entrepreneurial background in which he's used to bossing others around?

Often what you discover by asking yourself such questions can help you identify the best way to proceed. Here are several options.

Relax. If your associate has more experience and expertise than you do in certain areas, you don't need to take his or her efforts to explain, direct, or lead personally as an insult to you. Don't think of yourself as being "bossed" around. Think of yourself as learning from an expert and then appreciate the experience! Before you know it, having learned from a pro, you will likely be working on a par together in future discussions and decision making. And remember that any apparent imbalance in power can, and probably does, change when situations arise that call upon your strengths, expertise, and natural talents.

Claim your turf. No one can boss you around unless you allow it. If your associate is used to being in charge, he or she may simply be doing what comes naturally. You simply need to assert yourself. If, for example, an associate tells you to place a call for her, tell her that you're busy, and she'll have to place the call on her own. If an associate announces how things are going to be, tell him or her that since you are a team, you need to discuss the issue first. Often there's no need to talk about this issue; you simply need to demonstrate over several situations that you are not someone who can be bossed around.

Case in point: Four colleagues decided to open a small public relations firm together. They each had a home office, but they also rented a small office together and hired an administrative assistant. Whenever Gene was in the office, he quickly began ordering everyone around. Before they knew it, the whole office was rushing about taking care of Gene's needs. One person was placing calls, another was looking up files, while the third was running out to make copies. Then Gene would run off to a meeting, and those in the office would be left in a daze wondering what had hit them. Cheryl was the first to consciously notice this pattern and brought it up with her other two associates. They decided to put an end to it posthaste. "There was no need to discuss it," Cheryl said. From that day on when Gene swept in with his demands, they were all politely too busy to help out. "I'm sorry, Gene," Cheryl would say, "I'm working on a client deadline, too. If you need my help on a project, let me know in advance so I can schedule time to help out."

Gene ranted and raved for a few weeks, hurling off comments like "How am I going to get anything done around here without any help?" But before long, he began to realize he would have to plan his own time better and arrange for the help in advance when he needed it.

Have a progress meeting. If the more indirect approach doesn't work, you might want to discuss your feelings directly at a progress meeting (as described on page 309). During your discussion, remind your associates that you see your relationship as one among equals and that you need to be involved equally in decision making. Explain that you don't feel you're having the time you need to think about issues and decide together how you want to handle them. Ask your associate to take the time to check in with you before making a decision and make arrangements to coordinate your schedules so having such conversations is practical and easy for each of you. Agree to try doing this for a week or a month and then plan to check with one another to see how the new policy is working.

5. My Partner Is Noncommunicative. He/She Never Tells Me What's Going On and Acts Without Consulting Me

This problem is related to the last one. Instead of being overtly bossed around, you simply feel as if you're being left out of the decision making by virtue of not knowing what's going on. Not surprisingly, this complaint can be as annoying as not having a chance to share the power, because in today's age, *information = power.*

In fact, information is the lifeblood of many business activities today, so if you're intentionally or accidentally left in the dark, it's no wonder you're unhappy. Other than the occasional situation when someone "forgets" to tell you something, being left out of what's happening can leave you feeling embarrassed, ignorant, and even unable to make good business decisions on your own. You may even end up thinking that other people are "out to get you" by intentionally excluding you from information or decisions.

So if you believe your associates aren't telling you what's going on, consider taking the following steps to put your association back on track.

Agree on an "information exchange policy." Let your associates know that you feel you're not getting the information you need and suggest that you develop a plan together for the information each person needs to keep informed and work out how and when you can share pertinent information with one another (as described in chapter 5, p. 276).

Discuss the best means of communication. Most of us are so busy and stressed these days that it's hard to find the time to communicate regularly, and communication can easily slip through the cracks. But today there's such a wealth of communications technology available that if you think about it, there will undoubtedly be a way for everyone to be kept informed and part of the process. For example, consider which of the following would be the most appropriate ways for you and those you're working with to update one another on the various types of information you need to share with one another.

- One-to-one telephone conversations
- In-person meetings
- Telephone conference calls with everyone involved on the line at the same time

- Voice mail with private mailboxes on which you can leave messages for one another throughout the day
- Fax messages
- E-mail through an on-line service or the Internet
- Direct computer linkup via modem
- Video conferences via computer

Explore these options with one another and agree as to what methods are the easiest and most efficient for regularly exchanging information quickly and consistently among yourselves. (See p. 276 for the pros and cons of various ways to exchange information.)

Determine if you have a power struggle going on. Sometimes people withhold information to maintain control. If you feel this is the case in your relationship, discuss once again who has agreed to do what and make sure that those involved recognize that they need certain shared information to be able to accomplish their jobs. Sometimes this problem can arise from a lack of trust as well, so refer to the ideas discussed in the next issue below.

6. My Associate Doesn't Seem to Trust Me or Take What I Do Seriously

Because trust and respect are such personal matters, feeling that your associate doesn't trust or approve of your work is perhaps one of the most irksome conflicts that can develop between business associates. A lack of trust and respect can eat away at the very heart of a relationship because it is an absolute prerequisite for good teamwork. Here are a few signs that suggest a lack of trust and respect.

- Watching over someone's work and questioning what he or she is doing
- Asking that someone do things over again or double-checking his or her work
- Refusing to share "confidential" information
- Withholding information or not sharing it freely with others
- Asking someone to sign in and out or keep a written record of his or her activities for purposes other than billing
- Reviewing every decision someone makes and overriding some of them
- Calling on the phone to check on what someone is doing

If you're seeing any of these signs that your associate does not trust you, or vice versa, you need to reflect on why this lack of trust has developed. When did you first begin noticing it? Did your relationship begin with this lack of trust or was there some event that could have caused your associate to lose confidence in you or you in her/him? Consider the following possible explanations and what you can do to put such concerns to rest and rebuild the trust you need and want to have.

Is your associate secretive, suspicious, cautious, or distrustful by nature?
The person you're working with may not consider his or her behavior to be
indicative of mistrust or disrespect. Some people are naturally more distant,
cold, perfectionist, controlling, or curious than others and thereby may give
the impression that they doubt or distrust you. So observe the person's behavior in a variety of circumstances with a variety of other people and notice
if he or she has demonstrated this same seemingly "distrustful" behavior toward others as well. If so, you may find it easier to accept your associate's behavior knowing that it isn't directed toward you personally but is simply part
of her or his personality.

Have you done something that could have triggered a loss of trust and
respect? Sometimes lack of trust or respect can develop from a particular
event an associate believes was handled improperly. It may or may not be a
justified concern. But is it possible that you did goof up in some way or has
anything happened that could have led your associate to think you did? The
concern may even be irrational, unreasonable, or unnecessary, but is there
anything you can think of that could have been cause for concern? Have you
done anything that could have caused your associate to decide that he or she
needs to check up on you to make sure that nothing like that, or something
worse, ever happens again? Chances are, if so, when you think back over recent past events, you'll have some idea about what may have triggered the
problem and you can clarify or rectify the situation by reviewing the events
together and developing a mutual understanding of what actually happened.

For example, when Sharon began working on a project with an associate,
she accidentally erased an important project file the two had been working
on, and she'd made no backup copy. This caused a considerable problem, and
Sharon had felt terrible about it. She'd apologized profusely and assumed all
expenses to correct the problem. After it was all over, she thought nothing
more of it, feeling she'd rectified the situation in the best way she could, and
she knew she would never make that mistake again! But when their next project began, she noticed right away that her associate took over most of the
work, leaving only a small, insignificant element for Sharon to do and, of
course, a smaller, less significant fee as well. At first Sharon felt slighted; then
she realized it probably was the result of the previous error, so she brought it
up with her associate. "I called her," she remembers, "and told her that I
realized she probably had lost confidence in my computing abilities after the
mishap. I told her I understood why she would feel that way and wanted to
reassure her that I had been doing this kind of work for five years without
such a mishap and that she could rely on me to make sure it would never happen again."

Sharon's associate seemed relieved to have a chance to discuss the matter.
"She said she couldn't believe I had been so careless, and that she had been

very angry. But she'd really appreciated the way I took responsibility for the problem personally and financially and wanted to continue working with me in the future." And, indeed, she began including Sharon again in larger and larger aspects of projects. "In a way," Sharon admits, "I had to earn her trust again, and I was willing to do that."

In Damion's case, the situation was quite different. He and an associate had taken a booth together at a trade show, agreeing to split the costs and handle the trade show traffic they attracted. But the convention center misprinted instructions about the arrival times on the notice they sent Damion, so he arrived two hours late, after all the booths had been set up and the show had already begun. Damion was sorry about the miscommunication, of course, and explained the situation. Then he thought nothing more of it because the trade show went well for both of them from that point on. After the show, however, his associate became cold and distant and began canceling out on the other joint promotions they'd planned, saying he was "too busy." Thinking back, Damion realized the problem probably stemmed from the last trade show episode, so he called his associate to discuss the matter further.

"I told him I was concerned that he might still be feeling bad about the mess-up at the trade show, and he said that indeed he hadn't been happy about having to do all the setup himself and that he felt that I let him down. So I asked how he thought I could have handled it better." The associate told Damion he should have called to confirm the information. "I told him I hadn't thought of doing that and asked him if he'd called to confirm the information he received from the convention center. Of course, he hadn't, and he said, "Why would I? My information was right." At this point, they realized they'd received different information and, of course, assumed it was correct. They both broke out laughing and the discomfort between them dissolved.

Did your relationship start out in an unhealthy manner with less mutual trust and respect than you thought? Although you thought you'd entered into a relationship of mutual trust and respect, could it be that your associate has had a different view of your level of competence and expertise right from the beginning? When Renee graduated from her physical therapy training program, for example, she was flattered when one of the part-time instructors, Bruce, approached her about working together in a private clinic. Bruce was very complimentary of her work and seemed eager to have her as part of the clinic team. After they began working together, however, Bruce would only allow Renee to assist clients under his supervision. He didn't seem to trust her to work alone with patients. In fact, it seemed as if he still viewed her as a student.

"I finally decided to bring up this problem," Renee told us. "I asked if we could talk after work one day. When I told him I was eager to begin working with my own clients, he was surprised. He made it clear that he saw me as an assistant at this point but that he was sure the time would come when he would feel comfortable turning clients over to me, maybe in a year or so."

In this situation, there was clearly a misunderstanding about the relationship right from the beginning. Of course, had Bruce been willing to share responsibility more equally, Renee would have been willing to continue working with him but in view of his position, she decided to associate with another group who viewed her as teammate instead of as an assistant.

So, if you and your associate(s) have differing views of what your contribution can and should be, let him or her know what your expectations are for entering into your collaboration and that to continue you need to be trusted to perform your job and make decisions accordingly. Be open to whatever explanations your partner or associate may offer to explain his or her behavior but calmly insist on being shown the trust you deserve.

Are you dealing with a stereotype or role expectation that needs changing? Sometimes social or generational stereotypes or role expectations slip inappropriately into business relationships and erode the level of professional trust and respect you need to work well together. The most typical examples of this involve gender stereotypes and family role expectations.

Are you experiencing a gender stereotype? Sometimes the distrust that develops between people working together occurs because of an underlying gender bias. Usually it's a male associate who automatically assumes he should be in charge of a venture he enters into with a woman.

Dean was always so polite to Gloria, for example, that she felt like a "hothouse plant." He always opened doors for her, pulled out her chair, and got her coffee. At first she thought this was nice, but when he carried his chivalrous behavior into their business dealings with clients she felt embarrassed and discounted. She remembers,

> He would answer questions for me, reexplain what I said, assume that he would handle any of the challenging aspects of our work, etc. So I decided to confront these behaviors one by one every time they occurred. When he'd open doors, I'd smile and tell him, "That's okay, Dean, thanks but I can open the door for myself." When he answered questions for me, I'd interrupt and state my own opinions. And after such a meeting I'd tell him, "Dean, don't answer questions for me. Don't explain what I say. It makes me feel like a child, and I don't like it. It doesn't reflect well on us as a team."

He always apologized; it soon got to be that all Gloria needed to do was give him a look and he'd stop himself midstream. "It took awhile, but I guess you can say I've finally got him trained. It never happens anymore."

Of course, such biases aren't just a problem for women. Peter, for example, rented an art gallery with three other artists, all of whom were women. And before long, he found himself excluded from conversations and missing out on referrals, while being expected to do all the maintenance on the building and keep the financial records for their consortium. "At first I was angry and kept all the more to myself," he says, "but then I started to tell them how I felt. If everyone would stop talking when I came in the room, I'd ask what was going on. Then at one of the monthly meetings I told them I felt excluded and taken advantage of. They were shocked. They assumed I wouldn't want to hear their girl talk, that I'd want to be in charge of the money and building maintenance. They thought I'd be able to get plenty of work myself so I wouldn't need as many referrals." The group discussed each of his concerns and agreed to redistribute work and referrals more equally. They began including Peter in their social discussions, which turned out more often than not to be more about work and their lives than just "girl talk."

If you believe gender is a factor in the lack of trust and respect between you and a business associate, you might want to write down specific examples that illustrate the biases you're feeling. If you don't know your associate very well, it might help to talk with other men or women with whom your associate has worked to ascertain if they've also noticed such biases. Then, each time an offending behavior occurs, politely let your associate know that you don't like the behavior. If it continues, set up a meeting and discuss your concerns. If there's no openness to change, chances are you won't be able to work well with this person, and talking about it further will probably be a waste of time. For more information on handling gender stereotypes in the workplace see the resource list at the end of the chapter.

Are there family role expectations involved? In a family-run enterprise, what looks like lack of trust or disrespect can actually be generational biases or misplaced family role expectations. A father may relate paternalistically toward his son, for example; a husband may treat his wife as a helpmate instead of a partner; an older sister may treat a younger brother condescendingly; sons or daughters joining their father's business may feel their efforts are taken for granted or that they aren't allowed to take on the level of responsibility they want to assume because, from Dad's point of few, they're still "the kids." All such problems occur because habits from the way we relate in our personal lives weave their way into our business relationships. When this happens, as with gender stereotypes, it's usually a matter of "retraining" family members to interact with you more appropriately. Unfortunately, confrontation rarely works. If you tell Dad, for example, that he's treating you like a kid, he's just likely to become defensive and justify his behavior. "Retraining" family members more subtly usually works better.

Instead of calling his father "Dad" at the family auto shop, for example,

Brandon started calling his father by his first name the way everyone else did. Also, he told us,

> Dad had this habit of asking me to run family errands during the day. If my sister needed to be picked up from school, he say, "Hey, Brandon, run over and pick up your sister and take her to soccer practice." Or if someone needed to stay home to wait for the repairman to come, he'd say, "Hey, Brandon, you can come in late today." It bothered me a lot. All the other mechanics thought I was getting special privileges, and customers just thought of me as Ray's son.

When Brandon mentioned these concerns to his father, his dad would slough it off with a comment like "You're lucky to be part of this business. Most kids your age are still working at McDonald's."

So Brandon decided to "retrain" his father to see him differently.

> When he'd ask me to go get my sister, I'd tell him I couldn't because I was in the middle of a complicated job. If he asked me to stay home late, I'd tell him I couldn't because a particular customer was expecting me to be there. At first, he'd insist. But after a couple of jobs got messed up, he started taking me more seriously. Now I'm his right-hand man. He'd never think of doing those things.

When Georgia joined her husband as a bookkeeper in his new home-based accounting business, she had a few problems at first.

> At noon he'd say, "Where's lunch?" Or if he was going out of town to see a client, he expected me to pack for him. If things got messy around the house, as they did whenever we got really busy, he'd say, "How come it's such a mess around here?" At first I tried doing everything myself, but I started to feel angrier and angrier. So we talked about it, and he agreed: I couldn't do everything at home and work full-time in the business. But he never really changed, until I changed. When he'd say "Where's lunch?" I'd say, "I'm in the middle of a project right now, you'll need to get your own lunch unless you want to wait until I'm done." When he'd say "Will you pack my suitcase?" I'd say, "I can't right now, I'm on a deadline." When he'd say "How come it's such mess around here?" I'd say, "That's a good question. I haven't had time to clean up, have you?" Now we're truly partners, at home and in the business.

Of course, sometimes family role expectations can't be changed by such defining or "retraining" conversations. Sometimes changing role expectations to increase mutual respect and trust among family members will require bringing in an outside consultant or neutral third party to help solve the problem. For further information on working with family members, see the

Resource list of books and other sources that offer assistance for family businesses at the end of chapter 5.

7. My Associate Always Bickers, Argues, and Insists on Doing Things His/Her Way

If an associate constantly argues and bickers, it's a sign of three possible problems.

1. Your associate may lack listening skills.
2. Your associate may not know how to express his or her needs effectively.
3. Your associate may not know how to negotiate effectively, so he or she relies on coercive tactics instead.

Each of these problems can be a challenge in and of itself, but all three combined can obviously be damaging to any working relationship. The following steps can be helpful.

Encourage interactive listening. As we discussed in chapter 5, interactive listening makes both parties feel they are being understood because each person pays attention and encourages the other party to speak. If your associate is distracted, impervious to hearing your views, or an impatient listener, it is likely that he or she is not hearing your point of view. And chances are, that's because he or she is not feeling heard. So, the next time you want to be sure your opinion is heard, stop talking and make it a point to listen to and understand what your associate is wanting, needing, or thinking. Ask your associate to confirm that you understand their position fully. Then, once you have fully understood their point of view, ask if they would now be willing to listen to your point of view on the matter. When someone has been fully understood, they are usually willing to listen. But if, when you start talking, they jump back in to argue or restate their needs, remind them that you listened to their needs and that you understand them; then ask once again if they will listen until you finish explaining your concerns. You may have to do this repeatedly. Once you've explained your views, check to be sure your associate understands them, and if so, ask if he will help you find a way to meet both of your needs.

You may need to go through this process repeatedly before it comes naturally to your associate, but if you stick with it patiently and consistently, eventually it will become your habitual way of communicating with one another.

Help your associate communicate his or her needs. Bickering and arguing is usually an indication that someone doesn't know how to express their needs effectively or fears that they won't. They feel as if life is a battle of wills, and unless they beat you over the head, they'll probably lose. Such feelings are based on deep-seated conclusions that people hold about life in general and often are not related in any way to the situation or discussion at hand. Some people habitually argue with anyone who disagrees with them because that was how conflict was handled in their family when they were growing up. Other people feel threatened by any form of disagreement, and so in an effort to avoid conflict, they try to suppress differences of opinion in order to make a quick decision in their favor. Whatever the case, someone who's always arguing and bickering may need help expressing their feelings and thoughts calmly and clearly. You can help them by stressing that you really want to understand their concerns, views, etc., and asking that you both take a moment to talk it out in a more relaxed way, without internal or external pressure. If you and the associate have been bickering frequently, make it clear that you want to avoid this pattern from now on. Most people will be relieved and agree that bickering is both unpleasant and nonproductive.

When your partner blows up or starts yelling or lecturing, tell him or her directly that you don't understand what they're saying, but that you want to. Ask your associate if they can calm down so you can really talk about whatever is bothering them. You can use the five-step method on page 305 to manage conflict instead of arguing further.

Demonstrate win-win negotiation. When people use aggressive, combative, and coercive communication it's usually because that's what they think they need to do to win and they have a deep emotional need to "win" an argument at whatever cost. They may never have had experience finding a mutually agreeable solution to conflict. As we discussed in chapter 5, people who use argumentative and coercive tactics usually have a course of action already in mind and feel they must resort to threats, personal attacks, and exaggeration in order to have that position prevail. So you will have to demonstrate that their needs can be met and that they will be better served if you jointly find solutions that meet everyone's needs.

Remember, people who argue and bicker are concerned about themselves, so even though you want them to be concerned about your thoughts and feelings, the quickest route to what you want is to find out what they want and show them how they can have it by listening to your needs too. As you listen to them, be sure you understand the true need beneath whatever surface position they're expressing; tell them you would like to see them achieve that need too. Talk to them about how you could help if your concerns were met and see if they're willing to listen to your thoughts and concerns. Again, if people really feel understood, they will usually listen to you. Once they understand your perspective, you can begin brainstorming a solution that will work for everyone. For weeks or even months, you may have to stop the conversation frequently to remind your associate that you want his or her needs to be met fully and that if you keep brainstorming you can and will find a way that will work.

Granted, this approach takes patience, but in this case patience pays off. After you've reached several win-win solutions, you'll feel so good about each other and your ability to work together there will no longer be any problem with bickering. Of course, if a tough new conflict arises, the bickering and arguing may rear its ugly head again, but if you return to the process of finding out what your associate needs, get on his or her side, and ask him or her to get on yours, your new history of solving problems together will go a long way toward getting through even the toughest ones.

8. My Associate Is Always Criticizing Me, Whatever I Do

It's probably fair to say that most people have a problem with criticism. Usually we don't know how to productively give it or receive it. But the truth is, *constant* criticism is annoying and difficult to live with. It frequently creates a "toxic" environment for working together. Criticism is like a hot coal no one wants to hold for long; it burns if it's not passed on. So, in giving criticism, it's best to do so gently and with enough of a warning that whoever is catching it can put gloves on before you toss it. Basically, however, it's not a good idea to work with a chronically critical person. But of course, few people enter into teaming-up ventures expecting an associate to be highly critical, so here are three steps you can take to remove the sting from this problem.

1. Look for any valuable message buried in the criticism. Instead of dismissing the criticism or reeling off a defensive response, as most of us often do, listen for any grain of truth. Dismissing an associate's criticism entirely usually just leads to more criticism. Becoming defensive or countercriticizing just leads to an argument or bad feelings.

The fact is, most people are simply not very good at giving criticism, so we end up burying our valuable insights and feedback in inarticulate, accusatory, or even insulting comments. So if you can stop for a moment to reflect and pick out the pearl of wisdom in what the person intended to say, you may discover something interesting. Ask yourself, Is there any part of the criticism that is warranted? How could I improve the way I work based on the criticism? Finding the grain of truth in a criticism can actually be useful. And when you can do this, let your associate know that you appreciate her or his comment, and perhaps that you even agree with it. Such a response often short-circuits any potential conflict.

Example: "Your overheads are lousy. Too crowded . . ." Response: "I appreciate your feedback. I'm planning to simplify them."

2. Invite positive feedback and honest discussion. Encouraging a learning environment so that you and your associates are always aiming to improve your skills can be vital to the success of any venture. Since most people don't know how to give criticism constructively, you may be able to train your critical associate to share his or her ideas and feedback in an uncritical way.

Example: Each time you're criticized, you might say, "I want to hear your ideas and thoughts so I can learn more, but I personally hate to be criticized in those terms. Instead of telling me what's wrong, could you find a way to tell me what you'd like or what you think would be better?"

Another advantage of this approach to criticism is that it may uncover more quickly what the person really wants. A remark like "Your reports are dull and confusing" could actually mean "I wish you would take more time to make these reports sparkle," when you thought your associate wanted you to get the reports done as quickly as possible.

3. Deflect useless habitual criticism. Some people are by nature hypercritical and dislike any way of doing things other than their own. Marjory had just such an associate. He was a master potter who liked being loosely affiliated in an alliance with other artists. But he was hypercritical of everyone, always ready with a suggestion for a better way.

> He was always telling me I should keep my studio warmer, have less light in the room, work longer hours, make more customer calls, keep my dogs out of my studio . . . and so on. Since I was happy with the way I was running my own business, I found these incessant comments irritating. I finally said, "Jeffery, this is MY studio; let me run it the way that works for me!" From that point on, whenever he started criticizing my studio, I'd just hold up my finger and say, "OOPS! What did I tell you about that?" He still does this, but not nearly as often and by handling it this way, it doesn't bother me anymore.

If you believe your associate is such a person and you want to keep working with him or her, here are several "retorts" you can make to deflect chronic irritating criticism so you can continue working productively.
Examples:

- "Thanks, I'll think about that."
- "Thanks for the suggestion; I prefer to do it differently."
- "Would you like to handle this yourself? If not, let me do it my way."
- "Let's try it my way. If it doesn't work, I'll try yours."
- "Thanks, Commander" (with a smile).

However, in deflecting criticism in this way, be sure not to overlook valuable feedback you could benefit from. Sometimes it's wise just to try someone else's approach on for size; you actually could end up liking it better.

Special Skills for Preventing and Defusing Conflicts

The way we react to conflicts or potential conflicts often determines whether they develop in the first place and, if they do, whether they get resolved quickly or become even worse. Sometimes, unfortunately, the most natural, automatic response unintentionally makes matters worse. There are several ways you can respond to conflict, however, that can quickly defuse it instead of inflaming it.

Preempting Comments: Sometimes you can avoid a conflict altogether by preempting the negative feelings that can lead to problematic reactions. Preempting can be done by simply acknowledging the feelings and concerns you imagine your associate(s) will have before talking about an unpleasant subject. For example:

Problem: A legal problem you were responsible for taking care of has developed a snag that will prevent you and your associate from beginning long-awaited work with a new client.

Preempting Comment: Instead of announcing the problem without prelude, you can preempt negative reactions by saying something like: *"I have bad news. I'm sure you'll be as upset about it as I am."*

Preempting in this way allows people to prepare themselves mentally for bad news or problems. It can take a lot of the sting out of whatever difficulties need to be discussed. In fact, most people are actually somewhat relieved once you describe the actual problem because their thoughts immediately leaped to the worst possible scenario and, compared to what they imagined you were going to say, the actual problem seems quite manageable. Even in the worst possible cases, people have a few seconds to marshal their defenses and call upon their best coping behavior.

Preempting also allows others to postpone discussing developments they're simply not ready or willing to deal with at the moment. It gives them the opportunity to say, *"I can't deal with bad news right now. I'm on a deadline. Unless it relates to what I'm doing right now, please save it until I'm through."*

Agreeing: Many times you can defuse an intense conflict that erupts unexpectedly by simply agreeing with aspects of whatever concern the person is raising that you can honestly agree with. For example:

Problem: *"This report can't go out like this! It's a mess. As usual, you've dumped another mess in my lap."*

Agreeing Response: *"We certainly can't have a mess go out, and you shouldn't have to handle it all! Let's take a look at it and see what can be done now."*

Grooving: Many of the worst conflicts develop, grow, or continue because you and those involved get sidetracked from the issue at hand. Grooving, or what's also called "broken record" or repetition, is one way you can keep a discussion focused on the point at hand. It involves agreeing or acknowledging what someone is saying by then repeating the main message or issue that must be heard or addressed over and over again regardless of whatever else the person is saying. For example:

Problem: You and your associate have agreed to take turns staffing a trade show booth where you are exhibiting together. He was to take the morning shift and you were to take the afternoon shift. Although he had known for some time that you have a long-standing commitment in the morning, midafternoon on the day before the event he calls to say *"You'll have to handle things tomorrow morning because I've got to tend to an emergency with a client."*

Grooving Response: To keep the conversation focused on solving the problem at hand, no matter how many problems or issues your associate brings up, you can bring the discussion back to the key issue you must address together as follows:

"I understand that you need to handle a client emergency, but I'm not available tomorrow morning."

"But I've helped you out in a pinch before and this is a real emergency."

"I know you have, and I appreciate it. Unfortunately, as you know, I'm not available to help tomorrow morning. Is there something else you could do?"

"There's nothing I can do about it. This client is really in a tizzy. The whole project is at stake. Don't let me down. I've never let you down."

"I don't want to let you down, but since I'm not available tomorrow is there some other way I could help you deal with this problem?"

"Well, maybe you could get someone else to be there for me."

Now, at last, you're both focused on the same problem and can proceed to address it. You may be willing to take responsibility to make the needed arrangements, or you could suggest brainstorming other solutions if your situation doesn't allow you to take over the problem. For example:

"As I said, I would like to help you out, but right now I'm calling on a break from a meeting that's going to run all afternoon. I've got about ten minutes. Let's brainstorm how you could line up someone to back you up tomorrow."

Reframing: Most conflicts are focused on the negative aspects of whatever issues are at hand. However, by reframing the issues in a more positive light, you can make the prospect of taking time and energy to solve them more appealing. For example:

Negative Statement of Problem: *"You're spending too much time networking. It's a waste of our time and money. I need you here taking care of business."*

Reframed Statement: *"Let's take a look at our marketing plan and find out if networking activities are really bringing in enough business to make them worthwhile. Let's see if it's safe yet to cut back somewhat on the time and money we're putting into marketing."*

Blending and Redirecting: In their book *Dealing with People You Can't Stand*, Drs. Rick Brinkman and Rick Kirschner point out that the difference between conflict with a friend and conflict with a difficult associate is that with a friend the conflict is tempered by the personal bond you share. This bond provides a sound foundation from which to seek solutions to conflicts that arise. So Brinkman and Kirschner recommend using two skills based on neurolinguistic programming that they call "blending" and "redirecting" as a way to establish a common ground with someone when you don't have a long-standing personal bond from which to resolve conflicts.

• **Blending:** Have you ever noticed when someone is highly emotional and angry, the calmer and more rational you become the more agitated and irrational she or he becomes? Or have you ever noticed when an associate is feeling discouraged and depressed, your cheerful and upbeat response only makes matters worse? Such frustrating and confusing responses are examples of why it's helpful to use blending. In a conflict or emotional situation, people like to feel that they're being understood and, whether they are or not, they don't feel that they're being understood if your response or reaction is highly different from their own. So blending is matter of calibrating the tone, pitch, and movements of your response to match or mirror that of the other person's so they feel as though you're on common ground. For example:

Problem: Your associate comes charging into your office flailing, pacing and yelling wildly, *"You lost the airline tickets! We're going to miss the New York meeting! We'll lose the business! We're finished! Damn you!"*

Blending Response: Instead of reacting in a calm, cool, and collected fashion by saying something like "Just calm down. We'll find a solution," you might get up out of your chair and respond loudly and emotionally yourself: *"What? The tickets are lost? We can't miss the plane. We can't lose the business. Oh, no!"*

Often such nonverbal blending happens automatically and usually goes unnoticed by both parties. But consciously being sure to "pace" or match the intensity, style, and manner of someone in the midst of a conflict can create a greater sense of cooperation and synergy between you and other people.

• **Redirecting.** In situations like the one above, blending is only the first step to resolving a conflict. Without redirecting, you can both end up stuck in a negative, emotional state. After matching your associate's level of concern and emotion, you can redirect an argumentative and quarrelsome discussion by gradually shifting to another, more congenial and productive one. Returning to the above example:

Redirected Statement: Instead of continuing to flail your arms and yell about the missing ticket, allow your voice and manner to become increasingly calm and confident as you say, *"Let's see, what can we do? Oh dear, well, where were the tickets supposed to be? Could they be somewhere else? Where else could we look. Let's see if I accidentally left them in my briefcase."* Hopefully, by this time, both you and your associate can begin focusing on locating the lost tickets or otherwise solving the problem of how to get to New York on time.

Whenever you're faced with a bickering, argumentative, or otherwise difficult person, try using blending and redirecting to defuse the conflict and take your conversation in a more mutually productive direction.

9. My Associate Doesn't Seem to Understand What to Do, and I End Up Having to Make All the Decisions

Whereas most conflicts have to do with an associate who's intruding or inter-fering in some way with your productivity, it can be equally annoying to have an associate who isn't contributing in the ways you expected when you de-cided to work together. For example, let's say you and your associate are forming a joint venture and have divided up the labor so that you'll develop a marketing plan while your associate scopes out and purchases the equip-ment for your office. Three days later, though, he calls to say he hasn't pur-chased any equipment yet because he can't make up his mind about what model to buy and wants you to look over the product specifications and de-cide what you think. If this approach becomes a pattern, it won't be long be-fore you'll start to feel angry and frustrated about having to do so much more than your share of the work.

Habitual indecision, confusion, or failure to understand the issues at hand can seriously undermine any teaming-up effort. Again, it's best to avoid part-nering with someone who can't make decisions on his or her own, but if you've made a commitment to such a person and don't want to back out on your agree-ment, taking the following actions may help keep your venture moving forward.

When meeting together to make decisions, create a written journal or notes of your conversations. Most of us have a lot going on in our lives, and it's easy to forget things we've said or agreed to do even in a business enter-prise. So, when you meet with your associate to make decisions, bring along a notebook and ask him or her to do the same so you can each take notes as you talk. Write down all important decisions you make, including any as-signments each person agrees to take on. Fax follow-up copies of agreed upon action plans to all involved. In this way, your associate may get better at remembering and committing to what needs to be done.

Provide leadership. We each bring different levels of experience and ex-pertise to any teaming-up venture, and in general, it is best to turn over tasks to the person best equipped to handle them. However, when someone isn't as experienced as you and lacks the expertise or confidence needed, it's not un-reasonable for you to play a stronger leadership and decision-making role ini-tially. So when your associate turns to you for help, give it the best you can. Keep in mind, though, that one of the best ways you can provide leadership is to encourage your associate to make her or his own decisions. Offer your trust and support. In the case of the computer equipment, for example, you may not need to jump in and take several hours with him or her to review all the choices. You might suggest that your associate summarize his or her find-ings in written form and make a recommendation you can both go over quickly. Or in situations where a decision is not critical, such as which mail service to call or which credit card to sign up for, tell your associate simply to make a choice, and that you'll support it. Then together you can evaluate whether to change your decision at a later date.

Seek additional information together. When neither you nor your associate has sufficient confidence to make key decisions, take a course, read a book, or sign up for a seminar together to gain the expertise you need. By learning together, you can discuss business decisions jointly and directly encourage one another to be continually increasing your expertise and confidence.

Check to be sure you're not being critical, intimidating, or overbearing. Finally, consider the possibility that the problem lies at your feet. If you're a perfectionist or tend to be impatient or hypercritical, you may be intimidating your colleague into indecision. None of us wants to subject ourselves to criticism or look bad in the eyes of an associate, so your associate could be bringing you all the decisions because he or she knows you aren't satisfied unless things are done your way anyway. That's what happened to Carlo. He'd encouraged his wife, Betty, to leave her job and assist him in running his computer consulting company. She'd worked for ten years as an administrative assistant, so she decided to take him up on his offer. At first she seemed eager to take charge of all the administrative aspects of the business, but before long Carlo was complaining, "She leaves all the decisions to me and gets me involved in virtually everything in the office. She even checks with me before she'll file an invoice!"

He was baffled, but when they sat down to find out what was going on, she made the problem clear. "It doesn't matter what I do or how I do it, he has a so-called better way of doing it, and I just got tired of getting bawled out and having to do things over again and again. It's his business, so I let him run it." From that point on, Carlo took a hands-off approach to the office. "It wasn't easy," he admits. "I was used to being the boss and doing things my way, but I really wanted Betty to be a partner, so I realized I'd have to let her be in charge of the office. The result is, I don't always know where things are or how to track something down, but that's okay, because that's her side of the business and I've learned I can depend on her. Even if I don't agree with the way she goes about doing it, she gets it done well."

10. My Associate Never Follows Through on What He/She Has Agreed to Do

Most people don't intentionally drop the ball on what they agree to do, so don't assume the lack of follow-through is intentional. It's probably not. To deal with this problem, you have to figure out just what's going on.

Correct and avoid any underlying misunderstanding about what you've each agreed to do. One reason your associate doesn't follow through may simply be that you have a misunderstanding about just who is to do what. So, as in conflict 9, one way to correct this problem is for you to begin writing down all your decisions and expectations in a shared log or journal indicating who has agreed to do what.

Make sure your associate understands fully what the follow-through specifically involves. Your associate may not be aware that he or she's not following through. Many self-employed individuals have very little marketing, sales, administrative, or management experience, so their idea of following through may be considerably more limited than yours. Your associate may even hesitate to ask you for help or clarification for fear that you'll think less of him or her. In fact, some people have teamed up because they're new to running a small- or home-based business and are hoping to learn from their teammates. So if you notice that your associate isn't following through in the ways you expected, you can sit down and review the steps you believe should be included to turn your joint decisions into action.

For example, one new associate took on the assignment to research the competition on a joint venture. He called two companies he knew about who did something similar and thought that was sufficient. His associates concluded he was sloughing off until they began to query him about what he'd done and realized he was unaware that there was a local and national trade association and many other resources he could contact to complete his research. Once he knew about the resources, he was eager to continue following through.

Ascertain if your associate has agreed to do something he or she dislikes or disagrees with and is therefore proceeding to do things on his or her own terms. Carla agreed to chair the committee for lining up speakers for her monthly networking group. When she began recruiting the committee, however, she found that coordinating everyone's schedules was a pain in the neck, so she decided to book all the speakers herself—instead of forming a committee to do it as she as had been expected to do. She thought this approach was more efficient and productive. But other group members were angry. To them Carla wasn't following through on what she had agreed to do and was leaving the membership out of the decision-making process. When they discussed the issue with her at the executive committee meeting, everyone discovered that no one had wanted to cause any ill feelings. Carla has simply gone off on her own, thinking she was doing the best thing for everyone by streamlining the process. Since involving a committee in locating speakers was important to the membership, she decided she'd rather take on a different role in the organization, and they appointed a new committee chairman.

So if teammates seem to be heading off on their own instead of following through on joint decisions, set up a progress meeting and explore their rationale. You may need to reshuffle responsibilities, agree to carry them out differently, or perhaps discontinue working together if your objectives are no longer compatible.

11. My Associate Keeps Making Bad Decisions

If you believe your associate is making bad decisions about your business, consider taking these steps.

Take a more active role in the decision-making process. Instead of criticizing and disapproving of your associate's decisions, which will only cause more tension, get more involved in the decision-making process yourself. Whenever a decision needs to be made, make an effort to participate in analyzing the facts, evaluating and weighing the options, and selecting the best choices. By participating in this way, you can add your expertise and judgment to whatever decisions are made and be happier with the results.

If your partnership is intentionally set up so that you receive an unequal share of decision-making responsibility, accept that and learn to support your associate's decisions. Some collaborations are specifically intended to give one associate more weight in decision making. This is often the case when one person is contributing more money and the other is doing more of the actual work. If your collaboration is like this, you need to work within the guidelines you've agreed to and support your associate's decision or get out of the relationship.

12. My Associate Doesn't Have the Same Interest in Making Money That I Do

People have different ideas about the importance of money and what they'll do to get it. Some people want to make as much money as possible, and they're willing to work eighteen hours a day to do it. Others are completely satisfied to just get by financially as long as they have enough time free to do other things that are more important to them in life than work. We also place different values on the meaning we give to the money we make. For some of us, money is power; for others, it's prestige; for still others, money is simply a means to an end like paying the mortgage, sending the kids to college, or being able to pursue a hobby that's their real love.

The fact that many people are reticent to talk about financial matters exacerbates these differences. People often talk in vague terms about how much money they want to make without specifying exactly what they mean by "a good income" or "a lot of money." As a result, it's easy for people to think they agree on money matters when, in fact, they may be worlds (or bank accounts) apart.

So, if differences about money are a problem between you and your associate, it's absolutely vital that you sit down together and openly discuss your financial attitudes and goals. Discuss your personal responses to questions like these.

- How much money do you want to make per year from your venture?
- How many hours on average per week are you willing to work to bring in such an income?
- If you had to value your time or services on a per-hour basis, how much do you think they're worth?
- What are your goals for your joint venture over the next three years? The next five years?
- Do you believe in the adage "You have to spend money to make money"?
- What do you need your money for: mortgage/rent? college education for children? retirement? travel? business expansion?
- How much leisure time do you need and want each week?
- At what age do you want to retire?

Discussing your answers to such questions can then help you determine if you and your associate are aligned on money matters—if not, where you may differ. There are actually four specific financial areas where disagreement often puts a strain on a working relationship.

1. **Views about your current value.** Each person may have a completely different sense of what their work output is worth. Each person's view reflects his or her past earning power and current view of what he or she can charge as a self-employed individual. One person may think in terms of thousands per week, while the other is thinking in terms of hundreds.

2. **Financial goals for the next few years.** A teaming-up venture may have varying value to each person involved. One may have great expectations to grow into a full-time large company, while the other has minimal expectations of simply supplementing other ventures he or she has under way. Such a conflict in the way you view your collaboration will affect everything from how much time each of you is willing to commit to how much importance you place on the decisions you make.

3. **Views on how much money should be spent to make money.** Collaborators may have quite different ideas about how much money they are willing to spend up front to make money down the road. This view usually reflects personal attitudes toward risk. One person may believe it's perfectly natural to spend $5,000 on a marketing campaign that has the potential to bring in $20,000, while the other may insist on spending no more than $1,000 to test the waters, even if it means the ultimate reward will be smaller.

4. **What you will do to make the money.** Even when people share the same expectations about how much they want to make, they may have very different attitudes toward how much they're willing to work or what they're willing to do to make money. Some people are perfectly happy to cancel the rest of their life if working eighteen hours a day can earn them the new house or dream car they've always desired. Others believe that work

must have specific limits and going beyond those limits will ruin the quality of their lifestyle. Some people will travel or work weekends routinely, for example, whereas for others travel is out and weekends are sacred.

So if you suspect that you and your associate(s) have different financial objectives, discuss these areas together and find out where you agree or disagree. Share whatever concerns you have about one another's attitude in a thoughtful and considerate way. It's important to respect one another's views on money matters. Understanding your varying views can help you determine how you might better handle your workload, responsibilities, and profits. You may decide that the one of you who has greater expectations and is willing to work more hours at your venture should go ahead and do so and get a larger share of the results. On the other hand, you may decide that because of your different expectations and goals, your venture will be limited to a short-term collaboration as each of you moves on to find others to work with who more closely share your attitudes about money.

In one case, Miriam had great expectations for her company and wanted to see it become a million-dollar enterprise as quickly as possible. In contrast, her associate wanted to earn a decent living but wasn't interested in putting in the hours required to build a nationwide company. After consultation, Miriam agreed to buy out her associate so she could pursue her dreams on a grand scale.

Whatever your views, get your agreements about money down in writing. As we all know, money can lead to more problems and more bitter feelings than perhaps any other aspect of a business venture. Disagreements about money can bring out the worst in people, turning a seemingly generous, unselfish, and altruistic person into a stingy, greedy ogre. So, if you have serious differences about money, be sure you settle them and put whatever you agree upon in writing so that any "deal" breakers surface as soon as possible and you can redirect your efforts accordingly.

Joanne is a social worker and registered nurse. She has an excellent rapport with elderly women and dreamed of opening a center in every major city where women sixty-five years of age and older who could no longer care for themselves and had no family nearby could get the care they needed. Roger had a strong business background, having started and sold a variety of businesses over the years. When he met Joanne, he was impressed with her methodology and thought he could arrange the financing to launch a nationwide chain of centers for elderly women, who constitute a growing percentage of the national population. Partnering this venture seemed like a match made in heaven . . . until they opened the first center.

Joanne was making decisions based on the needs of the women who were referred to the center. She didn't care if she and her partner made very much money as long as they had enough to live on and their other expenses were covered. She didn't understand why they needed to make a "profit." In one meeting she even asked Roger, "Couldn't we just set the fixed salary we each want to make from this venture, maybe $50,000 or $60,000 a year and leave it at that?" Roger was flabbergasted. He was in the process of lining up venture capitalists who would be expecting millions of dollars a year in profit. Whereas they had begun their venture with good intentions and with the highest of respect for one another, their relationship deteriorated quickly.

Because they each believed so strongly in this project, however, they hired a business consultant who helped them agree to put Joanne on a salary to operate the first center and serve as a paid consultant to a professional board that would oversee the development of centers in other parts of the country. This arrangement is working so far, but because their financial motivations are so very different, the future of their relationship is not clear. Joanne has been talking about arranging to buy out the associate and operate her own center independently.

13. My Associate Is Always Busy Working on Some Other Project or Business and Doesn't Devote the Same Energy to Our Venture That I Do

There are many reasons why an associate will devote a different level of energy and time to a teaming-up effort, and each has its own solution.

Multiple Irons in the Fire. Your affiliation may be one of several ventures your associate is involved with, so there's no way he or she can devote as much time and energy as someone could if the venture were a primary focus.

Solution: If your associate is busy working on other projects because he or she has many irons in the fire, you need to sit down and honestly discuss one another's priorities. Ask your associate to be realistic and tell you how much time and energy you can actually count on his or her devoting to your venture. Also determine for how long your associate's other ventures will last; it may be that your associate is working under several temporary deadlines and will be able to spend more time on your venture in the future. With this kind of information, you can decide just what you can really expect from your associate. Be as specific as possible; e.g., two hours per week for six months, eight hours per week starting in a month, zero hours per week for the next three months. Depending on the outcome, you might offer to swap the extra time you can invest for a greater share of the profits. Alternatively, you might decide that your associate simply has too many things going at this time to continue your venture.

No Money Maker. If your venture is not yet profitable, your associate may need to spend a significant portion of his or her time and energy on other income-producing projects in order to maintain a livelihood.

Solution: If your associate is working on other projects because he or she can't afford to spend more time on your venture until it begins to produce more income, you need to revise your expectations and perhaps your agreement. Here are several possible solutions.

- You agree to take on more of the work until your collaboration is profitable, but in exchange you could get a higher level of profits during this time period.
- You hire someone to do the work your associate should have done, but the salary for that help is deducted from the associate's share of the profits.
- You keep track of the extra hours you must work and accrue them for later when your business is profitable to be used as vacation time during which your associate will do the work while you're gone.
- You could lend your associate enough money so that he or she could drop other projects and devote more time and energy to your venture; the loan could be repaid from your associate's share of the profits.

Different Skill Sets: Associates have different levels of skills, abilities, and expertise that influence how much time and energy they can contribute to different stages of a business relationship.

Solution: Sometimes an associate is more gifted at a particular aspect of business or has more experience and skill in a particular area than another. When this occurs, it could look as though your workload is unbalanced and that you're doing most of the work, when in fact, it's just that your business is in a stage where you are the one who is best suited to take the lead. As you move through this stage of your venture, the balance may shift and your associate may be the one who's doing the bulk of the work.

For example, when Glenna started a medical transcription business with her sister Genevieve, she felt overworked right away. Because of her strong sales and marketing background, she was keeping busy more than full-time while Genevieve, with her ten years of experience doing medical billing for hospitals, was spending lots of time at home with her family waiting for new business to come in. When Glenna began complaining, Genevieve offered to help out in whatever ways she could, and there were some things she could do to help, but it wasn't long before Genevieve was plenty busy. As their marketing effort began to pay off, Glenna got to relax a bit and had to pitch in to help keep Genevieve from feeling overwhelmed with all the work.

So review where each of your strengths lies, what stage your business is in, and how you think you can best balance your workload to use your differing skills to share your workload reasonably and fairly.

Different Energy Levels: It could be that your associate simply can't match your supercharged energy level. Individuals have differing levels of energy, work at varying paces, and need varying amounts of free time. We also differ in terms of our health, our family circumstances, and priorities. Often we need to account for such differences in appreciating what each person in a joint venture can reasonably contribute.

Solution: If you're cranking out more work than your associate because you enjoy working like a human dynamo and your associate doesn't or can't, you need to weigh your varying circumstances and contributions carefully and, if need be, honestly discuss your expectations with one another. In making this assessment, however, we suggest that you consider your own high level of energy as a gift, rather than thinking of it as a norm to be expected of everyone. The fact is, everyone can operate at only 100 percent of *their* capacity, but at any given point in time, not everyone has the same capacity to draw upon. Age, health, family circumstances, and individual physiology often determine how much energy we have to give to our careers.

Paulene is a single, twenty-four-year-old live wire who needs only four hours of sleep a night. She's in a position to contribute a lot more time and energy to marketing her sign-making business than her associate, Lucy, another sign maker, who's also single but forty-five years old and caring for two teenage children and an ailing seventy-six-year-old mother—all while recovering from emergency surgery she underwent two months ago. There's no way Paulene can expect Lucy to have the same level of drive and energy she has for their interdependent alliance. But Lucy has many more years of experience and many more contacts. Paulene realizes she has to make allowances for their differing energy levels in order for their relationship to work out, but she doesn't mind: "I figure if she's got the ideas and contacts, I've got the energy and the time."

So rather than expecting your associate to rev up to be more like you, see if you can't find a way to appreciate his or her energy level for what it is and focus on whatever valuable contribution your associate can make to complement your dynamic energy supply. It might be her or his analytic or organizational ability, insights, creativity, or networking contacts. Whatever it is, it's probably what attracted you to want to work together in the first place.

14. My Associate Keeps Involving His/Her Spouse or Other People in Our Business

In general, if your associate involves other people in your business venture who are not officially or professionally part of it, you're entitled to be annoyed. No matter what the excuse may be, there's no reason for people who aren't officially involved to play any role or have any influence over your official decisions unless you all agree that would be advantageous for some reason.

Many people who have tried teaming up in various ways mention this problem to us. During our research, someone told us about an associate who insisted on having her boyfriend attend their partnership meetings so he could contribute his ideas. In another case, an associate consulted with his father on a regular basis for general business advice and introduced the father's opinions and recommendations into their discussions expecting everyone else to automatically accept them. In a third situation, an associate constantly discussed her company's business with her husband and regularly quoted his opinion of why their venture wasn't proceeding as well as he thought it should.

If outside people are interfering in your business relationships, consider taking one or more of the following steps.

Request that all decision making be limited to your own opinions. Discuss with those involved in your teaming-up venture that outside information and opinions are always welcome as part of your research but all management decisions need to be based on your joint conclusions, not the views of spouses, parents, friends, siblings, and so on. Of course, such a dictum won't necessarily stop your associates from turning to others for outside opinions and ideas, but it alerts them that they should weigh whatever information they gather and then *reach their own conclusions*. If an associate is continually seeking outsiders' opinions, you might redirect the conversation as follows: "I understand that's what your husband thinks. What do you think? Do you agree? Why?"

Determine together when you want to officially solicit outside expert advice and opinions. Some spouses, parents, siblings, or friends have valuable counsel to contribute, so be open to drawing on such advice. It could be useful. But just make sure everyone fully agrees and understands when it's okay to bring on "Uncle Maxi's" counsel—and when it's not.

Clarify your views on confidentiality and proprietary information. Every venture has information that's considered confidential or proprietary such as the income, expenses, profit ratios, marketing plans, client names and circumstances and other strategic business information. You need to decide together what information regarding your business activities you believe should be considered confidential and ask one another not to discuss these matters with anyone who's not part of your venture. While it's natural for people to share challenges and problems with family and friends, in general, it's usually better to keep most of the key ideas, plans, and business dealings to yourselves rather than sharing them broadly with friends and family. As the old World War Two saying goes, "Loose lips sink ships."

15. I'm Fed Up and Want Out

When any one or a combination of the above problems continues on and on and never seems to get resolved, chances are you'll end up feeling that you want out. And when you do, it's clearly a sign that you're no longer in the right frame of mind to work creatively on a successful collaboration. But before you decide to terminate your relationship(s), ask yourself these questions.

- Have I played a strong enough role and made a sufficient effort to make this relationship work?

- Have I exhausted all possible remedies to communicate with my associate(s) and solve the problems we face?
- Can I learn to be more accepting of the relationship and make it work?

In other words, before you decide to call it quits, consider what your own role has been in making the relationship what it is today. Don't place all blame on your associate(s). Reflecting on your role in no way denies or denigrates your feelings of frustration and disappointment, but it can serve to remind you that, as the cliché goes, "It takes two to tango." It could be worthwhile to make further efforts to save your relationship. Maybe you can play more of a leadership role or take more responsibility for tasks your associate needs help on in exchange for her or his doing tasks you'd prefer not to do or don't do as well. Maybe you can use the five-step conflict management process mentioned on page 305 one more time to address the concerns that are dividing your energies and causing your disagreements. In short, there could still be other options to reduce your frustrations, resolve your problems, and redirect your venture toward the goals that initially brought you together.

So, consider the following actions before terminating your venture.

Consider going on a retreat with your associate(s) to refocus your venture in a more positive direction. Getting away from your daily routine and your usual environment for an afternoon, day-long, or weekend retreat might give you each a fresh perspective on your goals or reinvigorate your relationship. You can spend the time at such a retreat refocusing on your goals, and chances are any unresolved conflicts will surface. When they do, you can calmly and honestly discuss what you each see as the three most important issues you believe stand in the way of your working together successfully. Keep the focus on what you want and what you can do, not on what's wrong and who's to blame. Strive to find solutions, not dwell on problems. New solutions could create a new foundation upon which to build a more workable relationship. (See "Are You Ready to Change?" on page 338 and the ideas presented in chapter 8 on page 365 for tips on learning to change when you need to.)

Of course, such a retreat may also help you to discover that you no longer share the goals that brought you together, and the meeting can serve as an opening to discuss how you can amicably go your separate ways. (For more information on taking a business retreat, see p. 280.)

Hire an outside consultant. As we mentioned in chapter 5, a professional consultant can provide several types of assistance when a business relationship seems headed for self-destruction. You can gain:

- More objective analysis and evaluation of your difficulties
- Insight into how other companies in your field deal with the issues you're facing

- Additional information that might break the stalemate between you and your associate

In some cases, one session with a consultant is all you'll need to resolve the core issues that are dividing you. Other times you may need a series of consultations. But once you resolve your core issues, you can often resolve future disagreements on your own without further outside assistance.

Review your business plan, mission statement, and legal agreements. Taking time to review these key documents can serve two purposes. First, it might remind you of the vision you once had for your collaboration and reinforce its importance to you. Reading through your initial plans may reenergize you or help you realize that your differences are minimal compared with the benefits you hope to obtain from working together. Second, reexamining the agreements you've made for handling conflict and terminating your relationship may alert you to what action you need to take if you do plan to end your relationship and if doing so will be worthwhile. Sometimes terminating a business relationship can be more costly than you think. To end amicably, you may need to take the time to develop a plan for withdrawing or phasing out of your relationship.

Are You Ready to Change?

Do you know the old adage "Where you stand depends on where you sit?" The implication of this motto is that what you think about something often depends on the view from your particular vantage point. For example, if a customer gets angry at you for being late in completing a job, you may feel that he hasn't appreciated how hard you've worked on the project and that he didn't allow enough time for you to do it right. But later the same day, you may go to the cleaners to pick up your clothes and if they're not ready as promised, you may become angry just like the customer you encountered in your own business earlier that day.

The point of this anecdote is that when conflict occurs, it's helpful for each person involved to consider the vantage point of those on the other side and make an effort to understand their point of view. You may need to take responsibility for your role in whatever problem(s) you're having. For example, ask yourself these questions.

- Am I controlling?
- Am I a good listener?
- Do I apologize when necessary?
- Do I give compliments and positive feedback when needed?
- Do I learn from my mistakes?
- Do I control my anger?
- Do I make time to meet regularly with my associates?
- Do I build self-esteem in others?

Ultimately, the biggest and most important question is: Am I willing to change what I do and the way I do it to improve this relationship? Think about this question and what it may mean for you and your situation and review the following summary of problem-solving action steps before you decide that while breaking up may be hard to do, it could be best for you.

QUICK-REFERENCE TROUBLESHOOTING GUIDE

This table summarizes the fifteen most common problems that occur in teaming-up ventures of all kinds. We have used the word *associate* to mean anyone you've teamed up to work with, be it in an informal relationship, a collaboration, or a formal partnership.

---

1. My associate and I can never seem to agree on anything.

Actions

1. If your teaming-up relationship is new, get to know one another's thinking in more detail. See if there are unstated assumptions behind your disagreements. Also, look for decisions on which you do implicitly agree but perhaps have failed to state that fact to one another. Build your relationship on these small steps and seek compromise to help you get through the forming and storming stages of your effort.

2. If you have already been successful as associates for a while and find yourselves now disagreeing, frankly explore with one another to identify if something happened to cause one or both of you to feel that you no longer agree on *anything*. Try to go over the issue so you can remove the hurt and regain the path to success you were formerly traveling.

3. Learn the five stages of managing conflict so you get better at identifying your underlying positions, areas of agreement and disagreement, and how to search jointly for options.

---

2. My associate is a difficult person to work with.

Actions

1. Before taking any action, be more specific in understanding your complaint against your associate. Narrow your objection by finding what behavior your associate engages in that you find difficult.

2. Ask yourself if your actions play any role in the relationship that might cause the specific behavior you find difficult. Are you equally guilty?

3. Consider accepting and living with the person's quirks or foibles. Admit to yourself that you, too, have them.

4. Have a relationship meeting in which you try to resolve your problems by discussing with your associate a specific behavior or incident that you would like to have conducted differently in the future. Seek a constructive and creative solution. Avoid generalizations and abstractions.

3. My associate and I have different views of what our strategy and direction should be.

Actions

1. If you and your associate disagree on a key strategic direction for your firm, spend some time writing or rewriting your business plan so you can be sure you have developed your thinking to its fullest. Then review each other's plan and try to come to a consensus on your visions and management views. If you disagree, back up your opinions with market research and other concrete information so that you don't turn your professional dispute into a personal battle of egos.

2. If you cannot agree at all, hire a consultant to help you weed out the issues and evaluate the options based on market information and industry norms.

4. My associate is constantly bossing me around and making decisions without considering my opinions.

Actions

1. Determine which person has which expertise; divide up the power and decisions accordingly. Don't take it personally if one person has more expertise than the other. Each project or situation can differ in terms of whose expertise is required.

2. Claim your own turf. Be more assertive if you need to demonstrate that you should not be bossed around. Ask your associate to slow down and give you a chance to put forth your views and opinions.

3. Agree to share power equally by dividing up the leadership roles between clients or projects.

5. My partner is noncommunicative. He/she never tells me what's going on and acts without consulting me.

Actions

1. Let your associate(s) know that you feel you're not getting the information you need. Suggest that you develop a policy for what information each person needs to keep the other informed about.

2. Evaluate the best technology that can help you obtain consistent communications.

3. Determine if a power struggle is the real issue and take steps to curtail it.

6. My associate doesn't seem to trust me or take what I do seriously.

Actions

1. Determine if your associate is aware of his or her behavior that makes you feel distrusted. It may be that the person is naturally cold or critical, and you can learn to be more accepting of that character trait and see that it is not directed at you personally.

2. Determine if the lack of trust is related to a specific incident. If so, discuss the incident and come to agreement on how you can rebuild the trust.

3. Determine if your relationship is unhealthy and unbalanced. If so, have a relationship maintenance meeting in which you discuss your feelings and ask your associate to show you the trust you deserve.

4. Determine if there are any gender or role stereotypes causing the distrust, such as male/female bias or family pattern issues. If so, take steps to counter them and read more about handling stereotyping in the workplace.

7. My associate always bickers, argues, and insists on doing things in his/her own way.

Actions

1. Encourage interactive listening to make sure each of you recognizes the other's point of view. Ask your associate if he/she feels that you understand his/her position. If so, ask him/her to take the time to listen to yours.

2. Help your associate express his/her feelings calmly. Tell him/her that you want to understand his/her needs and avoid bickering.

3. Demonstrate win-win negotiation by explaining that both your needs can be met if you work together.

8. My associate is always criticizing me, whatever I do.

Actions

1. Ask yourself what fundamental message of the criticism may be useful for you to accept, rather than outrightly rejecting it. Some criticism is worth recognizing as valid.

2. Encourage an environment of positive feedback among all team members. Focus everyone involved on accepting well-mannered criticism so that you can develop a "learning" atmosphere whereby each team member can help improve others.

3. Discourage habitual critical comments that irritate and inflame and have no positive value. If someone on the team is a highly critical person, let her/him know that this attitude does not help people and distracts from your team efforts.

9. My associate doesn't seem to understand what to do, and I end up having to make all the decisions.

Actions

1. Keep a notebook or write memos summarizing your meetings and decisions. A written record can help your associate better remember what decisions were made and tasks assigned.

2. Increase the leadership you provide. Ask your associate to let you be project leader for a few months or take a greater role in decision making by preplanning and thinking in advance about your decisions.

3. Take courses together to develop your skills and emphasize the value of learning for all team members.

4. Consider that you may be at fault by moving too quickly or being too critical of your associates, which makes them feel that they can't make decisions alone. Slow down and listen to what others have to say before deciding that they can't make decisions or don't understand what to do.

10. My associate never follows through on what he/she has agreed to do.

Actions

1. Reflect on why the person does not do what was expected. He or she may have misunderstood the decision or may have insufficient business experience to properly assume his (her) responsibilities. If so, review your decision-making process and begin to record your meetings in writing through notes and memos. Organize your communications for greater clarity and increase the relationship between decisions and actions.

2. Determine if the associate doesn't do what was planned because he/she disagrees with the decision. Make it clear to a maverick associate that decisions reached by mutual consensus must be followed. If necessary, make a change if the person still refuses to do what was agreed upon.

11. My associate keeps making bad decisions.

Actions

This conflict often reflects the fact that you are not taking an active role in the decision-making process. Rather than blaming your associate for making "bad" decisions, you need to be more aggressive in participating in analyzing your options, weighing and evaluating them, and making the final choice. If your collaboration is set up so that you do not get an equal vote, you need to accept your position and learn to be a supportive player on your team—or get out of the relationship.

12. My associate doesn't have the same interest in making money that I do.

Actions

Have a money dialogue in which you honestly exchange your views on how much you want to earn, how much you feel you are worth, how much you are willing to work to get money, and what your views about spending money to make money are. If your attitudes diverge in a major way, come to an agreement on how that affects your level of effort and your adversity to risk. Seek either to reaffirm in writing your sharing of the profits, or to redistribute earnings if one person will work harder or longer, or to split apart if your views are incompatible.

13. My associate is always working on some other project or business and doesn't devote the same energy to our venture that I do.

Actions

Try to understand the reason that you and your associate have different energy levels.

1. If your associate has too many ventures going on, ask him to prioritize where yours fits in. Depending on the response, you can redivide up your time or make plans for an alternative arrangement.

2. If she/he has an immediate need for cash while you don't, and so gives other profitable projects priority over yours, see if you can come up with a creative solution to keep your collaboration going.

3. If you have different skill levels that account for the disparity in energy, try to find ways to divide up your work so that you both benefit in the long run.

4. If your energy level is higher than that of other people, give your associate the benefit of the doubt and look for ways she/he can contribute to your venture that don't involve sheer energy.

14. My associate keeps involving his/her spouse or other people in our business.

Actions

1. Make it a rule that that outside opinions are not welcome as part of your research. Make it clear that management decisions do not include the views of spouses, parents, friends, siblings, and so on.

2. Alternatively, decide which outside opinions are acceptable. Invite your associates to consult with these people and consider their opinions in your decision making.

3. Establish a policy regarding confidential and proprietary information. Ask everyone to respect this policy.

---

15. I'm fed up and want out.

Actions

1. Go on a retreat with your associate to get away from your usual environment where you can discuss without pressure the conflicts between you. Make it a goal to solve three of your most crucial problems.

2. Hire an outside consultant who might be able to help you with objective advice and comparative information based on how other companies handle problems similar to those you are having.

3. Review your mission statement and legal agreements to reenergize your vision of your relationship or to remind yourself of any agreements you have already made about withdrawing from your collaboration.

MOVING YOUR COLLABORATION TO HIGHER GROUND

We hope that, with skill and luck, the ideas in this chapter can help you get past the rough bumps along the road to successful collaboration. If not, chapter 7 will provide a road map for breaking up when that's your most positive alternative. And then in chapter 8, you'll see how you can make your teaming-up relationships even more successful.

RESOURCES

Building Team Power: How to Unleash the Collaborative Genius of Work Teams. Thomas A. Kayser. New York: Irwin Professional Publishing, 1994.

Can This Partnership Be Saved? Improving or Salvaging Your Key Business Relationships. Peter Wylie and Mardy Grothe. Dover, NH: Upstart Publishing Company, 1993.

Dealing with People You Can't Stand: How to Bring Out the Best in People at Their Worst. Dr. Rick Brinkman and Dr. Rick Kirschner. New York: McGraw-Hill, 1994.

Men and Women at Work. Katherine Kearney and Thomas White. Hawthorne, NJ: Career Press, 1994.

They Don't Get It, Do They? Communication in the Workplace: Closing the Gap Between Men and Women. Kathleen Kelly Reardon. Boston: Little, Brown, 1995.

Tongue Fu! How to Deflect, Disarm, and Defuse Any Verbal Conflict. Sam Horn. New York: St. Martin's, 1996.

7

When Breaking Up Is Best

You learn . . . and you learn. . . . With every good-bye, you learn.
—ANONYMOUS

IT WOULD BE UNREALISTIC to think that all teaming-up efforts will survive and thrive. For whatever reason, some business relationships don't work out. Some will wither on the vine and others will erupt due to personality differences, changing life circumstances, financial problems, lack of clients, poor product, or other business reasons.

For example, Risa Hoag, a PR consultant in New York, took on a partner to start a seminar company offering training on how to start and run a small business. When their seminars didn't get the number of enrollments they needed to be profitable, they decided to discontinue their joint venture and return to their own independent businesses. As Risa said, "This was a good example of forming a partnership to test the waters for a business idea. Unfortunately, it just wasn't profitable." As Risa's story illustrates, breaking up may be unavoidable, essential, and even desirable, but it need not be a negative experience, nor thought of as a failure.

ACCEPTING UNAVOIDABLE PARTINGS
Your teaming-up arrangement may come to an end due to factors completely beyond your control. For example, your associate may:

- Need to move out of state
- Get married and no longer want to work
- Have family difficulties that require his or her primary attention

- Get divorced and need to take a full-time job
- Develop financial difficulties and even go bankrupt

One person we talked with presented a more unusual reason for having to terminate his joint venture: the husband of his associate was jealous that his wife was spending more time with her male colleague than with him. While there was no sexual relationship between the business associates, the husband was simply annoyed at losing his mate and the mother of his children to an increasingly time-consuming partnership with another man. In another unusual case, a mutual-referral agreement came to a screeching halt when a new bride discovered that her husband's daughter was in the same business as her associate and the in-laws expected her to keep referrals in the family.

In such unintended and unavoidable situations, a business relationship may need to end regardless of how well it has been going or how much you enjoy working with someone. In such cases, it's always best to do whatever you can to support your associate in getting on with whatever new arrangements life has presented so you can remain on the best of terms. Of course, you may not always feel like "doing the right thing," but do it anyway. You won't be sorry.

Gladys was astonished when her associate announced that her husband was taking early retirement and that she wanted to drop out of their rubber stamp business. Gladys had been creating the designs each week, and her partner had been selling them at a swap meet every weekend. They'd split the profits and after five years were bringing in a decent income together. So at first Gladys was angry and felt overwhelmed by the prospect of having to run the entire business all alone while her associate was off traveling around the country with her husband. "It didn't seem fair. But I bit my tongue. I wanted to be happy for my partner. She'd been dreaming about having the freedom to travel all her life, and an unexpected downsizing had provided her with the chance to actually do it. She'd been my partner and best friend for so long I didn't want to spoil her plans by putting up a fuss." Making the adjustment was difficult for a while, but eventually Gladys's daughter-in-law joined her business and she was thankful to have handled things the way she did. "I still have my friendship and everything's working well again."

PARTING FROM INTOLERABLE SITUATIONS

There are also situations when you must end a relationship abruptly due to clearly intolerable circumstances. In such situations, you can't hesitate; you have to act fast and pull the plug at once, even if it involves a good friend or long-time acquaintance. Here are a few of the types of situations that require immediate action.

When a partner or associate:

- Steals, embezzles, or somehow manages to lose your money
- Lies or cheats on you or your customers
- Spreads rumors and false innuendoes about you or others behind your back
- Reveals your confidential information or proprietary secrets to others
- Has consistently not followed through on agreements despite every effort to clarify your joint expectations
- Has become involved in or arrested for any illegal activity or violates your expressed ethical standards
- Disappears or stops answering your phone calls
- Repeatedly alienates your customers
- Damages materials or property belonging to the business out of anger
- Injures your business reputation through unprofessional behavior

Unfortunately, you can never plan for such situations and they may arise even when working with a best friend or someone you've known for years, someone in whom you've had the greatest faith and trust. For example, an associate of ours was involved in a consulting business with a partner she'd known for many years. While our friend handled the marketing and consulting engagements, her partner handled all the bookkeeping and administrative aspects of their business. One day, our friend called and announced that she was ending her partnership because she had discovered quite by accident that over the past few years, the partner had been secretly transferring money from their business into her own bank account. When our friend confronted her partner, the woman was startled and clearly upset about having been discovered but offered no acceptable reason for having made the transfers. As much as our friend did not want to believe it, having known this person for nearly twenty years, she nonetheless realized that this situation had all the makings of embezzlement. She contacted her lawyer and immediately began the process of terminating their partnership.

Can This Relationship Be Saved?

As with a skidding car, it takes a lot of savvy maneuvering to keep a teaming-up effort from crashing once it's begun to spin out of control. Of course, as soon as you notice your business relationship is in trouble, you can take as many of the proactive steps discussed in chapter 6 as possible to try to get things back on track. But here are a few guidelines you can use to ascertain whether it's worth your while to keep trying to work things out.

_____ Do you both still share the goals that brought you together?

_____ Is your venture achieving those goals for both of you, or are there definite indications that it soon will be achieving them?

_____ Are there times when you and your associates still work well together?

_____ Do you have a long history of working successfully together?

_____ Have you resolved difficult problems successfully before?

_____ Do you still basically respect and trust one another?

_____ When you imagine the future, does it seem brighter if you see yourself working together?

_____ Have you taken responsibility for your role in the difficulties you're having and tried all appropriate methods for resolving them?

_____ Will dissolving your relationship create more business, personal, and financial problems than dealing with the problems of staying together?

_____ Have you given yourself several weeks to weigh a final decision before ending your relationship?

ENDING A RELATIONSHIP THAT JUST ISN'T WORKING

Most collaborations end when, no matter how hard the principals try to get along, they can't reconcile their differences and work harmoniously. Many people have told us about prior collaborations that ended poorly before they established their successful ventures. In the majority of these cases, "personality conflicts" were cited as the primary reason their teaming-up effort went sour. One person put it succinctly when he described the breakup of a partnership he had with himself, his wife, and a third party as follows.

> We formed a company with this fellow and put together several joint proposals. We contracted for a couple of projects that were successful, but we found we just didn't enjoy working with one another. What we learned was that the only way you can actually tell if you can work well with someone is by trying it out. Sometimes you just can't know if it will be right until you do it. And in this case, it wasn't.

For whatever reason, if you know in your heart that it's time to end a business relationship, give yourself permission to do so in the best possible way. Whatever difficulties or disappointments you've had, each collaboration is rich with learning and other valuable experiences, and each can be a stepping-stone to learning even more about yourself and your business. Most successful people have been involved in many business relationships, at least a few of which weren't successful. There's no reason for you to be like a teenage lover who keeps getting involved with the wrong associates. You can come to understand your own role in creating a good relationship by looking at how you became entangled in a negative one. Each relationship can help you become more flexible, creative, and willing to look at the world from another person's point of view.

So when the time arrives to end a relationship, accept it and develop a plan for how you can do it in the most positive way possible. Outline whatever legal and ethical steps are called for. Decide how you can provide your associate with as much advance notice as possible and what activities need to be carried out so you can close down your affairs with the least disruption to your clients and customers and one another's future success.

A BREAKING-UP CHECKLIST

For whatever reason you've decided to end a business relationship, use the following list to make sure you've taken all the steps you need to take to terminate your relationship appropriately. Naturally, the more formal your collaboration, the more specifically these steps will need to be carried out. But it's important that you end your relationship feeling confident that you've protected one another from future lawsuits or lost opportunities.

___ *1. Review any legal agreements you have made before taking any action.* Go over whatever written agreements you've made with your associates(s) or collaborator(s). Make sure you're fully aware of any commitments you've agreed to. Your legal agreement, be it a formal partnership agreement or informal letter agreement, may have stipulated how much notice you will provide, what you will and won't do for some specified period, how you will split profits and losses, and who gets control of any remaining assets from your venture. You may have also agreed to use mediation or arbitration to settle any disputes.

If you did not make a written agreement and you're involved in what by common standards and in a legal proceeding would be recognized as a partnership, find out what your state's Uniform Partnership Agreement (UPA) stipulates. If you and your associate are parting on less than cordial terms, and you have a lot of assets or debts, you may need to be prepared for the possibility of a legal battle over how the profits or losses will be split.

___ *2. Define your goals and objectives for ending your relationship positively.* Before announcing your desire to end a business relationship, identify what aspects of it you consider to be important to preserve and plan how you can best proceed to make your parting mutually beneficial. If at all possible, you don't want to leave with hard feelings. You don't want your reputation tarnished in any way by backing out on something others are counting on you for. And, of course, you want to preserve as much as you can of whatever benefits your relationship has produced—be it money, clients, contacts, reputations, access to opportunity, or other assets.

Sometimes with more informal agreements such as networking or mutual-referral agreements, the best way to end a relationship is to let it die a friendly, natural death by maintaining cordial contact but simply letting your interactions dwindle down of their own accord. Here's an example: Roger, a graphic designer, and Jim, an advertising consultant, had been providing mutual referrals to each other quite satisfactorily for several years, but gradually Jim's business began shifting to editorial work that involved little or no graphic design. At first Roger continued to send business to Jim, but as Jim's referrals dwindled, Roger began developing other, more useful referral relationships. While they never felt the need to actually discuss this shift, it just occurred naturally and their relationship remains strong to this day.

Most of the time, however, you will want and need to discuss or formally announce your plans to disengage from your work together. For example, when Stu decided to leave the holistic health center where he had practiced for five years, there were many things that had to be discussed including his rental agreement, his share of advertising that had been purchased for the upcoming year, how shared clients could best be handled, and how to deal with future referrals that came to the center for him. Naturally his first concern was his clients' well-being. But he also wanted to remain on good terms with the other practitioners at the center to protect his reputation and for professional contact and support. So he needed to make sure he met all his obligations.

____ *3. Meet with your associate(s) to announce your decision.* Out of respect for your prior relationship, it's preferable to make such an announcement face-to-face. As actor George Clooney said when he wanted to change his contract with the popular television show *ER* so that he could appear in a movie, "It's much easier and much better to look the guys you're working with right in the eye and let them know where you stand."

If you cannot do this, at least inform your associate by phone that you intend to terminate your work together. If your relationship has become hostile, vitriolic, or embittered, it's tempting to avoid this step and simply send a letter. If so, have your attorney send the letter or leave an answering-machine or voice-mail message. In most cases, however, making a final personal contact is the best, most respectful route to closure.

Usually your meeting should be followed up with a written document that spells out the terms of your termination. This is especially true if your venture involves any ongoing products or services. In either your prior legal agreement or this closing document, you should account for who will continue with which clients or projects, who owns any copyrights or trademarks you originated, as well as how your assets and losses are to be divided. In today's world, you can never predict when a product or service that's been struggling along for years will become a blockbuster success. So if you or your associates want a part in any such possible future success, you can avoid costly legal and financial hassles by accounting for such expectations now.

If your partner or associate has not been expecting your termination, be prepared to discuss your decision honestly and forthrightly. It is best to focus your explanation on only one or two primary reasons for wanting to end your venture. Frame your decision in terms of the positive steps you will be taking in leaving instead of on blaming or finding fault with anyone involved. Don't let your associate pull you into a new debate arguing the fine points of your termination. The truth is, when a collaboration has reached a high level of conflict and many attempts at reconciliation have been made without success, the parties intuitively know that splitting up is the best choice, but it can still be hard to admit it. So by not seeking to blame anyone or review in detail the chronology of negative incidents that led up to your conflicts, you can clear the air and leave on better terms.

___ *4. Consult a professional CPA or lawyer to help you and your associate if you have agreed to sell your share in the business or to have your venture appraised to determine its worth.* For formalized partnerships, there can be many tax implications when buying out a partner or transferring partnership assets from one party to another, so you will also want to assess any tax consequences involved in ending your relationship.

It will be in your best interest to conduct the entire termination process fairly and honestly with as little acrimony as possible. Don't be tempted to haggle over small details, go to the mat to see how much you can get from each other, or punish each other in the process of resolving the financial and tax issues. There will probably be temptations galore to act in ways that will make your relationship worse and keep you entangled in endless legal hassles. One or more things will probably raise your hackles and make you want to get even. But such responses are almost always a lose-lose proposition Here's an unfortunate example:

When Larry decided he no longer wanted to conduct seminars with Connie, she felt rejected, abandoned, and angry. Since it wasn't her idea to end the joint venture, she had her attorney stipulate that Larry would have to pay all the legal and accounting fees involved in concluding their partnership. When Larry saw that clause in the termination agreement, he was incensed and instructed his attorney that if that was how Connie wanted to do business, then he was going to demand a portion of revenues from all future seminars she conducted using any of the materials they had developed together. When she saw this clause in the agreement, she was enraged and decided to fight back further, taking the position that Larry should be precluded from any claim to ownership in their materials and prevented from using them in any way. And so on . . . and so on.

As you can imagine, the dissolution of their partnership continued from bad to worse to horrible over what began as a minor issue. The only people who can benefit from such an escalation are the attorneys on both sides. So don't do it. Small or even considerable amounts of money are usually not worth a legal hassle because attorneys' fees can gobble them up in no time. Get out as quickly, professionally, and cleanly as possible. Connie should have agreed, albeit reluctantly, to pay her own legal fees. But if she refused to do so, Larry would have been better served to pay the fees up to a specified amount and get on with his life.

SPECIAL CONSIDERATIONS
WHEN TERMINATION IS ONE-SIDED

While some endings are simple and straightforward because the parties agree to separate on the best of terms, others like Larry and Connie's aren't mutual, and, as we've seen, this can cause additional conflict and headaches as the associates squabble over whether or not to terminate, and if so, how to divide any assets and profits. To put it mildly, associates can sometimes be hard to get rid of. Just as a collaboration or partnership can start off like a wonderful marriage, it can also end with a bad divorce. But as a rule of thumb, you can expect your termination to proceed just about as well as your relationship has up to that point. If it's been an exceptionally good relationship, your termination will probably go equally well. If it's been an exceptionally rocky relationship, your termination may well be a rocky one too.

Here are some tips on how to handle a one-sided termination more smoothly, regardless of the circumstances.

If You Want to Terminate and Your Associate Doesn't

If your partner feels strongly about wanting to continue your collaboration, be willing to listen to his or her reasons and suggestions for doing so. At this point, you may hear at last the promising words you've been hoping to hear during past conflicts. Often people don't realize how much they want to keep a relationship going until they actually face losing it. Don't extort concessions that are not sincerely offered, however. The same old problems will most surely resurface, and you'll be right back to terminating. So make sure your partner doesn't feel as if he or she is being forced to give in. If he or she now wants to go along with what you've been asking for in previous discussions, however, accept the concession graciously and proceed working together with a clean slate.

If your partner agrees to the termination, but not your terms, be prepared to negotiate more effectively than you have been up to this point. If you and your collaborator haven't been able to resolve your conflicts in working to-gether, chances are you won't do any better working on terminating your re-lationship. Here are two rules of thumb for getting out fast.

1. If the amount of money or the dollar value of any assets that you are disputing is low, give in to your ex-associate. Consider this the cost of buying your independence and doing business in the way you want to: alone.
2. If the amount is high, consider hiring a mediator to help you determine how to settle the dispute. (See the Resources at the end of this chapter for obtaining more information on mediation.)

If Your Associate Wants to Terminate and You Don't

Perhaps you have a brighter vision for your joint activities than your partner does. If so, now is the time to describe that vision as convincingly and in as much detail as possible. If your working relationship has been plagued by conflict up to this point, however, regardless of who's responsible, you'll need to present a very strong case for why you and your partner should continue working together. In other words, at this point, the burden of proof is on you to demonstrate why it is worthwhile to stay involved.

If you want to terminate but don't like the terms being offered, first make sure that you are on good legal ground. Check any contract or agreement you've already signed. If the terms are in accord with your written agreement, you'll probably have to accept them. If your partner shows some flexibility, however, and you can make a good case for why you should get more than you're being offered, that's fine, but don't threaten a lawsuit at this point. As we described above, that may only escalate matters. Try instead to negotiate a settlement personally first, using whatever goodwill is left between you and your partner. Keep in mind, however, that if you are being offered less than you think you deserve, you're in a one-down position and you'll need to make a good case for why you should get more. Ultimately, mediation, arbitration, or hiring a lawyer to plead your case may be your only choice.

BUYING OUT A PARTNER

The need to buy out a partner, whether your venture is a formal or informal partnership, can be complex. Sometimes it arises when those involved don't get along and one person decides to take control by buying out the other's shares in the venture. But more often it's a mutually agreeable solution to changing realities. Here's a list of the kind of circumstances that motivate someone to buy out her or his partner(s).

- A partner becomes ill and can no longer work
- A partner decides to leave the business for personal reasons
- A partner moves
- A partner retires

- A partner no longer needs to work because the business has become so financially successful
- A partner no longer wants to be involved because the business is not successful enough

Unfortunately we've also heard about cases that might be described as "manipulative" buyouts. In one situation, an up-and-coming dress designer bought out her partner when she realized their company was soon going to be very successful. Part of her rationale was that she felt her partner was not pulling his weight in the company, but another part of her thinking was based more on pure greed: she no longer wanted to share the huge potential profits she was expecting, so she bought him out before the company skyrocketed in value from the many new orders she knew would be coming in.

Whether your buyout happens out of necessity, a personality clash, or as a manipulative tactic, you'll need to figure out what price to offer and how to structure your payout. If you're operating as a formal partnership with a written agreement, there are various tax laws that pertain to buyouts, so you'll need the services of an accountant because a buyout usually results in capital gains or losses for which there are specific tax implications.

When it comes to calculating the price for buying out your partner, there are no fixed guidelines. Much of your decision will depend on how long you've been in business, how long you've worked together, whether one of you intends to continue in the business and use the business name and its assets, and many other factors. Hopefully, your original agreement has stipulated the method of valuing your business in case of a buyout.

Some people offer to pay the amount of the person's original investment plus a percentage of the profits equal to a reasonable return on investment, such as 10 to 15 percent a year. But if your business has many assets and a good income, you may want to place a value on the business using one of several "valuation" methods.

Asset Valuation. In using this method, the market value (the price a willing seller and willing buyer would agree to), not the book value (the worth as it appears on your financial statement), of all the assets of the business (which include special treatment of accounts receivable) is tallied and then the market value of all debts is subtracted. The buyout partner then receives his or her share of the total while the remaining partners keep the assets. For example, consider a business that owns a building that was purchased many years ago for $100,000. Although years of depreciation may have lowered the book value of the building to zero, the asset value of the building is determined according to its market value.

Set-Dollar Valuation. Using the set-dollar method, the partners agree on a fixed price for the buyout. This is useful for businesses that have few assets such as service businesses where partners are getting along well and can mutually agree on the value of their business with one another.

Measure-of-Earnings Valuation. In using this method, the buyout is based on the business's projected annual income over a period of future time, based on its past performance and industry expectations. The amount of the buyout may then range from one year's projected future income to a "multiple" of anywhere from two to ten times the average annual earnings. Some industries such as restaurants and construction companies have even established traditional standards for setting the multiple. Multiples are not set in stone, however. Anything can be negotiated, and choosing the multiple should take into account how well the business is doing, what percentage of gross profit is net profit, projected earnings in coming years (that is, is the business growing or declining?), and if the multiplier will unduly strap the remaining partners while continuing to do business.

In some cases, a partner may lack sufficient cash to make a buyout, so the buyout offer includes ongoing payments over several years to the selling partner in addition perhaps to a small up-front payment. Naturally, if your company is successful, don't expect to get away with offering a small amount. A common rule of thumb in most financial matters is that a dollar today is worth more than a dollar tomorrow. In other words, people prefer the security of having the money in hand now rather than betting on the possibility of having it paid out at some future date. Because of this, whenever you offer to make payments over time or at a later date, you can expect to pay a principal amount plus interest on the unpaid balance to compensate for not paying the full amount up front.

MOVING ON

As we said earlier, the end of a business relationship need not be viewed as a failure. It can be a victory, a chance to demonstrate courage, compassion, determination, and persistence. It's also a beginning. As the old saying goes, for every door that closes, a new one opens to you. Freed from the limitations of a relationship that wasn't working or cannot continue, you can open yourself to a wealth of new opportunities for even greater success and satisfaction.

RESOURCES

Getting to Yes: Negotiating Agreement Without Giving In. Roger Fisher and William Ury. Boston: Houghton Mifflin, 1992.

How to Mediate Your Dispute. Pever Lovenheim. Berkeley, CA: Nolo Press, 1996.

8

Creating Magic Together

Out of clutter, find simplicity. From discord, find harmony.
In the middle of difficulty lies opportunity.
—ALBERT EINSTEIN

THERE'S ELECTRICITY in the air, and we're having fun. Yes, we're working, but you'd never know it. We're laughing. We're creating. We're spontaneously coming up with new ideas and tossing them back and forth among ourselves. That's how we three, Rick, Paul, and Sarah, feel when we meet to work on the many projects we have been doing together for many years. That's also how we, Paul and Sarah, feel when we work together as a couple, speaking at the podium together or appearing on radio or TV. And that's how we feel when we're discussing and planning how we'll work with the many other professionals we mentioned who are part of what we consider our virtual organization.

But we have to admit, this electricity and smooth working relationship have taken time to develop, both for us as a couple working together and for working with the other people with whom we frequently team up. Getting to this magic point when work seems like fun, ideas flow smoothly, and your business relationship is as productive as a new engine takes time.

For example, when we, Paul and Sarah, first started working together as a couple, we were completely out of sync. When we wrote our first book, we argued over the book's outline, the content, even whose version of a sentence to use. When we first started giving presentations together, sometimes we'd step on each other's lines or accidentally interrupt each other. And at first our different work styles made for frustrating decision making.

We actually don't remember precisely how and when our ability to work together changed, but we most certainly noticed when it had. We noticed that we started to have a lot more fun. We became much more creative. Disagreements became a rarity. People started joking about how we could talk as one person, finishing each other's sentences. And most noticeably our results improved dramatically. Our writing required less and less editing. Evaluations of our presentations went from good to glowing. And clips of our media appearances led to bigger and better-known shows.

What was happening? Essentially we had begun working synergistically. This is what every team needs to learn to do. And it takes time.

WORKING SYNERGISTICALLY

The word *synergy* derives from the Greek root *syn-* meaning "together," and *ergon* meaning "work." Taken together, *synergy* therefore means working together so that more is accomplished than those involved could accomplish working equally as hard alone. In other words, synergy is the *synthesis of energy*. When people work together, they merge their energies and create more than the sum of each individual's contribution, as in 1 + 1 = 3 (or more). And, of course, that's what we all hope for in teaming up with others. We don't want to simply do what we could do by working separately; we want the synthesis of our energy to create something extra, something special from the union that benefits everyone. And when that actually happens, there's always something quite magical about it. It feels magical and the results appear magical.

If you ever want a glimpse of the magic that's possible when two or more people truly work synergistically, watch a good sports team like the Chicago Bulls. You can see synergy in action anytime they are playing, but it's especially noticeable when they're playing at their best. Their moves look effortless, and the results are amazing and astounding. While your business relationships may never produce the spectacularly dramatic results the Bulls have attained, within the context of your own goals, they could be as extraordinary, enjoyable, and personally rewarding as any basketball championship.

Here's one teaming-up story that's a case in point. Close friends for sixteen years, Jack Canfield and Mark Victor Hanson were both successful professional speakers when they came up with the idea to write a book based on their lifetime collection of motivational stories and anecdotes they use in their seminars. The idea was to tell 101 inspirational stories that could serve as *Chicken Soup for the Soul,* which became the name of the book. Unfortunately when they pitched this idea, all the major publishers turned them down, but never to be deterred, the team traveled to the annual American Booksellers Association convention and went from booth to booth over two days shopping their grand idea. They found their publisher and thanks to a highly innovative marketing campaign the partners undertook together, *Chicken Soup for the Soul* has gone on to become a nationwide best-seller year after year. It's now been joined by *A Second Helping of Chicken Soup for the Soul* and *A Third Helping of Chicken Soup for the Soul,* both of which leaped immediately on to the best-seller list as well! As Canfield himself admits, "We thought it would do well, but we had no idea we'd get this kind of response."

As this story illustrates, an extraordinarily high level of synergy among teaming-up partners or collaborators doesn't happen overnight. It may look and feel like magic when it happens, but it doesn't happen by magic. And while you probably don't have a coach and a team owner investing time, money, and energy in making sure you will work well together, your teaming-up efforts may have more similarity to the Chicago Bulls basketball team than you think. The Bulls are a team of superstars. Individually they're the cream of the crop. But in your own way, so are you and your collaborators. As self-employed individuals, each of you is the star of your own business. So as with a team like the Bulls that means sparks can fly when stars collide or, if you work at working together, you can shine ever so more brightly.

When Phil Jackson started coaching the Bulls and introduced his new triangle offense, one of his goals was to channel the "superstar" power of the individual players into a team effort. So instead of the players competing with one another for a chance to get the ball so they could personally shine on the court, he wanted them to work together for the benefit of the whole team. He wanted them to be thinking and moving in unison, working synergistically without set plays, so anyone could make the most out of any moment's opportunity. But even with all the talent and resources Jackson and the Bulls had at their disposal, it took a year and a half before the team was comfortably working this way and over two and a half years before they had mastered the triangle offense's many nuances.

So while you and your collaborators may not be seeking a level of teamwork anywhere near as challenging as what's required to win four NBA championships, it's nonetheless reasonable to expect that you'll need both time and experience working together before you can begin to work synergistically. As with the Bulls, your success will be a matter of working together long enough and with sufficient devotion to make sure that the energy between you is constantly flowing, in sync, toward your unified purpose. This means you must develop ways to prevent your energies from becoming blocked so that you can maximize your mutual efforts. A synthesis of energy requires building as much energy as you can for your joint efforts and then harnessing its flow artfully toward your goals.

In other words, maximizing the flow of energy between you requires "getting on the same wavelength." This means not only synchronizing your goals and vision; it means getting the kinks out and learning what you need to do so you don't fade out when you need to shine, you don't drop the ball when you need to shoot, and you don't slow down when you need to step on the gas. It means making sure your energy doesn't get lost in minor miscommunications or confusion. And, of course, if you get involved in major disagreements, your energies become polarized and move away from—rather than toward—your goals until you get them resolved. Conflict thus wastes and dissipates energy. And when conflict occurs, people don't function at their best nor do they inspire one another to go on to greater heights. But as we mentioned in previous chapters, conflicts are inevitable and it's by resolving them satisfactorily that a new synergy can emerge. In other words, we needed to argue over our wording to write well together. We needed to step on each other's lines in order to learn how to speak well as a team. We needed to experience a clash of decision-making styles before we could find how we could work synergistically.

But how do you build synergy? How do you maximize your mutual efforts so your energy flows? How do you get your relationships to attain their highest potential? Here are seven ideas for creating true synergy. As you'll note, all these suggestions are based on learning how to keep your energies flowing toward your mutual goals instead of getting tangled up or blocking your progress by diverting your energies elsewhere.

Synergy-Building Techniques

1. Share your dreams, desires, and passions. As we have said in *Finding Your Perfect Work,* our most compelling personal desires and passions can provide the source of whatever energy we need to propel us toward our goals. In fact, what we do with our energy is what we become. And it's from pursuing our deepest desires that we each can tap into our own true personal power. So one of the easiest and best ways to achieve synergy is to recognize and link your individual desires. Recognizing, sharing, and linking up with your personal dreams, desires, and passions can provide the electricity to make your mutual efforts sparkle. Your dreams, desires, and passions are the core of your business, and by sharing them with one another, you'll strengthen and deepen your connection and open the channels for your energies to flow together.

2. Provide positive verbal support for each other. Building a collaborative relationship is like growing a garden of wildflowers. When your communication conveys respect, consideration, caring, and constructive thinking, the garden can blossom with lovely flowers you had no idea you'd planted. New ideas may sprout any day, some of which will blossom more beautifully (and profitably) than the ones from the day before. But when you lapse into critical, disrespectful, or angry communication, the air between you becomes noxious and toxic, nipping any blossoming possibilities in the bud.

Positive verbal support brings things to life, spurs growth and progress. It *creates* energy, whereas ignoring one another's needs *depletes* your energies. Similarly, insults, disrespect, and useless criticism *block* your energy and divert you from your goals. In fact, often conflicts arise needlessly from weeks, months, and even years worth of energy that's gotten dammed up behind stockpiles of negative communication. A regular diet of positive verbal exchanges keeps your energy flowing in the right direction, however, and invigorates and motivates you to reach your fullest potential. If you could hear the chatter among players on basketball courts or baseball fields from Little League to the pros, for example, you'd hear a constant banter of mutual encouragement. You can get the same kind of results for your "team" efforts by feeding each other regular doses of positive verbal feedback and encouragement.

Think of positive verbal support as the background music for your work. At the lower end of the dial positive verbal support can take the form of common courtesies like saying please, thank you, excuse me, and so on. You can tune in to these at any time, but you can and should turn up the volume regularly for even greater listening pleasure by:

- Complimenting others on work well done
- Noticing when someone is down and needs a lift
- Providing positive feedback about what's working even in the midst of failure
- Apologizing when you've made a mistake
- Being open to discussing feelings, issues, and concerns
- Acknowledging your own foibles and weaknesses
- Being an empathic listener

In his popular best-selling book, *Seven Habits of Highly Effective People*, noted writer and consultant Steven Covey comments on a wonderful synergistic experience he had with his business associates that illustrates the positive effects of turning up the volume on verbal support.

I enjoyed one particular meaningful synergistic experience as I worked with my associates to create the corporate mission statement for our business. Almost all members of the company went high up in the mountains where, surrounded by the magnificence of nature, we began with a first draft of what some of us considered to be an excellent mission statement. At first, the communication was respectful, careful, and predictable. But as we began to talk about the various alternatives, possibilities, and opportunities ahead, people became very open and authentic and simply started to think out loud. The mission statement agenda gave way to a collective free association, a spontaneous piggybacking of ideas. People were genuinely empathic as well as courageous, and we moved from mutual respect and understanding to creative synergistic communication. Everyone could sense it. It was exciting. As it matured, we returned to the task of putting the evolved collective vision into words.

It's been said that flowers grow faster and larger when music is played in the background. So it is with business relationships that the more you have supportive verbal dialogue playing in the background while you work the more productive your relationships will be.

3. Turn problems into goals. At heart, most of us don't *like* having problems. As enjoyable and challenging as it can be to solve them, it's hard not to feel that life would be better if we could simply go along our merry way without any problems. In particular, difficult problems, the ones that can't be solved on the spot, seem to divert us from our goals. They stop us in our tracks and cause us to reconnoiter around the options: Should we take this road or the other one? Should we handle it this way or that? So when problems arise, be they an internal dilemma between you and your associates or an external one between you and your customers, you may feel the energy begin draining out of your alliance. You can feel your momentum waning as you consider alternatives and figure out how to solve the dilemma.

But if you change the way you think about problems, they don't have to become a drain on your energy. Instead of viewing issues that arise as problems to be solved, you can redefine them as goals to be attained. Whereas having to stop to solve problems can feel like a drag on your energy, working toward new goals is positive and forward-looking in nature. Instead of blocking your energy, having new goals allows it to expand. Through this simple process of "reframing" your perception, you and your associates can preserve a feeling of forward momentum, sense progress toward your goal, and keep your energy flowing. For example, if you have a customer who is unhappy with the way you've handled a project, rather than feeling resentful and wishing the problem didn't exist, you could reframe by setting a goal to make sure your customers are 100 percent satisfied. Viewed in this way, the challenge becomes a way to advance your company by achieving a worthy goal instead of having to stop to "fix" a pesky problem. So, turning problems into goals is another way to build synergy.

4. Take reasonable risks. You've probably heard the maxim "Nothing ventured, nothing gained." It most assuredly applies to working synergistically. No collaboration can move forward without some risk taking. The very nature of working with others in such changing times as these requires us to take action even when the results can't be guaranteed. When you decide to work with others, there is a risk that it won't turn out as intended and you might lose something in making the effort. However, if you venture nothing, you have nothing to lose and there is no risk. If you go to a trade show as an observer, for example, you're venturing little and there's very little risk other than losing the modest fee you pay at the door. Taking a booth at the trade show, however, is another matter. You're venturing an investment in both time and money for a chance that you'll sell your goods or services. On the one hand, teaming up with others so you can afford the cost of exhibiting reduces your risk or makes it more reasonable. On the other hand, teaming up poses its own risks. What if your associate pulls out at the last minute? What if he or she attracts more of the traffic at the booth than you do? But, again, nothing ventured, nothing gained.

We urge you to take reasonable risks in your collaborations because risk taking keeps your energy flowing. That's essentially what *venture* means, as in *adventure;* it refers to casting forth energy without a certain outcome. A collaboration that risks nothing has no life, no energy. It may survive—but will it thrive? Eventually a riskless enterprise grows stale, as will the products or services and people involved. But by taking reasonable risks, you expand your vision and reach for new goals, thereby breathing life into your enterprise. Risk taking inspires you to create new ideas, meet new people, and explore new markets. And it's by winning in your ventures that you will thrive.

Naturally, it's wise to temper the amount of your risk by what you can afford to lose and what you have to gain. For example, risking the loss of your entire business is seldom worthwhile. But risking what you can survive losing will propel you forward. Spending $1,000 to have a booth at a trade show, for example, isn't likely to break your businesses, because even if you don't generate any new business at the show, your risk could pay off by following up on the contacts you've made from exhibiting.

And keep in mind, the more you undertake together, the better you'll get at doing it. You can't wait until you've got your act down so pat that there's no risk of failure. You'll never get your act down pat unless you risk doing it wrong. You can practice, of course. You can prepare, and you can select your initial audiences carefully, but ultimately you've got to start doing whatever it is you do and risk making whatever mistakes you need to make so you can learn together how to do it right.

5. Learn from errors. The corollary to daring to take reasonable risks is being willing to learn from your errors. Every business makes strategic mistakes, poor decisions, and less than stellar choices. In recent years, however, one management study after another has shown that those companies that chastise people for making mistakes create overly cautious employees who have ventured nothing and thus have nothing to gain. They may make no errors but they also have nothing to learn from, and thus such companies remain among the least progressive and innovative. Many of the organizations in these studies were once *Fortune* 500 companies, but by never taking risks on new ideas, little by little, their business was stolen from them by smaller, smarter upstart companies that were willing to take the needed risks. Such lumbering large corporations are like huge oil tankers that have to travel many miles to turn around and find a new heading.

The advantage of being a small or home-based collaboration is that you can usually recover from your mistakes quickly and less expensively than a large company—as long as you admit to your mistakes and learn from them. Self-employed individuals and small companies are like the sleek, highly crafted yachts in the America's Cup race; they can turn within a few hundred yards of a signal and correct their heading as needed. As you will see in the next section, that's just what we all must do to survive and thrive in times of rapid change and increasing complexity. In the end, taking reasonable risks and learning from your mistakes are essential energizing elements in continuing to achieve sterling results year after year.

6. Make room for fun and friendship. When you are deeply involved in the tasks of your business day, making decisions, dealing with customers, or analyzing goals, having fun is usually the furthest thing from your mind. However, paying attention to your mental, physical, and spiritual well-being will pay off on your financial bottom line. As in a dull marriage, when people lose their joy for life and for working with one another, their energy dissipates and even drains away. But laughing together, enjoying one another's company and your shared passion for life is like adding yeast to bread. It energizes whatever you do and creates greater synergy.

So, we mean this suggestion to be taken quite literally. Don't limit your business collaboration to all work and no play. Make sure you frequently do fun things with one another. Go to a movie, out to dinner, take a walk in the park, throw a party, play some tennis, or take a bike ride—anything to get you out of your business persona and into a recreational frame of mind. If you were not friends with your collaborators when you first began working together, you'll find that friendship develops easily from sharing fun experiences. And your emerging friendship will breed the loyalty, improved communication, and synergy you need for your relationship and your business to grow and thrive.

For example, Wally Bock went for walks with his joint venture partner every afternoon both to get exercise and to spend time thinking together. Dave Lakhani and Liane Lemon in Boise, Idaho, who do small-business consulting, join their families from time to time to be sure their social connection is as strong as their professional one. Risa Hoag and Mindy Hermann spend some time talking on the phone every day, and when that is not possible, they

E-mail messages to boost each other's spirits. When we, Paul and I, are writing and developing speeches together and need a fresh idea, we know we need to take a break and go for a walk, or maybe take a drive along the coastline. Some of our best ideas have popped up in our conversations while we're having fun together.

7. Focus on creativity. Combining the energy of several individuals doesn't ensure synergy; an additional element is always necessary—creativity. Creativity is the lifeblood of synergy. It is the spark that makes Energy + Energy turn into Synergy. In the same way that synergy reflects the process in which the sum of the parts is greater than the whole, creativity ignites the process that makes the combination of several old ideas become new ones. Here are some examples of how business relationships have tapped into this creative spark.

- Creativity led Chris Beal and several technical friends to realize that with so many old computers being abandoned, someone could develop a market for reconditioned used computers.
- Creativity led Mara Seibert and Lenore Rice to realize during their trip to Italy that the beautiful Tuscan pottery they saw was so unique it would be popular in the U.S.
- Creativity enabled Tim and Elisabeth Willey to recognize that as more and more people were moving to rural areas that had no electricity, there would be a market for small solar-based energy generators.
- Creativity led Eileen Glick and her partner to notice that Phoenix, Arizona, had a quickly growing population of home-based businesses and could use an association to help them meet one another and network.

We all have the seeds of creativity within us, but we must nurture them if they're going to grow. You can feed your creativity in many ways. For example, as we just mentioned, you can take a walk or a drive to an area you've never seen before, noticing the architecture, the landscape, or the people along the way. New experiences in particular often trigger new ideas by providing a fresh perspective, a way of seeing the world differently than while you're enmeshed in your ordinary routines. Another way to trigger creativity is to go to a newsstand and browse through several magazines you've never read. You may be surprised to find a wealth of valuable articles on topics you would never have imagined would relate to your business. As we said in chapter 1, attending professional meetings and networking groups can also spark new ideas by introducing you to new people with new perspectives.

In the popular creativity book *The Artist's Way,* writer Julia Cameron proposes that artists make a "creativity date" with themselves once a week. We suggest the same for any person who is running his or her own business. Make a date to go to a new place and observe whatever piques your interest. This kind of free-form, spontaneous exploration is crucial to developing a creative mind. Once you begin doing this, you'll be amazed at the "synchronicity" of events that will occur as you approach each adventure with an open mind. With an open mind, you'll begin to notice things you've never noticed before, much of which eventually can become fodder for your creative mind.

Naturally, you can take a creativity break alone, but whenever you're working in a collaborative venture, make an effort to take creativity breaks with your associates from time to time and ask yourselves, "what if" questions, as in "What if we took our business in this direction?" or "What if we made a proposal to this client for a contract?" Such hypothetical questions can lead to a surprising brainstorming session from which you may end up developing a new idea that will mean greater success for your business.

8. Go with the flow. The final suggestion for building synergy is to allow yourselves to go with the flow. Invariably at times, you and your partner will need to abandon an idea or a strategy you had in mind because you recognize it's not working or because a better opportunity presents itself. Instead of blaming one another or seeking to find fault with one another's lack of foresight, think of such about-faces as your chance to go with the flow and seize whatever opportunities you can jointly create from the reality of the moment.

Many people who have suffered through failed partnerships or unsatisfying collaborations told us their affiliation had worked fine for a while, but then for some reason it just "fell apart." Even when personality conflicts are involved, however, it's possible for such collaborations not only to survive but also to thrive if everyone involved is able to go with the flow and gallop in stride on the fast track of today's ever changing business environment. Fortunately, the more synergy you get going for you, the easier that will be to do.

GALLOPING IN STRIDE ON A CHANGING TRACK

One reason the Chicago Bulls basketball team has been so successful is that by playing synergistically, they're able to go with the flow. If the game isn't going as planned or as anticipated, they seize the moment and make the most of whatever is happening. And that's exactly what we have to do as self-employed individuals and small businesses. In today's changing and complex economic environment, long-range planning is not dependable. In fact, the need to be nimble and flexible and the ability to adjust quickly to unexpected changes are precisely what's fueling the development of "virtual organizations," "recombinant work teams," and a surge of other flexible and changeable teaming-up activities. By teaming up you can seize the moment more easily and make the most of whatever's happening, but only if your teaming-up relationships themselves remain sufficiently flexible to go with the flow.

Of course, the more quickly economic realities change and the more complex they become, the more it feels as though you're losing control. It's easy to feel that you can't adequately forecast what's going on and therefore can't adequately plan for what your next steps should be. So instead of going with the flow, it's quite tempting to struggle to maintain control by becoming all the more rigid and dogmatic. But keep in mind that the very change and complexity that's driving you crazy also produces some of your greatest opportunities. So, even though trying to respond flexibly when you're part of a team effort can be quite a challenge, at least at first, resist the temptation to become more fixed and controlling in the way you work. Instead of reining yourselves in, loosen up so you can respond flexibly to what's happening.

Here are several ways you can learn to go with the flow and work more synergistically in the midst of constant change.

1. Don't confuse "aims" and "goals." If you get too attached to any one strategy for achieving your goals, you won't be able to respond as flexibly as you may need to. In changing times, you need to remain focused clearly on where you're going (your goals), while realizing that you may need to continually re-aim in order to get there. In other words, to get where you want to go these days, you need to become more like a sailor, ready to shift directions when the wind changes so you can use the prevailing winds to get to your destination instead of being buffeted about on the churning seas of change.

This means that you and those you're working with need to be open to shifting your strategies and revising your plans. Don't let yourself get stuck looking for or hanging on to what seemed to be the "perfect" solution. In changing times, there isn't usually one "best" strategy, but rather a variety of desirable options. Considering many of them will provide you with more flexibility and choice and thus greater control. In other words, you can retain control by letting go of control.

But do stay focused on your goals, your shared vision, the horizon you're seeking together. Talk about it often together. Imagine it together. Begin anticipating it together. Let it feed your energy, drive, and commitment to one another. Whenever you begin to lose your way or lose focus, whenever things don't seem clear, return to your joint goals and vision.

2. Develop a tracking strategy. In the past, pursuing a strategy involved commanding and directing. In times of change, however, it's difficult, if not impossible, to command and direct. Instead strategy needs to be about monitoring and observing what's happening so you can respond effectively. Therefore one of your joint tasks needs to be keeping up with and tracking your results and what's going on around you, then sharing your observations with one another regularly.

3. Cast a wide net. In tracking what's going on, don't screen out all seeming irrelevancies. Of course, you can't attend to and track everything that's

Tracking Trends

If you and your associates each set aside one hour a day to keep up with events of the world through a combination of the following media and discuss the insights gained from what you've noticed at least once weekly, you should be able to stay abreast of changing realities and opportunities.

1. Read one good daily newspaper to follow broad consumer and business trends both locally and nationally.
2. Watch or listen to one local and one national news report on television or radio each day.
3. Read one national weekly news magazine where you can pick up more detailed market trends.
4. Read through the weekly local business journal in your area to track who is doing what and to identify possible valuable business connections.
5. Review the major trade journal or newsletter in your field to keep abreast of the latest developments, problems, and needs of your customers and clients.
6. Read one monthly trend magazine or newsletter to become familiar with the most recent demographic changes and changes in business and consumer habits.

You don't have to read these publications from cover to cover. Simply skim the headlines and look for articles about what people are buying, what your competition is doing, and how the economy is affecting them. And you don't have to get this information in print. Many publications are available on-line, and electronic clipping services can bring the articles you're looking for to your attention from multiple publications at no cost or a modest one.

By reviewing these sources of information regularly, in print or via computer, you'll be surprised how quickly and easily you can keep up with events that will affect the success of your business.

happening. But it's important to cast a wide enough net that you pick up on activities and events on the horizon before they affect you adversely and in time to seize their possible advantages. So take the time to identify what you believe you should be tracking, split the workload among you, and encourage one another to let your interests and hunches guide you into investigating seemingly extraneous topics of interest.

Tom and Wendy Eidson, the couple who started the Mo'Hotta, Mo'Betta condiments catalogue, cast a very wide net when they were first identifying a new business for themselves. As they told us, they investigated many types of industries but settled on the food business. They then looked into many aspects of this business and again narrowed it to food catalogues. One day, Wendy came home and announced that she had found their target: watermelon pickles and canned gooseberries. Upon reflection, though, they realized that this idea was too narrow, so they kept researching and researching until they found a niche market that no one in the food industry had thus far identified: hot sauces. Once they began their company and realized they could make it successful, they continued casting a wide net to identify new products they could add to their catalogue, and new ways of marketing and distribution. Their ability to keep abreast of trends and to continually refresh their catalogue has allowed them to weather the years, despite a spate of competitors who have sought to imitate their success.

Casting a sufficiently wide net prevents you from getting boxed in. It allows you to keep a rich array of options at your fingertips. And it enables you to make more holistic judgments by taking into account more all-encompassing ideas and trends as well as more narrow and pressing concerns.

4. Rely on your intuition. In an uncertain and unpredictable world, the logical, orderly approach may not always take you where you want to go. What worked yesterday may no longer apply tomorrow, and the seemingly obvious next step today may be the wrong path for the future.

It has been said that we use only 1 percent of the capacity of our brains, and whether that's true or not, we most certainly can make better use of what we call our brain's "unconscious processing" abilities to guide us through fast-changing realities. The brain takes in, stores, and processes vast amounts of information every day, and this wide array of "unconscious processing" is often what allows our intuition to provide us with hunches and "bright" ideas. If you've been tracking developments as suggested above, you and your associates have been ingesting ample amounts of information and data for your intuition to draw upon. The key is to trust your own and one another's hunches and gut feelings by checking and testing them out and let them guide you to the best decisions.

One way to encourage using your intuition is for you and those you're working with to formulate and write down the biggest decision, question, or issue you're faced with, and then begin noticing answers or next steps the events you're presented with suggest. It often happens that life will throw an answer out to you through a chance encounter or a sudden realization as you go about your normal business. But you need to pay attention to this potential for serendipity and keep an open mind to anything and everything. Fortunately, as you will see, the process of drawing on your intuition is greatly enhanced when done collaboratively, so attend carefully to your personal hunches and the coincidences you encounter, but be sure to discuss them with each other. You may be surprised at the synchronicity of ideas that flow when you use this approach.

5. Accept that everyone will be operating from self-interest and that's okay. Everyone is and should be looking out for her or his own future. The best teams become vehicles for each person to pursue her or his own self-interest while simultaneously working toward the team's shared goals. So, in any teaming endeavor between independent individuals, we all need the elbow room to be ourselves and do our own thing. It's important that we provide ample opportunities for one another to capitalize fully on our particular strengths and give one another room to grow and develop within our relationships. If you don't, your energies will begin seeping in other directions and into other activities, draining energy away from your joint ventures. You're not only codeveloping your work, you're also coevolving as individuals. So it's important to never turn down an associate who wants to volunteer to do something that might help your joint goals. In fact, when someone starts to take an initiative, be ready to make needed shifts to harvest the results. It's this kind of flexibility that creates generative relationships. If someone feels hog-tied, he or she won't be able to generate the many opportunities you undoubtedly have teamed up together to reap.

6. *Get accustomed to moving at a gallop.* One of the advantages of being on your own is that you can make decisions and take action much more quickly than larger organizations. In fact, as we've said, larger organizations are paring down and flattening their hierarchies so they, too, can respond more quickly to fast-changing times. This partly accounts for why recombinant work teams have become so popular. Companies can pull in and deploy whatever resources they need whenever they need them and quickly cut off expenses that are no longer needed. So, the more quickly you can pool or redirect your resources to the opportunities at hand the better. This means recognizing that you may have to act quickly and being willing and able to do so. There may not be time for long-drawn-out discussions and planning. You may need to make decisions on the spot, trusting your instincts and learning from your mistakes. The more synergy you and your associates can get going among you, the easier this will be. But you also need to create a structure for relating to one another that will enable you to do what you need to do as quickly as possible.

Obviously being able to gallop at lightning speed in sync along a moving track will take some time. As the old saying goes, first slow, then fast. But don't be tempted to settle into thinking slow is good enough. Invest the time, money, and energy you need to get what you do down well enough so that you do it as quickly, if not more quickly, together as you could do it alone.

7. *Develop requisite variety.* While it's important to draw upon each other's strengths in order to respond quickly and effectively to whatever arises, it's equally important that each of you develop a sufficiently wide range of abilities that you can pinch-hit for each other and step into whatever roles you're called upon to carry out. In other words, you need to support one another in developing what's called "requisite variety," the ability to summon whatever skills, abilities, talents, and behaviors are required to respond effectively in the moment to whatever circumstances bring your way. You should encourage your associates to learn from you while you remain open to learning from them.

One way Phil Jackson has helped the Chicago Bulls and other basketball teams he has coached to go with the flow and seize the moment has been to make sure everyone can do everything that needs to be done. Of course, he makes strategic use of each player's strengths and gives him the role he can best carry out, but Jackson also sees to it that players are rotated so everyone can play under a variety of circumstances and in a variety of positions. This is one reason his second teams can be as effective as his first teams. When the big stars foul out, burn out, or become injured, the backup players can come in and perform like big stars. You'll never be able to come through like that for one another if you hoard what you know and fear letting one another take over the reins.

While reading *Hoop Dreams* and learning how Jackson has gone about building the Bulls into a record-breaking world championship basketball team, we were excited to discover that we (Paul and Sarah) have been following the same principles in developing our ability to work synergistically together. This seems to be a formula that works.

- Share a goal.
- Share the money.
- Share the stage.
- Share the glory.
- Make yourselves interchangeable.
- Have a system but no set pattern.

When we started working together, Paul was best at doing research, gathering and using statistics, and making presentations; Sarah was best at writing, motivating, and formulating overriding concepts. Paul, with his background in law, was better at negotiating; Sarah, as a psychotherapist, was better at facilitating. This combination of skills made us a great team, but over time we've helped each other become strong in the areas in which the other excels, so now either one of us can step into whichever roles we need to. We've also supported each other in acquiring skills neither of us had. For example, neither of us was strong at selling, so we've taken classes and hired consultants to build our sales skills.

In speaking and writing together, at first we planned and outlined everything. But such a structure approach put serious limitations on our ability to go with the flow. If things didn't go as planned (and they usually didn't), we'd be somewhat off our game. But now we have a system, a general way of operating, so we know we're on the same page, but we have no set pattern.

Every speech or interview is completely different from every other one because instead of sticking to a preset plan, we can respond to whatever the circumstances call for. We can tailor each presentation to the needs of the audience. That not only makes us more effective, it also makes our work infinitely more fun. It's never boring, and it's usually exhilarating.

8. Synthesize your understanding of how life works and evolve a shared language for talking with one another about what's happening to you and your businesses. It has been said that the limits of our languages are the limits of our world. But the longer you work together, the more likely you and your associates are to quickly and almost intuitively understand one another. You can further this process by consciously developing a shared view of the way the world works and having a common terminology you can refer to to talk about your goals, your strategies, your procedures, concerns, and issues. Many delays, conflicts, and problems arise because people think they're talking about the same thing when they are actually talking about different things.

Holding regular progress meetings (see page 309), as discussed previously, is an excellent means of grasping each other's points of view and evolving a shared perception of the way things work. Continually ask yourselves, "How is what he or she is saying *like* something I think or believe?" If there are differences, ask if they are important ones and discuss them in an effort to truly understand. Often, however, our differences are differences without distinction. In other words, they don't have to affect our ability to work well together.

As you talk and review your work, look for the patterns in your problems, your performance, and your perceived needs. Find ways to talk about these patterns. You may need to coin new terms or at least redefine existing ones to describe what you are discovering together about your work.

9. Let it be okay to change or part ways. With constantly changing realities, often relationships must change as well. We cannot assume that a relationship that works for everyone today will work equally well for everyone tomorrow. While our self-interests may merge today, they may diverge at any time. So it's vital to accept and respect each other's needs to move on in other directions. So many conflicts arise unnecessarily when people take an associate's decision to move in a new direction personally instead of realizing that circumstances have changed and others have to look out for their own interests. Here's an example:

Before deciding to team up, Georgia and Claire had their own businesses. Georgia bred and raced thoroughbred horses; Claire was an animal trainer. They met at a horse race and began working together informally at first, then as associates, and later they became formal partners. They worked effectively as a team until Claire's father died and left her a sizable inheritance, part of which she used to follow her lifelong dream of owning and racing several horses of her own. She bought her first horse from Georgia, and they raced it together quite successfully. When that horse gave birth, however, Claire began racing the new horse as well. At that point Georgia was miffed. She felt as if Claire had gone into competition with her and she angrily broke off the partnership.

Of course, both parties have the right to do as they choose with their lives, but it's unfortunate Georgia couldn't make room for Claire to spread her wings either within or outside of the partnership without harboring bad feelings. In a world of recombinant work teams, it's best to redefine relationships in a positive way so you can work synergistically together within new realities. Sometimes that means working cooperatively with new competitors who were once collaborators. Those new competitors could open other doors for you or become collaborators once again when circumstances change in the future.

The whole nature of recombinant work teams means that we can anticipate moving in and out of a variety of business relationships, bringing each other into opportunities as they arise and moving on as opportunities shift. Sometimes that means we have to work less formally with someone, letting the other move on and seemingly leave us behind. But when this happens, avoid letting your fears or anger override your best judgment; this will help you to part on good terms. You never know when there will be a chance to reconnect and bring each other along on a new opportunity that neither of you would have ever imagined at the time you parted. So whenever possible, leave the door open and a welcome mat out between you.

Parting Ways on the Best of Terms

When priorities and needs shift, here are several steps you can take to make sure you can come to a parting of the ways on the best possible terms.

1. Be open and honest about your need to move on as early as possible. When you need to move on, be up front about it. Whenever possible, in making changes, be sure you allow ample time for others to adjust to your new plans. Express your regret about not being able to continue working together and assure your associates that you'll be looking for ways to work with them again in the future. Ask for their support in taking this next step in your own development.

2. Be happy for each other's successes. When your associate has an opportunity to move upward or onward in a way that doesn't include you, as long as everything has been handled ethically and legally, set aside feelings of jealously, fear, anger, resentment, or abandonment. You will be best served to handle any such feelings yourself or by expressing them to friends, loved ones, or a professional counselor. With your associate, express only your regret that you'll no longer be working together accompanied with heartfelt best wishes for his or her future success. This will demonstrate that you're a professional, someone who can move effectively in and out of teaming-up relationships in a fast-changing world. Then your former associate will have no reason to resist or fear involving you in future opportunities.

3. Explore new ways to continue supporting each other. While you may not be able to work together in the way you have been, there are probably other ways you can be mutually supportive. Work out how, and then do it. Maintaining positive contact with past associates can be one of the best routes to getting included in future activities.

4. Take responsibility. If you're leaving a relationship behind, do so responsibly even if it means passing up an opportunity. It's your responsibility to find whatever options exist for you to move on without violating any written or verbal agreements you've already made. Practically speaking this is true even if you could "get away with" breaking them, because in a recombinant world, what goes around most definitely does come around. You need to have a reputation as being someone who can be counted on. This applies equally when your associate is the one who's moving on. Don't be tempted to "make him or her sorry" for leaving. Follow through on your part right to the end and try to be as accommodating as possible of her or his needs.

5. Let go of the little stuff. There will always be something or other you can be mad or resentful about. But why spoil the soil? Past relationships are such fertile ground for seeding new opportunities, why leave with a bad taste in your mouths? Before making a big deal about something, ask yourself how important it will be a year from now, five years from now, or ten years from now. Don't make a mess out of anything that can be best left neat and clean.

10. Work to continually uplift and energize each other. There is always ample opportunity to sink into doubts, fear, and confusion. Fear in particular is a common reaction to change and uncertainty, but it leads us to make poor decisions and have extreme reations. One thing that can keep your relationship functioning at its peak, however, is helping each other past such feelings when they arise. Here are several ways you can do this for each other.

- At times when you feel your associates' confidence waiver, listen intently to them, focus your attention on what they're saying, lend them your energy, and when need be, lend them a hand.
- Remember your successes. Celebrate and feed off of your successes, no matter how small, and return to them especially during the most difficult times. Remind yourselves, "We can do this." "We've done this before." "We'll find the answer. It will come to us."

- Review and identify the ideas and techniques in this book that could be most helpful to you and those you're working with. Develop a checklist of options you can call upon whenever need be; e.g.:

_____ Progress meetings (p. 309)	_____ Creative conflict resolution (p. 305)
_____ Retreats (p. 280)	_____ Synergy-building techniques (p. 359)
_____ Your shared language (p. 371)	_____ Trend tracking (p. 367)

EXPANDING YOUR TEAMING-UP EFFORTS

Success may motivate you to formalize what has been an informal collaboration into a formal arrangement, or you may want to expand your joint efforts to involve more people. When such a time comes, there are several options you can explore.

Formalizing an Informal Arrangement

When people have been working informally through networking groups, mutual referrals, or interdependent alliances, and these relationships go especially well, the question inevitably comes up, "Should we formalize our relationship into a partnership or joint venture?" Of course, making this decision is entirely up to you, but it's important to consider the advantages and disadvantages of moving to a more formal arrangement.

Advantages
- A formalized partnership often recognizes what is already happening in a working relationship. Like two people who live together and decide to get married, it officially acknowledges the bond between you in a legally binding manner.
- A formalized partnership can remove the uncertainty and lack of security that often occur when people work together without a written agreement and makes official the decisions you've made such as how to split profits and expenses.
- A formalized partnership can increase your visibility and credibility in the marketplace. It adds a level of professionalism to your business you may not have from working together more informally.
- A formalized partnership obligates your partner to help you in whatever ways you specify in your written agreement. This is useful when your partner's investment in time and energy has been fluctuating sporadically. When lapses occur, you can point to the agreement and remind your partner of what he or she has agreed to do.

- A formalized partnership clarifies the relationship between you, so you can avoid potential conflicts over the strategy or management of your firm. Especially when you've agreed to be equal partners, an agreement reduces the ability of one person to unconsciously "control" the enterprise.

Disadvantages

- A formalized partnership changes your legal and financial relationship. Under a partnership, you are now fully responsible for all the business's debts, regardless of who incurs them. If your partner buys $5,000 of computer equipment for your business, for example, and does not pay for it, you will be obligated to pay the bill.
- A formalized partnership ties you to a specific partner or group of partners. It may be harder to extricate yourself from such ties if you decide it's no longer advantageous to work together. You could have a harder time responding flexibly to unexpected changes and opportunities. You may have to buy out someone or ask someone else to buy you out if you want to go your own way.
- It may cost money to formalize your relationship if you need to use a lawyer and/or accountant to discuss your agreements.
- More formal relationships require an additional investment of time and energy to manage and administer.

Whether you decide to execute a formalized partnership or not, our view is that if you're beginning to work with someone on a consistent basis, you'll be best served by at least developing a written agreement. In addition, if you're working very closely with others and your enterprise generates substantial profits on a consistent basis, for your protection, you should seriously consider operating under a partnership agreement.

Expanding Your Collaboration by Hiring Employees or Adding New Partners

Every increasingly successful enterprise gets to the point where they need to decide if they want to continue growing, serve more customers, bid on more contracts, or take on new projects. Of course, if you're a solo enterprise, this may be exactly why you're teaming up in the first place. But now that you're working with others, deciding if you want to continue growing becomes more complex.

First, you must decide if your joint efforts have the potential to grow to the point that you'll have enough new business to cover the costs involved in adding new people. That decision can be made by examining your past business growth and making a reasonable prediction about the likely growth rate you believe you can maintain in the future. Typically, you would calculate this projected growth rate over a two to five year period so you can be sure the need truly exists to hire staff or bring in new partners. But knowing how rapidly things change, think carefully about the reliability of such forecasts before making long-term commitments to add overhead costs.

In most cases, you'll want to maintain maximum flexibility so you can continue to work most effectively. It's usually easier to use subcontractors or temporary workers, for example, than to hire full-time employees. Using temps or subcontractors enables you to get the help you need when you need it without jeopardizing your flexibility to change directions or cut back on expenses quickly if you need to. Also, it's generally easier to use subcontractors or temps, hire employees or affiliate more informally with other professionals than to disturb the status quo of a successful partnership by taking on other formal partners. In other words the more flexible your expansion options, the less the risk in the event that your projections are inaccurate and your business does not grow as quickly as you thought it would.

Bill Grumbine, who manufactures custom-designed wood pens, has found a variety of ways to get help in expanding his home-based business, Wonderful Wood. He has three children and the older they get the more they have been helping him out and learning about how the business operates. In the process they are able to earn more money than they would earn at most jobs teenagers could get. In addition, he subcontracts out some work that he can't or doesn't want to do himself. For example, he subs out laser engraving because the machine required to do it costs $80,000. He's also thinking about subbing out manufacturing his custom-designed boxes, but he says, "This brings up a concern. Subbing out work like this requires releasing proprietary information which could backfire if the relationships goes sour. There's nothing to stop anyone from copying my designs, but why give them the specs to make it easy?"

Certainly it is easier to release an employee than to discharge a partner. However, as in our review of teaming-up options in chapter 2, there are many tax regulations and considerable paperwork involved in hiring employees. So if you do decide you need an employee, another option is to hire one through a leasing agency. When using an employee leasing company, you usually pay a somewhat higher wage to the agency which handles all the state, federal, and social security taxes as well as benefits and unemployment insurance. Finally, if you bring in employees of any kind, be sure to preplan who will be responsible for supervising them. If you and your collaborator both try to provide supervision, you may inadvertently give conflicting signals.

Deciding to bring in a new partner or additional collaborators can add a new perspective and energy to your efforts. If your business has really taken off, you might add a new partner to fulfill a specified area of needed expertise, such as administrative management or marketing. For example, Joe Ely and his partner from West Lafayette, Indiana, run a debt intervention service for agribusiness throughout the farm belt from Ohio to Montana. They are retained by farmers and ranchers when they have a conflict with a vendor, supplier, or bank about repayment of a debt. A year after buying this business, however, they found they needed more expertise in negotiating larger operating and land loans with banks. So when a former bank examiner from Decora, Ohio, seven hours away expressed interest in joining them, they were interested. The prospective new partner could extend their market considerably and he needed their marketing reach, so they decided to expand their partnership and the new relationship has worked out well.

Sometimes, while by no means always, adding a partner can even save a partnership from the jaws of defeat. Having invested a lot of money to launch a direct mail business specializing in women's lingerie, two women were nearing a painful end to their dream when they ran into a woman they'd known only vaguely who wanted to invest in the business. She thought she could turn it around. For a sizable share of the business, her new energy catalyzed their venture. As one of the original partners told us, "She sees things I could not see, hears things I could not hear, and corrects wrongs I had no patience with."

Keep in mind, however, adding a new member to your team means modifying any agreements you already have. You will need to decide how the new partner will fit into your management and decision-making structure. You'll need to determine what role he or she will play and how much authority he or she will have. Will this person be an equal partner or become a minority partner, for example? As was discussed in chapter 4, splitting profits and/or decision making unequally can cause difficulty, regardless of whatever written agreement you may negotiate to spell it all out. So as your enterprise grows, you'll want to decide whether a minority partner would truly accept being a "backseat driver" who can be overruled at any time.

To save yourselves a lot of needless strain and tension, it's crucial to reflect on these kinds of questions before deciding to add others to your team as either employees, associates, or new partners. Usually, as in choosing any teaming-up option, your choice will be highly personal. For one travel writer, finding the right solution took some time. As his business grew, he began acting as a satellite subcontractor, contracting out work he was too busy to handle to other freelancers. But since he writes in a highly intuitive way, he found subcontracting frustrating. He told us,

> I do very little subcontracting now. It cut me off from the intuitive development process I usually go through, so in the end I didn't save much time or make much money. In fact, I barely broke even on work I contracted out. So, now when I get more work than I can handle, I refer it to one of a handful of other writers I know are top-notch. I've found that the potential clients appreciate my forthrightness and it hasn't prevented them from approaching me again in the future with other work. In fact, in sending business to other writers, some return the favor later on.

Expanding Your Business by Raising Outside Capital

In general, home-based and small businesses usually grow during their first few years solely through their own capitalization and by reinvesting profits. However, the time may come when you will need additional money to expand your business to a new level of success. You may need money to purchase needed equipment, open an office in another location, or to hire employees. Fortunately you have several options for bringing in additional capital.

Personal Contacts. The easiest, most common way to get investment capital is to tap into your personal contacts such as family and friends who are willing to loan you the money you need after seeing the track record you have established and how successful your collaboration has become. Naturally, you'll need to pay interest on any such loan or you can offer a percentage of your revenues, but interest is generally a far better choice.

Banks and Savings and Loans. There was a time that getting a bank loan as a small or home-based business was virtually impossible. Loan amounts used to start at over $100,000 and obtaining one involved meeting tough credit reviews and offering extensive collateral. Increasingly, however, banks and savings and loan companies are recognizing that very small business is good business, so they're beginning to offer "LowDoc" loans and lines of credit for smaller amounts of money from $2,500 or less to over $100,000. Usually such loans are available only to individuals or companies that have a three-year track record of success, but if you qualify you can obtain the money you need quickly and easily.

Small Business Administration Loans. The SBA has many loan programs available for small businesses, as well as assistance in learning better management techniques. Most SBA loan programs are called *guaranteed* loans in which the enterprise actually obtains the loan from a bank but the SBA guarantees the loan in the event of default. The application process thus involves going first to your bank to apply for the loan; if the bank approves your application, it then passes it along to the SBA for their approval on the guarantee. See page 380 for more information on SBA loans.

Offering an Investor a Limited Partnership. In chapter 4, we described limited partnerships in some detail and pointed out that in the beginning of a teaming-up enterprise, this method is often not pursued. Once your business is under way and ready to grow substantially, however, this option may make more sense.

Limited partnerships have actually been around since the twelfth century when they were used by Italian merchants to obtain outside capital for their trading ventures. Historically, in a limited partnership, a silent partner was literally silent; he or she remained anonymous and played no role in the business except to furnish capital. Today, silent partners don't necessarily remain anonymous, but by law they cannot play an active role in managing the partnership if they want to obtain the legal and tax benefits of a limited partnership.

Investors find a limited partnership desirable because they can earn money from loaning their money without assuming any liability for partnership debts beyond the amount of their loan. Limited partnership investors also don't have to take on the responsibilities for managing an enterprise they invest in or take any responsibility for any of its daily operations. Typically limited partners receive a return on their investment either as a fixed percentage of their principal each year, such as 15 percent or 20 percent, or they may get a percentage of gross income or a percentage of profits. Whichever method is used should be stated in your limited partnership agreement.

You can obtain financing from limited partners in several ways. They may either give you a lump sum up front, or make periodic investments such as once a month. Limited partners may also contribute property or equipment to your collaboration. Note, however, there are many special tax and legal provisions affecting limited partnerships that you should be aware of including the following.

1. Just as partnerships are subject to the Uniform Partnership Act (UPA), limited partnerships are subject to what is known as the Uniform Limited Partnership Act (UPLA). This act, which has been adopted for most states, stipulates many requirements that limited partnerships must follow in the absence of a written agreement of their own.

2. Most states require limited partnerships to file a "certificate of limited partnership," which ranges from a simple document in some states to a very detailed document in others.

3. Limited partners are not allowed to use their names in the name of the business unless their name is the same as one of the general partners, or was already in use before becoming a limited partner.

4. Offering an interest in a limited partnership can be construed as selling a security under certain circumstances. This means that inviting investors is like selling stock, and is thus subject to regulation by the Securities and Exchange Commission (SEC). Complying with SEC regulations is a major legal challenge and will cost you dearly. Fortunately, most of these regulations exempt small businesses as long as the offering is only to "intrastate" investors, meaning that your investors are not from out of state or that your offering is private, not public. The latter requirement is a function of how many people receive your offering to become a limited partner, and generally if you are offering the opportunity to ten or fewer people, you are exempt from federal securities laws in all states.

As you can see, forming a limited partnership can be quite a complex undertaking, but for an excellent and detailed discussion on the legal and financial ramifications of using a limited partnership to finance your collaboration, see *The Partnership Book* by Denis Clifford and Ralph Warner.

Venture Capitalists. The term *venture capitalists* has come to be used in the context of raising large amounts of capital for fast-growing high technology companies, but venture capitalists also fund businesspeople in other types of industries. Venture capitalists (VCs) differ from investors who take a stake as limited partners in several ways. In general, venture capitalists also want an ownership position (what's called an equity stake) in the company. However, most venture capitalists are seeking companies that show potential for very large profits such as $50 million within three to five years, instead of the slow steady growth many small and home-based businesses attain. In addition, VCs usually expect to take the company public through the sale of stock once that growth level is achieved. Because of this, VCs look for highly experienced management teams with a track record for getting a business to sales of several million by the time the VCs are called in. VCs typically invest a minimum of $500,000 or more.

Often you can locate venture capitalists by simply looking in the business section of your local newspapers where many VCs advertise. Most specialize in certain industries they have expertise in themselves. Many cities also have venture capital clubs. For more information and to locate a club in your area contact the Association of Venture Clubs, 265 East 100 South, Suite 300, P.O. Box 3358, Salt Lake City, UT 84110-3358 or call 801-364-1100.

Tapping Into the SBA for Loans and Advice on Growing Your Collaboration

The Small Business Administration (SBA) is a federal agency that's dedicated to helping small businesses. The SBA's definition of a "small" business, however, is actually quite large: any enterprise with fewer than 1,500 employees and revenues of less than $17 million qualifies as a small business! But since many small businesses still can't qualify for bank loans on the owner's personal credit, the SBA offers loans geared to providing small business with seed capital for start-up or business expansion. Most SBA loans are guaranteed loans in which the SBA guarantees to repay the bank up to 90 percent of the loan in the event of a default. The SBA also has one direct loan program for businesses that do not qualify under the guaranteed loan programs.

For obtaining most SBA loans, the lending process begins with the potential borrower contacting a financial institution. The small business owner is required to explain the need for and planned use of the loan, and to submit financial statements for the previous three years, as well as a detailed business plan and a cash budget for the enterprise. The bank then performs a credit check on the applicant. If the borrower meets the definition of a small business, the financial institution will then help the owner obtain the SBA loan guarantee. You must fill out and sign several SBA documents, and submit income tax data along with your application. Note that your information is checked with the IRS to verify that you are not engaged in any tax fraud. In general, the approval process may take from ten days to three weeks.

There is an additional requirement imposed by the SBA that you should be aware of. The SBA now requires all investors owning more than 20 percent of a small business to pledge their personal assets against the guaranteed loan. This can be a problem for borrowers who have previously obtained outside financing such as loans from relatives or venture capitalists who do not want to accept this additional risk.

The major SBA programs utilized by small businesses include:

1. The Microloan Program. This program is intended for entrepreneurs and small business owners who need only a small amount of money, from just a few hundred dollars up to $25,000. This program was created because it hasn't been cost effective for most financial institutions to process such very small loan requests. Under the microloan program, a business owner applies for financing from a nonprofit organization selected and funded by the SBA for this purpose. The interest rate on microloans is limited to a maximum of 4 percent above the prime rate and the loan must be paid back within six years. The credit terms and collateral requirements vary from one lending organization to another. In general, however, the debtor must exhibit good character, management expertise, and an ability to repay the loan. Collateral may or may not be required, but personal guarantees of the loan usually are. The proceeds from a microloan must be used to purchase machinery, equipment, or furniture and office supplies, or to provide working capital. The funds cannot be used to repay existing debts.

2. The LowDoc Program. The LowDoc program is designed for very small new companies. The maximum loan size is $100,000. The name "LowDoc" loans originates from the idea that loans through this program require only a simple one-page application. The company negotiates terms with the lender, applies to the SBA, and the SBA guarantees up to 90 percent of the loan if it's approved. The LowDoc program has two other advantages for borrowers. First, response time is quick, usually a matter of two to three days. Second, the approval criteria for a LowDoc loan focuses on the creditworthiness of the applicant rather than on the value of any collateral. This can be especially important to small start-up companies with few fixed assets.

3. The 7(a) Program. In this program, the SBA guarantees loans made to a participating small business by a private financial institution. The 7(a) program is the most popular program administered by the SBA because banks like the way this program reduces their risk.

4. The 8(a) Program. The 8(a) program began in the 1970s to help minority businesses bid for government projects. Admission into the 8(a) program is based on strict regulations: at least 51 percent of the firm must be owned by members of socially and economically disadvantaged groups, including African Americans, Hispanic Americans, Native Americans, Asian Americans from the Pacific islands or the Asian subcontinent, or other groups periodically designated by the SBA. In addition, the applicants must prove that they suffer from economic disadvantages. Generally this means they must have a net worth of less than $250,000.

Membership in the 8(a) program is not permanent. Firms receive the 8(a) designation for nine years—a four-year development period and a five-year transitional phase. At the end of the nine years, the firm is expected to compete in the open market. The future of the 8(a) program may be affected if federal legislation modifies affirmative action rules.

5. The Direct Loan Program. Under this program, there is no private lender or loan guarantee. The SBA simply provides the funds to selected borrowers and then collects the payments as they come due. However, in recent years the direct loan program has been largely replaced by the guaranteed loan programs above because the direct loan program was subject to extensive fraud. At this time, the only direct loan program still available is for small businesses headed by handicapped individuals, and even this program has limited funds.

6. The 504 Program. This program is designed to help established small businesses with fewer than five hundred employees, a net worth of less than $6 million and a net income of less than $2 million for each of the last two years. It enables such businesses to make investments in property, plant, and equipment that increase or retain employment. A 504 financial package generally involves three participants.

1. The borrowing firm, which provides 10 percent equity
2. The participating bank, which provides 50 percent of the loan
3. A Certified Development Company (CDC), which is sometimes a private organization or one of the economic development entities created by the SBA to facilitate development projects. The CDC contributes 40 percent of the funds.

Loan repayment begins on the first day of the month following the signing of the contract. The property, plant, and equipment purchased by the firm are used as collateral for a 504 loan. If the business defaults on the loan, the financial institution is the first mortgage holder, the SBA holds the second lien, and the CDC is the last to be repaid.

7. *The Small Business Institute Program (SBI).* This program is intended to help small-business executives learn more about management. The program utilizes teams composed of students and faculty from over five hundred participating institutes located at college business schools who perform in-depth analyses of your business such as market studies, accounting evaluation, personnel policy development, product design, and strategic planning. The SBA funds the entire program at minimal cost. Of course, the value of an analysis depends in large part on the diligence of the students who work on your project.

8. *The Women's Network for Entrepreneurial Training (WNET) program.* This program is designed to help female entrepreneurs. It matches successful businesswomen with female entrepreneurs who are just starting out. The mentor provides business advice and networking contacts to her protégé.

9. *The Service Corporation of Retired Executives (SCORE) Program.* The SBA sponsors SCORE to tap into the expertise of retired businesspeople. SCORE matches participating small businesses with one or more counselors who have prior experience in their field. The SCORE volunteers then provide advice to the business owner free of charge. There are more than twelve thousand SCORE counselors; the average person has more than thirty-five years in business.

To learn more about these SBA loan programs, call the SBA hotline at 800-827-5722 and use their automated system to find out about all the SBA services available. Their voice mail system offers immediate information on:

- Financing your business
- Counseling and training
- Minority-owned businesses
- Many other matters

In addition to the SBA, the federal government also has a grant program called the Small Business Innovation Research (SBIR). This program offers small businesses funding to do government-related research on many topics such as agriculture, high technology, aerospace, and so on. The government's research needs are announced quarterly in a publication called the SBIR Pre-Solicitation Announcement. The awards range from up to $100,000 for initial (Phase I) research to $750,000 for follow-up (Phase II) research. You must get a Phase I award before getting a Phase II award. For additional information on the SBIR program, write to the Office of Innovation, Research, and Technology, U.S. Small Business Administration, 409 3rd Street, 8th Floor, Washington, DC 20416 or call 202-205-7777.

Finally, the SBA jointly funds with state governments the Small Business

Development Center (SBDC), which host conferences, seminars, and counseling on issues of importance to small businesses. These seminars are generally held either free of charge or for a nominal fee. There are more than 750 SBDCs in the country, most of which are located on college campuses. Each state has a lead SBDC that oversees the subcenters. You can locate your state's lead SBDC center by calling the SBA number above and selecting the voice mail choice called Counseling and Training.

SUCCESS HAS A SCHEDULE OF ITS OWN

Every collaboration travels its own path to success—at its own speed. For some, like husband-and-wife team Sandy and Gerald McDevitt, the magic of teamwork comes quickly. They founded their company, Creative Computer Products, when Sandy realized that most software programs had too many commands to remember, so she invented a template that could be laid over the keyboard to remind users of each program's set of commands. Within a few months, they were getting more than thirty orders per day and were forced to rent space outside of their home for their inventory. A year later they had to rent even bigger space. Michael Hakimi and Joshua Schneider, mentioned earlier in chapter 1, founded their Internet service in June 1994, and by year's end they had generated revenues of $250,000.

For other teaming-up efforts, making magic takes longer. It did for Steven Jobs, founder of Apple Computer who was reported as saying, "Everything I've done has taken a long, long time. I'm impatient. But that doesn't make it happen any faster." Some ventures seem to have to plod along, making a little money here and a little there over several years, beginning as a sideline activity and building slowly until they develop sufficient momentum to become full-time ventures.

Whichever is the case for you, how you handle your success is crucial to your health and well-being, and your willingness to carry on. The more successful you become, the more of everything else comes your way—more money, more business, more phone calls, more social invitations, more mail, more bills and, if you allow them into your day, more annoyances. As a result, you and your associates need to be prepared to handle all that your success brings—the good and the bad. It's helpful to define your priorities and values clearly and keep them in mind so you can work together to keep success in bounds, allowing only those things which nurture and keep you healthy to dominate your working days.

Of course, having greater choice over what fills your waking hours is one of the primary benefits of being your own boss. You can elect to take only those clients and projects that make sense to you, and refer others elsewhere. And as you grow, you can hire outside services or staff to take over aspects of the business you no longer enjoy, but you should always remain involved in the core of your business.

Ironically, partnerships often break up once they've achieved stellar success. In some cases, the owners have done exceptionally well, and as in winning the lottery, once they have enough money to retire at an early age they don't want or need to work anymore. But sometimes success causes people to exaggerate their contributions and forget their shortcomings. As Michael Jordan has said, "Success turn we's back into me's." But, it doesn't have to. If you pay as much attention to maintaining healthy, resilient, flexible, and supportive relationships as you pay to achieving a healthy bank balance, success can make your relationships all the more enjoyable and creative. Your affiliations can evolve to new levels of success for all of you whether it means working together more or less. As long as you keep the magic alive in your ventures, you can continue to create all the success you can truly enjoy!

RESOURCES

The Artist's Way. Julia Cameron with Mark Bryan. New York: Tarcher/Putnam, 1993.

Finding Your Perfect Work. Paul and Sarah Edwards. New York: Tarcher/Putnam, 1996.

The Hiring and Firing Book: A Complete Legal Guide for Employers. Steven Mitchell Sack. Merrick, NY: Legal Strategies, Inc., 1993.

Hiring Independent Contractors: The Employer's Legal Guide. Stephen Fishman. Berkeley, CA: Nolo Press, 1996.

The Partnership Book: How to Write a Partnership Agreement. Denis Clifford and Ralph Warner. Berkeley, CA: Nolo Press, 1996.

Sacred Hoops. Phil Jackson and Hugh Delehanty. New York: Hyperion, 1995.

The Second Curve: Managing the Velocity of Change. Ian Morrison. New York: Ballantine, 1996.

Unconventional Wisdom: Twelve Remarkable Innovators Tell How Intuition Can Revolutionize Decision-Making. Ron Schult. New York: Harper Business, 1994.

Do You Have Questions or Feedback?

Paul and Sarah Edwards want to answer your questions. They can respond to you directly, usually within twenty-four hours, if you leave a message for them on the Working from Home Forum on CompuServe Information Service. If you have a computer and access to CompuServe, simply type "GO WORK" at any "!" prompt; their ID is 76703,242. You can also visit Paul and Sarah's resources offered on the Internet's World Wide Web at http://www.homeworks.com

If you do not have a computer, you can write to Paul and Sarah in care of "Q&A," Home Office Computing magazine, 730 Broadway, New York, NY 10003. Your question may be selected to be answered in their monthly column or they may respond to it on their radio or TV show. However, they cannot respond to every letter.

OTHER BOOKS BY PAUL AND SARAH EDWARDS

Use the table below to locate other books that contain the information you need for your business interests.

Subject	Best Home Business for the 90s	Getting Business to Come to You	Secrets of Self-Employment	Making Money with Your Computer at Home	Working from Home	Finding Your Perfect Work
Advertising		Yes				
Business opportunities					Yes	
Business planning				Yes		
Children and Child Care					Yes	
Closing sales		Yes	Yes			
Credit					Yes	
Employees					Yes	
Ergonomics				Yes	Yes	
Failure			Yes			
Family and marriage issues					Yes	
Financing your business			Yes	Yes	Yes	
Franchise named					Yes	
Getting referrals		Yes			Yes	
Handling emotional/ psychological issues			Yes			
Housecleaning					Yes	
Insurance					Yes	
Legal issues					Yes	
Loneliness, isolation					Yes	
Managing information				Yes	Yes	
Marketing	Specific techniques by business	Yes Focus of book	Yes Attitude	Yes Technology tools	Yes	
Marketing materials		Yes		Yes		
Money			Yes	Yes	Yes	
Naming your business		Yes				
Networking		Yes			Yes	
Office space, furniture, equipment					Yes	
Outgrowing your home					Yes	
Overcoming setbacks			Yes			
Pricing	Yes Specific			Yes Specific	Yes Principles	
Profiles of specific business	Yes			Yes		
Public relations and publicity		Yes			Yes	
Resource directory			Yes			
Selecting a business career	Yes			Yes	Yes	Yes Focus of book
Software				Yes	Yes	
Speaking		Yes				
Start-up costs	Yes			Yes		
Success issues			Yes			
Taxes					Yes	
Time Management			Yes	Yes	Yes	
Zoning					Yes	

INDEX

COMPLETE YOUR LIBRARY OF THE WORKING FROM HOME SERIES BY PAUL AND SARAH EDWARDS

These books are available at your local bookstore or wherever books are sold. Ordering is also easy and convenient. To order, call 1-800-788-6262, prompt #1, or send your order to:

Jeremy P. Tarcher, Inc.
Mail Order Department
PO Box 12289
Newark, NJ 07101-5289

For Canadian orders:
PO Box 25000
Postal Station 'A'
Toronto, Ontario M5W 2X8

Price

_____ The Best Home Businesses
for the 90s, Revised Edition   0-87477-784-4 $13.95
_____ Finding Your Perfect Work   0-87477-795-X $16.95
_____ Getting Business to Come to You   0-87477-629-5 $11.95
_____ Making Money with Your
Computer at Home   0-87477-736-4 $13.95
_____ Secrets of Self-Employment   0-87477-837-9 $13.95
_____ Working from Home   0-87477-764-X $15.95

Subtotal _____
Shipping and handling* _____
Sales tax (CA, NJ, NY, PA) _____
Total amount due _____

Payable in U.S. funds (no cash orders accepted). $15.00 minimum for credit card orders. *Shipping and handling: $3.50 for one book, $1.00 for each additional book. Not to exceed $8.50.

Payment method:

☐ Visa   ☐ MasterCard   ☐ American Express

☐ Check or money order

☐ International money order or bank draft check.

Card # _____ Expiration date _____

Signature as on charge card _____

Daytime phone number _____

Name _____

Address _____

City _____ State _____ Zip _____

Please allow six weeks for delivery. Prices subject to change without notice. Source key WORK